Jesus the Hero Family Devotional

ASHLAND EDITION

Written and Compiled by
David E. Prince and Members of
Ashland Avenue Baptist Church

General Editor: Jon Canler

CONTRIBUTORS

CONTENT RESEARCH AND DEVELOPMENT

Joe Abdelghany – Seminary Student/Pastoral Intern at Ashland Oldham County

Nate BeVier – Pastor of Worship and Community at Ashland Lexington

Justin Camblin – Accountant/Member at Ashland Lexington

Jon Canler – Church Administrator at Ashland Lexington

Wayne Cole – Vice President of Operations at Ad-Venture Promotions/Foster Care Mentor/Member at Ashland Lexington

Josh Crawford – Auditor at The Rawlings Group/Seminary Student/Pastoral Intern at Ashland Oldham County

Jake Hancock – Access College Minister and Facility Administrator at Ashland Lexington/Seminary Student

Josh Hancock – Member of Ashland Lexington

Jeremy Haskins – Pastor at Ashland Church in Madison County

Aaron King – ESL Teacher/Member of Ashland Church in Madison County

Chad Lindon – Toyota Team Member/Seminary Student/Ashland Lexington

Joe Martin – Instructor/PhD Student at University of Kentucky/BFG Leader at Ashland Church in Madison County

John Martin – Business Manager/Deacon at Ashland Church in Madison County

Todd Martin – Pastor of Mission and Children at Ashland Lexington

Casey McCall – Campus Pastor at Ashland Oldham County

David Prince – Pastor of Preaching and Vision at Ashland Lexington

Tyler Smith – Berea College Major Gift Officer/Ashland Lexington

Clay Tabor – Worship Leader at Ashland Church in Madison County

Ryan Tenges – Highway Safety Engineer/BFG Leader at Ashland Lexington

Eric Turner – Member of Ashland Lexington

Thomas Walters – Veritas Student Ministry Director at Ashland Lexington/Seminary Student

Adam York – Administrative Coordinator at Blessed Earth/Pastoral Intern at Ashland Lexington

FOR THE KIDS

Kellyn Clayton – First Grade Teacher/Nursery Coordinator at Ashland Lexington

Kenneth Clayton – Landscape Administrator/BFG Leader at Ashland Lexington

Mollie Cole – Wife and Mom/Member of Ashland Lexington

Krissa Finch – Wife and Mom/Preschool Coordinator at Ashland Lexington

Kathy Kendrick – Retiree/Member at Ashland Church in Madison County

Amelia King – Wife and Mom/Journey Children's Ministry Team Member at Ashland Church in Madison County

Andy Stevenson – Graphic Designer/Member of Ashland Lexington

Julie Stevenson – Wife and Mom/Member at Ashland Lexington

EDITING

Zac Lewis – Lecturer at University of Kentucky/Access College Ministry Coordinator at Ashland Church in Madison County

Hannah Shultz – Administrative Assistant at Sojourn Community Church/Seminary Student/Member of Ashland Lexington

FOREWORD

David E. Prince

Jesus is the Hero.

The Hero of what? The Hero of the self-revelation of God in the Bible. The Hero of the created order. The Hero of world history. The Hero of redemptive history. The ultimate Hero of all things. Paul explains, "He is the image of the invisible God, the firstborn over all creation, for all things in heaven and on earth were created by him—all things, whether visible or invisible, whether thrones or dominions, whether principalities or powers—all things were created through him and for him. He himself is before all things and all things are held together in him. He is the head of the body, the church, as well as the beginning, the firstborn from among the dead, so that he himself may become first in all things" (Col. 1:15-18). Christ is the one in whom God will ultimately sum up the entire cosmos (Eph. 1:10), and we are called to sum up all things in Christ right now (1 Cor. 10:11; 2 Cor. 1:20; Heb. 9:26). Every text of Scripture is about Jesus because, in reality, *everything* is ultimately about Jesus.

The *Jesus the Hero Family Devotional* is an attempt to help followers of Christ in the task of summing up all things in Christ right now. The work of the Father and the Spirit is centered upon the Son; the focus of Scripture is also centered upon the Son (Luke 24:27, 44-47). As we read, study, memorize, hear, and pray Scripture, the Spirit makes application of his own Christ-centered Scripture to the heart of the believer. As the believer embraces Scripture by faith, he or she begins to experience the pattern of Jesus' life as his or her life-pattern. Paul describes this as conducting life "consistently with the truth of the gospel" (Gal. 2:14). Walking in line with the gospel is not simply a matter of pulling isolated truths out of the Bible to apply to our lives; but rather, it is determining to apply our lives to the biblical gospel story. We cannot claim any of the promises of God apart from Christ and his gospel because there are no promises of God apart from Christ and his gospel.

There is a world of difference between reading Scripture while rummaging for facts to fix self-defined problems and reading Scripture as adopted children of God who desperately want to know their history and family identity as a child of God. We must not simply attempt to learn information from the Bible but seek to live within the story of the Bible—the gospel story. Paul asserts that the story of our "adoption as his sons through Jesus Christ" (Eph. 1:5) began before the foundation of the world and extends into eternity (Eph. 1). In Christ, all of the stories in biblical redemptive history are our stories. We must long to develop a familial gospel identity and accent, finding our identity in Jesus, who is not ashamed to call us brothers (Heb. 2:11). Thus, obedience is never a matter of performance but is "the obedience of faith" (Rom. 1:5; 16:26) as adopted children who have their identities formed by their familial gospel story.

The *Jesus the Hero Family Devotional* was written and compiled by members of Ashland Avenue Baptist Church (Lexington, Kentucky), Ashland in Oldham County (LaGrange, Kentucky), and Ashland Church (Richmond, Kentucky) under the excellent editorial supervision of Jon Canler. The original devotional included a few excerpts from other authors whose writings the editor and contributors have consistently benefited from; however, all of the content in this Ashland Edition was developed exclusively by Ashland members. The best way to use this devotional is to use it. I mean that using the devotional in whatever way you find helpful is better than it sitting on a shelf collecting dust. Below I will explain each of the basic components of the devotional, but you should figure out what works best for you. It would make sense that a person who has not previously had a consistent devotional time in the past will approach it a bit differently than someone who has had a consistent quiet time for four decades. I would also remind you to avoid a false guilt complex using the devotional. If you miss a few days, just jump back in and get started again, and continue to do so if the pattern repeats. It is satanic logic that says, "If you miss a few days, you might as well give up."

Week: Day
The *Jesus the Hero Family Devotional* is designed to be used five-days-a-week, which provides a couple of days of cushion each week.

6

Bible Reading

Each day has a primary Bible reading. The daily reading is usually one chapter from the Bible or a couple of chapters when it is perceived that multiple chapters are needed to keep a story, an event, or a character's life tied together. The 260 readings have been chosen to help the reader understand the flow of the Bible's storyline.

Key Text

The key text is the verse(s) that best embody the core meaning of a day's Bible reading. If you are just starting a devotional time or if you find yourself in a time crunch, you might simply read the key text for that day.

Biblical Storyline Idea

The heading and devotional reading are designed to help the reader gain insight into the meaning of the chapter(s) in the context of the Christ-centered biblical storyline. The reading also attempts to guide the reader toward understanding how the reader can apply one's life to the biblical gospel story.

Connection with Older/Newer Testament

Each day also provides texts that connect the day's reading to particular texts in the other testament. We have intentionally chosen to use the language of Older and Newer Testaments instead of Old and New Testaments because we want to emphasize that, while there are important elements of discontinuity between the testaments, there is an overriding organic, Christ-centered unity in the Bible. Jesus did not come to abolish the Old Testament but to fulfill it (Matt. 5:17-20).

For the Kids

The "For the Kids" section provides simple and creative ways to communicate the message of the daily Scripture reading to children. This section is a blessing to parents because it removes the need for time-consuming planning, allowing parents to focus on the text and their children.

Prayer Prompts

This section provides a couple of simply-worded prayer prompts to help the reader think about effectively praying the Scripture, which is a vital spiritual discipline.

The Puritans viewed the family and the household as a "little church."[1] Lewis Bayly taught, "What the preacher is in the pulpit, the same the Christian householder is in his house."[2] Christians and parents, we must not shirk our God-given responsibility to teach ourselves and our family about God. In Matthew 22:21 in response to a question, Jesus says to his disciples, "Then give to Caesar the things that are Caesar's, and to God the things that are God's." We must render ourselves and our children to God. The only alternative is to sit passively back and, by inaction, render ourselves and our families to the world. Caesar's image was stamped on the coin; God's image is stamped on us and our children. May we, by God's grace, awake from our slumber and, for the sake of the glory of God and for the good of the next generation, call ourselves and our families to hope in God (Ps. 42:5, 11, 78:7; Acts 24:15; 1 Pet. 3:5).

---

[1] Leland Ryken, *Worldly Saints: The Puritans as They Really Were* (Grand Rapids: Zondervan, 1990), 128.

[2] Lewis Bayly, *The Practice of Piety*, Primary Source Edition (Charleston, SC: NABU Press, 2013), 153.

WEEK 1: DAY 1
Genesis 1

Key Text
"In the beginning God created the heavens and the earth." Genesis 1:1

The King Creates His Kingdom

In the beginning, God created. He spoke and the cosmos sprang into existence. The word *created* is a particular Hebrew word which is only used in reference to God. We, as God's image bearers, can (and should) create things from objects found within his created order, but we cannot create out of nothing. Only God creates this way—he speaks and it happens. The instantaneous and almighty power of the word of God described in Genesis 1:1 provides an introductory framework for understanding the biblical narrative, as we must acknowledge the Creator's authority over the entirety of his creation. The Hebrew word used here for God is *Elohim*, meaning "The Almighty." This name of God highlights his inherent dissimilarity compared to his creation. Unlike us, God has no beginning; he is eternal. Unlike us, he is sovereign over all; he is King. We, as his created image bearers, have a responsibility to worship and obey our Creator-King. A king's authority is confirmed by the obedience of his people to his word, while his righteousness is maintained through retribution against those who disobey. Regardless of personal opinion, God *is* the king of the universe. Every part of the created order is accountable to him, including us. Ultimately, we will be held eternally responsible for how we respond to the command of his word.

David Prince, "The King of the Cosmos," Preached 3/15/2015, Prince on Preaching Website, Accessed 4 December 2015, Available from http://www.davidprince.com/2015/03/15/the-king-of-the-cosmos-genesis-1/.

Connection with Newer Testament
John 1

For the Kids

Share with your children how much you enjoy the things they make. Then, ask if they are able to make you something with no crayons, paper, or supplies of any kind at all. Explain that only God can make something out of nothing at all; he's our maker.

Prayer Prompts

1. In what ways do you struggle to obey the word of God, the Creator-King? Ask the Spirit to reveal and vanquish sin which has taken root in your soul.
2. Thank the Lord that he has provided a perfect Savior to atone for your rebellion against God. If you're a child of God, then Jesus has absorbed punishment for your rebellion on the cross.

◆

WEEK 1: DAY 2

Genesis 2

Key Text

"The LORD God said, 'It is not good for the man to be alone. I will make a companion for him who corresponds to him.'" Genesis 2:18

God's Image Bearers Created to Rule Under His Authority

The Bible paints an incredible picture of mankind's created purpose—complete and utter kingly dominion on earth under the authority of *the* King. God uniquely created us in his image to serve him as vice-regents, as we are to physically mirror the kingship of God on earth in our very person and nature. Man and woman are both charged with the creation mandate to multiply and exercise dominion over the entirety of the created order. However, man and woman, while working together towards the same goal, fulfill this command through differing means. In Genesis 2, the text emphasizes the nature of these complementary responsibilities as man serves as leader—chiefly responsible before God for his family's obedience to the king—and woman serves as helper—lending her gifts to strengthen the man's weaknesses in this endeavor. Furthermore, the creation mandate includes man's responsibility to work (vv.

8-15). Issued prior to the fall, God's command to work is inherently a *good* thing, functioning as the essential act by which man subdues the world to the glory of God. God gifts his image bearers with the unique responsibility to rule the earth, caring for it and using it to provide for those under their care. It was, and is, a responsibility of protection and leadership.

David Prince, "The Manliness of Adoption: Testosterone and Pure Religion," Published 9/9/2010, Prince on Preaching Website, Accessed 4 December 2015, Available from http://www.davidprince.com/2010/09/09/the-manliness-of-adoption-testosterone-and-pure-religion/.

Connection with Newer Testament
Colossians 1

For the Kids
Help children think about what responsibilities you have given them—making their bed, etc. That is the work they are given to do. Explain that when God created us he gave us responsibilities. Share with them Dad's and Mom's responsibilities, and then pray together for each to honor God in his or her role.

Prayer Prompts
1. Thank God for the opportunity and blessing of work in your daily life as the means of providing for your family and fulfilling the creation mandate.
2. Consider areas in your life in which you've failed to exercise dominion. Pray for repentance, and commit to submit every circumstance to the rule of Christ.

◆

WEEK 1: DAY 3
Genesis 3

Key Text
"Now the serpent was more shrewd than any of the wild animals that the

LORD God had made. He said to the woman, 'Is it really true that God said, "You must not eat from any tree of the orchard"?'" Genesis 3:1

Rebellion in the Kingdom and the Promise of Messiah

Not every voice is worth listening to, including your own. In Genesis 1, God's voice declares that he alone possesses all authority in the cosmos. The Creator-King speaks and creation appears due to the sheer power of his word. However, Genesis 3:1 provides the first instance in the Bible where we hear a competing call in the Garden: *Did God actually say?* The serpent intends to use *his* voice to undermine and misrepresent the voice of the sovereign God of the universe. Satan distorts the good command of God, subtly accusing the King of lying to his children and withholding good things from them. Ultimately, mankind buys into the destructive distortions of the voice of Satan, both historically in the Garden and today. However, God, in his great mercy, speaks of a future hope for mankind—the Messiah, the seed born of woman who will conquer sin and defeat the evil one. Unlike the rebellious kingship of Adam, this Messiah-King will one day rebuke Satan and his lisping temptations fully and finally. We easily forget the reality of God's promise and its fulfillment in the person of Jesus. Each day, we must fight to listen to the voice of God, drowning out the voice of the serpent through daily worship and praise to our great King.

Casey McCall, "The Seed," Preached 5/3/2015, Ashland Avenue Baptist Church Website, Accessed 4 December 2015, Available from http://www.ashlandlex.org/podcast/the-seed-genesis-3/.

Connection with Newer Testament
Matthew 4

For the Kids
Have a child sit in the middle of the room with his or her eyes closed or blindfolded, and tell the child to follow your voice. Now, let everyone start giving him or her instructions even while you call the child to where you are. Explain that, as they grow, they must listen to God's word above all other

messages. Every time they disobey, it's because they have not followed God's word.

Prayer Prompts

1. Are you listening to God's voice as proclaimed through his word? Or are you listening to Satan's voice by following the desires of the flesh? Ask God to guide you to his voice.

2. Thank God for Jesus, the seed of woman, who overcame evil for us by choosing obedience to God's voice over the lisp of the subtle serpent.

◆

WEEK 1: DAY 4
Genesis 4

Key Text
"Cain said to his brother Abel, 'Let's go out to the field.' While they were in the field, Cain attacked his brother Abel and killed him." Genesis 4:8

Cain and Abel: Enmity Between the Seeds

In Genesis 4:4, the Lord had regard for Abel's offering but not for Cain's. There are two reasons for giving an offering: (1) hope for something in return or (2) in response to what's already been given. As believers in Jesus Christ, we should make an offering in response to the great gift we've been given—forgiveness of sins.

Hebrews 11:4 tells us that, by faith, Abel offered to God a more acceptable offering than Cain. Cain had a sense of works-based entitlement, the opposite of grace, and he received the punishment for failure to walk in worshipful humility before God—judgment. An entitlement mentality leads to bitterness toward others around you. Cain saw himself as the righteous one and saw Abel as the problem; he, therefore, did away with the problem. Do not be like Cain (1 John 3:12)—imaging his father, the devil—but instead, trust in Jesus, who was the perfect and ultimate offering for our sins. Christianity is built on grace, which snuffs out the entitlement division between brothers.

13

David Prince, "Raising Cain in the Church," Preached 2/13/2013, Prince on Preaching Website, Accessed 4 December 2015, Available from http://www.davidprince.com/2013/02/13/raising-cain-in-the-church-genesis-41-10/.

Connection with Newer Testament
John 8

For the Kids
Explain or demonstrate the difference between a child's sincere "thank you hug" and a "getting ready to ask you for something hug." Our worship of God should be like the first kind of hug, a thankful response to Jesus for forgiving us and giving us eternal life.

Prayer Prompts
1. Ask God to reveal any entitlement attitudes in your heart today. Could it be that you are giving in order to get something from God?
2. Are you harboring bitterness in your heart toward others? Perhaps someone got promoted instead of you. Maybe someone has more money or better health. Ask God to help you find your satisfaction in him and him alone.

◆

WEEK 1: DAY 5
Genesis 5

Key Text
"This is the record of the family line of Adam." Genesis 5:1a

Adam to Noah: The Seed of Woman Marches On
Consider what immense mercy it is for Adam to have descendants. God's prized creation, the only one made in his image who was given dominion over all other life, despised his good provision and swallowed disobedience with arrogant indifference. At that moment, God had every right to end

humanity. He would have been perfectly justified to do so because he's perfectly just.

And yet, we read this astounding statement: "This is the record of the *family line of Adam…*" God *didn't* eradicate humanity. No, instead, he *blessed* them.

In Psalm 127:3, God tells us that children are "a gift from the LORD, the fruit of the womb is a reward." Children are a beacon of God's mercy and blessing, and so the continuation of Adam's line is evidence of God's mercy and kindness to us. God is "compassionate and merciful; he is patient and demonstrates great loyal love" (Ps. 103:8) and so decided to give life not only to Adam, but also to his posterity.

While we certainly see the merciful blessing of God in Genesis 5, we also see the just judgement of God. Take note of the last three words of each listed generation: "…then he died." Adam's legacy is tainted by the curse of death. If Adam had rejected the lies of the serpent, those three words never would have been written.

But, we don't have to look back and think, "If only Adam hadn't sinned." The beauty of God's grace is illuminated in Romans 5:19: "For just as through the disobedience of the one man many were made sinners, so also through the obedience of one man many will be made righteous."

The disobedience of Adam led to separation from God and death, but the obedience of Christ leads to reconciliation and life! In the garden, Adam brought a curse on us. On the cross, Jesus bought everlasting life for us. Under Adam, our legacy is death, but in Jesus, our legacy is life.

Clay Tabor

Connection with Newer Testament
Luke 3:23-38

For the Kids
Tell your children about a distant relative, perhaps a great-great grandparent, you never knew who died before you were born. Tell your children of distant relatives you did know who your children never knew because the relative died

15

before your children were born. Help your children understand that ever since Adam and Eve, people have been growing up, getting old, and then dying (with just a few exceptions like Enoch). But, God is eternal, and he has given us eternal life for all who believe in Jesus.

Prayer Prompts

1. Praise God that through Christ, the perfect seed of woman, we will walk in the presence of God for eternity, enjoying his full presence.

2. Ask God to deliver you from evil today so that you may walk in a manner worthy of your reconciliation with him.

◆

WEEK 2: DAY 1

Genesis 6-8

Key Text

"Now the earth was ruined in the sight of God; the earth was filled with violence." Genesis 6:11

The Seed of the Woman Preserved Through Noah

The flood represents the most significant and sweeping act of judgment God has ever inflicted upon his creation. When reflecting upon this event, it is especially important for those who have had the blessing of growing up in the context of the church and in Christian homes to divorce the historical flood from cartoon drawings and coloring book pages. This is not a children's story.

Perverting the command of Eden to "be fruitful and multiply" (Gen. 1:28), man has multiplied (6:1) for unparalleled and unceasing evil (6:5). Though there is disagreement among scholars about the expressions "the sons of God" and "the Nephilim," it is clear that violence, along with perverse and evil sexual acts, was taking place and that the seed of the serpent was strong and spreading through these unholy unions.

The flood God sent in response marks another instance in Genesis where creation was sacrificed for the sake of man. Just like God clothed Adam and Eve with the skins of slain animals (Gen. 3:21), here nearly all life on earth is sacrificed for God's redemptive purposes for man. Undoubtedly, these twin events served as powerful indications to Adam and Eve, as well as to Noah and his family, of the grave seriousness of sin.

Ultimately the flood was a decisive, although grim, victory against the seed of the serpent. At a time when evil appeared to reign unchecked, God solemnly acted to preserve "the seed of the woman." And though destruction of this magnitude may be hard to comprehend, we must remember that God always has redemption in mind. He not only redeemed Noah and his family, but he preserved and protected their descendants for generations until "Jacob the father of Joseph, the husband of Mary, by whom Jesus was born, who is called Christ" (Matt. 1:16).

Joe Martin

Connection with Newer Testament
1 Peter 3:20; 2 Peter 2:5

For the Kids
Remind your children of a time when they disobeyed. Explain to them that Mom and Dad did not teach them to disobey. We were all born with a know-how to do wrong (a sin nature), and, no matter how hard we try, we will never be perfect. We deserve God's judgment. Yet, God in his mercy chose to save all who trust in Jesus.

Prayer Prompts
1. In what ways have you sinned today and reflected the rebellion of the flood generation? Confess those sins and repent before the Lord.
2. Because of our sin, we deserve to be swept away in the flood of God's judgment. Praise the Lord for his daily mercy. Praise him for saving a remnant and for including you. Praise him for Christ who is our ark, the one in whom we have shelter from judgment because of his body and blood poured out for us.

◆

Genesis 9

Key Text

"Then God blessed Noah and his sons and said to them, 'Be fruitful and multiply and fill the earth'… When he drank some of the wine, he got drunk and uncovered himself inside his tent." Genesis 9:1, 21

Noah: A New Adam, a Failed Messiah

From the very beginning, God's design was for man to reign on earth. In Genesis 1:28, immediately after the creation of man and woman, God gives the command, "Be fruitful and multiply! Fill the earth and subdue it! Rule over the fish of the sea and the birds of the air and every creature that moves on the ground." Yet, the first Adam failed in this task. Instead of exercising his dominion over the beasts, he was himself subdued by the craftiness of the serpent. From this time until the flood, humanity spiraled deeper into sin. And, while mankind was "multiplying" (Gen. 6:1), man's numbers only increased their capacity to sin so that God, deeply grieved, regretted creating man (Gen 6:6). But, Noah "found favor in the sight of the LORD" (Gen. 6:8) and was spared from the destruction of mankind.

Thus, it is no accident that God said to Noah and his sons when they stepped off the ark, "Be fruitful and multiply and fill the earth," echoing the command to Adam. God had dramatically "reset" the world and put in place a new, second Adam to exercise dominion over the re-creation. This new Adam, however, failed as the first did. Though Noah's fall into shameful drunkenness under the fruit of the garden was not exactly immediate (planting and reaping the fruit of a vineyard would take some time), it was definitive. The Bible clearly teaches here that a physical change in the people one is surrounded by and a change of physical circumstances cannot change the sinfulness in man's heart. A flood of God's grace into the human heart is needed to overcome sin. Fortunately, though God's representative had once again failed in his duty, God would not abandon humanity. A day was coming and is now here in which the last Adam, Jesus Christ, would come to defeat sin for his people and to righteously rule over the cosmos with his redeemed people as the perfectly obedient image bearer of God (Rom. 5:12-21, Col. 1:15).

Joe Martin and Jon Canler

Connection with Newer Testament

Romans 5:12-21

For the Kids

Ask your children what would happen if you put a scoopful of sand and grass into a brownie mix and baked it. Would they eat it? Why not? Help them understand that our sin—even just a "little" sin—is like the sand and grass. It ruins the whole batch of brownies. Even if we just sin once, we have broken God's law and are worthy of God's punishment. Thank God that he chose to send his Son to offer salvation to us despite our unworthiness.

Prayer Prompts

1. Life after the flood reminds us that sin cannot be remedied through external circumstances apart from heart change. Praise God that Jesus, the last Adam, lived a sinless life and established the new covenant under which our hearts are made new to love the lord and to hate sin.

2. The command to exercise dominion over the earth and to fill it for God's glory is still binding. Ask the Lord for grace to be diligent about kingdom work. Filling the earth certainly now includes making disciples of Jesus from all nations, not just physical reproduction. Pray that you would be faithful to preach the gospel to those God brings in your path.

◆

WEEK 2: DAY 3

Genesis 10-11

Key Text

"Then they said, 'Come, let's build ourselves a city and a tower with its top in the heavens so that we may make a name for ourselves. Otherwise we will be scattered across the face of the entire earth.'" Genesis 11:4

The Seed of the Woman Preserved from Noah to Terah

Before the first stone was laid in the Shinar plain, two dangerous ideologies were in the hearts and minds of the people there, both of which are relevant to our time. First, there was a misplaced confidence in the promises of technology. Advances in building materials brought with it the erroneous belief that, suddenly, anything was possible, even rising to "the heavens." In a time like the one in which we live (where bricks and bitumen are no longer even worthy of the designation "technology"), Christians must be careful to leverage the unsurpassed technology around us for the purposes of God, not merely for the advancement of mankind or our personal desires.

Second, a perverse understanding of the purpose of man on earth prevailed. God had explicitly instructed Adam and Eve to "Be fruitful and multiply! Fill the earth and subdue it" (Gen. 1:28). God also clearly instructed Noah twice after the flood to do the same (Gen. 9:1, 9:7). Not only was the tower under construction in Shinar for the purpose of increasing the glory of man instead of God, it was also built to prevent being "scattered across the face of the entire earth" (11:4). This insular and self-glorifying act ran completely contrary to the purposes of God for man.

It is important for us also to properly understand Genesis 11:6. This is not a picture of God threatened by man but rather God protecting man from himself and from the seed of the serpent. Man was not created to be all-knowing or all-powerful. Earlier in Genesis, Eve was tempted by the hope of wisdom that brought the quality of being like God (Gen. 3:5), and here, the tower builders hope not for wisdom, but for a God-like power. Considering the propensity of wickedness in humanity, God preserves the seed of Eve by checking the power of man and effectively forcing the dispersal of man across the globe.

Joe Martin

Connection with Newer Testament

Acts 2

For the Kids

Talk to your children about their reactions when they get a good grade in school, win a game, or receive praise for completing a chore. Remind them that God gave them the ability to do everything they do, and he deserves the praise. Pray with your children asking God to help them do all to the glory of God.

Prayer Prompts

1. Repent of trying to make a name for yourself, and find your identity in the name the Lord has provided: Jesus Christ.
2. Praise God for his mercy, faithfulness, and patience with humanity despite our sin. Praise him for salvation through the seed, Jesus.

◆

WEEK 2: DAY 4

Genesis 12:1-9

Key Text

"'And I will make you a great nation, and I will bless you, and I will make your name great; and so you shall be a blessing. And I will bless those who bless you, and the one who curses you I will curse. And in you all the families of the earth will be blessed.'" Genesis 12:2-3*3

Abram Called: The Curse Answered by the Promise

Wickedness once again reigns among mankind, coming to fruition in the construction of the Tower of Babel. The nations had come together for the purpose of making "a name for [themselves]" (Gen. 11:4). After dismantling their perverse endeavors, Yahweh puts into motion his contrary plan. Rather than the people uniting around the common purpose of making their own name great by their own power, God calls Abram and declares to him, "I will

---

3 * indicates the editor's translation

21

bless you, and I will make your name great" (v. 2). God has great plans for humanity, but this greatness is to originate from God's power, not man's (Matt. 23:12).

This blessing that God places on Abram does not exist solely for Abram. Instead, the blessing exists in part so that in Abram all the families of the earth shall be blessed (v. 3). This blessing marks the beginning of God's plan to reverse the curse of sin as the curse on the ground is matched by a promise for Abram to become a nation—which implies ground, as the difficulties in childbearing are matched by a multitude of descendants, and as the enmity between the seed of the serpent and the seed of the woman is matched with blessings on the nations in Abram. The curse was ultimately overcome as the promise made to Abram was ultimately fulfilled in Christ (Rev. 5:9-10). As we share the gospel and as people come to faith in Christ, the families of the earth receive the fulfillment of Abram's blessing.

Joe Martin and Jon Canler

Connection with Newer Testament
Galatians 3:10-14

For the Kids
Tell your children about the last time you changed your mind due to circumstances, weather, sickness, etc. Tell them that we often change our minds and sometimes are unable to keep promises. However, God never changes; he is the same today, yesterday, and forever. Because he never changes, we can rest assured he will always keep his promises to us.

Prayer Prompts
1. Praise God for the gospel. In Christ, the seed of Abraham, the curses for sin have been overcome once and for all, for all who believe in the promise as Abraham did.
2. Like Abraham, who trusted in God's gracious promise of a nation, we must cling to the promises of God that are for us in Christ. Pray for faith to press on and fight well in the daily struggles of your Christian walk.

◆

WEEK 2: DAY 5
Genesis 12:10-13:18

Key Text
"'Get up and walk throughout the land, for I will give it to you.'" Genesis 13:17

Abram Prospers and Is Promised the Land of Canaan

Aren't you glad that God doesn't only use perfect people? As a matter of fact, the more we read the great drama of the Bible, the more we see that God specifically uses the foolish, the weak, and the despised (1 Cor. 1:27-28). Abram has been chosen to receive God's favor in the form of a child, a land, and a blessing. However, up to this point in the story, he has received none of those things. He is supposed to be walking by faith, but he keeps taking matters into his own hands. He foolishly devises a scheme to keep himself out of harm's way, even at the cost of putting his wife in the middle of trouble (12:11-13)! It's a faithless act of shameless self-protection.

God could've easily wiped the slate clean at that point. He could've easily concluded that Abram was not worthy to be the "father of many nations," but he doesn't. Instead, he spares Abram and Sarai from the wrath of Pharaoh and takes Abram to get his first glimpse of the promised land (13:14-17). God uses severely flawed people. The genealogy of Jesus is filled with them. And that's really good news for you and me.

Casey McCall

Connection with Newer Testament
1 Corinthians 1:27-28; Matthew 19:29

For the Kids
Help your children understand that they don't have to be the best at something to be used by God. Remind them that Moses couldn't speak well, but God used him to speak in front of the most prominent person in the nation: Pharaoh.

23

Emphasize that when we aren't good at something, or when we make mistakes and fail, God is still able to use us for his glory.

Prayer Prompts

1. Praise God that he saves severely flawed people, like us, and uses us for his glory in his kingdom.
2. In Christ, we've received a promise greater than a plot of land in the Middle East. We've received the promise of eternal life in the presence of God. Praise God for blessing us with such riches in Christ.

◆

WEEK 3: DAY 1
Genesis 14

Key Text

"He blessed Abram, saying, 'Blessed be Abram by the Most High God, Creator of heaven and earth. Worthy of praise is the Most High God who delivered your enemies into your hand!' And Abram gave Melchizedek a tenth of everything." Genesis 14:19-20

Abram Blessed by Melchizedek

While the raids and alliances described in the first portion of Genesis 14 were a fairly common feature of ancient Near Eastern life, the events retold in Genesis 14 relate to the family of Abram and, therefore, to redemptive history. When the four-king-alliance overtakes the five-king-alliance (that includes Sodom and Gomorrah), Lot, Abram's nephew, was carried off with the spoils of war. This prompts Abram to pursue the armies in order to recover the captives (his nephew among them) and property.

Upon returning from the victory, Abram is met by the king of Sodom and the king of Salem. This second king is one of the most mysterious characters in all of Scripture. He is called "Melchizedek," which means "King of Righteousness," and many believe that Salem is a shortened form of Jerusalem. Melchizedek is mentioned only one other time in the Old Testament and a few times in Hebrews. In the Messianic Psalm 110, David declares "You

24

are an eternal priest after the pattern of Melchizedek" (Ps. 110:4b). And, the author of the letter to the Hebrews tells us in Hebrews 7 that Jesus himself is a priest, not of the line of Aaron, but of the line of Melchizedek. Jesus has arisen "in the likeness of Melchizedek, who has become a priest not by a legal regulation about physical descent but by the power of an indestructible life" (Heb. 7:15-16).

Though the person of Melchizedek may leave us with many questions worth exploring, one thing is clear: Abram paid homage to this great priest-king called Melchizedek. Let us pay homage and give glory to the greatest prophet-priest-king: Jesus Christ.

Joe Martin

Connection with Newer Testament
Hebrews 7

For the Kids
Ask your children to spell Melchizedek. Give them paper and pencil, and let them try their best to spell this odd name. Then tell them they can see how to spell it by looking in the Bible, but only in a few places. Then explain that, though the name is rare in the Bible, it is still very important. Melchizedek points to most important person of all, Jesus Christ, the King of Peace!

Prayer Prompts
1. Praise God for the ultimate Priest-King, Jesus, who even now intercedes for us before the Father and will one day rule over all when he returns to fully consummate his kingdom.
2. Pray for your friends, family, and co-workers who do not yet know this great Priest-King. Pray that God would soften their hearts to the gospel message, and pray for opportunities to boldly share the gospel with them.

◆

WEEK 3: DAY 2
Genesis 15

25

Key Text

"And he brought him outside and said, 'Now look toward the heavens, and count the stars, if you are able to count them.' Then he said to him, 'So shall your offspring be.' Then he believed in the LORD, and he reckoned it to him as righteousness." Genesis 15:5-6*

Abrahamic Covenant: A People and a Place Sworn by Oath

We tend to envision our lives happening the way we want, and when they don't, we are miserable. God made a promise to give Abram land and a seed. All people would be blessed through him (Gen. 12:27). Abram only saw that he was childless and did not have an heir (v. 3). What was Abram doing here? Instead of seeing God's promises, he was complaining about what God hadn't done.

This is where we live our lives—constantly looking at what God is supposed to do instead of delighting in what he has already done on our behalf. We think we deserve more than what God is providing, and we get frustrated when he doesn't give us everything that we want.

God showed Abram a sky full of stars that couldn't be numbered as a physical symbol of the great multitude of his future offspring. He believed the Lord, and it was counted to him as righteousness (v. 6). Faith is believing that God will do what only he can do. Abram was full of flaws, but his faith gave him the righteousness he needed. It's the same with us. The faith that saves you is the faith that transforms you! Knowing that God loves you and accepts you drives you to obedience. How do we know? A bloody cross seals the deal.

Jeremy Haskins, "The Promise," Preached 11/4/2014, Ashland in MC Website, Accessed 3 December 2015, Available from http://www.ashlandmc.org/podcast/the-promise/.

Connection with Newer Testament

Romans 4

For the Kids

Let your children take turns guessing how many stars are in the sky. Teach them that God's promises are as innumerable as all those stars and sometimes just as hard to imagine. His plans for us are always better and often very different than what we can imagine. Encourage them to trust the Lord that his plans for them are best.

Prayer Prompts

1. Consider the areas in your life where you think God is failing to give you what you "deserve." Ask God to break your entitled heart and forgive you for not trusting his promises daily.

2. Are you trying to live the Christian life by performing good works like Bible study, holy living, and evangelism, instead of trusting in God's gift of grace secured in the death, burial and resurrection of Jesus Christ? Pray for God to cause you to live by faith in Christ in all aspects of life.

◆

WEEK 3: DAY 3
Genesis 16

Key Text

"So Hagar gave birth to Abram's son, whom Abram named Ishmael." Genesis 16:15

Ishmael Born: Abram and Sarai Doubt God's Promise of Offspring

As humans, we tend to be impatient. Even when we know that something is likely to happen, we don't want to wait! We want to take things into our own hands to make sure that an event takes place in *our* timing. In this passage, time seemed to be running out on Abram and Sarai to have the child through whom God had promised to bless the whole world (Gen. 12, Gen. 15). Abram and Sarai were getting older, and they saw no sign of the promised child. Sarai finally allowed her frustration to overcome her, and she told Abram to have a child with her servant, Hagar (v. 2). Abram listened to his wife whose voice came with an echo from the garden (Gen. 3:6). As sin does, this sin sparked more sin when Hagar got pregnant and "despised Sarai" (v. 4) and

27

when Sarai treated her harshly (v. 6). So the promise from God turned into a sinful mess because of man's pride and impatience.

We see the same thing happening on this side of the cross. We tend to want to try to earn our salvation by our own efforts, by impressing others with our works. Instead of trusting in Christ's works and waiting for *his* timing in our lives, we want to do things our own way. This always leads the same place—away from the promise.

Chad Lindon

Connection with Newer Testament
Galatians 4:21-31

For the Kids
Ask your children how they would feel if you promised them dessert after dinner but you got up from the table without getting dessert. Ask them if they would they be tempted to go to the cabinet to get dessert on their own rather than trust your promise that dessert would come sometime (maybe two hours) after dinner. The desire to make things happen on our own is the temptation Abram and Sarai faced. Remind your children that the Bible calls us to trust God, even when we may be tempted to think God has forgotten his promises. Remind them that Jesus has paid the penalty for our sin, including distrust of God, if we repent of sin and turn to Jesus by faith.

Prayer Prompts
1. Thank God for his faithful care over all of humanity, not just over those descended from Abraham. In Christ, be thankful that you who once were likely outside of the promises of God have been brought in.
2. In what ways have you grown blind or numb to God's awesome work of grace in your life? Pray for a renewed heart to more fully see and worship him.

◆

WEEK 3: DAY 4
Genesis 17:1-18:15

Key Text

"When Abram was 99 years old, the LORD appeared to him and said, 'I am the sovereign God. Walk before me and be blameless. Then I will confirm my covenant between me and you, and I will give you a multitude of descendants.'" Genesis 17:1-2

Circumcision and the Seed of Promise

Names don't mean much in our culture today. But when God gives someone a new name, it means something big. God gave Abram a new name, Abraham, which means father of the multitude, and he gave Sarai a new name as well, Sarah. These new names were given to confirm the promise that had been given to Abram many times before that he would be the father of a multitude of people (Gen. 12:2, 13:16, 16:10). Then God made an eternal covenant with Abraham and commanded circumcision as a sign of the covenant. At around one hundred years old, Abraham and Sarah both struggled with the thought that they would have a child at such a late age (17:1, 18:11). Abraham thought that God should establish the covenant through Ishmael, but God insisted that the covenant would pass through Isaac (17:21; Rom. 9:7).

So many times, we want to have faith only in what we can see, but God wants to show his power by accomplishing the impossible. We know the end of the story. The end is that Jesus would come as the seed of woman from the line of Abraham through Isaac to crush the head of the seed of the serpent (Gen. 3:15) on the cross finally and forever. Now if we come to Jesus by faith, repenting of our sins and trusting in him, we too will receive new names with new identities as sons of the living God (Rom. 9:26, Rev. 2:17).

Chad Lindon

Connection with Newer Testament

Romans 9

For the Kids:

Share with your children the meaning behind their name and why you chose that name for them. Ask them what name they would chose for themselves if they could choose any name they want. Then share with them that, when someone gets a new name in the Bible, it is important. A new name usually means that the person is being included in God's covenant promise, just like Abraham and Sarah. Then tell them that everyone who follows Christ will receive a new name (Rev. 2:17). Jesus is the pinnacle of God's promise to his people. Jesus will give us a new name because, in him, we are new creations (2 Cor. 5:17).

Prayer Prompts

1. God gives Abram a new name which reflects his new identity in his covenantal relationship with God. We too have been given a new identity and name through the cross of Christ. Thank God that he has adopted you into his family, made you an heir with Christ, and given you every spiritual blessing.

2. God takes the initiative to rescue us and willingly chooses to dwell with us in spite of our sinful state. Though we, along with Abraham, forget and doubt God's promise to us, he still keeps us. Praise God!

◆

WEEK 3: DAY 5
Genesis 20

Key Text

"Abraham said about his wife Sarah, 'She is my sister.' So Abimelech, king of Gerar, sent for Sarah and took her." Genesis 20:2

Abimelech: The Covenant Threatened Through Abraham's Sin

Abraham, acting with the sole purpose of self-preservation, has once again threatened the dignity of his wife and his promise of fathering the chosen seed (Gen. 18:10). Just as with Pharaoh in Genesis 12:10-20, Abraham has lied about the identity of his wife so that so that she falls into the hands of a pagan king. Yet once again, despite the apparent faithlessness and self-serving tendencies of Abraham, God is faithful and ready to supernaturally intervene. We see in this text God's ability to act both covertly and explicitly. He not only prevents Abimelech from inappropriately from taking advantage of Sarah (v.

6), but he also speaks directly to Abimelech about the matter (v. 3). The duality of God's approach here speaks to the importance of protecting Sarah and the bloodline of the promised redemptive seed.

Yahweh, in his infinite power and wisdom, is able to take a moral failure on Abraham's part and work it out for good (Gen. 50:20). At the beginning of the account, Abraham and his wife are in a hostile place in which there is no fear of God at all (v. 11). By the end of it, King Abimelech and all his men are "terrified" (v. 8) of the God of Abraham, Sarah is returned untouched to Abraham, and with her are some of Abimelech's servants, livestock, and a thousand pieces of silver (vv. 14-16).

While it is easy for readers to recognize Abraham's apparent faithlessness and preference for dishonor before death, we must not fail to identify similar tendencies in our own hearts. Let us rejoice that God is as faithful today as he was in the time of Abraham and that he promises "all things work together for good for those who love God, who are called according to his purpose" (Rom. 8:28).

Joe Martin

Connection with Newer Testament
Acts 3:11-26; Romans 8:28

For the Kids
In a quiet moment, ask a child to share a time when they felt like they let God down. Then, challenge him or her by asking if he or she thinks God's plan was stopped in any way by his or her sin. Nothing he or she can do will prevent God's will from being carried out, and God can and will use our bad circumstances to fulfill his plan. Thank the Lord for the beautiful things he's made out of our lives despite our sin.

Prayer Prompts
1. Praise God that the fulfillment of his promises is not forfeited due to our failures. His promises come to pass because of his faithfulness in spite of our faithlessness.

31

2. Glory in the sovereignty of God. He works all things for the good of those who love him and are called according to his purposes. He turned Abraham's sin into riches. He turned Joseph's slavery into salvation for Israel. He turned Jesus' murder into our salvation. Evil doesn't thwart God's plan because God is sovereign.

◆

WEEK 4: DAY 1
Genesis 21

Key Text
"But God said to Abraham, 'Do not be displeased on account of the boy or your female slave. All that Sarah says to you, listen to her voice, because through Isaac your offspring shall be named.'" Genesis 21:12*

Covenant Fulfillment Begins: The Birth of Isaac
The alarm heralding the fulfillment of God's promise to Abraham that he would be the "father of a multitude of nations" (Gen. 17:4) was the wailing of a crying infant. For twenty-five years, Abraham and Sarah (impatiently) waited for God to carry out his word, but now the promised child was here. This was the child with whom God would establish his "covenant…as a perpetual covenant for his descendants after him" (Gen. 17:19). Despite their unfaithfulness, sinfully seeking to prematurely catalyze the fulfillment of God's promise (through Hagar), God remained faithful to his promised word.

Thousands of years later, another baby cried out, broadcasting the fulfillment of the promise God made that one would come to bruise the head of the serpent (Gen. 3:15). This snake-crusher named Jesus didn't solely disarm Satan's power; he also reversed the curse of sin and death, securing righteousness and eternal life for all who trust in him.

We live in a world of unfulfilled promises. Political leaders neglect to make good on campaign trail pledges. Spouses deny their vows and leave their marriages. We miss work deadlines saying, "I got busy with something else." Friends commit to "getting together soon," but "soon" never comes. Sons don't repair the kitchen sink they guaranteed they would fix. The list goes on.

But, God's promises aren't like our promises. His never fail. They can't, for the steadfast love of the LORD "never ceases; his compassions never end. They are fresh every morning" (Lam. 3:22-23). God made a promise that all nations would be blessed, and he sealed that promise with the blood of his Son. In Christ, "every one of God's promises are 'Yes' in him" (2 Cor. 1:20a).

Clay Tabor

Connection with Newer Testament
Romans 9:6-9

For the Kids
Make a promise to your children about something fun you will do for them sometime this week (two days from now, but don't tell them that). Explain that a promise is a guarantee that you will follow through, even when they don't see you actively working on it. Explain that we can be certain of God's promises (far more than a human promise), even when we don't see how he will bring them about.

Prayer Prompts
1. Do you trust the Lord even when he doesn't seem to be working on your timetable, perhaps even when it seems impossible by all human means for him to be faithful to you? Ask the Lord for faith to trust him when your logic tells you otherwise.
2. Yet again, God is faithful. When, again, it looks as if the seed of woman might be defeated, the Lord provides. He is faithful to Abraham, providing the miracle life of Isaac when Abraham's body was as good as dead. The Lord fulfills his promises. Praise him for his faithfulness.

◆

WEEK 4: DAY 2
Genesis 22

Key Text

"Abraham looked up and saw behind him a ram caught in the bushes by its horns. So he went over and got the ram and offered it up as a burnt offering instead of his son." Genesis 22:13

The Sacrifice of the Seed of Promise and the Provision of God

Men break promises. That's why we don't have much faith in the promises of man. But what about the promises of God? Can we always trust God? This question must have crossed the mind of Abraham as he saddled his donkey and packed the supplies for the burnt offering of his son Isaac—the son of the promise. But, Abraham didn't hesitate when he was commanded by God to take Isaac to the land of Moriah to sacrifice him as a burnt offering. Even though he couldn't have understood why God wanted him to kill his beloved son, he prepared to do it anyway. *That is faith* (Heb. 11:17-19).

Faith is following God's command even when we don't understand why or even how it will be accomplished. Faith is putting God first above your own understanding in every situation in your life.

Isaac knew something strange was going on because he didn't see the lamb for the sacrifice (v. 7). But, Abraham assured him in a fatherly way that God would provide (v. 8). And as Abraham lifted the sharp blade of the knife in defiance of all worldly logic to kill his own son, he heard the saving words of the angel of the LORD telling him to stop (vv. 11-12). Then Abraham looked and saw the substitute sacrifice of a ram caught by his horns in the thicket (v. 13). The LORD will *always* provide. The LORD provided a substitute sacrifice that day on that hill in Moriah, and he did it again, this time for the sins of his people, through a bloody cross on a hill outside Jerusalem.

Chad Lindon

Connection with Newer Testament

Hebrews 11:17-19

For the Kids

Ask your kids about the promise you made yesterday. Are they worried you

34

might change your mind? Are they confused when your actions don't match their expectations? Explain how God always fulfills his promises, sometimes in very unexpected ways.

Prayer Prompts

1. Praise God for Jesus, the perfect Son, whom was sacrificed on the cross for us. God willingly crushed his Son in order to make a way for us to be reconciled to him.

2. Ask God to help you live every day with the God-given faith of Abraham, trusting God to provide in even the most difficult and trying of circumstances.

◆

WEEK 4: DAY 3
Genesis 24-26

Key Text

"'Stay in this land. Then I will be with you and will bless you, for I will give all these lands to you and to your descendants, and I will fulfill the solemn promise I made to your father Abraham." Genesis 26:3

Promise Continues: God's Covenant Established with Isaac

Having grown old, Abraham began to focus on the continued fulfillment of God's promises to him through his son, Isaac. But this meant that Isaac would need a wife. Abraham charged his most trusted servant with the task of finding a wife for Isaac from among Abraham's country and kindred (24:4), thereby avoiding the moral risks of Isaac marrying a Canaanite. Upon arriving in the city of Nahor, Abraham's servant prays for and immediately receives supernatural confirmation that Rebekah is God's chosen bride for Isaac, whose family prays prophetically upon her departure, "may your descendants possess the strongholds of their enemies!" (24:60).

In seeming contradiction to God's prior signaling that Rebekah was his intended wife for Isaac, Rebekah is found to be barren. Yet, as he so often does, God restored to Rebekah the ability to conceive, and she did: twins. Although Esau was the firstborn, and rightful heir of Isaac, Esau infamously sells his birthright to Jacob in exchange for a bowl of lentil stew. While this event may seem inexplicable, one can find modern parallels in people who sacrifice wealth, power, family, and reputation for the fleeting pleasures of, say, an adulterous affair.

Despite Isaac's propensity to engage in identical acts of faithlessness as his father (disowning his wife as his sister in the presence of King Abimelech of Gerar), God maintains his covenant faithfulness to Isaac and promises him, "I will fulfill the solemn promise I made to your father Abraham" (26:3). Though the blessings of God are being poured out on Isaac, this passage ends with the ominous note that Esau took a Hittite for his wife, and "they caused Isaac and Rebekah great anxiety" (26:35). Later, Esau would approach Jacob with a force four hundred men strong (Gen. 32:6), but faithfulness and protection of the covenant seed would prevail as the two brothers were reconciled (Gen. 33).

Joe Martin

Connection with Newer Testament
Romans 9:6-13

For the Kids
Today, keep your promise that you made two days ago. Explain how keeping the promise had nothing to do with *their* behavior—no matter whether they were good or bad, you would have kept the promise anyway. Explain how God's promises to us depend on his perfect faithfulness toward us, and (thankfully) not our faithfulness toward him!

Prayer Prompts
1. Praise God that our sin doesn't thwart his promises.
2. Repent of any Isaac-like self-preservation tactics you enact that doubts the goodness of our faithful God (e.g., grumbling).

◆

WEEK 4: DAY 4
Genesis 27-28, 35

Key Text

"'May he give you and your descendants the blessing he gave to Abraham so that you may possess the land God gave to Abraham, the land where you have been living as a temporary resident.'" Genesis 28:4

Promise Continues: God's Covenant Established with Jacob

If you read the Bible looking for exemplars of morality, you'll be sorely disappointed. The Bible is full of selfish, faithless, and deceitful people seeking their own benefit, loved by a selfless, faithful, and true God working all things for their good and his glory.

At this point in his life, Jacob is a sniveling, weak scoundrel. A con artist, he fools his father, Isaac, into believing that he is his brother Esau, the firstborn son who was intended to receive God's blessing, thus snatching it for himself. Breaking the cultural code, Isaac commits the Abrahamic blessing to Jacob and sends him on his way to find a wife for himself. On his journey, the Lord appears to him in a dream, repeating the promise he made to Abraham, "'And in you and in your offspring all the families of the earth shall be blessed.'" (28:14*). God reassures Jacob, "'I am with you! I will protect you wherever you go...I will not leave you until I have done what I promised you'" (28:15).

God looked at a whining swindler and committed his covenant to him. Why? Is it because he saw potential in Jacob? No. The Word of God is clear about what resides in man: "the hearts of all people are full of evil, and there is folly in their hearts during their lives" (Eccl. 9:3). God covenanted with Jacob because he's faithful to his word.

Each of us, every single day, fail the Lord. We lie. We gossip. We deceive. We do things we would never tell a soul! Isaiah 53:6 tells the truth about us: "All we like sheep have gone astray; we have turned—each man—to his own way."* But there's good news, for that text continues, "but the LORD violently placed on him the iniquity of us all."* For though we "all have sinned and fall short of the glory of God," we are "justified freely by his grace through the redemption that is in Christ Jesus" (Rom. 3:23, 24). Reject embracing your moral performance before God, and rest in the gospel of Jesus Christ.

Clay Tabor

Connection with Newer Testament
Hebrews 11:20

For the Kids
Have your children select a colored crayon or marker for you to use. Begin drawing a picture of your family on a piece of paper. Every thirty seconds, pause and have them select a new color. When you finish, show how you were able to complete the drawing in spite of their color choices. In the same way, our sin grieves God, but it does not surprise him. In his sovereign power and wisdom, God uses it to complete his plans in spite of our choices.

Prayer Prompts
1. Praise God that his providence extends over our sinful activity. Though the sin of favoritism, lying, and deceit are not pleasing to the Lord, it does not stop God from accomplishing his purposes of redemption. Through Jacob, Jesus was born.

2. All people, even those who are children of Abraham by faith, are prone to sin. Confess your sins and ask the Lord for forgiveness. Ask the Lord to increase your faith so that you might be an obedient child of faith in all aspects of your life.

◆

WEEK 4: DAY 5
Genesis 37, 39-41

Key Text
"Now Joseph's brothers saw him from a distance, and before he reached them, they plotted to kill him." Genesis 37:18

The Sovereignty of God in the Suffering of Joseph

It is so easy for us to grumble about the bad situations in our lives, but we shouldn't. We suffer because the world is broken by sin (Rom. 8:21). As we read of Joseph and his brothers, the story should give us a peace knowing that God is sovereign in all suffering. Joseph was sold into slavery by his brothers, set up by Potiphar's wife, thrown in prison, and forgotten by the royal cupbearer. Yet, Joseph still persevered through all of that to become the second in command over all of Egypt. How? *The LORD was with Joseph* (39:2, 21; 41:39).

God never causes evil, but he uses it for his glory and for man's good. When we look back on our sinful lives, it can be hard for us to understand how God could use our sin for his glory or how any good could come from it. But when we read stories like Joseph's and when we read Scripture passages like Romans 8:28, "all things work together for good for those who love God, who are called according to his purpose," we have to trust that God is in control of everything—*even evil.* Nothing sums this up better than the cross of Jesus Christ. The cross was the most heinous crime ever committed, but it was also the most gracious and loving act that God could ever allow (Acts 2:23). When we find ourselves in a seemingly insurmountable situation, we should think about the cross. Jesus took the wrath, paid the price and traded his perfect righteousness for our horrible sin so that we may have eternal life (2 Cor. 5:21, John 3:16).

Chad Lindon

Connection with Newer Testament
Romans 8:26-30

For the Kids
Ask your children about something difficult or sad that happened to them this week. Write these in one column. In a separate column, help them list the ways that God might use those things to provide for them. For example, maybe God is using a scary situation to make them more courageous. Maybe they had to keep returning to a boring chore because God wants them to learn diligence or obedience. God uses all situations, even difficult ones, to perfect and provide for his people.

Prayer Prompts

1. Repent of any grumbling words you have spoken about your life's circumstances, and ask the Lord for grace to help you trust in his good providence in all affairs of your life.

2. Praise God that he works good in and through both evil and the suffering of his righteous servants. Praise God for Jesus, whose unrighteous suffering at the hands of his "brothers" resulted in the salvation of people from every tribe, tongue, and nation, including you.

◆

WEEK 5: DAY 1
Genesis 42-44

Key Text

"When Jacob heard there was grain in Egypt, he said to his sons, 'Why are you looking at each other?' He then said, 'Look, I hear that there is grain in Egypt. Go down there and buy grain for us so that we may live and not die.'" Genesis 42:1-2

Famine in Canaan and the Survival of the Offspring of Abraham

In Genesis 42-44, we see an incredible transformation take place in the hearts of these brothers. Years ago, they willingly sold their brother, Joseph, into slavery, only after nearly consigning him to death. Because of their jealous hearts, they would rather see Joseph a slave (or worse!) than to endure his condescending dreams of their bowing to him.

Now, they are bowing to Joseph, completely at his mercy. But the greatest surprise came when Joseph granted their freedom, requiring only Benjamin to be left behind in Egypt as a slave. Joseph had put them in the same scenario as before. They could walk away from their problems and one brother, for only the price of their father's grief for his favored son. But this time Judah intercedes and offers himself in Benjamin's place. He would become a slave for life to save his brother and protect his father.

Throughout Joseph's time in slavery, his confusion and despair could only be relieved by trusting in God's sovereignty. As the events in these chapters unfold, he begins to see God's plan become clear. His prophetic dream was coming true, but he never could have concluded that, through his slavery, he would become the salvation for his entire family during a devastating famine that would result in the transformation of his brothers' hearts. Further, the chosen people would survive to one day see the Messiah come from their nation. God's sovereignty is much greater than we can imagine, even in the midst of devastating loss.

John Martin

Connection with Newer Testament
Acts 4:23-31

For the Kids
Ask your child to think about his or her favorite book. Explain the difference between real stories and made up stories. Discuss with your child how God is the author of all our stories, from people in the Old Testament to people in the New Testament and today. Only he knows the whole story, and he is able to work both hard times and good times for his glory and our good.

Prayer Prompts
1. God used the difficult means of Joseph's slavery to preserve the line of the seed of the woman from death. Yet how often do we grumble at his providence when life is difficult or injustice seems to be present? Repent of desiring to be God.
2. Rejoice in the sovereignty of God. The surety of God's faithfulness is rooted in his all-powerful ability to accomplish his will, even when everything you see looks dismal and bleak. The hope of your salvation rests in the sovereign power of God, so rejoice that no one and nothing is more powerful than God.

◆

WEEK 5: DAY 2
Genesis 45-47

Key Text
"'Don't worry about your belongings, for the best of all the land of Egypt will be yours.'" Genesis 45:20

Provision and Prosperity: Israel in Egypt
The LORD will provide for his people. The LORD will provide. In today's text, the sons of Israel are in Egypt seeking help that will keep them from starving to death under a brutal famine that had come upon the land. So much is at stake here. Israel's very existence is at stake. If Egypt does not extend mercy with respect to food, Israel could be destroyed. Furthermore, the very promises of God are at stake here. God promised Abraham that he would be given land and that he would be the father of a great nation (Gen. 12:1-2). The same blessing of offspring and land was given to Isaac (Gen. 26:1-5) and to Jacob/Israel (Gen. 35:11-12). These promises have not been fulfilled. Also, what about the promise of the seed of woman made in Genesis 3 who would come and crush the seed of the serpent to overcome sin? If Israel dies, the LORD will prove himself untrustworthy, as impotent to keep his word. If Israel dies and the promises of God fail to come to pass, we can say with certainty that there is no hope in the Bible.

But, the LORD does provide for his people. He is faithful. He is trustworthy. The LORD provides for his people through the nation of Egypt because of Joseph. But it's not just provision that Egypt gives; Egypt lavishes blessings on Joseph's family. They are given food to eat (45:11). They are given the best of the land of Egypt (45:18). The people of Israel will be so cared for that they are not even to have concern for their own goods (45:20). Through God's sovereign working in Joseph in Egypt, Israel is saved from famine, provided for, and blessed. The LORD is shown to be trustworthy to his word and good to his people. He can and is to be trusted at all times and in every circumstance.

Ultimately, the LORD would one day provide again for his people who were dying and, in so doing, would fulfill his promises. He would send his Son, Jesus Christ, to die on a cross and to be raised from the dead as the seed of the woman from the line of Abraham so that his people might be rescued from the eternal death that our sin brings. And not only would the LORD provide, he would lavish the riches of his life-giving grace upon his people (Eph. 1:7-8).

Jon Canler

Connection with Newer Testament
Ephesians 1:7-8

For the Kids
Explain how God used Joseph's position to protect his people and to keep his promises. God always fulfills his purposes and uses his people to do his work. Pray and discuss ways your family can serve others physically and spiritually under the life-giving gospel of Jesus Christ—perhaps a neighbor, a teacher, a friend, or even someone at the grocery store. Talk about how God wants us to serve others and be a blessing, not to think primarily of ourselves.

Prayer Prompts
1. Praise the Lord that, in Christ, we will inherit "the best of all the land" in the new heavens and the new earth. We need not have any concern for earthly things because we will dwell forever in the presence of the Lord.
2. Ask the Lord for grace to help you live out your eternal blessing in Christ toward others. Ask the Lord to help you be a blessing to other Christians. Repent of selfishness and greed in your own heart.

◆

WEEK 5: DAY 3
Genesis 48-50

Key Text
"'Judah, your brothers will praise you. Your hand will be on the neck of your

enemies, your father's sons will bow down before you.'" Genesis 49:8

The Blessing of Jacob and the Coming Kingdom of Judah

Jacob (Israel), nearing death, lies ill in bed. His sons stand around him, waiting to hear his final, prophetic words to them. He looks to Reuben, his firstborn, the one who's "outstanding in dignity, outstanding in power," and he slams him as unfit to lead (49:3). He's "destructive like water" and has forsaken his birthright (49:4). Jacob then looks to Simeon and Levi and pulls no punches. His rebuke comes as a jackhammer to the heart as Jacob harshly asserts, "O my soul, do not come into their council, do not be united to their assembly, my heart" (49:6). Sweat beads on the back of every remaining son as they anxiously wonder what kind of curse will befall them.

Jacob's tired eyes land on Judah, and we see a glorious reverse. A kingly blessing is trumpeted over Judah promising that "the nations will obey him" (49:10). The ripples of this prophetic blessing would be known all over the earth. Years later, a king would arise from Judah's descendants—David. He would rule with authority and bring peace to Israel.

But, this peace was temporal. David was not the final fulfillment of this word. No, there was one from the line of Judah far greater than David. This word of Jacob pointed to the Word of God, the Messiah, the one from whom the ruling "scepter will not depart" (49:10)—Jesus the Christ.

Raised from death, blazing whiter than the sun (Rev. 1:16), the "Lion of the tribe of Judah" (Rev. 5:5) sits on his everlasting throne. Jesus stooped down from his heavenly throne to walk in the dust of the earth, crouched as a lion against Satan and his hell-bent kingdom. His pierced hands grabbed the serpent by the neck and choked out the power of death. His garments are dipped not in wine, but in blood (Rev. 19:13), securing eternal prosperity and blessing for his people, and one day all people will bow down before him in obedience.

Clay Tabor

Connection with Newer Testament
Revelation 5

44

For the Kids

Ask your children if they know their grandparents' first names. If so, ask if they know the names of their great-grandparents. Chances are, they will not know. We rarely ever know the names of the generations of family that were before us. Jesus, however, is known by the name of a descendant from millennia earlier. He is called the "Lion of Judah." Jesus was descended from Judah's family. God's redemptive plan is seen in people from the first book of the Bible.

Prayer Prompts

1. Praise Christ, who is not ashamed to call us brothers, because he has crushed the head of sin and Satan as the Lion of Judah.

2. Praise the Lord that the scepter will not depart from Judah. The kingdom to which we belong is eternal. The reign of the rulers and principalities of evil will be finally crushed, but the reign of our righteous King will not cease.

◆

WEEK 5: DAY 4

Exodus 1

Key Text

"The Israelites, however, were fruitful, increased greatly, multiplied, and became extremely strong, so that the land was filled with them." Exodus 1:7

The Covenant in Conflict: Multiplication and Oppression of Israel

God has called children blessings from the beginning of the Bible to the end. But there is a struggle in our hearts that tempts us to view children as a threat to our own kingdom-building agenda. Even in the church, there is uncomfortableness about children. People ask snide questions to parents like, "How many children do *you* have?" Why? Because in our hearts is a war—a battle. So often in our lives, what God calls a blessing is seen as a curse. In Exodus 1, God is bringing about life in the land of sin and death. His people are multiplying in spite of Pharaoh's efforts to kill the male children. We have to be very careful how we speak about children in the church; if we're not careful, we can end up sounding a lot like Pharaoh. Are these children a blessing or a burden to us? When we hear a child's laughter, we should be reminded of life in the gospel. God produced one baby who has already crushed the head of the serpent (Gen. 3:15). On the cross, Satan's hiss was silenced—forever. Now we yearn for the day of his return to rescue us from sin and death—eternally.

Jeremy Haskins, "VBS as Warfare in a Foreign Land," Preached 7/21/2013, Ashland in MC Website, Accessed 3 December 2015, Available from http://www.ashlandmc.org/podcast/vbs-as-warfare-in-a-foreign-land/.

Connection with Newer Testament
Matthew 2

For the Kids
Talk with your children about how Satan has been threatened by life since the Garden of Eden and how he is always seeking to destroy life. Explain, too, that God is in control over the evil plans of Satan. Tell them how much King Jesus loves them and how he has made them, just as they are, and desires for them to live eternally in his kingdom. Share with your children what a blessing they are to you as God's good gift.

Prayer Prompts
1. Ask God reveal any selfish desires that cause you to view children as curses, perhaps to your own kingdom-building program, rather than as God's blessings.
2. Jesus loves children. Satan hates them. Pray for the world that is torn apart by the exploitation of children. Abortion, child abuse, child abandonment, divorce, and child trafficking run rampant in the world today. Pray for gospel transformation in the hearts of those who hate children.

◆

WEEK 5: DAY 5
Exodus 2-4

Key Text

"Moses said to God, 'Who am I, that I should go to Pharaoh, or that I should bring the Israelites out of Egypt?'" Exodus 3:11

Moses: A Messiah is Called

"Who am I" (3:11)? It's a critical question that exposes more about us than it asks. So often we are saturated with messages to convince us of our significance. Advertising inundates us with the message that we deserve better service, more attention, and greater respect. Social media sometimes looks like the whole world consists of individuals clamoring to have their voice heard.

But Moses doesn't want to be heard. He is reeling from an encounter with the Living God and seems to recover himself only when he realizes he is supposed to be God's spokesperson. Moses is fearful to the point of disobedience as he considers himself completely unworthy and incapable of being of any use to God. How can someone who lacks eloquence be expected to influence countless Hebrews, much less the king of the nation that enslaves them? Ultimately, he is nothing special.

We might say that God uses Moses in spite of his inadequacies, but it may be more accurate to say it is *because* of them. Moses knows he can't count on his political influence, charisma, or communication skills, and he is terrified. Why? Because Moses thinks success depends on him. When it comes to serving God, pleasing God, and—most importantly—being restored to God, fear exposes something in our hearts: What if I'm not good enough?

God doesn't answer Moses' self-oriented identity question with any assurances that he was special or gifted. His answer was, "I will be with you" (3:12), an answer that should give us great peace and greater courage.

John Martin

Connection with Newer Testament

John 15:5

For the Kids

God is our creator, and he made us just as we are: our hands, feet, eyes, mouths, minds, etc. Because God made us, he knows best how to use us. Apart from him, we can do nothing. Have your children draw a picture of themselves as God has made them. Pray and thank God for making them, and ask God to direct their path to honor and worship him.

Prayer Prompts

1. Ask the Lord to constantly remind you of your inadequacy in serving him so that, through humility and in the power of the Spirit, you might be used to make much of Christ.

2. Praise the Lord that Jesus Christ lived a humble life, without sin yet fully dependent upon the Lord, and delivered us from the bonds of sin and Satan that we are unable to free ourselves.

◆

WEEK 6: DAY 1
Exodus 7-10

Key Text

"'Pharaoh will not listen to you. I will reach into Egypt and bring out my regiments, my people the Israelites, from the land of Egypt with great acts of judgment. Then the Egyptians will know that I am the LORD, when I extend my hand over Egypt and bring the Israelites out from among them.'" Exodus 7:4-5

The Plagues: Judgment on God's Enemies

Why wouldn't he give up? Stubbornness is sometimes valued in our culture, and the person who refuses to give up—even in the face of insurmountable opposition—is often praised. But here, Pharaoh finds himself facing the Living God and even acknowledges that he has sinned (10:16). Still he refuses to admit that he was wrong. He cannot offer any submission to God's will or accept God's authority. He would rather see his entire country come to ruin under the plague judgments of God (10:7) before acknowledging his helplessness before the God of the Hebrews.

Scripture says God hardened Pharaoh's heart but also that Pharaoh hardened his own heart. Pharaoh did exactly what he wanted to do: defy God and maintain his autonomy.

Humanity is called to surrender to God. We must see ourselves as sinful, needy, corrupted, guilty before God, and worthy of judgment. In our weakness, God's strength will rescue. In our cry for rescue, he sends a savior. In our guilt, he offers Jesus as payment. But in our stubbornness, we, like Pharaoh, can only expect wrath.

Giving up sounds like defeat. But for those who give up on being lord of their lives and who surrender their lives to Christ, it is a victory more glorious than any temporary kingdom we can establish.

Joe Martin

Connection with Newer Testament
Revelation 16

For the Kids
Pharaoh would not listen to God's commands through Moses, and it led to death. Listening to God's word spoken to us and following his commands by faith leads to life. This is why we are quiet when Mom, Dad, or the pastor is teaching from the Bible. Have your children practice listening as you read a Bible verse from today's passage, and talk about what obedience by faith to the verse looks like.

Prayer Prompts
1. Rejoice in the fact that God will judge all those who oppose his people, ultimately vindicating his people for his glory. Evil does not win; it will not go unpunished.
2. Have you repented from sin and placed your faith in Jesus Christ? If not, you are just like Pharaoh in your rebellion. Know that the God of the Bible is the Lord. Turn to Christ and find salvation through his atoning death on the cross.

WEEK 6: DAY 2

Exodus 12

Key Text

"'The blood will be a sign for you on the houses where you are, so that when I see the blood I will pass over you, and this plague will not fall on you to destroy you when I attack the land of Egypt.'" Exodus 12:13

Passover: Saved Through the Blood of the Lamb

The air was thick with a musty, metallic odor as blood dripped from the doorposts of every Israelite household. Wide-eyed mothers, clutching their firstborn, stared out the window into the darkness of night, waiting for dawn. Fathers wiped the blood from their hands and kneeled over a fire to prepare the slain lamb for the first Passover dinner. Families huddled together in fear as the cries of the Egyptians howled throughout the city. The sound of death echoed through the night sky.

This gruesome scene is to strike terror into our hearts. God's judgment against sin isn't a slap on the hand—it's death. The pride of Pharaoh led all of Egypt to enslave the people of God, and the Lord put an end to it.

But this horrifying display of God's wrath against sin is colored with mercy: "when I see the blood I will pass over you" (v. 13). God's people are saved by the blood of the lamb. What a glorious gospel promise!

As God's people ate the flesh of the slain lamb, we are reminded of the words of our Lord in Matthew 26:26, "Take, eat, this is my body." The slain lamb was to be fully consumed, pointing to the slain Lamb that was fully consumed by God's fierce wrath against sin for us. God struck the firstborn of all those not covered by the blood of the lamb. On the cross, God struck the firstborn (Col. 1:15), and we are covered by his blood. The Israelites were evacuated from the kingdom of Pharaoh by the strong hand of God. We are welcomed into the kingdom of God by the pierced hands of Christ.

Clay Tabor

Connection with Newer Testament
Matthew 26:26-29; Mark 14:22-25; Luke 22:15-20

For the Kids
Discuss with your children why we eat every day. Help them see that many meals are about much more than giving our bodies food (birthday meals, Thanksgiving meals, meals with relatives). Talk to them about the Lord's Supper (many smaller children have not seen it practiced). Let them know it is a meal like the Passover where we remember what God has done for us in Christ.

Prayer Prompts
1. Praise the Lord that Jesus Christ, the Lamb who takes away the sins of the world, has been slain, and his blood has been applied to us so that we might live when the Lord comes to execute judgment on the world.
2. The Lord's Supper replaces the Passover. It reminds us of the great work of God on our behalf so that we may press on in faith and obedience. Thank the LORD for this means of grace in the Christian life. Pray that parents would use the Lord's Supper as a teaching moment to share with their children the significance of the event and the glory of the gospel.

◆

WEEK 6: DAY 3
Exodus 14-15:21

Key Text
"So the LORD saved Israel on that day from the power of the Egyptians, and Israel saw the Egyptians dead on the shore of the sea." Exodus 14:30

Deliverance Through Water: Rejoicing at the Red Sea
Israel's enslavers are destroyed. As Israel scans wide-eyed over the Red Sea, remnants of chariots, swords, and spears wash ashore, and fear of the Lord strikes their hearts. As their new life dawns, a victorious song of praise flows from their mouths: "I will sing to the Lord, for he has triumphed

gloriously…The Lord will reign forever and ever" (15:1-18). The Israelites passed through the waters unharmed while the Egyptians drank the judgment of the Lord and were destroyed. The weight of God's power is displayed in Egypt's devastation and Israel's liberation—judgment and salvation harmonize to declare the glory of God. The wicked men bear the wrath of God, and the undeserving rabble are granted a wondrous salvation from the mighty hands of God.

What a greater vision of the Exodus we have than those who experienced it! On this side of the cross, we know this salvation foreshadowed the far greater salvation accomplished by Christ, where God's people are freed not from political tyranny but from their own sin and, ultimately, from death! At the cross, we see again the harmonization of God's judgment and salvation as Jesus exhausts the wrath of God towards our sin on our behalf, securing for us life eternal. The Egyptians were washed away in a torrent of judgment in the Red Sea. Our sin is washed away by the torrent of blood from our savior. One day, we will join with all the saints before the throne of God in continuing the song of Moses and the song of the Lamb (cf. Rev. 15:3). How much more are we to rejoice, for God himself has become our salvation in Emmanuel!

Clay Tabor

Connection with Newer Testament
Colossians 1:12-14; Revelation 15:3-4, 21:1-22:21

For the Kids
Ask your children what good heroes do. Tell your children how Jesus has saved you, about the judgment curses you would have without him, and about the future you have with him instead. Then, as a family, celebrate by singing "God is so Good," "Amazing Grace," or simply by praying with thanksgiving to God for salvation through Jesus.

Prayer Prompts
1. God has miraculously delivered you from sin through the judgment of Christ

on the cross if you believe the gospel. Praise the Lord for his saving and judging work on your behalf.

2. Pray for those you know who don't know Christ—that they might turn to him to find salvation instead of judgment.

◆

WEEK 6: DAY 4
Exodus 15:22-17:7

Key Text
"He called the name of the place Massah and Meribah, because of the contending of the Israelites and because of their testing the LORD, saying, 'Is the LORD among us or not?'" Exodus 17:7

A Pilgrim People Failing to Live by Faith

God is patient. If you don't believe that, just dwell on Exodus 15:22-17:7. God's people had just been rescued out of hard slavery in Egypt by God (Ex. 12:51), and they had been miraculously taken through the Red Sea (Ex. 14:22) while their enemies perished in the same waters (Ex. 14:26-28). Now, Moses was leading Israel through the wilderness toward the promised land, but all the people wanted to do was grumble (15:24, 16:2, 17:2-3). God hates grumbling!

As sinful human beings, we always tend to want to grumble about our situation even if it is better than it was before. This is sin. We don't always know what is best for us. When we don't appreciate what God has provided for us (i.e. job, spouse, finances, etc.), we are not just grumbling against our situation; we are grumbling against God. He is sovereign and all knowing; yet, we think that we know what's best for our lives. That is a wrong way of thinking. Like a child who grumbles because we remove him from playing in a busy intersection, so our grumbling against an all-knowing and all-powerful God is just as ridiculous.

Be glad that God is patient and merciful, and be thankful that Jesus obeyed the Father and never grumbled as he was going to the cross for our sins. Just like the mercy that God gave his ungrateful people in the wilderness,

God's mercy is seen in Jesus, who went to the cross willingly for us. Though we grumbled, Jesus died for us anyway. That's grace.

Chad Lindon

Connection with Newer Testament
1 Corinthians 10:10

For the Kids
Talk to your children about things we tend to grumble about and how God hates grumbling. Explain that God provides all we need and has provided us with his Son, Christ Jesus. When we grumble, it shows we don't believe he has provided all of our needs. Encourage your children to remember this when they start to grumble about what seems like a big deal to them.

Prayer Prompts
1. In light of God's goodness to you in Christ, where are you grumbling against God when he doesn't work according to your preferences? Repent and thank God for the undeserved favor you have received in Jesus Christ.
2. Praise God that he did not destroy you the first time you grumbled. He was and is patient with you when you don't deserve it. Thank him for such mercy. Ask him for mercy to be so gracious when others grumble against you, perhaps at home or in the office.

◆

WEEK 6: DAY 5
Exodus 19-20

Key Text
"God spoke all these words: 'I, the LORD, am your God, who brought you from the land of Egypt, from the house of slavery. You shall have no other gods before me.'" Exodus 20:1-3

The Law: Covenantal Living as the Lord's Redeemed People

In Exodus 19-20, the stipulations of the Mosaic Law/Covenant are set forth for God's covenantal community. Consider the following truths as you meditate on the word of God delivered at Sinai.

First, the Mosaic Law was given by God to Israel as an act of grace to set forth conditions pertaining to how a redeemed Israel should live in obedience to the LORD who redeemed them. So often we associate the Law with legalism, with the idea that God gave the Law so that people could attempt to keep it in order to gain favor with the LORD, because legalism is condemned throughout the New Testament. However, we must remember that God gave the Law to Israel after he redeemed them (20:1-3). God favored his people by saving them, and then he graciously gave them the Law so as to set forth conditions by which his presence and grace would be maintained among his redeemed, albeit sinful, people. We must reject any belief that attempts to gain favor and right standing with God through works of obedience (Gal. 2:16).

Second, the Mosaic Law is summed up in the Ten Commandments. How should the LORD's redeemed people live? First and foremost, they should love God by worshipping him alone, by worshipping him apart from images, by honoring him and his name as holy, and by keeping the Sabbath (20:1-11). Consequently, Israel should love their neighbors as themselves by respecting God-given authority in honoring one's parents, by honoring the value of God's image bearers by not murdering, by honoring God's design for marriage and family by not committing adultery, by trusting in God's provision by not stealing, by reflecting the truthful character of God by not bearing false witness, and by being grateful in one's heart for what God has provided by not coveting (20:12-17). Israel has been redeemed to live as a holy people to the LORD so that God's glory might shine to the nations through their lifestyle.

Third, the Law is gracious because it ultimately shows humanity our need for God's grace. Have you ever tried to keep the Law on your own? It's impossible. God's righteous standard is impossible to attain by people stained with a sinful nature. Consequently, the Law points sinners to grace for salvation. It points us to God and leads us to call upon the Lord for mercy and salvation from sin. It points us to Jesus Christ, to the righteousness of God who fulfilled the Law on behalf of sinners through his life, death, and resurrection so that sinners like us could be redeemed from our sin, given new hearts, and live a life full of new covenant obedience to God (Matt. 5:17-20, Gal. 3:24).

Jon Canler

Connection with Newer Testament
Matthew 5:17-20

For the Kids
Ask your children to list as many of the Ten Commandments as they can while helping them as needed. Remind your children that the Ten Commandments represent how we should live before God. Ask your children if they have ever disobeyed any of the commandments. Give them of an example in their own life if they need help. Give them an example from your life too. Use this as an opportunity to show them that both you and they fall short of God's moral standards as law-breakers and that both you and they need Jesus as savior in order to be made right with God.

Prayer Prompts
1. Are you trying to keep God's Law to earn his favor? Or do you feel that, because of grace, you don't have to follow the commands of Christ? Ask God to help you follow him in love-based, joy-filled obedience to the law of Christ. 2. Pray for God to reveal any lack of reverence, fear, or awe of him in your heart. Ask God to forgive you for your idolatry and to draw you closer to him through Christ.

◆

WEEK 7: DAY 1
Exodus 25-27

Key Text
"'Let them make for me a sanctuary, so that I may live among them.'" Exodus 25:8

The Tabernacle: The LORD Chooses to Dwell Among His People

Beginning in Exodus 25, the LORD calls for an offering to be taken up from the people of Israel so that a sanctuary could be constructed. While it is easy to get lost in the details of the sanctuary and of its individual parts that God instructs the Israelites to make, do not miss the significance of what the tabernacle represents. The tabernacle represents God's desire to dwell among his people. The tabernacle represents a step back toward Eden, to that place where God and man dwelt in communion together. God chooses to dwell among those he redeems.

Hundreds of years later, God would take on human flesh in the person of Jesus Christ to tabernacle among his people (John 1:1-14). As the tabernacle, Jesus would also be a priest who offered his own body as a sacrifice before God so that sinners from every tribe, tongue, and nation could be received into the presence of God (Heb. 8:5-6, Rev. 5). Now that he has ascended into heaven, Jesus has sent the Spirit of God so that the Lord not only dwells among his people but dwells in them (John 14:17).

God's salvation is rooted in his presence with his people. Do you delight in the presence of God? Would salvation be just as good for you if the presence of God in Christ was absent? For those redeemed of God, his presence ought to be our greatest joy.

Jon Canler

Connection with Newer Testament
John 1:14; Hebrews 8:5-6

For the Kids
Ask your children what shows them that Dad and Mom are present in the house (clothes in the closet, food in the kitchen, a spot for you at the table, etc.). Ask that if all of your needs were met but Dad and Mom were never with them, would they miss you? Explain that you want them to long for God's presence in their lives and not just long for the things God provides for them.

Prayer Prompts

1. Ask God to help you understand his presence in your life through his Son Jesus Christ. Ask him to reveal to you what a blessing it is for a Holy God to dwell amongst sinners like us. Worship him in light of this.

2. Thank God for sending his Son Jesus to dwell amongst us and save us. Ask him to cultivate and grow his presence in your heart and mind.

◆

WEEK 7: DAY 2
Exodus 28-29

Key Text

"'And you, bring near to you your brother Aaron and his sons with him from among the Israelites, so that they may minister as my priests—Aaron, Nadab and Abihu, Eleazar and Ithamar, Aaron's sons.'" Exodus 28:1

The Priesthood: How the Lord Tabernacles Among a Sinful People

Yesterday, we examined the instructions for building the tabernacle, and we thought about how the tabernacle represented God's presence among his redeemed people. Today, the subject matter is the priests who work in the tabernacle. If the tabernacle represents the place where God chooses to dwell among his people under the old covenant, the priests indicate how the Lord can tabernacle among a sinful people like Israel: through the shedding of blood. The priests function as mediators between God and man who offer sacrifices so that sinners can dwell in the presence of a holy, sinless God (29:42-46).

Thousands of years after the Aaronic priesthood was established under the old covenant, a greater priest came on the scene to offer his body as a once-for-all sacrifice for sins, a sacrifice that actually purifies one's conscience before God (Heb. 9:11-14). No longer would sinful men offer up the blood of bulls and goats. A new and greater priest, not in the temporal order of Aaron but of the eternal order of Melchizedek, would arise in the person of Jesus Christ to make a final sacrifice for sins to draw men to God. By faith in this Great High Priest, you will dwell in the gracious presence of God forever.

Jon Canler

Connection with Newer Testament
Hebrews 4:14-5:10

For the Kids
Remind your children what sin is (rebellion against God) and that its penalty is death. Explain to them that we need to be cleaned from our sin in order to live with God. Tell your children that God provided priests who would sacrifice animals so that God could dwell with sinful Israelites. Then point them to Jesus by telling them that we can be forgiven and cleansed from our sins through Jesus who is both our sacrifice and priest before God.

Prayer Prompts
1. Praise God for his grace. He has made a way for sinners, like us, to dwell in his presence through Jesus Christ, the Great High Priest.
2. Ask God for courage to boldly preach the gospel wherever your feet are, knowing that Jesus is the only high priest who has earned our access to the Father. All other types of "priesthoods" in which people serve—such as money, works, and other gods—will not satisfy God's wrath or humanity's desires.

◆

WEEK 7: DAY 3
Leviticus 16

Key Text
"'for on this day shall atonement is to be made for you to cleanse you from all your sins; you must be clean before the LORD.'" Leviticus 16:30

The Day of Atonement: A Reminder of Sin and the Need for a Substitutionary Sacrifice
The reality of animal sacrifice offends our modern sensibilities. God created a 1400-year river of animal blood and all kinds of restrictions and

59

requirements associated with it. It seems barbaric. It seems complicated. And it was. And you know what else it was? It was visual. It was a constant visual teaching reminding the people that they were sinners. But what was God doing? God spent all of this time convincing us that without the shedding of blood there is no remission of sin. He spent all of this time, all of this sensory activity that was recorded for us, so we could read and feel the weight of the moment when it is proclaimed: "Behold! The Lamb of God who takes away the sin of the world." There is Christ! He is the priest! He is the sacrifice! It is his blood! All of it to bring us to that moment—the body of Christ offered for us and the end of the river of blood. And he says to all who look to him: "Your sins are forgiven. I will remember your sins and your lawless deeds no more, and there is no more need for the sacrifice for sins." It's been offered once for all.

David Prince, "Why Gospel Movies are Not Visual Enough," Preached 9/13/2009, Prince on Preaching Website, Accessed 4 December 2015, Available from http://www.davidprince.com/2009/09/13/why-gospel-movies-are-not-visual-enough-leviticus-161-16/.

Connection with Newer Testament
Hebrews 9-10

For the Kids
Ask your children what they think about their house. When they are riding in the car and you pull into the driveway, what thoughts come to their minds? The house serves as a visual for their family just as the shedding of blood was a visual reminder of sin and of God's grace. Instruct your children about the Lord's Supper and baptism. Remind them that these ordinances are visuals to the church that picture the gospel.

Prayer Prompts
1. Praise the Lord that he has provided a full and final atoning sacrifice for our sins in Jesus Christ rather than leaving us to die in our sins.
2. Perhaps you need to confess your sin and repent before the Lord. You are a

sinner, but the Lord provides forgiveness through the shed blood of the Lamb of God.

◆

WEEK 7: DAY 4
Exodus 32

Key Text
"When the people saw that Moses delayed in coming down from the mountain, they gathered around Aaron and said to him, 'Get up, make us gods that will go before us. As for this fellow Moses, the man who brought us up from the land of Egypt, we do not know what has become of him!'" Exodus 32:1

The Golden Calf: The Mosaic Covenant & Need for New Hearts

Isn't the heart of man interesting to think about? Thousands of years ago, Israel was delivered from Egyptian bondage by the grace of God and was given guidance through Moses, their mediator with God. However, the moment their circumstances became difficult and uncertain, Israel attempted to find their joy and security on their own apart from God. The people of Israel were so quick to turn toward idolatry despite the grace of God. God extended grace, but the people of Israel refused his grace by holding to their own desires.

Something we need to realize is that we are no different than the people of Israel. In fact, we may be worse! We have received grace from the Lord through Jesus Christ in a greater measure than Israel. We are a new creation. We are a holy priesthood. We have direct access to the creator of the cosmos; yet, we so easily turn back to our own desires and sin when it simply becomes convenient. The beauty of the cross and of the new covenant made through the blood of Jesus is that we have God's law written on our hearts. By the Spirit, God has made us alive in Christ so we would no longer be enslaved to sin.

Jake Hancock

Connection with Newer Testament

Romans 6:12-14

For the Kids

Ask your children to name a rule in your house. Ask them if they have ever disobeyed the rule. When the answer is yes, remind them that just because you have laws in your household does not mean that you have the "want to" desires needed to obey them. It's the same with God's law. God must change our hearts to give us the "want to" needed to obey him, which he does by the Holy Spirit. Ask the LORD to give your children new hearts that delight in Jesus and that delight in obediently following him by faith.

Prayer Prompts

1. Praise God for the new covenant in Jesus' blood; it provides what the Mosaic covenant failed to provide—new hearts that desire God.
2. Ask God to reveal where your heart is being pulled away from his grace and mercy. Repent of any idolatrous tendencies, and put them to death.

◆

WEEK 7: DAY 5

Exodus 33-34

Key Text

"The LORD passed by before him and proclaimed, 'The LORD, the LORD, the compassionate and gracious God, slow to anger, and abounding in loyal love and faithfulness, keeping loyal love for thousands, forgiving iniquity and transgression and sin. But he by no means leaves the guilty unpunished, responding to the transgression of father by dealing with children and children's children, to the third and fourth generation.'" Exodus 34:6-7

Covenant Renewal and the Character of the LORD

We all deserve wrath. God is holy and just. We are all sinful (Rom. 3:23). Therefore, we deserve his wrath. But God is not only just. He has other attributes, like patience, mercy, and love. In our passage today, God told the people of Israel that he would not go up to the land of milk and honey with them without consuming them because of their sin (33:3-5). This was bad news. The people were distraught and so was Moses. Moses said that he didn't want to go without the LORD (33:15), so he interceded for the people, begging God to go up with Israel (33:16). God then renewed the covenant by giving Moses the Ten Commandments on stone tablets again (34:28).

But what about the justice of God? How can God be righteous if he overlooks the sins of the people without punishment? Exodus 34:7 says that God will by no means leave the guilty unpunished. How can this be reconciled? At the cross! When Jesus died on the cross, the sins of God's people were punished finally and forever. Jesus was put forth as a propitiation (or wrath-bearer) for all who receive him by faith (Rom. 3:25). Romans 3:25 continues, "This was to demonstrate his righteousness, because God in his forbearance had passed over the sins previously committed." God sent his Son to be our perfect intercessor so that we could be free from his wrath, which we deserve. God's mercy does not violate his justice because of the cross!

Chad Lindon

Connection with Newer Testament
Romans 3:24-26

For the Kids
Ask your children to make a list of words that describe Dad or Mom. Read today's key text with your children, and explain to your children that these verses contain God's own list of words that describe who he is and how he acts. Discuss the characteristics of God with your family. Use them to teach your children about sin, justice, forgiveness, and grace found ultimately in Jesus.

Prayer Prompts
1. Praise the Lord for his character: for his mercy, grace, patience, love, forgiveness, and justice. Praise him for the cross in which love and justice met to provide your forgiveness in a way that upholds the Lord as righteous.

2. Confess and repent of sins you've committed today. The LORD will forgive through the cross of Christ.

◆

WEEK 8: DAY 1
Numbers 1

Key Text
"All the Israelites who were twenty years old or older, who could serve in Israel's army, were numbered according to their families. And all those numbered totaled 603,500." Numbers 1:45-46

From 70 to 2 Million: The Lord Fulfills His Promise to Abraham

There are numbers out there that will always be engrained in our minds, be it anniversaries, how long one's been married, your favorite team's number of championships, and so on. Numbers matter to us because they tell a story. There are few numbers that can tell a story like 603,550 in Numbers 1.

It has been approximately one year since the Lord parted the Red Sea and the Israelites escaped the clutches of Pharaoh in Egypt. The Lord was a mighty warrior for his chosen nation. The Israelites experienced salvation and deliverance from Egypt, but the promise of God extended past salvation to a land flowing with milk and honey.

When the descendants of Jacob found their way to Egypt, they were a mere seventy people; 430 brutal slave-driven years later, they had grown to over two million descendants. After the Exodus, God tells the Israelites to count everyone. He wasn't just giving them a monotonous task but, instead, was pointing them to see the two million blessings he'd given. God's promise from Genesis 15 was coming to fruition in the eyes of the Israelites as they counted each and every tribe. But this story also points to something much greater.

The monotonous counting isn't the point of this narrative. Rather, the counting tells a story of the gospel promised to Abraham (Gen. 12:1-3). Galatians 3 tells us of that promise coming to fruition through a man named Jesus. God not only chose to keep his promise to Abraham, but he has kept his promise to us. The numbers not only tell the story of the Israelites, but also our story as sons and heirs through the promise of God.

David Prince, "In the Wilderness with Jesus," Preached 10/27/2013, Prince on Preaching Website, Accessed 4 December 2015, Available from http://www.davidprince.com/2013/10/27/in-the-wilderness-with-jesus/; David Prince, "Blessed Warriors," Preached 11/3/2013, Prince on Preaching Website, Accessed 4 December 2015, Available from http://www.davidprince.com/2013/11/03/blessed-warriors/.

Connection with Newer Testament
Galatians 3

For the Kids
Have your children count to one hundred in different ways (racing one another, counting by fives, etc.). For younger children, count to ten. Talk about numbers significant to your family—the number of children, dates of birthdays/adoption days/wedding anniversaries/baptisms, etc. Tell your children that these numbers remind us of God's faithfulness and goodness in each situation.

Prayer Prompts
1. Count daily. Count the many blessings God has given to you and be thankful for them.
2. Pray that God would grant you joy in the seeming "monotony" of daily life.

◆

WEEK 8: DAY 2
Numbers 2, 10:11-36

Key Text
"So the Israelites did according to all that the LORD commanded Moses; that is the way they camped under their standards, and that is the way they traveled, each with his clan and family." Numbers 2:34

The Preeminence of Judah and the Centrality of God in Israel's March to the Promised Land

The Israelites come out of bondage from Egypt screaming, "Where's God?" They questioned where he was in light of all the torment they were experiencing. We are reminded that the promise of God wasn't just that they would get out of Egypt, but that he would bless them by giving them a land. God was committed to restoring Eden. God was committed to dwelling with his people on the journey to the promised land.

God dwelt with his people in battle and at home. God formed a system of dwelling. It began with the tabernacle in the center of the camp where the almighty God dwelled with his people. It represented God's active presence with his people. From there, the Levites dwelled. The Levites were a people who had sinned yet uniquely trusted God in important ways. They were totally dedicated to defending the worship of the one true and living God. They were part of a different warfare, a spiritual warfare. From there the twelve tribes surround the tabernacle facing the tabernacle. Why? To focus on God. They aren't to look out at the world and decide what needs to be done. They were to look back and rely on God to help them. The God that is dwelling with them will decide what needs to be done; he is their only hope.

The problem remains. As much as God being at the center and the focus of all of our lives is meant to be a blessing, sometimes we would rather him be on the outside of the camp so we can rule our own lives. We then try call him to help us accomplish our dreams and plans. The question that needs to be asked in our lives is simply this: is God a means to an end put outside the camp, or is he the end at the center?

David Prince, "God-Centered Living," Preached 11/10/2013, Prince on Preaching Website, Accessed 4 December 2015, Available from http://www.davidprince.com/2013/11/10/god-centered-living-numbers-147-234/.

Connection with Newer Testament

John 14:15-31

For the Kids

Discuss why your family lives where you do. Look around your home for what it says about your family—maybe the toys on the floor show the age of the children, or the flowerbeds show that Mom likes to garden, etc. Explain to your children that the Israelites' houses tell us about their lives too. Where their houses were and which direction they faced showed that God was the center of their lives. Talk to your children about ways you order your home and your lives that are meant to physically reflect and remind one another of the centrality of Christ.

Prayer Prompts

1. Pray that God would completely consume our lives as Christians as we live daily for him.

2. In what areas of your life are you attempting to use God as a tool to achieve your own purposes? Repent and place your whole-hearted trust in the person of Christ.

◆

WEEK 8: DAY 3

Numbers 11-14

Key Text

"The LORD is slow to anger and abounding in loyal love, forgiving iniquity and transgression, but by no means clearing the guilty, visiting the iniquity of the fathers on the children until the third and fourth generations." Numbers 14:18

Grumbling, Rebellion, and the Failure to Enter the Promised Land

Why do we question God? Why would we grumble against the almighty Creator of the universe? The answer is simply found in pride. Pride is much easier seen than it is to define because it can be rooted in so many areas of our life.

Pride can be wrapped up nicely in a box that looks very similar to spirituality. This is what the Israelites came up against in Numbers 11-14. Within three days of their journey, they began to grumble and complain over their food sources. They believed God wasn't providing. Miriam and Aaron used their advantages for their own advancement, which brought God to anger. The Israelites were given a task to go to Canaan to bring back a report of the promised land. They were meant to be witnesses to how great the land was that God had provided. They were to go and marvel at how large the fruit was, but instead, all they saw were how large the enemies were. All except for two came back not declaring good news, but declaring bad news. Their pride left them hopeless. They rejected humble faith in God for what their eyes saw.

We struggle with pride on a daily basis as Christians. Pride says, "I deserve more." When humility is the root, thankfulness is always the fruit. Humility is looking at the world and saying, "I've been given more than I deserve." You might be going through a difficult time in your life, but at the end of the day, you've been saved by grace. If you've been saved, there's no circumstance that can change that. You've been given more than you deserve.

David Prince, "Treacherous Tongues," Preached 7/13/2014, Prince on Preaching Website, Accessed 4 December 2015, Available from http://www.davidprince.com/2014/07/13/treacherous-tongues-numbers-11/; David Prince, "Grumbling Against God," Preached 7/27/2014, Prince on Preaching Website, Accessed 4 December 2015, Available from http://www.davidprince.com/2014/07/27/grumbling-god-numbers-12/.

Connection with Newer Testament
Hebrews 3:7-19

For the Kids
Ask your children if they've ever looked at a meal that was cooked for them and said, "Yuck! I don't want that!" Then tell your children that this was how Israel responded when they heard about the promised land. Show them that such a response is prideful as it fails to give thanks for a good gift and as it focuses only on self. Remind your children that both God and parents are

pleased when we respond to good gifts with thankfulness because good gifts are better than what we sinners deserve.

Prayer Prompts

1. Pray for a humble heart that would seek to serve Christ on a daily basis
2. Pray that God would remind you that you have been given more than you deserve when you are tempted to grumble and complain about God's good plan and provision in your life.

◆

WEEK 8: DAY 4

Numbers 20

Key Text

"Then the LORD spoke to Moses and Aaron, 'Because you did not trust me enough to show me as holy before the Israelites, therefore you will not bring this community into the land that I have given them.'" Numbers 20:12

Striking the Rock: The Sin of Moses and the Need for a Greater Messiah

The first ten chapters of Numbers is a time of rejoicing for the Israelites. Everyone was positive. Unfortunately, chapters 11-19 are marked with Israel's constant grumbling. Each step they took towards the promised land was littered with fear of death instead of a right fear of God, who dwelt with his people. The pressure was exposing what was in their hearts.

In chapter 20, Israel is reminded, and we as Christians are reminded, that the wages of sin is death. The people can see it all around them. They can smell the stench of death in the wilderness, and it finally gets to Moses. Moses seems to be questioning what God has said in regard to receiving water from the rock. God tells Moses to speak to the rock; yet, he hits the rock twice, disobeying God's command. Moses acts faithlessly, going beyond the command of God, as if what God has provided is not enough. Moses is putting himself above God. Moses was prideful.

69

Pride trusts in self and attempts to use God. Humility trusts God and surrenders self to God, however he sees fit. What do you choose?

Thankfully, we know that the ultimate Rock is Christ, who will provide living water so that those who drink will never thirst again. Christ would be struck once on the cross but would be raised to provide all-satisfying, eternal provision for his people. Trust and obey him!

David Prince, "Just Say Something," Preached 9/28/2014, Prince on Preaching Website, Accessed 4 December 2015, Available from http://www.davidprince.com/2014/09/28/just-say-something-numbers-20/.

Connection with Newer Testament
Romans 6:23

For the Kids
Collect some rocks, and have your children try different ways of extracting water from them. Of course, none of them will work! God acted supernaturally to provide the Israelites water from a rock. We must be humble enough to trust God instead of ourselves, even when we don't understand his ways.

Prayer Prompts
1. Pray that God alone would be the center of your daily life. Pray for the boldness to seek and kill self-exalting sin in your heart.
2. Fight to choose sovereignty over sentimentality. Consider the places in your life where you are not walking humbly before our sovereign God, and ask for strength and wisdom to correct your course.

◆

WEEK 8: DAY 5
Numbers 21

Key Text
"And the Lord said to Moses, 'Make a fiery serpent, and set it on a pole. And

it shall be that everyone who is bitten, when he looks at it, shall live.'"
Numbers 21:8*

The Bronze Serpent and the Need for Faith in God's Provision

After conquering the Canaanite king of Arad by turning to the Lord, the Israelites immediately gazed upon their own hearts. Verse 5 states that they "spoke against God." God had provided for them, but the Israelites saw his provision as worthless. So, the Lord provided a reminder of their bondage to Egypt—the fiery serpent. Over and over throughout the book of Numbers, we see how grumbling leads to discipline and how this discipline leads to death. In the end, the Lord had mercy on his people. The Israelites pleaded with Moses to have God take away their bondage yet again. God told Moses to build a bronze serpent. Those who looked upon it after being bitten would be healed.

Israel was stubborn, but so are we as Christians. Do you find yourself never really satisfied and tempted to grumble? God has provided another bronze serpent in the form of his Son, Jesus Christ. All who look to him and bow their knee will be saved.

What do you grumble about? We stand in front of our full closets and think we have nothing to wear. We stand in front of our full pantries and think we have nothing to eat. People across the globe would rejoice for our advantages. In our own spiritual lives, we say, "God hasn't given me enough light. God is not satisfying." Instead of thinking, "I deserve more," think instead: "I've been given more than I deserve in Christ Jesus and him crucified."

David Prince, "I'm Snakebit," Preached 10/5/2014, Prince on Preaching Website, Accessed 10/5/2014, Available from http://www.davidprince.com/2014/10/05/im-snakebit-numbers-211-9/; David Prince, "Pilgrims March," Preached 10/12/2014, Prince on Preaching Website, Accessed 4 December 2015, Available from http://www.davidprince.com/2014/10/12/pilgrims-march-numbers-2110-35/.

Connection with Newer Testament
John 3:14

For the Kids

Confess to your children something that you have grumbled about recently, and show them how you have repented of that grumbling and chosen to trust God instead. Help them think of when they have grumbled, and if appropriate, lead them in repentance.

Prayer Prompts

1. What is it that you grumble about? Understand that grumbling is hellish. Confess your sins and repent of them.

2. Ask the Lord to grant you daily reminders of his grace in Christ so that, in dwelling upon his grace, you might be a grateful person rather than a grumbling person.

◆

WEEK 9: DAY 1
Numbers 22-24

Key Text

"'I see him, but not now; I behold him, but not close at hand. A star will march forth out of Jacob, and a scepter will rise out of Israel. He will crush the skulls of Moab, and the heads of all the sons of Sheth.'" Numbers 24:17

Balaam and the Blessing of Israel: A King from Abraham is Coming to Crush His Enemies

We look at Numbers 22-24 and the first thing we see is God's chosen people on the plains of Moab with the promised land in sight. It's been an incredible journey from Egypt. Two generations have made a habit of grumbling, but still God is keeping his promise to the next generation. Things are beginning to turn: the Israelites actually trusted the promise of God in the face of battle. Now a king named Balak is terrified of Israel.

What's in the background of the text is Israel, the people of God, on the very cusp of the promised land. And yet, the scene shifts away from them, and the first person we see is the fearful king Balak. Instead of placing his hope in Almighty God, Balak places his hope in a man named Balaam, someone who was thought to have the ability to see into the future and enact cursing or blessing for a fee. Three times we see Balaam blessing Israel when he was actually paid to curse Israel. Fortunately for the Israelites, God's people can't be cursed.

Throughout this entire section of Scripture, Israel was hardly even mentioned. God was interceding for his people even without their knowledge. Thankfully, God continually intercedes for us as well. There has come a King from the line of Abraham who took the curse on our behalf. Christ was cursed though he had no sin. Through paying the penalty for our sin, Christ killed the curse of sin on his people. You're un-curse-able. Everything that happens in your life, the difficulties that you face, is positioned in the midst of the reality that you are un-curse-able in Christ.

David Prince, "When a Donkey Talks," Preached 10/19/2014, Prince on Preaching Website, Accessed 4 December 2015, Available from http://www.davidprince.com/2014/10/19/donkey-talks-numbers-22/; David Prince, "Blessed! No Matter What," Preached 10/26/2014, Prince on Preaching Website, Accessed 4 December 2015, Available from http://www.davidprince.com/2014/10/26/blessed-matter-numbers-23-24/.

Connection with Newer Testament
2 Peter 2

For the Kids
Ask your children if they can imagine how strange it was to hear a donkey talking? God used a talking donkey to stop a man from causing harm to his people. If God will even use a donkey to protect his people, you can be sure that, if you trust Christ, you are always and forever safe in him!

Prayer Prompts
1. Give thanks that Christ has become the curse on our behalf so that we may not be cursed.
2. Praise the Lord that he continues to intercede and intervene in our lives, even

in spite of our ignorance to his working. Pray for a faith that sees beyond the difficulty of present situations and anticipates the goodness of God's plan.

◆

WEEK 9: DAY 2
Numbers 25-26

Key Text
"Phinehas son of Eleazar, the son of Aaron the priest, has turned my anger away from the Israelites, when he manifested such zeal for my sake among them, so that I did not consume the Israelites in my zeal." Numbers 25:11

A New Generation to Receive the Fulfilled Promises of God

Numbers 25 paints a busy picture. God had been working on behalf of Israel, dealing with pagan kings and pagan seers. The people of God had also been busy, albeit in a differing manner. They had been busy serving their own appetites—obeying their guts and their instincts.

Israel is at a crossroads. They are stuck between two generations, seen through the dichotomy of Phinehas and Zimri. One trusted in God while the other trusted in his own appetites. One had moral courage while the other lacked moral backbone. Phineas was driven by his commitment to the character of God. His reaction was on behalf of God for the people. He was passionate and zealous. He embodies the new generation. He was willing to put God first, no matter what he thought it would cost him.

We tend to read these verses about Israel's faithlessness and shake our heads. How could they do that? Don't they know how God has acted on their behalf? It's just happened. They can see the promised land. And yet they continue to disobey. However, Phineas acts in faith, disregarding his own safety. What will make us safe? The answer is the cross of Christ, which teaches us that we don't even know how to provide satisfaction for ourselves. Jesus says, "If a man wants to save his life, he will lose it." If you're living for safety, you're living a very dangerous way. If you're zealous for God, if you have self-control shaped by the cross and matched with moral courage because your life is rooted in the word of God, that is far more safe than trying to ensure your own safety. That is how we ought to live daily.

David Prince, "Zeal & Hope," Preached 11/2/2014, Prince on Preaching Website, Accessed 4 December 2015, Available from http://www.davidprince.com/2014/11/02/zeal-hope-numbers-25/.

Connection with Newer Testament
1 Corinthians 10

For the Kids
Discuss whether God ever asks us to do something scary? Yes, all the time! When we wonder about doing something, we should only ask the question, "Is this what God would have me do?" If so, then we should do it, no matter how scary it seems to us.

Prayer Prompts
1. Pray that we would have a moral conviction to stand up for what is right, no matter the consequence.
2. Pray that we would not live by our gut, but by the cross of Christ.

◆

WEEK 9: DAY 3
Deuteronomy 2-3

Key Text
"'Get up, make your way across Wadi Arnon. Look! I have already delivered over to you Sihon the Amorite, king of Heshbon, and his land. Go ahead! Take it! Engage him in war!'" Deuteronomy 2:24

Land Conquest Preview: Sihon and Og Defeated
When God is fighting for us, we can't lose (Rom. 8:31)! No matter how terrible a foe we may seem to be battling against, that foe is nothing compared to the all-powerful God of the universe. When God told Moses that

his people would conquer Sihon and Og, there was no doubt that they would. Even though they seemed to be formidable opponents, there is no force that can stand against God Almighty. Consequently, God's victories for his people led to the Israelites acquiring the land east of the Jordan as a preview of the coming conquest of the promised land that had been promised to them since the days of Abraham.

In the New Testament, things are the same, although the battle is different. Ephesians 6:12 says, "For our struggle is not against flesh and blood, but against the rulers, against the powers, against the world rulers of this darkness, against the spiritual forces of evil in the heavens." In Luke 10, Jesus sent seventy-two men out like "lambs surrounded by wolves" (Luke 10:3), meaning that they were going up against great odds in the evil forces of the world. But when the men returned they rejoiced! Why? Because the evil forces of the world are nothing compared to the strength of the Lord (Luke 10:7). Jesus said, "I saw Satan fall like lightning from heaven. Look, I have given you authority to tread on snakes and scorpions and on the full force of the enemy, and nothing will hurt you" (Luke 10:18-19).

So, what does this mean for us today? It means that we can go boldly into the world carrying nothing but the gospel of Jesus Christ as our weapon. Satan has already been defeated on the cross. The territory of human hearts across the globe will be conquered by the power of God in Christ.

Chad Lindon and Jon Canler

Connection with Newer Testament
Luke 10:1-20

For the Kids
Ask your children who they think is the strongest person they know. Then ask, "Do you think that person can beat a whole army by himself or herself?" How strong would one person have to be to beat a whole army by themselves? That person would have to be infinitely strong! That is just what God is. He is infinitely strong, and the Bible tells us that God is on the side of anyone who loves his Son, Jesus. In Jesus, God is infinitely strong *for* us!

Prayer Prompts

1. Praise God that he fights for his people and delivers to them what he has promised! He has done so supremely in Jesus, defeating Satan so that, by faith, we might inherit eternal life with him.

2. Just as in Deuteronomy, Joshua, and elsewhere in the Bible, God calls his people to fight in large battles with courageous faith in his leadership. Ask the Lord for courage to battle spiritual enemies, boldly proclaiming the gospel of Jesus Christ under the leadership of the Holy Spirit.

◆

WEEK 9: DAY 4

Deuteronomy 4

Key Text

"'Indeed, ask about the distant past, starting from the day God created humankind on the earth, and ask from one end of heaven to the other, whether there has ever been such a great thing as this, or even a rumor of it.'" Deuteronomy 4:32

Moses' Final Instructions: Keeping the Covenant & Threat of Exile

Did you know that remembering is a spiritual discipline? As the Israelites were set to enter the promised land, Moses called on the people to remember all that God had done for them. Remember how it all started. God did not look down from heaven and find the most numerous people. No, he started from scratch with one guy who was worshipping the moon. In his sovereign grace, God picked Abraham. It is important for Israel to remember that. They were not always a mighty people. They did not free themselves from slavery. They did not swim across the Red Sea to escape the Egyptian army. God did it all.

It is important for us to remember where we began as well. When we forget the sovereign grace of God, we will begin to think we have done more than we have. We will begin to think we deserve more than we have. But when we remember where we started, recalling that we too were once apart from

77

Christ and headed to hell, we are protected from thinking that we deserve more than what God has provided.

Entitlement is the deadly enemy of grace. When we forget where God has taken us, when we forget the lavish grace he has poured out on us, we will give in to entitlement and only grow bitter when God does not give us what we think we deserve. We reduce God, making him a means to another end. So, let us remember all that God has done. Let us dwell upon the cross. Let us remember the darkness that blinded us before we knew Christ. And may our remembering protect us from an entitlement mentality.

Jeremy Haskins, "The Spiritual Discipline of Not Forgetting," Preached 4/27/2014, Ashland in MC Website, Accessed 3 December 2015, Available from http://www.ashlandmc.org/podcast/spiritual-discipline-forgetting-deuteronomy-4-32-40/.

Connection with Newer Testament
Ephesians 2:11-22

For the Kids
Guide your children to remember all of the good things Mom or Dad has done for them. Tell them we should do the same with God – we should remember all the good things he has done for us. We should also remember all the good things he did for the people who lived before us, too.

Prayer Prompts
1. Remember your life before Christ, and thank God for showing you mercy and saving you.
2. Think about problems you face, and ask God to help you view them through the lens of the gospel, not through the lens of an entitlement mentality.

◆

WEEK 9: DAY 5
Deuteronomy 5-6

Key Text

"'Hear, O Israel: The LORD our God, the LORD is one! You shall love the LORD your God with all your heart and with all your soul and with all your might. And these words that I am commanding you today shall be on your heart.'" Deuteronomy 6:4-6*

Reminding a New Generation of the Mosaic Covenant

When God established Israel as his chosen covenant people, he established responsibility for parents to nurture their children in the faith. This is a clear charge given by the Lord God to moms and dads.

The key text cited above is known in Jewish tradition as the Shema (vv. 4-5). It is named after the first word in verse 4, *hear*, which is the Hebrew word *shema*. The word is a command, which denotes the urgency of what is about to be said. Also, in the Hebrew mindset, "to hear" is tantamount to "to obey" because to hear God and not to obey him is really not to hear him at all. Everything about the context reveals the weightiness of the command.

It is interesting to note that it is Moses who is God's instrument to convey this command to his people. When God first came to Moses and called him to speak as his messenger, Moses said, "I am slow of speech and slow of tongue" (Ex. 4:10). God quickly reminded him who it was that was giving him the command—"who gave a mouth to man" (Ex. 4:11). Many parents need to be reminded that it is God who gives this command for them to teach their children the faith. All of the excuses ("I'm not smart," "I don't speak well," "I am shy," "Others are more qualified") fade away in light of this reality. God reminds parents: "Who created you? Who gave you those children?" Moses, the one who could not speak, now proclaims the word of God: "Hear, O Israel: The Lord our God, the Lord is one!" Many parents who are not now speaking the word of God to their children need to *hear* and obey.

David Prince, "Family Worship," Published 3/23/2013, Prince on Preaching Website, Accessed 4 December 2015, Available from http://www.davidprince.com/2012/03/23/family-worship/.

Connection with Newer Testament

Matthew 22:34-40

For the Kids

Families have all kinds of traditions: eating Sunday dinners, watching ballgames together, traveling to Grandma's house at Christmas. Discuss your family's special traditions. Tell them that, when Mom, Dad, or a grandparent teaches you about God, they are continuing a "tradition" that was commanded long ago. It's the best tradition that they can continue with their own children when they are grown up too!

Prayer Prompts

1. Pray for families in the church as they seek to train their children in the faith.
2. Pray for fathers in the church—that they would lead their families in worship regularly.

◆

WEEK 10: DAY 1

Deuteronomy 7, 9

Key Text

"'It is not because you were more numerous than all the other peoples that the LORD favored and chose you—for in fact you were the least numerus of all peoples. Rather it is because of his love for you and his faithfulness to the promise he solemnly vowed to your ancestors that the LORD brought you out with great power, redeeming you from the place of slavery, from the power of Pharaoh king of Egypt.'" Deuteronomy 7:7-8

Grace as the Foundation of God's Kindness to His People

The people of Israel were not chosen to be the people of God because they were special, important, powerful, smart, or many. They were chosen to be the people of God simply because God wanted to lavish his love on them. God is in the business of using the unexpected and insignificant to create something powerful and magnificent. God used Israel to display his might and his grace to the rest of the world. His grace and mercy is unchanging! The same God who chose Israel is the same God who looked upon you and chose you, not because of your intelligence or strength, but simply because of his love.

As to the election of God's people, we know that the "secret things belong to the LORD our God" (Deut. 29:29). What a comforting thought! Our salvation and sanctification are not dependent upon our own ability; rather, they rest solely on the ability of our amazing God! Despite our foolish and unfit hearts, God declares, "You belong to me and I will be your God."

God chose Israel because he wanted to show them his immeasurable love and power, even though they consistently ran away from his presence. No matter how far you have run from the love of God, he will pursue his own until the end. Psalm 139:7-8 says, "Where can I go to escape your spirit? Where can I flee to escape your presence? If I were to ascend to heaven, you would be there. If I were to sprawl out in Sheol, there you would be." Rest in the sovereign God who chooses his people and who chases his people to conform his people into his likeness.

Jake Hancock

Connection with Newer Testament
Ephesians 2:1-10

For the Kids
Ask your child, "If we were to have a big family basketball game and chose teams, who would you want on your team?" Show them that even though we choose the tallest, fastest, and strongest, God isn't that way. When God chose the people of Israel, it wasn't about how good they were; it was about how good God is in using them to send Jesus for us all.

Prayer Prompts
1. Celebrate that your salvation is not dependent upon your ability to save yourself, but is fully dependent on the work of Christ! Praise God for seeking you out and chasing you down until he made you his own.

2. Repent of any notions you have about earning or deserving the love and grace of God. We are totally stubborn and rebellious apart from the grace of God.

◆

WEEK 10: DAY 2
Deuteronomy 10

Key Text
"'Therefore, circumcise the foreskin your heart, and do not stiffen your neck again.'" Deuteronomy 10:16*

Loving the Lord & Circumcised Hearts: What the Lord Requires

What does the Lord demand from his people? In Deuteronomy 10, Moses lists what God requires of his people: fear the Lord, walk in his ways, love him, serve him, and keep his commandments (vv. 12-13). These are all good things that actually would make the lives of his people better. These are not things that Israel would have to do to earn salvation, but they are things Israel should do because they already belong to God. The problem is that, though physically free to worship the LORD, Israel doesn't have the moral ability to choose to fully obey God. That's why Moses later says that Israel should circumcise their hearts and no longer be stubborn (v. 16). The outward circumcision of the flesh means nothing without the inward circumcision of the heart because obedience to the covenant is impossible without a purified and circumcised heart (Rom. 2:29).

Today, as Christians, we are circumcised through Christ by faith. Paul tells Christians, "You, who were dead in your trespasses and the uncircumcision of your flesh, God made alive together with him" (Col. 2:13). Only by faith in Christ can we please the Lord our God, and the faith that God requires through circumcised hearts comes as a gift through Jesus (Eph. 2:8-9). Praise God that he graciously provides what he requires of his people.

Chad Lindon and Jon Canler

Connection with Newer Testament

Colossians 2:8-15

For the Kids

Explain or demonstrate the difference between a hug for an unfamiliar relative in obedience to one's parents and the spontaneous run-and-hug that happens when grandma comes in the door. Our life with God should be like that second kind of hug. God wants us to worship and obey him from the heart. Pray for such hearts for your children if they are not Christians.

Prayer Prompts

1. Praise the Lord that, in Christ, he has given us circumcised hearts that enable us to joyfully obey the law of Christ. What the Lord requires, that he has provided.

2. The Lord is still a God of justice who loves the fatherless and the widow (Jas. 1:27). Ask the Lord to provide opportunities to serve these people having first been served yourself by God in Christ.

◆

WEEK 10: DAY 3

Deuteronomy 17

Key Text

"'When he sits on his royal throne he must make a copy of this law on a scroll given to him by the Levitical priests. It must be with him constantly and he must read it as long as he lives, so that he may learn to revere the LORD his God and observe all the words of this law and these statues and carry them out.'" Deuteronomy 17:18-19

A Scepter-Wielding King Is Coming: Rules for Righteous Rulers

Moses was convinced of Israel's future dwelling in the promised land and of a righteous king of God's own choosing. This king was to reject the prevalent privilege of ancient kings in lavish living and was, instead, to use his power for the benefit of those under his rule. He was to be an Israelite ("among your fellow citizens," v. 15) so as to identify with those whom he rules. His throne was to be established upon the foundation of the Law of God, which he was to know, meditate on, and delight in so that he may fear the Lord and do what's righteous, reigning in wisdom (cf. Prov. 9:10).

Instead of trusting the Lord, Israel sought a king of their own choosing, and many (most) of their successive kings presumptuously trampled on the Law of God, using their rule for self-centered gain. Israel longed for a king that would love the Law of God and would vanquish their enemies and rule in power, wisdom, and righteousness.

When this King came, his rule was nothing like Israel imagined. He flipped Israel's notion of kingship upside down: greatness was found in weakness, glory in sacrifice, and victory in death. He came not simply to follow the Law of God, but the Word of God came and accomplished for us all the Law of God requires of us. He became flesh and blood, made like his brothers in every respect (Heb. 2:17), identifying with us in our weakness. Jesus is the holy King from eternity past who *is* immeasurably greater than we and, yet, used his power, rule, and authority for our greatest benefit—eternal life with God. Jesus is the true, promised King, who never turned "either to the right hand or the left," but went straight on to the cross.

Clay Tabor

Connection with Newer Testament
John 18:28-40

For the Kids
Let one of your children pretend to be ruler over your house for a few minutes. Have them make decisions about what needs to happen in the house and who in the house should be responsible for each task. Afterward, talk with your children about their decisions as ruler. Were any decisions mean? Did your child make decisions that were best for the family, or was there ignorance? Were any decisions selfish, like not assigning work to themselves? Then explain to your children that the king of Israel was to know the Law to keep him from making bad, selfish, mean, ignorant decisions that were sinful and/or bad for

God's people. Tell them that kings and rulers aren't perfect, then share with them how Jesus is the righteous king who obeyed the Law and uses his authority to serve us for our good by saving us from our sins.

Prayer Prompts

1. Thank God for the King, Christ, who perfectly fulfills the requirements of God and reigns even now as King of all.

2. Think about the coming kingdom of Christ, and ask God to expose areas of your life that are in rebellion to the reign of King Jesus.

◆

WEEK 10: DAY 4

Deuteronomy 18

Key Text

"'I will raise up a prophet like you for them from among their fellow Israelites. I will put my words in his mouth and he will speak to them whatever I command.'" Deuteronomy 18:18

A New Moses: Longing for Another Prophet

Most of us long to hear from God. People will try all sorts of ways to determine God's will for their lives or to figure out what God's trying to say: an affirming feeling, an internal "calling," a spontaneous message in alphabet soup. But, God's word in the world has been consistent since the Word created the world.

At the time of today's text, the Lord spoke to his people through Moses, who was one of many in a long line of men called prophets to be God's mouthpiece. Prophets pronounced God's plans and purposes to his people. At Mount Horeb, the Lord displayed his thunderous might in violent cloud and lightning, and the people trembled, begging Moses to speak to God on their behalf, to mediate between them and the Almighty. In Deuteronomy 18:15, Moses prophesies that another prophet will come in the future and speak the words of the Lord, just as he did for the people then.

Jesus is the greater Prophet. He came not as a mouthpiece for God, but as God himself. Hebrews tells us that long ago "God spoke to us by the prophets, but in these last days he has spoken to us by his Son." Jesus *is* God's Word in the world. He is the promised Prophet of old, whose voice is synonymous with the Father, because he and the Father "are one" (John 10:30). The warning of the Lord through the lesser prophet, Moses, about the greater Prophet, Jesus, should be carefully heeded: "I will personally hold responsible anyone who then pays no attention to the words that prophet speaks in my name." (Dt. 18:19). Today, trust the Word of God.

Clay Tabor

Connection with Newer Testament
John 5:16-30; Matthew 17:5

For the Kids
Think of a simple message you want to convey to one of your family members through one of your children. Whisper that message to the child and have them deliver the message, perhaps in person to another family member in your house or perhaps by phone to a family member not present. Once delivered, tell your children that they were like prophets. Explain to your children that a prophet is a person who speaks to people words from God. Tell them that Moses was a prophet and that Jesus is also a prophet—the best prophet ever. Instruct your kids that Jesus speaks the words of eternal life! "You must listen to him" (Dt 18:15)!

Prayer Prompts
1. Praise the Lord that God has given us gospel words of eternal life in Jesus.
2. Ask the Lord to deeply root you in the Bible so that you may not be led astray by false teachers into practices, such as legalism or licentiousness, which are detestable before the Lord.

◆

WEEK 10: DAY 5

Deuteronomy 29-30

Key Text

"Moses proclaimed to all Israel as follows: 'You have seen all that the LORD did in the land of Egypt to Pharaoh, all his servants, and his land. Your eyes have seen the great judgments, those signs and mighty wonders. But to this very day the LORD has not given you an understanding mind, perceptive eyes, or discerning ears!'" Deuteronomy 29:2-4

The Future of Israel: Exile, Redemption, New Hearts

Our inability to obey does not negate our responsibility to obey. In Deuteronomy 29:4, Moses tells the people of Israel, "But to this very day the LORD has not given you an understanding mind, perceptive eyes, or discerning ears." The old covenant perfectly laid out what God required of his people, but it did not provide the ability to obey. However, the defect did not lie with God but within the sinful hearts of God's people. God's standard does not lower to compensate for our sin. God's perfect righteousness simply does not allow his perfect standard to be lowered to a level we can keep. As a result, the requirement of obedience remains in spite of our heart defects.

The just consequence for Israel's disobedience is alarming: "The generation to come—your descendants who will rise up after you, as well as the foreigner who will come from distant places—will see the afflictions of that land and the illnesses that the LORD has brought on it. The whole land will be covered with brimstone, salt, and burning debris; it will not be planted nor will it sprout or produce grass. It will resemble the destruction of Sodom and Gomorrah, Admah and Zeboiim, which the LORD destroyed in his intense anger." (29:22-23). Exile, judgment, and plague will fall upon God's disobedient people. However, he will not write them off forever; if they repent, he will restore them again (30:1-5). And, in spite of all their sin, Moses tells of a better day coming, a day when "the LORD your God will circumcise your heart and the heart of your offspring, so that you will love the LORD your God with all your heart and with all your soul, so that you may live" (30:6*). Under the new covenant in Jesus Christ, God would not only require perfect righteousness, he would change the hearts of his people to love him and obey him. Today, we get to have a relationship with God through this new covenant in Jesus' blood (Luke 22:20).

Casey McCall

Connection with Newer Testament
Hebrews 8:7-13

For the Kids
Demonstrate for your children that, on one hand, God told the people that, if they obeyed, their futures would be good (we call those blessings). On the other hand, if they disobeyed, then bad things would happen (we call those curses). Jesus always obeyed [gesture with the first hand]. We have disobeyed [gesture with the second hand]. But, Jesus took our bad things on the cross, so we can experience the good things [cross hands] (Gal. 3:13). As a result, when we believe, he changes our hearts and puts his love in them!

Prayer Prompts
1. Ask the Lord to grant you a daily remembrance of new covenant mercies that are in Jesus' blood so that you may be equipped to faithfully obey the LORD.
2. Praise the Lord that we will never experience the judgment of exile for our sins like Israel because Jesus was exiled for all of our sins on the cross. For those in Christ, our future is filled not with thoughts of a new exile but with thoughts of a new Eden in the presence of God.

◆

WEEK 11: DAY 1
Joshua 1

Key Text
"After Moses the LORD's servant died, the LORD said to Joshua son of Nun,

Moses' assistant: 'Moses my servant is dead. Get ready! Cross the Jordan River! Lead these people into the land which I am ready to hand over to them.'" Joshua 1:1-2

Joshua Replaces Moses: The Need for a Savior Continues

What happens when the leader of a group dies? At the beginning of Joshua, Moses is dead and the people of Israel are in desperate need of a leader. Every time a leader dies in the Old Testament, uncertainty and crises arise. Who will take over? Will the new leader be a good leader or an evil one? Will the new leader be blessed by God or cursed?

At the beginning of Joshua, these questions are answered. Joshua takes on the role of leading Israel. Just as Moses took the people of God through the Red Sea on dry land, so Joshua preforms the same miracle by leading the people of God on dry land through the Jordan River. Moses was feared because he feared God. The people followed Moses because they knew God was with him and that God was with them. Now, Joshua fulfills Moses' place in leading the people of God to the promised land.

Both Moses and Joshua point to the God-man who will lead all nations out of darkness and into his marvelous light. Where Joshua and Moses were only able to save the Israelites from imminent death, the God-man, Jesus Christ accomplished what no man could do. He died to defeat death itself for all eternity.

Jake Hancock

Connection with Newer Testament
Matthew 28:18-20

For the Kids

When the sun goes down and the day ends, do we sniffle and cry because it's over? Of course not! We know tomorrow is coming, and it will be a new, exciting day. In the Bible, even when all of the days of Moses were finished and he died (that is a sad day!), it's still true that new and better days were coming in Jesus. Even today, with all the mercies of God we have in Christ through the

Spirit, the best days are still ahead of us. Jesus is coming soon! So be strong and courageous.

Prayer Prompts

1. Praise the Lord that Jesus is the greater than Joshua, the Savior whose broken body and shed blood defeats all of our enemies and leads us into the kingdom and presence of God for all eternity.

2. The Lord was with Joshua as the Lord was with Moses. Praise God that Jesus is with us always, even to the end of the age. Fear not. Serve the Lord faithfully.

◆

WEEK 11: DAY 2

Joshua 2

Key Text

"'When we heard the news we lost our courage and no one could even breathe for fear of you. For the LORD your God is God in heaven above and on earth below!'" Joshua 2:11

Rahab: A Convert to the Lord from the Nations

Salvation is offered to all peoples. There is no better proof of that than this passage from Joshua 2. Rahab was a Gentile. Not only was she a Gentile, she was also a prostitute. She would be considered lower class scum by most of society. But God used her, and he used her in a big way. He sent his spies to her to be protected from the king of Jericho (v. 1).

Why would God use a prostitute to help his spies when he could've used some upstanding citizen or maybe even an Israelite hiding out in the city? Because God wants to show that he is the one who saves! Salvation is not about people being perfect. Instead, it is about imperfect sinners repenting and trusting a perfect God. That is what we see here.

Rahab knew the true God of the universe who had saved his people from slavery in Egypt by drying up the Red Sea and who later defeated Sihon and Og (v. 10). She knew that the LORD was her only hope. She figured that, if she protected God's spies, he would be merciful to her just as he was to his own people. That is exactly what happened. By protecting God's spies, she showed her allegiance to God Almighty by faith (Heb. 11:31). Today God doesn't ask us to hide spies, but instead to repent and trust in Jesus Christ as Lord and Savior.

Chad Lindon

Connection with Newer Testament
Hebrews 11:31

For the Kids
Imagine how someone who had done something bad would feel if he thought he was being brought to jail, but, instead, was brought to the king's birthday party. Do you think he would feel like he belongs there? In the same way, we've all disobeyed God, like Rahab, and we deserve punishment. No one belongs in his perfect kingdom, but God made a way for Gentile sinners like us to be there through Jesus. We call this grace.

Prayer Prompts
1. Praise the Lord for his exceedingly great grace in Christ to all who repent of their sins and trust him. Such grace is for sinners like us, prostitutes and rebels. Such grace is for all who turn to the Lord, even pagan Gentiles like us.
2. Saving faith results in godly works, just like Rahab's faith led her to protect the spies of Israel. Do the works in your life reflect and result from your faith in Christ? Repent of faithless works. Ask the Lord for grace to live in radical obedience to him, even when such obedience may be costly.

◆

WEEK 11: DAY 3
Joshua 3-4

Key Text
"The priests carrying the ark of the covenant of the LORD stood firmly on dry ground in the middle of the Jordan. All Israel crossed over on dry ground until

the entire nation was on the other side." Joshua 3:17

Crossing the Jordan on Dry Land: The Lord Will Provide

The Lord God provides! As we witness what took place in the book of Joshua, we see that God brought his people through the Jordan River: on dry ground! God swore to his people that he would deliver them into the promised land, and the LORD has never once broken his promise to his people. We see that truth continued in Joshua chapters three and four as Israel walks on dry ground through the Jordan River.

In these chapters, Israel's trust is found rooted in the provision and faithfulness of their God. God did not call Joshua to be the greatest leader that ever existed, but he did call Joshua to be faithful and obedient. The people of God were also called to be courageous, strong, and obedient to whatever Joshua demanded (Josh. 1:16-18). Their obedience was an act of trusting in their God to deliver on his promise.

The God Israel served thousands of years ago is the same God we serve today. The God who brought Moses and his people across the Red Sea, the God who brought Joshua and his people across the Jordan River, is the same God who asks for our trust today. Moses and Joshua were simply men who God saw fit to lead his people to the promise land. Today, we have someone greater than Moses and greater than Joshua—the God-man, Jesus Christ, who provides for us deliverance from sin to the new heavens and the new earth where sin ceases to exist. God himself, in Christ Jesus, commands us to follow him by faith (Luke 9:23). We get the privilege to trust God with our very lives today.

Jake Hancock

Connection with Newer Testament
Mark 6:45-52

For the Kids
Have your children close their eyes and imagine what it would be like if the family was at the lake/river and God allowed everyone to walk to the other side

by moving the water out of the way. How would the children feel? In the same way, two different times, God moved the water out of the way for the people to give them the promised land. Nothing can separate us from the future God wants to give us through faith in Jesus!

Prayer Prompts

1. Jesus' miraculous acts are meant to remind us of the Exodus and the glorious provision of God's salvation, calling his people out of Egypt and into the promised land. In feeding the multitudes and in walking on water, Jesus declares that he is providing a new exodus for all who trust in him—an exodus from sin and death into eternal life in the new heavens and new earth. Praise the Lord that he has provided us entrance into his eternal kingdom through his power in Christ.

2. Israel left stones at Gilgal to be a reminder of God's grace and power so that Israel might teach their children to fear the Lord forever. Today we have baptism and the Lord's Supper that remind us of God's grace. Pray that parents will use these ordinances and other life events to instruct their children to fear the Lord.

3. How are you not trusting in the provision of the Lord? It may be related to your job situation, your marriage, or with finances. Pray that the Lord will grow your trust in his provision.

◆

WEEK 11: DAY 4
Joshua 5

Key Text
"At that time the LORD told Joshua, 'Make flint knives and circumcise the Israelites once again.'" Joshua 5:2

The Obedience of Faith: Circumcision, Passover, and the Commander of the Lord's Army

As the Israelites crossed the Jordan River, stories exalting the greatness of God were being proclaimed across the land of Canaan. All the powerful

Canaanite kings trembled in fear when they heard about the mighty deeds of Israel's mighty God. Yet, it was not just the people of Canaan who were humbled by the might of God.

As Joshua was camping by Jericho, he looked up and saw a man with his sword drawn. After he introduces himself as the commander of the army of the LORD, this man commands Joshua to take off the sandals from his feet (v. 14). In this instant, Joshua falls on his face before the LORD, bowing down in worship at God's greatness.

Joshua knows that even as Israel's leader, the nation is not great because of his own wisdom or strength, but rather because of God's mighty acts. In verse 1, it is not the stories of the Israelites that bring mighty kings to trembling, but the stories of the Israelites' God. How much more should our great and awesome King Jesus, who has delivered us from the deep waters of sin, cause us to continually bow before him!

One day, our great King Jesus will return to the world with a sword of judgment for the rebellious, and even the mightiest king on earth will bow his knee in worship. Until then, may we live in faithful obedience to King Jesus—no matter the cost—to declare to the nations the excellencies of Jesus in word and deed.

Thomas Walters

Connection with Newer Testament
Revelation 19:11-21

For the Kids
Have your children do something that they know is dangerous, perhaps something they would never do on their own, something that might be uncomfortable where you have to ask them to trust you that this act is for their good. Once they do it, explain to them that Joshua 5 is about the Israelites doing uncomfortable things in obedience to God because they trust God's goodness to them no matter what. Instruct them that such obedience to Christ, even in the midst of difficulty, is the obedience of faith that is pleasing to God. Pray for your children to be given such faith in Christ.

Prayer Prompts

1. Ask the Lord to cause you to be obedient to him, even when obedience appears foolish, costly, or painful.

2. Pray for our pastors—that they, like Joshua, would be reminded that their leadership in the church is rooted in their worship of Yahweh and that they would lead accordingly.

◆

WEEK 11: DAY 5

Joshua 6

Key Text

"'Have all the warriors march around the city one time; do this for six days. Have seven priests carry seven rams' horns in front of the ark. On the seventh day march around the city seven times, while the priests blow the horns.'" Joshua 6:3-4

The Foolishness of Faith and the Fall of Jericho

The Lord is keeping his promise. He is leading the Israelites into the land he has promised them. Jericho was the first stronghold that the Lord commanded the Israelites to conquer in this land; however, the Lord did not accomplish victory over Jericho by means of weapons of war. Rather, Israel's victory came through the Ark of the Covenant being carried around the city by the priests, accompanied by the men of war, once a day for six days while the priests blew trumpets. On the seventh day, the people marched around the city seven times. When they finished marching, the people shouted, and the trumpets blew, and the walls of Jericho came tumbling down!

Israelites marching around the city for seven days probably looked foolish to the people of Jericho. The Israelites had no weapons to take the city! This is no way to siege a city. But, such an approach showed that the Lord was a mighty warrior who destroyed the city on behalf of his people. Instead of the people of Israel acting in their own strength, they acted according to faith in what God told them to do even though it seemed odd. Victory came by faith in the Lord, not by the force of man.

Just as God triumphed over Jericho on behalf of Israel, Jesus triumphed over Satan through a foolish cross for all who, by faith, trust in him as Lord. Just as we must trust Christ to be the conqueror of our sin for salvation, we must also trust him daily—by faith—to accomplish his work in us and around us. We are to trust and obey as we look on to see the mighty works of God. The Lord has chosen folly in the eyes of men to be the way he often accomplishes his mission, and though it may be contrary to what the world likes or expects, he is the one in control. We are simply to follow him.

Josh Crawford

Connection with Newer Testament
1 Corinthians 1:18-31

For the Kids
Have your children walk around the perimeter of the room or run a lap around the house. Have them do it again. Have them do it four more times. How did they feel? How did the Israelites feel marching in a circle around the city for six days in a row? Couldn't they skip to the seventh day? In the same way, we do not choose how to be saved, but God has chosen it. Our job is just to follow him.

Prayer Prompts
1. The Lord fights for his people and provides for those who trust in him, even when his means of victory seem foolish. He has provided salvation for you through the folly of the cross. Praise him.
2. Perhaps you need to ask the Lord to increase your faith so that you may trust him and his ways in all circumstances, especially when you are tempted to fight him for control of your life.

◆

WEEK 12: DAY 1
Joshua 7-8

Key Text

"But the sons of Israel acted faithlessly concerning the devoted things, for Achan, the son of Carmi, the son of Zabdi, the son of Zerah, from the tribe of Judah, took some of the devoted things. And the anger of the LORD burned against the sons of Israel." Joshua 7:1*

Ai: Defeat and Victory on the Basis of Faith in God

For the majority of my childhood I played baseball every spring and most fall seasons. Though the only shot I had at getting to first was through a walk or getting hit between the shoulder blades, I enjoyed the game year after year. That was, until the year of Coach King. Coach King was a kind man until cleats were laced to his feet—a true Jekyll and Hyde. Worst of all, he preferred communal punishment. You miss an easy pop fly because you weren't paying attention, everyone runs. You don't get your glove down and you miss a slow grounder, everyone drops for ten push-ups. Looking back, he was the greatest coach I ever had. His greatest coaching accomplishment? Unknowingly teaching us the communal effects of sin.

Sin does not exist in solitude. The arms of sin often have far-reaching repercussions. In the case of Achan, his faithless covetousness wrought grave consequences for all of Israel. The Lord decreed that no items devoted to destruction during Israel's conquest were to be owned by the Israelites. Achan did so, nonetheless, and the anger of God burned against him, his family, and even on all of Israel. This resulted in the Israelites losing an embarrassingly easy battle and the death of Achan's entire family. One man's sin affected the whole community.

We tell ourselves that our sin is our problem, only affecting us. Scripture says that's a lie. Sin often harms others no matter how secretive we believe it to be. Paul exhorts the Corinthian believers to deal with the sin of certain persons in their congregation corporately because "a little yeast affects the whole batch of dough" (1 Cor. 5:6). Wickedness produces wickedness. Take time to pray that the Lord would help you repent of the sin you're struggling with or refusing to turn from.

Remember the gospel. In the garden, Adam's sin fissured man's relationship with his Creator. One man's sin led to the degradation of all things.

But thanks be to God that just as "through the disobedience of the one man many were made sinners, so also through the obedience of one man many will be made righteous" (Rom 5:19). At the cross, Jesus' sacrifice revived man's relationship with his Creator for those who turn to Jesus by faith.

Clay Tabor

Connection with Newer Testament
Acts 5

For the Kids
Remind your children that their sin brings discipline so they will learn to do what is right. Explain that believers are God's children, and God expects obedience from his children. When we do not obey, he disciplines us. Pray with your children and thank God for the discipline he brings when we do wrong so that we will learn how to more obediently trust and serve him.

Prayer Prompts
1. Repent of any sin you've committed that you have yet to confess. Ask the Lord for grace to live a life faithfully devoted to him.
2. Praise God that Jesus perfectly walked in faith before the Lord. In him we receive forgiveness for our unfaithfulness.

◆

WEEK 12: DAY 2
Joshua 9

Key Text
"Joshua summoned the Gibeonites and said to them, 'Why did you trick us by saying, "We live far away from you," when you really live nearby?'" Joshua 9:22

Joshua's Folly: Covenanting with the Gibeonites
          In their defeat to the army of Ai, Israel learned the necessity of fully obeying the Lord and the communal consequences of sin, but they had yet to

learn to consider him at every step in their life under his rule. Joshua, along with other leaders of Israel, were conned into establishing a covenant with the Gibeonites. From Joshua's observation, the Gibeonite tricksters looked the part of a weather-worn people from a far-off land: threadbare clothing, stale bread, and busted wineskins. Even after questioning them, the sincerity of their lie led the leaders of Israel to covenant with the deceivers. But it wasn't the bread, the clothing, or the wine that made a fool out of Joshua; it was his pride. The Israelite leaders, when met with the Gibeonite imposters, relied on their own wisdom instead of seeking "the LORD's advice" (v. 14).

Deception isn't a full-frontal assault. Rather, it's a sneaky poison. Many a follower of Christ have unwisely and hastily jumped into decisions without first heeding Proverbs 3:5: "Trust in the Lord with all your heart, and do not rely on your own understanding." All too often, the path of wisdom becomes blurred by our own self-assured pride so that we are instead deceived into the coaxing arms of sin.

We won't always seek the Lord's counsel in every circumstance. We may be deceived by the evil one towards sinful pursuits. Fortunately for us, Truth has come in Jesus (John 14:6), and, as a match to a dark room, he exposes falsehood and calls us to follow him into his marvelous light.

Clay Tabor

Connection with Newer Testament

James 1

For the Kids

Ask your children to count the number of hairs on their heads. If they can't do it, then ask them if they can count all the stars in the sky. Emphasize that our knowledge and wisdom is limited, but there is One whose knowledge and wisdom is limitless. In fact, Psalm 147:5 says, "Our Lord is great and has awesome power; there is no limit to his wisdom." Remind them to daily read God's word for guidance and understanding wisdom to follow Christ, our wisdom (Col. 2:1-3).

Prayer Prompts

1. Ask God, the giver of all good things, for wisdom in the decisions that you make on a daily basis, both large and small.

2. Ask God to grant wisdom and conviction to the pastors, so that they might lead our church to follow after Christ all the more.

◆

WEEK 12: DAY 3

Joshua 10-11

Key Text

"So Joshua took all of the land, according to all that the LORD had spoken to Moses. And Joshua gave it for an inheritance to Israel according to their divisions by their tribes. And the land had rest from war." Joshua 11:23*

A Return to Eden: God's Rest for God's People in God's Place

There was a time when one's status in society was measured largely by how much land he or she owned. Land ownership has always been a sign of wealth and blessing. The book of Joshua is all about land, but this land is not just any land. The land that Joshua is leading Israel to conquer is the promised land, the specific land that God promised to Abraham (Gen. 12:1; 15:7). This land's value does not lie in its size or its fertility. This land is special precisely because it is the land that God had promised to his people. Possessing this land represented, for Israel, receiving the blessing of God's kingdom.

The biblical story has always involved land. When Adam and Eve sinned, they were exiled from Eden, the physical locale of God's blessing (Gen. 3:23-24). The story of God's coming kingdom is the story of God bringing his people back to his land. Vaughan Roberts defines God's kingdom as "God's people in God's place under God's rule and blessing."[4] Jesus came to save God's people and to reign over them forever. But this wonderful salvation also

---

[4]Vaughan Roberts, *God's Big Picture: Tracing the Storyline of the Bible* (Downer's Grove, IL: InterVarsity Press, 2002), 22.

has a location: "Then I saw a new heaven and a new earth, for the first heaven and earth had ceased to exist" (Rev. 21:1).

Casey McCall

Connection with Newer Testament
Hebrews 4:1-13; Revelation 21:1-4

For the Kids
Ask your children to tell you where they would go if they could go anywhere. What would they describe as the best place to be and why? (Wait for answers such as Disney World, Grandma's house, the zoo, etc.) Explain that the promised land was that place for Israel. Then explain that there is even a *much* better place than the promised land and the place they described. When Jesus returns to earth, he will bring a new heaven and a new earth where there is no sadness, tears, or pain because the Lord Jesus Christ will rule over it.

Prayer Prompts
1. Praise God that, in Christ, we can look forward to dwelling in God's land in God's presence for all eternity.
2. In the New Testament, the Lord conquers and gives rest to the people who are the inheritance of Jesus, the true Israel. Pray that the gospel would continue to march forth in conquering power to give rest to sinners from every nation.

◆

WEEK 12: DAY 4
Joshua 13-14

Key Text
"The following is a record of the territory assigned to the Israelites in the land of Canaan by Eleazar the priest, Joshua son of Nun, and the Israelite tribal leaders." Joshua 14:1

God's Inheritance: The Promised Land Divided Among Israel

If you were to travel down Highway 53 in Ballardsville, Kentucky, you'd find a small, red-brick house with a paltry shed out back. In the backyard, you'd find weathered 2 x 4's nailed high up in a maple tree, remnants of an ambitious eight-year-old's attempt at a tree fort. A clothesline (see also: makeshift zip-line or perilous rope bridge) paralleled a chain-link fence that attempted to contain a dog far too large for the quarter acre the house rested on. You'd drive by this unassuming house without a thought or care, just like anyone would. Why wouldn't you? It bears no significance to your life. But to me it's where I spent my pre-adolescent childhood, dreaming up all sorts of ridiculous adventures with the neighbor kids. Places have no meaning without context. Think of the house you grew up in or of a family heirloom you possess. Those places or objects carry significance in our lives because of the stories surrounding them.

It's easy to gloss over these passages of Scripture. Reading territory boundaries of cities we can't pronounce can seem like drudgery. But these seemingly obsolete cities are screaming, "Promise fulfilled!" The allotment of this territory signifies the realization of the ancient promise given to Abraham (Gen. 15:18-21). This is the moment for which the Israelites have longed! God, through the giving of this inheritance, is confirming the promise he made to his people from the start.

In Christ, the Lord promises us an eternal inheritance (Eph. 1:11-14; Heb. 9:15; 1 Pet. 1:4). His faithfulness to his word long ago encourages us to believe that promise even today.

Clay Tabor

Connection with Newer Testament
Ephesians 1

For the Kids
Show your children something you have inherited from a family member or something that a friend has given you. Explain why it is important to you. Teach your children that these verses in Joshua 13-14 were important to Israel

because they pointed to God's faithfulness to his promises. Remind your children that we have a much greater inheritance in Jesus Christ because we will spend eternity in the presence of God.

Prayer Prompts

1. Praise God for his faithfulness in fulfilling his promise of land to the Israelites. He was and is worthy to be trusted.

2. Praise the Lord that, in Christ, we too have a rich inheritance. We have been given every spiritual blessing and are permitted to dwell in the presence of God for all eternity as his sons.

◆

WEEK 12: DAY 5

Joshua 24

Key Text

"Then Joshua said to the people, 'You are not able to serve the LORD, for he is a holy God. He is a jealous God; he will not forgive your transgressions or your sins. If you abandon the LORD and serve foreign gods, he will turn and do you harm and destroy you after he has done good to you.'" Joshua 24:19-20*

An Ominous Future: Inability to Serve the Lord

In Joshua 24, we find the Israelites at the end of an epic journey. As Joshua traces the steps of their humble history, one thing becomes increasingly apparent. The story of Israel is not Israel's story, but God's. It was not the military might of the people that drove their enemies out of the promised land, but God's. It was neither Moses nor the people who made possible the parting of the Red Sea, but God. It was not the supernatural power of the people that plagued their captors of four hundred years with all kinds of devastating plagues unto their release, but God's. Their story did not even begin with a man who sought God, but with a man named Abraham who worshiped other gods! With every step of this epic journey, the LORD had—with his power and might—brought his people to where they now stood. And as Joshua stood to give this history lesson, he challenged the people to recall whose story theirs really was. It was the story of their faithful God.

With this history lesson fresh on their minds, Joshua confronts the people with a choice: either turn your backs on the God in whose story you now live, or serve him alone by forsaking the gods of the people in whose land you now dwell. Joshua thunders forth the command, "choose today whom you will worship" (v. 15). The people responded as we would imagine they would, "Far be it from us to abandon the LORD so we can worship other gods" (v. 16). Yet Joshua's response reminded them, and reminds us today, that God's story was neither theirs nor ours to accomplish. "You are not able to serve the LORD" (v.19). They (and we) needed one who would serve the LORD according to his holiness—the one whom God alone could provide. The story of Joshua ends by pointing to a greater Joshua (YAHWEH is salvation) who would come bearing a very similar name, "Yeshua" (Jesus) our salvation.

Nate BeVier

Connection with Newer Testament
Romans 12:11

For the Kids
Ask you children if they've ever been told that their eyes are bigger than their stomach. Tell them that some adults say this to their children at dinner time after a child put a bunch of food on his or her plate but realized that he or she really couldn't eat all of the food. Teach your children that the Israelites at the end of Joshua were, spiritually speaking, like a child who said they could clean their plate but couldn't. They said they would obey the Lord, but the reality is that they didn't have the heart ability. The heart ability comes through Jesus.

Prayer Prompts
1. Praise God that he has overcome the problem within the Mosaic covenant, namely the lack of new hearts, in Jesus so that we who believe in Jesus are able to serve the Lord.

2. As you think about God's past grace to you in Christ, ask him to sear the gospel on your mind so that his past grace might spur you to faithfully serve him in the present and in the future.

◆

WEEK 13: DAY 1
Judges 1-2:5

Key Text
"Now the angel of the LORD went up from Gilgal to Bochim. And he said, 'I brought you up out of Egypt, and I brought you in to the land I swore to your fathers. I said, "I will never break my covenant with you, and you shall not make a covenant with those who dwell in this land. You shall tear down their altars." But you have not obeyed my voice. What is this you have done?'" Judges 2:1-2*

A New Fall: God's People Fail to Exercise Dominion
Despite the fact that Joshua is nearing death, the promise of the Lord continues. Judah has been handed the baton of responsibility for the removal of the Canaanites from the land. He is faithful to the Lord at the beginning of his conquest, devoting each city to destruction just as the Lord commanded. But notice what happens as the chapter progresses: the Israelites begin to hedge the commandment of the Lord by accommodating, rather than eradicating, the people living in the land the Lord gave them. Even still, by all appearances everything seems to have gone well enough as the Israelites "forced the Canaanites to do hard labor, but they never totally conquered them" (1:28). In fact, to the Israelites this may have seemed like an even better deal. Not only did they get the land promised to them, but now they have a workforce to work it for them.

By blurring the words of God, we accommodate our sinful desires and don't fully obey the Lord (which isn't obedience at all). This leads to disastrous consequences. For the Israelites, their unwillingness to do as the Lord said by driving out the Canaanites would lead them to practice pagan idolatry and to abandon faith in the Lord altogether. "Little" disobediences eventually compound, leading to apostasy, for unrighteousness suppresses the truth (Rom. 1:18). When we allow "minor" sins to roam freely, we join with Satan in asking, "Did God really say?"

Jesus was faithful to the last iota of the Law of God on our behalf. As the Father said, he did. He did not falter or stumble. In our daily missteps, there's grace to be found in the footsteps of Jesus. He walked the path of righteousness for you.

Clay Tabor

Connection with Newer Testament
Luke 19:11-27

For the Kids
Ask your children if they have ever heard of a "white lie." Discuss whether a white lie is better, worse, or the same as a "regular" lie. Show them how when we begin to accept minor sins as not a big deal, we open the door to allowing sin to rule us in more significant ways, like the Israelites in our passage today. Sin is sin, and we deceive ourselves when we believe otherwise.

Prayer Prompts
1. In what "little" ways are you unfaithful to the Lord? Confess your sins, and ask God for the grace of faithfulness.
2. Praise the Lord that we have a Messiah in Jesus Christ who is faithful to God, who fully kept the Law of God on our behalf. Praise him for his faithfulness, which has redeemed us from our fall into sin.

◆

WEEK 13: DAY 2
Judges 2:6-3:6

Key Text
"Then the LORD raised up judges who delivered them from the hands of those who plundered them. But they did not listen to their judges, for they played the

harlot after other gods and they bowed down to them. They quickly turned aside from the way that their fathers had walked in obeying the commandments of the LORD; they did not do so." Judges 2:16-17

Covenant Transgression and Salvation: Judges as Micro-Messiahs

After Joshua died, "a new generation grew up that had not personally experienced the LORD's presence or seen what he had done for Israel. The Israelites did evil before the LORD by worshipping the Baals." (2:10-11). Thus began a long, spiraling descent into wickedness and idol worship traced throughout the remainder of Judges. The people forgot the God who rescued them out of bondage and, instead, returned to the bondage of serving other gods. They did what was right in their own eyes rather than doing the right that God had prescribed. The consequences of their rebellion were in accordance with his warning: "the LORD did them harm" and they "suffered greatly" (2:15).

In their despair, the people would begin to call upon the name of the LORD, and he would have pity on them and answer their needs by sending a judge who would rescue them from the hands of their enemies (2:18). Judges records a sad history of Israel, but it's a history that describes the state of each of Adam's ancestors. For even after deliverance, the people would again forget the works of the LORD and, instead, worship false gods. Perhaps no other Old Testament book better illustrates man's need for a greater Adam, a perfect Judge to come in power to defeat, once and for all, the enemies of God's people. Jesus is that final Judge, and by his death and resurrection, he has defeated with finality our greatest enemies. "Where, O death, is your victory? Where, O death, is your sting? The sting of death is sin, and the power of sin is the law. But thanks be to God, who gives us the victory through our Lord Jesus Christ!" (1 Cor. 15:55-56).

Nate BeVier

Connection with Newer Testament

1 Corinthians 15:55-56

For the Kids

Comic books often tell a story about a person with great power called a superhero. These heroes use their great power to rescue people from some evil. Use Superman as an example. In Judges, God raises up heroes to rescue his people from evil. The people are called Judges, and they have power only because God makes them powerful. Also, amazingly, the evil that God rescues the people from was self-caused. God used his power through the judges to rescue the Israelites from the consequences of their sin. Just like Israel, we need a hero to rescue us from our sin. Jesus is that Hero, and he rescues us once and for all by conquering the enemy of sin and death!

Prayer Prompts

1. Thank God for all the ways that he has faithfully loved and cared for you by sending the ultimate Messiah-Judge in the person of Jesus Christ.

2. Ask God to reveal areas of your life where you have been content with Israelite-like religious emotionalism rather than true repentance. Confess your sins and strive to walk in love-motivated obedience.

◆

WEEK 13: DAY 3

Judges 3:7-31

Key Text

"When the Israelites cried out for help to the LORD, he raised up a deliverer for them. His name was Ehud son of Gera the Benjaminite, a left-handed man. The Israelites sent him to King Eglon of Moab with their tribute payment." Judges 3:15

A Left-Handed Man and an Oxgoad: The Lord Saves His People in Unexpected Ways

What do we do with a story like Ehud? How do we make sense of it? Many deal with it by ignoring it. But we ignore it to our peril. It's a dangerous thing to come to the Bible and judge it by your own ethics. And to do so with the story of Ehud is to miss the point, which is that God continues to send deliverers despite the fact that the people are sinful rebels. We need that story.

This story is recorded in the Bible because there is a sinful people, and the LORD has provided a double-edged sword to defeat the enemy. When we see that the people did evil in the sight of the LORD, we are to see ourselves and remember that we have done evil in the sight of the LORD. But notice also that as soon as the people cried out, God sent a deliverer. He did not delay with Israel. Immediately, God raised up Ehud to deliver Israel. And he will not delay for you either. If you cry out to the Lord in the repentance of faith, there is a deliverer for you. His name is Jesus Christ. And the Bible tells us that when he returns, a double-edged sword will come out of his mouth to strike the nations. His victory will be complete and final, and his people will enjoy an eternal rest.

David Prince, sermon series on Judges sent via text message link to Dropbox to editor 5/27/2015.

Connection with Newer Testament
Revelation 19:11-21

For the Kids
Talk to your child about their favorite superhero and the different ways that superhero might save them from all types of peril. As you think together about these superheroes, tell you children about sin and about our need for a savior. Then tell them about Jesus, reminding them that Jesus came to save us in an unexpected way: by suffering and dying on a cross. Now resurrected, there's nothing he could not save us from when we cry out to him. Like with a left-handed swordsman and with a donkey jaw bone, the Lord saves in ways foolish to the world that make him look great (1 Cor. 1:18-31).

Prayer Prompts
1. Thank God that he has provided a Deliverer for you through the unexpected means of a cross.
2. Ask God to help you read the Bible with Jesus as the Hero of every story.

◆

WEEK 13: DAY 4
Judges 4-5

Key Text

"The most rewarded of women should be Jael, the wife of Heber the Kenite! She should be the most rewarded of women who live in tents. He asked for water, and she gave him milk; in a bowl fit for a king, she served him curds. Her left hand reached for the tent peg, her right hand for the workmen's hammer. She 'hammered' Sisera, she shattered his skull, she smashed his head, she drove the tent peg through his temple. Between her feet he collapsed, he fell limp and was lifeless; between her feet he collapsed and fell limp, in the spot where he collapsed, there he fell imp—violently murdered!" Judges 5:24-27

An Unexpected Deliverer: Jael and the Head-Crushing Defeat of Israel's Enemy

If you thought Ehud, the left-handed assassin, was a wild story, Jael and her tent-peg reach a whole new level. And what are we to learn from this story? Two things: God will save you, and God will use you.

No matter where you came from or what you have done, you are not beyond the saving power of God. Again, in our text, we read that Israel did evil in the sight of the LORD. And again, when Israel cried out, God sent a deliverer. Again and again, Israel strays from God's commands, but God does not ultimately abandon them. He is always ready to send a deliverer. The same is true for you. In Jesus Christ, God has sent a Deliverer for you. All you need to do is put your trust in him.

God will also use you. Barak is called a hero of the faith in Hebrews 11:32. But what we see from him in our text is weak faith. He goes but does not go courageously. And God still uses him to defeat the army of Sisera. Think also about Jael. Her husband was in alliance with Sisera, but she feared God more than her husband. She crushed the head of Sisera. Likewise, God has sent Jesus to crush the head of the serpent, and he calls us to join his mission to proclaim the end of the serpent's kingdom and the coming of his own kingdom.

And we are promised in Romans 16:20 that God will soon crush Satan underneath our feet.

David Prince, sermon series on Judges sent via text message link to Dropbox to editor 5/27/2015.

Connection with Newer Testament
Hebrews 11:32; Romans 16:20

For the Kids
Summarize the story of Jael to your children. Point out the truths we learn from the story found in the devotion. Then, ask your children to think about the different ways God might use them in their lives right now. Help them to really stretch their imaginations to come up with all kinds of scenarios (even unlikely ones). Pray with them that God would help them to be aware, all through their days, for ways that he might want to work through them for accomplishing his kingdom purposes in Christ.

Prayer Prompts
1. Ask God for opportunities to share the gospel with those you know who are not believers so that they may live rather than perish as enemies of God.
2. Ask God to reveal to you sins in your life, then ask for gospel grace to crush those sins having died to sin and having been raised to new life in Christ.

◆

WEEK 13: DAY 5
Judges 6-8

Key Text
"The LORD's messenger appeared and said to him, "The LORD is with you, courageous warrior!"" Judges 6:12

Gideon: A Humble Deliverer like Moses, But Not Above Idolatry
Do you think God can use your life in a mighty way? When you look

at your life and you see the sin and the flaws, do you think that God could not use you? When you go through difficult things, do you wonder why God would allow you to go through it? Do you ever find yourself questioning whether God will take care of you if you obey his commands? If you have ever asked questions like these, then you have asked the same questions that Gideon asked.

In our reading, we see God graciously answering Gideon's questions. And he has provided even more clear answers to us than to Gideon. If God really cares, would you face difficulty? Yes. But you will not go through it alone. He promises you his presence. Can God use someone like you? Yes. He promises you his strength, his victory, and his peace. Will God really take care of you if you obey him? Yes. He promises his provision, the provision of his own Son, Jesus Christ. If we only put our faith and trust in Jesus Christ, we will know God's presence. We will be supplied with God's strength and God's victory, and we will have nothing to ever fear. For the One who gave us his Son on the cross will not spare us anything. We will inherit the kingdom of God. So fear not!

David Prince, sermon series on Judges sent via text message link to Dropbox to editor 5/27/2015.

Connection with Newer Testament
Luke 14:26; Romans 8:32; Hebrews 11:32-34

For the Kids
When the Lord is on our side, we have all we need to be prepared for battle on his behalf. Have your children make a list of all things they would take into a traditional battle, then have them brainstorm what God gives us when we live for him. Pray that God would free them from trusting lesser idols in order to trust him and his glorious provision for them in Christ.

Prayer Prompts
1. Ask God to reveal any false humility that is seeking to cover up unbelief in your heart.

2. Think about the gift of Jesus on the cross, and then ask God for the help to live each day knowing that, in Jesus, we have everything we need to lead a godly life.

◆

WEEK 14: DAY 1
Judges 11-12

Key Text
"Now Jephthah the Gileadite was a brave warrior. His mother was a prostitute, but Gilead was his father." Judges 11:1

Jephthah and the Continued Corruption of Israel
Jephthah had the Spirit of the LORD upon him, and yet he bargained with God for military success. The LORD promised Israel he would conquer all their enemies, and time and time again, God tells them he's already given their enemies into their hands. Yet, the spiritual condition of Israel is such that now a judge, a leader in Israel, instead of trusting the word of the Lord, makes a tragic, foolish, and wicked vow before the LORD. He approaches the LORD not as a recipient of gracious blessing, but as a politician. What the LORD freely gave, Jephthah sought to control. Jephthah, even though zealous for the LORD, did not know the LORD as he revealed himself. Jephthah was unfamiliar with the Law of God, and his perpetual foolishness led to the killing of his daughter and the ruin of any chance of a legacy, and it drove Israel into further spiritual, moral, and ethical decay.

And so it is with some of us. In Christ, we've been given "every spiritual blessing in the heavenly realms" (Eph. 1:3), and yet we approach the Lord as if he doesn't desire to give us all things (Rom. 8:32). Oftentimes this is due to a misunderstanding or forgetting of the gospel. We forget who we are as recipients of grace, and our flesh pulls us away from mercy and back into works-based bargaining with God: "God, if I do this, will you give me this?" Disbelieving the gospel only leads to spiritual rot. The Lord has given you everything in Christ. Believe it!

113

Connection with Newer Testament

Romans 8:32; Ephesians 1:3-14; Hebrews 11:32-40

For the Kids

Share an example from your life when you acted sinfully—maybe even with what you thought were good intentions. Even the best leaders still commit sin. Explain that only someone with no sins of his own can remove our sins, and ask your children if they can think of anyone whom that might describe. Then pray for your children to cling to Jesus.

Prayer Prompts

1. Jephthah was a mini-messiah who needed the Messiah to cover his sins. By faith, Jephthah received such mercy. Praise God that his saving mercy flows to all who put their faith in Jesus.

2. Jephthah's foolishness flows from his sacrificial vow, knowing the object of the sacrifice might be a human. And he was more foolish and wicked for actually keeping the vow! Ask God for grace to keep you from wicked and foolish decision-making as you abide in Christ.

◆

WEEK 14: DAY 2

Judges 19-21

Key Text

"In those days Israel had no king. Each man did what he considered to be right." Judges 21:25

In Need of a King: Sodomy, Slaughter, and the Grace of God

As we have read through Judges, we have been shocked by the overwhelming weight of sin that we see in Israel. Our reading for today is no different. But the shocking nature of the sins committed is not the point of Judges. Rather, the point of Judges is to teach us that God's grace is more shocking than sin. If we are not shocked by God's grace, we have not fully understood God's grace.

The story in Judges 19 should remind us of another. We should immediately think of Sodom (Gen. 19). Gibeah, the city of the tribe of Benjamin, is the new Sodom. The people who were to rid the land of Canaanites is now indistinguishable from them. And because of their rebellion, the LORD defeats and almost destroys Benjamin (20:35). But he leaves a remnant, and what we find in Judges 21 is shocking. We find Israel repenting through sacrifice and God responding in grace. Benjamin was provided wives so that the tribe could continue. We see in chapter 21 that God remains doggedly committed to his people in spite of their sinful rebellion.

Aren't you glad that God is doggedly committed to you in spite of your sin? Aren't you glad that God chastises those he loves? We know God's ultimate commitment to us in that he sent Jesus to live and die on our behalf so that we could enter in his presence. No matter what you face today, know that God is so committed to you that he was willing to send his only Son to die on a cross in your place. God has not abandoned you. Today, you can face anything because you know that God is totally committed to your good.

David Prince, sermon series on Judges sent via text message link to Dropbox to editor 5/27/2015.

Connection with Newer Testament
Romans 8:32; Philippians 3

For the Kids
List some sinful actions, then ask your children what they think the consequences of those actions would be. Finally, ask what they think the consequences would be for someone who rebelled against God and his law. Then tell them about Jesus. Are they surprised to hear that God doesn't give his people what we deserve but decided to save us and give us the gift of eternal life instead?

Prayer Prompts

1. Remember your sin, and thank God for his complete commitment to you displayed in the cross of Jesus.

2. There are most likely people in your family who are far from the Lord. Remember the shocking grace of God, and pray that they would be reconciled to the God of shocking grace.

◆

WEEK 14: DAY 3
Ruth

Key Text

"Then the women said to Naomi, 'Blessed be the LORD, who has not removed a redeemer from you today. May his name be exclaimed in Israel!'" Ruth 4:14

The Lord's King is Coming!

The book of Ruth is a love story, but not the kind of love story to which we are accustomed. Like many love stories, it begins with loss and difficult circumstance. We are introduced to Ruth through Naomi. Naomi and her husband, Elimelech, move from Jerusalem to Moab due to a severe famine during the time of the judges. With them travel their two sons. Both sons take Moabite women as their wives. One of those women is Ruth.

Tragedy befalls the family. Naomi's husband dies along with both her sons. She instructs Ruth and her other daughter-in-law to return to their people and their homeland's gods. Naomi plans to return to Israel broke and desolate. Naomi wants to free the women from the poverty she will experience. Ruth, however, is faithful. She tells Naomi, "Stop urging me to abandon you! For wherever you go, I will go. Wherever you live, I will live. Your people will become my people, and your God will become my God." (1:16).

Ruth follows her mother-in-law to Israel where she is forced to scavenge grain for their survival, but God directs her steps. While she is gleaning, she meets her future redeemer: Boaz. Boaz, a distant relative, falls in love with Ruth, and he takes her as his bride. This act is not the greatest picture of love in the story. For from this union between Ruth and Boaz comes the linage from which King David springs. While that in itself is important, it is not nearly as amazing as the fact that from this same linage Jesus was born. Jesus, the one who was to save his people from their sin was foreshadowed in the life of a poor Moabite woman. The greatest act of love in this book is God working centuries before to send his redeemer, Jesus, for his bride, the church.

Adam York

Connection with Newer Testament
Matthew 1

For the Kids
Ask your children to name a few fairytales where a prince rescues a princess and the two live happily ever after. Then, describe to them that Jesus is the Prince of Peace who loved his bride, the Church, so much that he died for her. Yet, remind them that he was raised from the dead so that the church does not have to fear death. Show your children how the story of Ruth leads to Jesus.

Prayer Prompts
1. Praise the Lord that, like Ruth, we Gentiles have been brought into the fold of God through faith in the promises of God.
2. Ask the Lord for grace to trust his providence. He can turn bleak circumstances, like famine, death, and daily difficulties, into circumstances that lead to your great joy, to great good for his kingdom, and to great glory for his name.

◆

WEEK 14: DAY 4
1 Samuel 1-2:11

Key Text
"The LORD shatters his adversaries; he thunders against them from the heavens. The LORD executes judgment to the ends of the earth. He will strengthen his king and exalt the power of his anointed one." 1 Samuel 2:10

Hannah's Song: Interpreting the World Upside Down

Hannah, the barren wife of Elkanah, desired nothing more than a son, a son whom she vowed to give to the Lord in service should the Lord choose to bless her request (1:11). And in the midst of the wickedness of Israel, in the midst of wicked priests serving before the altar in Shiloh, God granted Hannah's passionate plea and gave her a son whom she named Samuel, meaning "God has heard." This child would grow to be Israel's last judge and would eventually anoint a king (David) upon whose throne would one day sit the Messiah, the Judge, the Prophet, Priest, and King of the cosmos.

Hannah's response to God's provision is a song of victory (2:1-10). Her fervent response to God was one of confidence and joy in God, her salvation. He is one who is faithful to lift the needy from the ash heap, to raise the poor from the dust, and to give them a seat with princes. Hannah's humility becomes her crown of glory as she foreshadows the King whom God will supply—and this before a king had ever been seated on a throne in Israel. "The LORD executes judgment to the ends of the earth. He will strengthen his king and exalt the power of his anointed one" (2:10). She sings a song of praise in Jesus' name. Christ's exaltation as the ultimate anointed King of the LORD is her sure foundation.

In a fascinating development, Hannah's song is a song with lyrics of striking similarities to the song the virgin Mary sings in Luke 1:46-55 while the Lord Jesus Christ was still within her womb. God's provision of the prophet/judge Samuel pointed ahead to the all sufficient provision of Jesus Christ.

Nate BeVier

Connection with Newer Testament
Matthew 5:1-12; Luke 1:46-55

For the Kids
Have your children stand on their heads or lean upside-down off of the couch. Remark how funny everything looks from this perspective, with the furniture clinging to the 'ceiling' and nothing but a few light fixtures on the 'floor'.

Explain how, for God's people, everything is upside-down. Those in this world who are wealthy and strong but wicked will come to nothing, while the weak and brokenhearted who trust in God are called blessed.

Prayer Prompts

1. Thank God for what he has provided you and thank God for the things he has withheld, knowing that one day, we will lack for nothing in his kingdom.

2. Ask the Lord to help you see the world upside down—to help you understand that those who trust in the Lord will be vindicated and that those who don't trust the Lord will be judged, even when it may appear to be the opposite in the present moment.

◆

WEEK 14: DAY 5
1 Samuel 9-10

Key Text

"There was a Benjaminite man named Kish son of Abiel, the son of Zeror, the son of Becorath, the son of Aphiah of Benjamin. He was a prominent person. He had a son named Saul, a handsome young man. There was no one among the Israelites more handsome than he was; he stood head and shoulders above all the people." 1 Samuel 9:1-2

Saul: The Lord Appoints the Worldly King that Israel Desires

At the end of 1 Samuel 8, the Israelites reject the prophet Samuel's warning against establishing a worldly king, crying, "No! There will be a king over us! We will be like all the other nations" (1 Sam 8:19b-20a). The Israelites traded the rule of the One who holds every molecule together for a man who couldn't find his father's donkeys. They placed a man on the throne of their own choosing who only looked the part, impressive in stature and appearance. But Saul would ultimately reject the Lord, joining with those he was to lead in doing what was right in his own eyes, using the blessings of the Lord for his own personal gain. God's reign over his people was effervescent (lively), and he lavishly gave them all they needed and more. His kingship was one of blessing. Saul's kingship was one of bondage.

Each day we are faced with the same decision the Israelites faced at the end of 1 Samuel 8: do we submit to the rightful King on the throne, or do we fight to place our own king (our own self) on the throne? We rule in the vein of Saul—self-serving, vying for control. Jesus, the true King, is not like Saul. Jesus' reign is self-sacrificial for the benefit of the ones he loves. He proved that with his own blood, securing an eternal kingdom for us through his sin-atoning death.

Clay Tabor

Connection with Newer Testament
Philippians 2:1-11

For the Kids
Ask your children to name their favorite sports team. What if the players on that team stopped doing their jobs and each started pretending to be the coach, making their own teams, and making up their own rules? It wouldn't go very well! Tell them the example of Saul and Israel. Remind your children that when we sin, we are taking God's place and acting as if we are king, which leads to death. Thank God that he restores us to his 'team' through repentance and faith and that he helps us see our proper roles!

Prayer Prompts
1. Praise the Lord that he has provided us with a righteous King from the line of Judah who has delivered us from our sins. Unlike Saul, this King does not garner the attention of the world, but rather lives fulfilling the Law as an unassuming ruler who perfectly seeks the Lord.
2. Ask the Lord to guard you from making sinfully foolish decisions that reject the Lord as King in favor of serving your own desires.

◆

WEEK 15: DAY 1
1 Samuel 12-13

Key Text
"So Saul said, 'Bring me the burnt offering and the peace offerings.' Then he offered a burnt offering." 1 Samuel 13:9

A Sinful Sacrifice: Saul Unfit to Be King of Israel
The world we live in today tells us we must live our best life now. The world will tell us, "Here are a few steps to maximize your happiness." There's something that the world doesn't tell us. It doesn't tell us about warnings, but the Bible is full of them! The problem with the warning about foolishness is that we never really believe that we are foolish.

In 1 Samuel 13 there was a need for leadership. The people of Israel were crying out for a king. In God's grace, he gave his people an earthly king, Saul. Saul was from a nowhere place. He was unfit to be king, but the people demanded a king from God. Saul was not a king who listened to the voice of the LORD, but he was given to the people. During the few years Saul reigned as king, he offered a sacrifice against the will of the LORD. Saul walked away from the voice of wisdom from the LORD and became a fool. He knew the command of the LORD, but he thought his way was more advantageous.

Anytime we believe our way to be better than Almighty God's way, we become fools. When obedience requires trust, we act as if God has asked too much. We want to be obedient only when we know we will benefit from being obedient. Obedience means you have to trust something outside of you—someone outside of you—Christ. Saul did not understand this and, too often, we don't either. Only when we realize our foolishness towards God can we repent and trust in Christ. For true wisdom is doing what is right in God's eyes. Praise be to God that he has revealed what is right and good.

David Prince, "Your Foolish Life Now! One Easy Step into a Life of Folly," Preached 1/25/2009, Prince on Preaching Website, Accessed 4 December 2015. Available from

Connection with Newer Testament
1 Corinthians 3:18-23

For the Kids
Saul knew his role as king wasn't also to be the priest, but he wanted victory for himself in battle and thought he could use God to get what he wanted. Explain how disobedience can never lead to wisdom or joy. Pray God would give you and your children the grace to follow the voice of Wisdom instead of folly.

Prayer Prompts
1. Praise the Lord that he is in control. If you had his authority, you would destroy yourself and the world in your folly.
2. Repent of your foolishness before God and cling to his wisdom, wisdom which often appears foolish according to our worldly standards.

◆

WEEK 15: DAY 2
1 Samuel 16

Key Text
"So Jesse had him brought in. Now he was ruddy, with attractive eyes and a handsome appearance. The LORD said, 'Go and anoint him. This is the one!'" 1 Samuel 16:12

The Lord's King: David is Anointed King
Everyone is in pursuit of power. We want to look powerful and to be powerful. The question is: Do we pursue power that honors God or that doesn't honor God?

In our text, Israel wanted a power that was contrary to God's honor. They wanted a power that they could see! Never mind that they had a God who was all-powerful and controls the cosmos. They said, "We want a king like the other nations!" So, God appointed Saul to be king. But it wasn't long until God ripped the kingdom of Israel from Saul.

How do you think about power? God defines power as this: "The fulfillment of my purposes." God says, "Look back on all that I have done and see my hand guiding you."

Too often we want to see that we are in control. We want to exercise our power over our lives, but that only leads to folly. The only way we will ever know true power is when our lives are in perfect alignment with God's grace.

When God anointed David as king, he was a sinner that deserved the judgment of God. But, according to God's purposes, David was used in the most powerful way possible. David was used in a mighty way as king that made much of Jesus. No one can be *you* surrendered to Jesus except *you*. God is in the habit of using the outcast to make much of himself when we align ourselves to his will and his power for our lives.

David Prince, "Seeing God's King: Understanding Power in the Kingdom of Christ," Preached 2/22/2009, Prince on Preaching Website, Accessed 4 December 2015, Available from http://www.davidprince.com/2009/02/22/seeing-god's-king-understanding-power-in-the-kingdom-of-christ-1-samuel-161-13/.

Connection with Newer Testament
1 Corinthians 1:27-31

For the Kids
God didn't look at David from the outside. David wasn't the biggest or strongest or oldest (which was pretty important back then). God chose David because of his heart. He uses what we think is upside down to show that he is all-powerful. Then teach your children how silly it appears from the outside that salvation would come through Jesus crucified. Then show them how powerful God is as you tell them about the resurrection. Even more, tell your children that God offers salvation to anyone who will repent of sin and trust in Jesus, not just those who appear attractive or rich or famous or strong.

Prayer Prompts

1. Praise God for his all-powerful wisdom over your life.

2. Maybe you need to repent of desiring worldly power that exalts yourself and not the Spirit-filled power that makes much of Jesus.

◆

WEEK 15: DAY 3

1 Samuel 17

Key Text

"'This very day the LORD will deliver you into my hand! I will strike you down and cut off your head.'" 1 Samuel 17:46a

The Lord's Warrior: David Strikes the Head of Goliath

We all know the story of David and Goliath. But could we be reading that story, along with other texts of the Bible, wrongly? The Bible is often taught, preached, and read as if it is all about you. There is a tendency today to jump straight from the text to your life. When you do that in 1 Samuel 17, you see Goliath as any type of general problem in your life. You look at your own problems and Goliath represents your problems. Goliath might be your financial struggle. Goliath might be a health issue in your life. He might be the next hurdle to a new promotion. When we see Goliath as our problems, we make ourselves David. We often like to be the protagonist of the story—so it's only fitting, right? David had courage, so I must have courage. David was clever, so I must be clever. I have to slay the Goliath in my life. But that couldn't be further from the truth.

We cannot forget who David is. We cannot read 1 Samuel 17 as if we have not seen what God has done in 1 Samuel 16 and the rest of the Bible. David did not look much like a king. He was a young man, a man after God's own heart. He was a shepherd from Bethlehem. And David removed the head of the enemy, just as Jesus crushed the head of the Serpent. The Bible is a book about our God magnifying his Son. That means we must first ask the question, "How does this passage magnify Christ?" If you don't do that, you will read the entire Bible wrong. Don't walk away from reading this passage and think you should have more faith in your strength, your intellect, and your courage. We are to see ourselves as Israel—a cowering people who were faced with an enemy too great to overcome in their own strength. David was the only hope of Israel. Christ is your only hope.

David Prince, "David and Goliath We Never Knew You: The Good News that the Bible is Not All About You," Preached 3/8/2009, Prince on Preaching Website, Accessed 4 December 2015, Available from http://www.davidprince.com/2009/03/08/david-goliath-never-knew-good-news-bible-1-samuel-17/.

Connection with Newer Testament
Romans 16:20

For the Kids
The story of David and Goliath is exciting. There is a hero and villain, a good army and bad army. The hero is a young man, and the villain is a giant. With skill, craftiness, and trust in the LORD, this young hero (David) defeats the big, nasty villain (Goliath). It is an amazing story, and we all want to be like the hero. In truth, rather than being the hero, we need a hero. Just like God raised up David to rescue Israel, we need God to raise up a Hero to defeat our big, nasty enemy that we cannot defeat. God sent his son Jesus to be our Hero to defeat our enemy, sin. Praise God his Hero is victorious!

Prayer Prompts
1. Praise the Lord that the battle has already been won! You do not have to work for approval, you simply get to rest in the grace of God.
2. Perhaps you need to confess your sin and repent before the Lord. You may have been trying to earn your place in God's kingdom, but he has already earned it for you.

◆

WEEK 15: DAY 4
1 Samuel 21-22

Key Text

"So the priest gave him holy bread, for there was no bread there other than the bread of the Presence. It had been removed from before the LORD in order to replace it with hot bread on the day it had been taken away." 1 Samuel 21:6

David and the Holy Bread: Life over Legalism

News about God's kingdom coming has always led to paranoia. In our passage, we see a paranoid King Saul murder the priests of the LORD for ministering to David. Saul knew that David, God's chosen future king, represents the end of his kingdom and the beginning of God's. Many years later, news concerning the son of David, Jesus of Nazareth, would lead King Herod to murder innocent children in David's and Jesus' hometown of Bethlehem (Matt. 2:16-18). God's kingdom threatens every other kingdom.

The Pharisees ruled over a kingdom of their own; it was not a visible kingdom, but they had established themselves as kings in the eyes of the people through a strict policy of rule-keeping and judgmentalism. Jesus threatened their self-righteous kingdom with his radical message of grace. In Matthew 12:1-8, a group of paranoid Pharisees critique Jesus for plucking heads of grain on the Sabbath and eating. Jesus takes the opportunity to remind them of how the priest-king David had eaten the bread of the Presence on the Sabbath (21:1-6). His point is clear: Jesus is the Priest-King who is also "lord of the Sabbath" (Matt. 12:8). No other kingdom will stand in his way.

Casey McCall

Connection with Newer Testament

Matthew 12:1-8

For the Kids

Ask your children why they think you give them rules. Listen to their answers (it may help expose some parental weakness). Then, explain that you give them rules because you love them and desire their good. You believe your family's rules are for their provision and protection. Yet, your love for them never depends on their rule keeping. The Pharisees in Jesus day believed that they could win God's approval from following rules. In reality, God loves us through Jesus Christ. God's love for us comes through his Son, Jesus.

Prayer Prompts

1. Repent of any legalistic requirements you enact on yourself and on others in light of the fact that God desires mercy more than sacrifice.

2. Praise God that he values life over legalism and that, through his mercy, he provided food for David and his disciples. Likewise, his life-giving mercy provides salvation for us all through the Lord of the Sabbath: Christ.

◆

WEEK 15: DAY 5
2 Samuel 2

Key Text

"The men of Judah came and there they anointed David as king over the people of Judah." 2 Samuel 2:4a

The Scepter Arises from Judah: David Anointed King of Judah

If you read too quickly, you will miss it. In Genesis 49, Jacob is on his deathbed, and he calls his twelve sons, the ones who would become the twelve tribes of Israel, to his bedside to bless them. When he gets to his son Judah, his blessing takes on a prophetic tone: "The scepter will not depart from Judah, nor the ruler's staff from between his feet" (Gen. 49:10). We don't begin to see what this blessing means until 2 Sam. 2 when David, from the tribe of Judah, is anointed king over Judah. God's king will apparently come through the line of Judah.

Just like every other member of the family of Judah, David will soon show that he is a sinful man and not worthy to inaugurate the kingdom of God. There must be another. And so, we keep following the line of Judah through Solomon, who fails, and Jehoshaphat, who fails, and Hezekiah, who fails. Generation after generation come and go, and Judah's kin keep falling short. Then, one day, a Judahite named Joseph adopts a son named Jesus, the fruit of the womb of his virgin wife Mary. And finally, Jacob's words to Judah are fulfilled: "The scepter will not depart from Judah, nor the ruler's staff from between his feet."

Casey McCall

Connection with Newer Testament
Luke 3:23-38

For the Kids
Ask your child to remember a time when they said they would do something they wound up not doing or maybe a promise made to them that someone wasn't able to keep. Explain that God is not like us; he always keeps his promises in his timing. Tell your children that 2 Samuel 2 is about God keeping his promises to Judah, Jacob, Isaac, Abraham, and Adam. Thank God for being faithful and trustworthy to what his word teaches us.

Prayer Prompts
1. Praise God that the Lion of the Tribe of Judah has been anointed King of Kings and Lord of Lords and has brought us into his everlasting dominion through the shedding of the blood of King Jesus.
2. Praise God that he is faithful to his promises. What he promises will come to pass in his timing. His word never fails.

◆

WEEK 16: DAY 1
2 Samuel 5

Key Text
"Previously, when Saul was king over us, you brought out and brought in Israel. And the LORD said to you, 'You will shepherd my people Israel, and you will be a ruler over Israel.' So all of the elders of Israel came to the king at Hebron, and King David made a covenant with them at Hebron before the LORD, and they anointed David king over Israel." 2 Samuel 5:2-3*

David of Judah Made King of Israel

At last, David is anointed king over the kingdom of Israel. One of the primary reasons the elders of Israel anointed David as king was because they believed that God had chosen him: "And the LORD said to you, 'You will shepherd my people Israel, and you will be a ruler over Israel.'" (v. 2b.)

No two positions could be more different in the ancient world. Shepherds were part of the lowest class of society. They stayed out in the fields with their sheep. They were smelly, got dirty, and even slept on the ground. Princes were part of the highest class of society. They stayed in lavish palaces with their families, wore soft clothes, washed in perfumes, bathed in glimmering pools of water, and slept in luxurious beds. God chose David as king so that he would be the best of both shepherds and princes.

As Israel's shepherd, David was to be humble, hard-working, and serve God's people like a flock of sheep. As Israel's king, David was to be a strong warrior, decisive, and rule God's people like a mighty nation. As he did so in submission to God's will, the text says he became greater and greater "for the LORD God who commands armies was with him."

In eternity past, God anointed his Son, Jesus Christ, to be the Shepherd-Prince over his people. As the King of Kings and Prince of Peace, Jesus Christ came and humbled himself and was born in a smelly, dirty stable surrounded by sheep and other animals. He is the ultimate Shepherd-Prince from the line of David who is the rightful and eternal King of all nations who will rule and serve for all eternity.

Eric Turner

Connection with Newer Testament
John 10

For the Kids
Explain what a shepherd is. Our #1 shepherd, the Good Shepherd, is Jesus! Explain that those who repent and believe in Christ are sheep, and talk about why sheep need shepherds. As we all follow Jesus, our church has certain men

who God has given us as under-shepherds called pastors. Tell your children who the pastors are, and encourage them to pray for them.

Prayer Prompts

1. Thank God for the under-shepherds at our church. Pray for them as they seek to faithfully lead this flock to which God has called them.
2. Praise God that the faithful ruler of Israel has come in Jesus, through the line of David, to reign in righteousness over God's people forever.

◆

WEEK 16: DAY 2

2 Samuel 6

Key Text

"When David finished offering the burnt sacrifices and peace offerings, he pronounced a blessing over the people in the name of the LORD of hosts." 2 Samuel 6:18

A Priest-King: King David Offers Levitical Sacrifices

We tend to put a lot of stock in good intentions. "At least he meant well," you might hear someone say. In 1 Samuel 6:7, we see that God doesn't feel the same way about good intentions. The ark of the covenant, which represents the presence of the LORD in the midst of his people, has been in exile in Philistia, but now it is returning to Israel. It's an exciting day, and there's music, singing, dancing, and laughing. And then the unthinkable happens. The oxen carrying the ark stumbles, and a well-intentioned man named Uzzah reaches out his hand to catch it. God immediately strikes Uzzah dead in judgment for his well-intentioned act.

"That's not fair!" we exclaim. But we only feel this way because we don't understand the depth of our sin and the magnitude of God's holiness. We assume that Uzzah's hand is less polluted than the ground, and we assume wrongly.

In a surprising scene later on in the chapter, King David acts as a priest and lives to tell about it (v. 17). David wasn't sinless, but he points us ahead to the future Davidic King, the One without sin, who would follow his ancestor as a royal priest. However, the sacrifice Jesus made of himself would be the last sacrifice ever needed.

Casey McCall

Connection with Newer Testament
Revelation 11:15-19

For the Kids
Ask your kids why people wash their hands before they eat. We wash them because we believe that they are dirty from the world around us. We want clean hands before we touch our food. Likewise, Uzzah grabbed the ark of the covenant because he wanted to keep it clean from dirt even though touching the ark was disobedient to God. What we see is that the dirt of the ground is cleaner than the disobedience of Uzzah. The Bible tells us that we need clean hearts that will obey God. There in nothing we can do to clean our heart from the stain of sin and to keep it clean, no matter how good our intentions. Because we have sin-stained hearts, we are separated from God. However, God loves us and sent Jesus to remove our sin. Obeying Jesus is the only way to be clean.

Prayer Prompts
1. Ask the Lord to help you understand the objectivity of sin. Good intentions do not nullify the sinfulness of rebellion.
2. Praise the Lord that he has provided for us a sinless Priest-King in Jesus who covers us, once and for all, from our sin.

◆

WEEK 16: DAY 3
2 Samuel 7

Key Text
"'Your house and your kingdom will stand before me permanently; your

dynasty will be permanent.'" 2 Samuel 7:16

The Davidic Covenant: An Eternal Kingdom in the Seed of David

David was burdened that he lived in an elegant, expensive palace made of cedar, and he looks at the ark of the covenant, the very presence of God, and it dwells in a tent. His desire was to see God's presence live in a place worthy of his glory. David says, "This doesn't seem right. I dwell in a palace, but my God lives in a tent!" But the LORD says, "Would you build me a house to live in? I have not lived in a house since I brought my people from Egypt. I have moved with my people because I dwell with my people."

Do you get what God is saying? He is a God who dwells with his people. This must shake you. God is so doggedly determined to dwell with his people that he says, "This tent will be my dwelling place. I will live in a smelly, moldy, musty, tent because I am with you." God will not distance himself from his people, nor will he distance himself from you. He does not define his relationship with us by what we can do for him, but our relationship with him is defined by his grace. If any relationship is defined by your ability, you will ruin it. Your relationship with God is not defined by your works but only by his grace. What glorious news!

When Christ came in flesh and dwelt among us, he was born in a smelly, moldy stable, but he dwelt with his people because his kingdom was to be established forever with death and sin destroyed because of his grace. God's presence has nothing to do with what we can do for God, but what God has already done for us!

David Prince, "The Temple (David)," Preached 12/2/2012, Prince on Preaching Website, Accessed 4 December 2015, Available from http://www.davidprince.com/2012/12/06/the-temple-david-2-samuel-74-19/.

Connection with Newer Testament

John 2:13-22

For the Kids

Talk with your children about how you all live together under one roof. Tell them how God lives with his people. He will not leave them. His people never have to be away from him. He will live with us and draw us to himself by the Holy Spirit.

Prayer Prompts

1. Praise the Lord that he is near and desires to be with his children!
2. Have you been distant from God? Perhaps you need to confess your sin and repent before the Lord because he is near and desires to dwell with you.

◆

WEEK 16: DAY 4

2 Samuel 11-12

Key Text

"David sent some messengers to get her. She came to him and he had sexual relations with her. (Now at that time she was in the process of purifying herself from her menstrual uncleanness.) Then she returned to her home." 2 Samuel 11:4

David and Bathsheba: David Isn't the Sin-Defeating Messiah

We tend to look at others and judge their actions and see them in black or white. The person either did the right thing or they did the wrong thing. But we don't see our own actions that way. Instead, we have reasons why we do the things we do. We place the facts in the best possible narrative for our benefit. We want to be the good guy of the story. Therefore, others become an instrument for our storyline. We begin to see people as tools for our use, and if they don't perform to our expectations, we get angry and frustrated.

In our portion of Scripture, we see David commit adultery with Uriah's wife and impregnate her. Then David has Uriah killed in battle to cover up his sin. David tries to paint himself as the good guy in the story. David used his power to manipulate the circumstances so that he looked good and benefited from other peoples' actions. Earlier in Scripture, God calls David a man after his own heart (1 Sam. 13:14). This is the same King David that obeyed God and defeated Goliath! But now God shows another side of David and calls him a despiser of his words and an evil doer (12:9). Is God changing his mind? No, not at all. We see that David was only meant to point us to the greater than David, Jesus Christ.

God reveals himself in a story. He doesn't give a list of facts about himself. Instead, he reveals facts about himself through the powerful storyline of redemptive history, of which Jesus is always the fulfillment.

David Prince, "The Problem—We Take," Preached 12/14/2014, Prince on Preaching Website, Accessed 4 December 2015, Available from http://www.davidprince.com/2014/12/14/problem-take-2-samuel-121-7a/.

Connection with Newer Testament
Romans 3:23

For the Kids
Ask your children who their heroes are. Talk about how all heroes besides God have weaknesses. Only Jesus Christ is the perfect hero who rescues us. He is the hero of the Bible.

Prayer Prompts
1. Praise the LORD for Jesus, the greater than David who obeyed God the Father even unto death.
2. Repent for trying to make yourself the good guy of your story. Jesus is the only one who is good.

◆

WEEK 16: DAY 5
Psalm 2

Key Text
"The one enthroned in heaven laughs in disgust; the Lord taunts them."
Psalm 2:4

A Coming King Who Conquers Nations

"I am the master of my fate; I am the captain of my soul," says every person apart from Christ.

We so badly want to rule over our own lives. We want to be in control over each situation that comes our way. Every day, God calls us to be reminded that we are not in control. There is only one Lord, and his name is Jesus. It's not that we disbelieve God, it's that we inherently hate God. We want God to leave us alone, so that we can do it our own way!

Psalm 2 pictures all the nations apart from God saying, "Let's do it our own way. We don't need God!" But God does not negotiate with the rebels. He simply reaffirms his sovereign, royal plan: he is setting his king on Zion, his holy hill. God promised David that there would be a King who will overcome death, sin, and time. In our portion of Scripture, we gain a clear picture that Jesus Christ will set up his kingdom and that there will be no other lords but the LORD.

Therefore, serve the Lord with fear, and rejoice with trembling. Take refuge in Jesus Christ, for he is our only hope. Without Jesus, we will want to be the master of our fate, and we will find our fate to be hell. As believers, we take refuge in our great God, for his wrath has been set upon his Son so that we can rest in the joy and grace that has been offered.

David Prince, "History," Preached 6/2/2013, Ashland Avenue Baptist Church Website, Accessed 4 December 2015, Available from http://www.ashlandlex.org/podcast/history/.

Connection with Newer Testament
Acts 2:36

For the Kids
Ask your children if they would like to be kings of their own kingdom. Ask them how they would rule it. Talk about how Jesus is a better king and has a better kingdom than we could ever imagine. We can be a part of his kingdom and be under his loving rule by faith.

Prayer Prompts

1. Praise God for being a better King than we could ever dream of being!

2. Repent for desiring to be in control over your own life.

◆

WEEK 17: DAY 1

Psalm 8

Key Text

"What is man that you are mindful of him, and the son of man that you care for him?" Psalm 8:4*

The Glory of the Son of Man

Have you lost the wonder of the cross? Do you feel the weight of God's glory in your life? Or do you walk about day-to-day forgetting everything? It is so easy to get caught up in the daily rhythms of life. Do you ever stop for even two minutes to just think about what God has done for you? The Creator of all things died. The Creator of all things rose again. And now he desires to dwell in you. This should place us on our faces in awe! There is nothing more important going on in your life than you seeking the face of God.

We see that David understood this in Psalm 8. David has seen the creation of God before. In fact, he's lived in God's creation his entire life, but David can look up and still say, "How majestic is your name in all the earth! When I see your heavens, a work of your fingers, the moon and the stars, which you established, what is man that you are mindful of him, and the son of man that you care for him?" (vv. 1, 3-4*). David had a big view of God. When David thinks about the universe, he sees the hand of God in it all!

Everything you see in the universe was created for, by, and through Jesus Christ. He is in control of the heavens and the earth. He is even in control over the smallest details of your life. The mighty hand of God governs even the mundane of your life, and we should be struck by God's involvement in our mundane story.

Casey McCall, "The Majesty of Mundane," Preached 8/11/2013, Ashland Avenue Baptist Church Website, Accessed 4 December 2015, Available from http://www.ashlandlex.org/podcast/the-majesty-of-mundane/.

Connection with Newer Testament
Matthew 21:15-17

For the Kids
Walk around and outside your home. Have the children point out things that are common to them and things that are amazing to them. Remind them that God made it all and that we do not want to forget that God governs all things, even the simple things in our lives. Praise God for his wonderful creation, for his wonderful gift of new creation in Christ, and for his mindfulness of us.

Prayer Prompts
1. Pray that you are struck by the majesty of the mundane.
2. Repent for not rejoicing to God about the life that you've been given.

◆

WEEK 17: DAY 2
Psalm 22

Key Text
"My God, my God, why have you abandoned me? I groan in prayer, but help seems far away." Psalm 22:1

God's Anointed One is Forsaken
David, the author of this Psalm, is expressing an emotion that many have felt in times of distress. In those moments, it can feel as if God is not there. David himself would not be immune to those times. During his life, both King Saul and his son Absalom attempted to murder him. David was forced to flee into the wilderness and to take refuge in caves. Even worse, the murderous intentions of David's adversaries were unjust. Suffering unjustly only increases the feeling of being forsaken by God.

Yet, even in the midst of feeling forsaken, David reminds us to combat those emotions with truth. He still calls out to God, trusting that God is his deliverer (vs. 19-21). David is correct. God is the deliverer, not just of David, but also of all of us. We see this truth in the New Testament account of Jesus' crucifixion. Good Friday gives this psalm its fullest meaning.

Jesus, God's Son, unjustly suffers on the cross, crying out, "My God, my, why have you forsaken me?" (Matt. 27:46). The mocking that accompanies the suffering in the psalm (v. 8) Jesus experiences himself (Matt. 27:43). If the psalm is about unjust suffering, then Jesus is the ultimate sufferer. In quoting the psalm, Jesus voices the suffering that accompanies injustice. No death has ever been so unjust. Yet, no other death can bring us justification. Jesus undeservedly took upon himself the just wrath of God so we may receive the unmerited favor of God. Jesus' suffering is good news for us.

Adam York

Connection with Newer Testament
Matthew 27:46-50; Mark 15:34-39

For the Kids
Ask your children how they would feel if you punished them for the behavior of another child. Ask them how they would feel about you as a parent at that moment. Would they feel a little betrayed? Tell them they would be right to feel that way. They do not deserve to be punished for something someone else did. Then describe to them how Jesus took the punishment for our behavior. Jesus suffered for our sin and disobedience. Remind them that the reason he did that is because of how much he loves us.

Prayer Prompts
1. Thank God that he never leaves us nor forsakes us.
2. Ask God to help you remember that, even in difficulty, he is with you.

WEEK 17: DAY 3
Psalm 31

Key Text

"Into your hand I commit my spirit; you have ransomed me, O LORD, faithful God." Psalm 31:5*

The Anointed One Wholly Trusts Father God

The calling to walk faithfully before God is not an escape from difficulty. The Christian life is beset with those that oppose it, not to mention that we have an adversary in Satan whose sole purpose is to steal, kill, and destroy us. In those moments when the attacks of our enemies seem overwhelming and we are wearied from the battle, how should we pray? This psalm is the answer.

David penned this psalm as a prayer for someone in that very circumstance. It is a reminder that, no matter the difficulty of the trial, God is our refuge and fortress. He is the rock of our salvation. He is our God whose steadfast love does not fail. He guides our paths. The answer to our difficulties is not to escape them but to entrust ourselves to the one who is our strong fortress. When we have that trust, we can say with confidence, "Into your hand I commit my spirit; you have ransomed me, O LORD, faithful God" (v. 5).

This truth applies in all circumstances, even unto death. It is this level of trust that Jesus demonstrates on the cross. As he takes his last breath, he cries out, "Father, into your hands I commit my spirit!" (Luke 23:46). Jesus, God's anointed, trusted wholly in the goodness of his Father. God's goodness was on display in Jesus' death. Only through his death can we walk faithfully before God.

Adam York

Connection with Newer Testament
Luke 23:46-48

For the Kids

Ask your children to remember a time they felt alone or scared. Remind them that, even in those times, God is faithful to his promises. He will not turn away from those who believe in him. Knowing that truth will help us face the hard and scary times in the future with commitment to Christ.

Prayer Prompts

1. Praise the Lord that Jesus trusted the Father unto death; his faithfulness and believing trust, even unto death, is the righteousness that covers our sins before a holy God.

2. What needs do you have? What difficult circumstances are you facing? Don't trust in yourself or in your stuff. Ask God to help you trust more in him when you are in difficult situations.

◆

WEEK 17: DAY 4

Psalm 53

Key Text

"Fools say to themselves, 'There is no God.' They sin and commit evil deeds; none of them does what is right." Psalm 53:1

Humanity's Greatest Problem: Unregenerate Hearts

David opens the psalm stating, "The fool says in his heart, 'There is no God'." It is hard to consider ourselves among these fools who deny the very existence of God. Yet, the next few verses make clear we are just as foolish. The psalm describes God searching the earth for anyone who understands and seeks after him. God concludes everyone ignores him. Everyone is corrupted and has fallen away. There is not one who seeks him.

That is a harsh reality. Perhaps we do not think to ourselves that there is no God, but our actions often say otherwise. For, if we refuse to seek God, we are treating him as if he does not exist. By failing to seek God we are voicing with our lives that the creator of the universe does not deserve our attention. Rather than giving him the honor he is due, we ignore him. We treat him as if he is not there. That is the epitome of foolishness. Note, this is not a failure of action. It is corruption of the heart. As David stated, our foolishness begins in the heart.

Since it is a heart issue, the correction is not a behavioral change. We need a change of heart. We need a new heart. A new heart is what God offers us as part of the new covenant through Jesus (Ezek. 36:26). With that new heart, we confess Jesus is Lord (Rom. 10:9) since "his mouth speaks from what fills his heart" (Luke 6:45).

Adam York

Connection with Newer Testament
Romans 3:9-26

For the Kids
Talk to your kids about a heart transplant and why some people need new hearts. Tell them that doctors remove the sick or injured heart and give the patient a healthy heart. Now let them know that we are all born with something worse that a sick heart. The Bible tells us we all have a heart of stone that is dead to the things of God. Yet, God loved us enough to send Jesus so that we may get a new heart that is alive to God.

Prayer Prompts
1. Thank God that he offers us a new heart and life through Jesus.
2. Pray that you will have the courage to share with others the amazing grace related to your new heart.

◆

WEEK 17: DAY 5
Psalm 60

Key Text
"Gilead belongs to me, as does Manasseh! Ephraim is my helmet, Judah my royal scepter." Psalm 60:7

The Scepter in Judah

Have you ever felt spiritually dry? Have you ever experienced what some call "the silence of God"? You may be in such a spot right now. Perhaps you are going through difficult trials or even a tragedy. Perhaps you have been praying to God for something with no resolution in sight. The Bible contains a book that provides language for these times: Psalms. The psalms are filled with honest and searching questions. These prayers and songs free us to be honest about the emotions and experiences we are facing. There's no hiding the pain here. There's no pretending like everything is alright, and that's refreshing.

But here's the vital truth. The questioning and lamenting of the psalmists is the questioning and lamenting of faith. They haven't given up on God. They may feel dry and lonely and forsaken, but they're still searching and waiting. They still believe that God is good and trustworthy in spite of their circumstances. They still have hope that God will keep his promises. Psalm 60 is a good example of such faith. The circumstances are certainly not good, but David still believes that God's kingdom is coming and that the line of Judah will provide a Savior (v. 7).

Casey McCall

Connection with Newer Testament
Matthew 2:1-6

For the Kids
Have your children identify a person/group for which your family has been praying. Remind your children that, even though God has perhaps not answered our prayers that we know of or in the way we desired, that does not mean he has forsaken us. If we have to pray for them for a long time, that is all right. We know God is faithful, and we are praying because we trust that he is faithful to his people and able to more than we ask.

Prayer Prompts
1. Ask the Lord for grace in times of trouble that allows you to question and

lament in faith.

2. Praise God that, through many trials and afflictions, the long-awaited king from Judah has come in Jesus Christ to bring salvation to sinners like us.

◆

WEEK 18: DAY 1
Psalm 67

Key Text

"Let the nations be glad and sing for joy, for you judge the peoples with uprightness, and you guide the nations on the earth. (Selah)" Psalm 67:4*

Missions in the Old Testament: That the Nations May Be Glad

Are you called to missions? Many Christians would think this could be answered with a 'yes' or a 'no'. But if you are a believer in Christ, there is only one answer for you: yes. Missions is not just for goers, it also for senders. The Bible calls you to be a part of missions, whether that means you are to personally go to the ends of the earth or send others to the ends of the earth. Worship drives both our going and our sending. Missions is worshiping Christ in the church. We exist to see the nations worship our great God.

David writes in Psalm 67, "Let the peoples praise you, O God; let all the peoples praise you!"* Jesus Christ has bought you with his blood, and it was at a costly price. His life, death, and resurrection have made a way for all peoples to look at God and call him Father. Wanting to see more worshipers of Jesus Christ should fuel our life.

David says, "May God bless us and make his face shine upon us."* The biggest blessing God could ever give you is to know him and make him known. Do you see that it's twofold? God's blessing is not just for you to know God, but the blessing is fully experienced when you realize it's not only about you. It's about your neighbor, it's about your co-worker, and it's about the nations knowing Jesus Christ as Lord. Do you believe that?

Jeremy Haskins, "Worship is the Mission," Preached 6/22/2014, Ashland in MC Website, Accessed 3 December 2015, Available from http://www.ashlandmc.org/podcast/worship-mission-psalm-67/.

Connection with Newer Testament

Luke 24:44-49; Romans 15:7-13

For the Kids

Make a list with your children of people your family knows who are not believers. Share a story of how you've shared the gospel with one of them recently. Talk about the role each person in your family can play in sharing Jesus with those people, and pray that God would save them. Remind them that God saves people who look, sound, and act differently than one another. Pray that your family members, and even people around the world, may be glad in Jesus through you.

Prayer Prompts

1. Pray that you would see that God has saved you to be a blessing to others.
2. Pray that your heart is moved to desire that the nations would know Jesus Christ and worship him forever.

◆

WEEK 18: DAY 2

1 Kings 4

Key Text

"The people of Judah and Israel were as innumerable as the sand on the seashore; they had plenty to eat and drink and were happy. Solomon ruled all the kingdoms from the Euphrates River to the land of the Philistines, as far as the border of Egypt. These kingdoms paid tribute as Solomon's subjects throughout his lifetime." 1 Kings 4:20-21

King Solomon's Reign: Initial Fulfillment of Abraham's Covenant

Solomon's rule was a time of great prosperity for the Israelite people.

Solomon's God-given wisdom made his rule fruitful and effective. This prosperity meant that, at least for a time, the Israelite nation dwelt in peace. The time of peace allowed the people to flourish, so much so that they became numerous enough to be described as "sand on the seashore."

This description is an important one. The Israelites are living into the promise God made to their great patriarch. Recall the promise made to Abraham centuries before. God made a covenant with Abraham. He assured Abraham, "I will indeed bless you, and I will greatly multiply your descendants so that they will be as countless as the stars in the sky or the grains of sand on the seashore" (Gen. 22:17). Now, under Solomon, the people are described as exactly that: numerous as the sand.

At first glance, it seems that God fulfilled his promise to Abraham under Solomon, but there was more to the promise. God promised Abraham that all nations of the earth would be blessed in his offspring (Gen. 22:18). That blessing did not come about for roughly another millennium when another of Abraham's offspring would arrive in Jerusalem.

Jesus entered Jerusalem on a donkey as a servant king. He came to serve and give his life as a ransom for many. Jesus the Christ is the fulfillment of the Abrahamic promise. Through Christ and his work, all the nations of the earth can be made right with God. Therefore, anyone believing in Jesus is a child of Abraham, making his offspring as numerous as the sand on the seashore.

Adam York

Connection with Newer Testament
Galatians 3:7-9

For the Kids
Show your kids a bag of rice and ask them how long they think it would take them to count all the grains. Now ask them to imagine counting all the grains in a bucket of sand and then counting the sand on the shore of a beach. Then, tell your children that the promise God made to Abraham about his descendants is as big as the number of sand grains on the seashore. Then tell

them that this promise is only possible if Abraham's descendants are more than just physical children. Let them know that if anyone believes in Jesus they are considered a descendent of Abraham's faith.

Prayer Prompts
1. Thank God that he blesses all the nations through King Jesus
2. Ask God to give your family a gospel vision for the nations.

◆

WEEK 18: DAY 3
1 Kings 5

Key Text
"'So I have decided to build a temple to honor the LORD my God, as the LORD instructed my father David, "Your son, whom I will put on your throne in your place, is the one who will build a temple to honor me."'" 1 Kings 5:5

The Temple: God and Man in the Garden Again
Solomon sets out to accomplish the task that was denied to his father David. Because of the wars in which David participated, God ordained that Solomon would be the one to construct a house for God's presence. Solomon's temple would be so beautifully crafted by the finest craftsmen with the finest materials that it would be the glory of Jerusalem and all of Israel. The center of Israel's kingdom was the temple with the presence of the God of Abraham, Isaac, and Jacob.

This glorious temple was both a reminder and a foretaste. Not since the Garden of Eden had God's people dwelt with him in such peace and beauty. Now Israel was experiencing peace on all sides. Additionally, not since they walked with God daily in the Garden of Eden could they experience God's presence daily in such a setting of magnificent beauty. The temple was a just a small, imperfect, temporary taste of the original paradise.

The temple is also a foretaste of an everlasting paradise. This paradise will be realized in the new heaven and new earth. For only then will it be said, "The residence of God is among human beings. He will live among them, and they will be his people, and God himself will be with them" (Rev. 21:3). The only way to experience this restored paradise is through Jesus Christ. Only through believing in him can your name be written in the book of life, which is the guest book of the new paradise. Will you, like the thief on the cross, hear Jesus' promise that you will be with him in paradise?

Adam York

Connection with Newer Testament
John 2:13-22; Revelation 21:9-26

For the Kids
Give your kids crayons or pencils and paper, and ask them to draw a house where they think God might want to live. Once they finish, ask them why they choose to include certain things. Then talk to them about how God wants to live with us, and what he's done in Jesus to do so. In Jesus, we are temples where God's Spirit lives, and in the new heaven and new earth, we will live with God forever.

Prayer Prompts
1. God's presence with his people is a consistent theme throughout Scripture. Now, for anyone in Christ, we are indwelt with God's Spirit. God is ever with us. Praise God that he lives in you and will never forsake you.
2. The Spirit living in Christians is the means by which we can be fruitful for God and his kingdom. Yet, our sin can quench and grieve the Spirit. Ask God to reveal where you have sinned. Repent, and ask to be filled afresh with the Spirit.

◆

WEEK 18: DAY 4
1 Kings 10:14-11:43

Key Text
"The LORD was angry with Solomon because he had shifted his allegiance

147

away from the LORD, the God of Israel, who had appeared to him on two occasions and had warned him about this very thing, so that he would not follow other gods. But he did not obey the LORD's command." 1 Kings 11:9-10

Violations of a King: Solomon's Sins and a Divided Kingdom

A cursory reading of the end of chapter ten gives the appearance that King Solomon has been blessed of God and has achieved greatness. As we read into chapter eleven, we see that King Solomon has not been blessed but cursed. His amassing of great wealth, gold and silver, horses, and women is in direct violation of God's commands concerning kings in Deuteronomy 17:16-17, which states, "Moreover, he must not accumulate horses for himself" and "he must not marry many wives lest his affections turn away, and he must not accumulate much silver and gold."

God knew what would happen to the king who acquired many of these earthly treasures: his heart would be turned away from dependence on God in order to find protection and power in things such as horses, chariots, and offspring. That is precisely what we see happening here. The wisest man in the world still has a sinner's heart; thus, Solomon's disobedience leads to God's judgment. God raises up enemies to oppose Solomon, and God promises to tear the kingdom away from Solomon's descendants. The kingdom will be divided, and all of God's people will suffer.

The wisest man on earth failed God's people, proving that wisdom apart from obedience is worthless. Israel needs someone with God's wisdom and with God's holiness. No such man has ever walked the earth, except for one: Jesus, the Son of God. Jesus, the Wisdom of God, is the King God's people need. He alone perfectly combines wisdom with holiness. He alone can and will unite God's kingdom as one for all of eternity.

Eric Turner and Jon Canler

Connection with Newer Testament

Matthew 12:38-42

For the Kids

Ask your children how their friends influence them. Do these friends help them serve other people? Do these friends encourage them to disobey a teacher? Explain to them that the people they spend time with affect them and that they should choose close friends wisely. You may want to explore how to relate with friends who do not follow Christ. If appropriate, explain to them the importance of choosing godly spouses who will pursue Christ with them instead of pulling them away from him.

Prayer Prompts

1. Thank God for Jesus, the perfect King whose kingdom will prosper for all eternity. Praise him that, according to his indescribable grace, you are allowed to enter into his perfect inheritance.

2. Ask God to reveal any good desires in your heart which you are converting into idols. Pray for God to tear down the high places in your heart which are not bowing down in submission to Christ.

◆

WEEK 18: DAY 5

Proverbs 1

Key Text

"The fear of the LORD is the beginning of knowledge; fools despise wisdom and instruction." Proverbs 1:7*

Wisdom: Wise Men and Kings Fear the Lord

Know, understand, receive, hear. The book of Proverbs opens by drawing attention to our desperate need to respond appropriately to words. However, these words are not just any words. We are to know, understand, receive, and hear words of wisdom. Wisdom enables us to live in harmony with the world that God has created. Wisdom does not come from our own understanding. It does not come from the world around us. Wisdom comes from God. He reveals to us the right way to live.

Proverbs reminds us that there are many false wisdoms. "There is a way that seems right to a person, but its end is the way that leads to death" (Prov. 14:12). There are always other voices that seek to drown out true wisdom. The serpent's voice was heard over God's voice in the garden when Adam and Eve rebelled. Solomon warns us about the words of "sinners" who seek to "entice" us (v. 10). The other voices come from all around: media, friends, school, family, and our own twisted inner logic.

Which voice will you heed? To whom will you listen? God is not hiding his voice of wisdom. He does not whisper: "Wisdom calls out in the street, she shouts loudly in the plazas" (v. 20). When we heed the voice of wisdom, we heed the voice of Jesus, who is "wisdom from God" (1 Cor. 1:30).

Casey McCall

Connection with Newer Testament
1 Corinthians 1:30

For the Kids
Set up a small obstacle course for each child to attempt blindfolded. Tell them to listen to one family member for the correct directions to complete the course, but have other family members call out incorrect directions and nonsense at the same time. Discuss the importance of listening to the correct voices in our life. Only in seeking and listening to the wisdom of God can we follow the correct path of the Lord.

Prayer Prompts
1. There are always multiple voices calling out to us. Ask the Lord to help you hear only his voice (John 10) and obey him, both for your good and for his glory.
2. Pray for family, friends, co-workers, peers, and both international and cultural leaders to find true wisdom in Christ and to reject the enticing folly of the world.

WEEK 19: DAY 1

Proverbs 2-3

Key Text

"For the upright will reside in the land, and those with integrity will remain in it, but the wicked will be removed from the land, and the treacherous will be torn away from it." Proverbs 2:21-22

Living in Wisdom: The Difference Between Blessing and Cursing

Sin's allure is found in its false offer of pleasure. Eve ate the fruit of the forbidden tree only after examining it and seeing that it was "attractive to the eye" (Gen. 3:6). Likewise, the adulteress of Proverbs 2:16-19 tempts with her "flattering words." She wants us to believe that following her will lead to joy. Sin wants us to look at God's ways as boring, irrelevant, and unexciting. Meanwhile, sin presents itself as exciting and pleasurable.

However, when was the last time that sin came through on its promise? When was the last time you obeyed sin's overtures and were glad you did it? The truth is that sin has never fulfilled what it promises. Eve was promised that she would be like God, and she got exiled from his very presence. The adulteress may have smooth words, but following her leads to destruction: "None who go in to her will return, nor will they reach the paths of life" (2:19). Sin has only ever led to misery, suffering, and death. It is not able to deliver the pleasure it promises.

Wisdom, however, is "attractive" to your soul (2:10). Following the Lord's path will lead to a more pleasurable life now (3:2) and, more importantly, for eternity. To live in wisdom is to live in Christ. This path coincides with the way the world was created (3:19-20). When we fear the LORD, we live in harmony with the created order, and life is simply better. Wisdom generally leads to good reputation (3:4), success (3:6), health (3:8), and wealth (3:10). Wisdom always leads to eternal life and blessedness (3:18).

Casey McCall

151

Connection with Newer Testament

James 3:17

For the Kids

How does a wise person live? Help your children understand that wisdom begins with knowing who God is and having a healthy fear of him. A wise person will run away from sin and try to live by faith according to God's word in Christ. What if we do sin? The wise person will ask God for forgiveness and trust in him.

Prayer Prompts

1. Praise God that his wisdom has been manifestly revealed in Jesus Christ. Through faith in Jesus, you are eternally blessed, never to be cut off from God.
2. Ask the Lord to cause you to live on the basis of his cross-shaped wisdom in every circumstance you face, trusting that the wisdom of God is infinitely superior to your own wisdom.

◆

WEEK 19: DAY 2

Ecclesiastes 3:9-22, 12:13-14

Key Text

"Having heard everything, I have reached this conclusion: Fear God and keep his commandments, because this is the whole duty of man." Ecclesiastes 12:13

A Good Life in a Fallen World: Fear the Lord and Be Content

"A mother's womb is now one of the most dangerous places in the world." I once heard that quote and got chills. A mother's womb is supposed to be a place of nurture, protection, and love. However, because of the legalization of abortion, this place of safety has become a place of danger. Solomon is reflecting on similar absurdities in the book of Ecclesiastes: "I saw something else on earth: In the place of justice, there was wickedness, and in the place of fairness, there was wickedness" (3:16). How do we get by in such a messed up and absurd world? Where do we turn when our sin has made even the safe places dangerous?

The message of Ecclesiastes is clear: our help must come from outside of us. Our world does not supply the solution; it is not able to straighten out the absurdities. No amount of human money or pleasure or work can bring this world under our control. But God has embedded within our hearts the desire to look outside of ourselves: He has put eternity into man's heart (3:11). God alone knows the end of things. He alone knows how to right this ship. We must look to him in fear and obedience (12:13), gratefully receive his gifts (3:12-13), and trust that he will judge the wickedness all around us (Eccl. 2:17; 12:14).

Solomon knew that the answers to the human dilemma were found in God, but his vantage point was limited. He had no idea that one of his relatives would be the key to making all things new (Rev. 21:5).

Casey McCall

Connection with Newer Testament
1 Peter 2:17

For the Kids
God knows that we live in a sinful world, a hard world that is often difficult for us to understand. But God also desires for his people to be joyful as we live in the world. The author of Ecclesiastes tells us our lives will be more content and joyful if we obey God and if we practice gratefulness for what we do have rather than greediness for what we don't have. Think of the many good things you do have that are gifts to you. Thank God for the many good gifts he's given, especially for the gift of forgiveness of sins in Jesus. Ask him to help you fear him. Ask him to help you find joy and contentment in him.

Prayer Prompts
1. Ask God for wisdom to live today in light of the gospel and for mindfulness concerning the brevity of your own time on earth. Ask for intentionality to live every day with a laser focus on the glory of God.

2. Thank God for how he has provided for you throughout your life. Consider how you may use God's means of provision in your life to help you provide for others.

◆

WEEK 19: DAY 3
Job 1-2, 40-42

Key Text
"Then Job answered the LORD: 'I know that you can do all things; no purpose of yours can be thwarted'" Job 42:1-2

Job: The Suffering of the Righteous and the Glory of God

Job, like Ecclesiastes, presents us with the darker side of life. While Proverbs shows us the general realities of wisdom's benefits (i.e. "The wise will be blessed"), Job and Ecclesiastes remind us that we still live in a fallen world. We have no guarantee of a trouble-free life of ease and comfort. In fact, sometimes God's people must endure inexplicable tragedy and senseless suffering. There's not always a clear reason for such instances. Unlike Job's friends, it may be better not to speculate. Our world is broken, and we will inevitably taste that brokenness to some degree during our earthly sojourn.

While we may not be able to explain exactly why certain things happen to us, we can rest assured that none of our sufferings are meaningless. God is in control, and he is working out his purposes even in the midst of the most senseless tragedies. Nothing catches him off guard. Satan can't even act without God's divine permission (1:12; 2:6). The pain we experience here is real and it hurts, but God is always at work. He took the most senseless tragedy in history, the crucifixion of the sinless Son of God, and used it to bring about the salvation of the world.

The book of Job allows us to follow Job through unspeakable tragedy as he seeks answers. Job doesn't always land where he ought. Sometimes it's painful to watch as he listens to foolish friends who think they have the world figured out. But in the end, we see God at work. We see a broken man realize the power of God before coming to trust him on a whole new level.

154

Connection with Newer Testament

Hebrews 12:1-11

For the Kids

Sometimes we don't understand why bad/sad things happen. But, we should worship God in good and bad times. Our God created and can destroy the mightiest creatures (Behemoth and Leviathan). We can be confident in always trusting our Mighty God. All things work together for good for those who love God, for those called according to his purposes (Rom. 8:28).

Prayer Prompts

1. Ask God to help you to trust his goodness in the midst of your suffering. Remember the faithfulness of God to bless and restore Job in his own time. Through the cross, you are already infinitely blessed and awaiting future glory! 2. Ask God to strengthen those whom you know are suffering. Unlike Job's three friends, pray for gentleness and wisdom as you minister to them in their pain.

◆

WEEK 19: DAY 4

1 Kings 12, 14:1-20

Key Text

"After the king had consulted with his advisers, he made two golden calves. Then he said to the people, 'It is too much trouble for you to go up to Jerusalem. Look, Israel, here are your gods who brought you up from the land of Egypt.'" 1 Kings 12:28

Jeroboam and Idolatry: Rebellion Among the Northern Tribes of Israel

God chose Jeroboam to lead the ten northern tribes of Israel after Solomon's disobedience (1 Kings 11:35). God promised to be with Jeroboam and to build him a "lasting dynasty" like David if he would faithfully obey him (1 Kings 11:38). What becomes quickly apparent is that Jeroboam has no intention of trusting and following God's desires but, rather, intends to trust and follow his own desires. Jeroboam, king of Israel, is afraid that when the people go to the temple in Jerusalem to worship God, their hearts will turn in favor toward Rehoboam, king of Judah, such that they will follow him instead. So, Jeroboam erects two golden calf idols to serve as gods for the people of Israel in the place of the invisible God, declaring the same lie Aaron spoke at Mt. Sinai in Exodus 32:4: "These are your gods, O Israel, who brought you up out of Egypt."

Instead of submitting to God's will and purposes, Jeroboam invented his own gods to serve his will and purposes. Idolatry has always worked this way. Since God won't submit to our plans and do things our way, we make our own gods out of created things and use them to further our will. God will not stoop to do our will and serve our purposes, nor will he allow us to give his praise and glory to idols. God despises our idols because God's glory is not seen in images of golden calves or on the face of dollar bills. God's glory is seen in the face of Jesus Christ (2 Cor. 4:6). The cross smashes all of our idols, and Jesus calls us to repent of our idolatry and to trustingly follow him as Lord.

Eric Turner

Connection with Newer Testament
Mark 12:29-31

For the Kids
Have you ever been given a special honor like Jeroboam (line leader, captain of the team, mom's helper for the day, etc.)? When we think we are "special" for being chosen and begin to make our own rules instead of following the adults' rules (like Jeroboam did toward God), we are being disobedient to God. We must remember that we are to obey God's instructions because he is our Ruler. We must remember also that, when we disobey God, we can find forgiveness in King Jesus.

Prayer Prompts

1. We're all prone to act idolatrously, like Jeroboam, for the sake of protecting our own kingdoms. Ask the Lord to reveal your idols, then repent of them. Take active steps to distance yourself from the sin of your heart.

2. Praise God that he called forth a King in the line of David—Jesus Christ. Though tempted in every way, he failed to succumb to idolatry so that he might free us from idolatry's power.

◆

WEEK 19: DAY 5
1 Kings 17-19

Key Text

"Then fire from the LORD fell from the sky. It consumed the offering, the wood, the stones, and the dirt, and licked up the water in the trench." 1 Kings 18:38

Elijah Proclaims the Supremacy of the Lord

The Lord is greater than hunger and thirst, death is no obstacle to the display of his resurrecting power, and he is supreme over all things! The Lord showed his kindness in providing food to strangers and foreigners through the account of the Zarephath widow and her family (17:8-16). Even after providing sustenance for her whole family, her son became ill, and the Lord raised him from the dead through Elijah the prophet. These were strangers in the land of his people; yet, he provided for them miraculously!

This kind and powerful God showed himself to be the only one, true God in the showdown between Elijah and the prophets of Baal. The people of Baal gathered against the Lord; yet, the Lord displayed his supremacy over the false god and its priests. The whole purpose in this showing of God's power was so "these people will know that you, O LORD, are the true God and that you are winning back their allegiance" (18:37). The Lord makes it very clear that it is he alone who is God and that it is he alone who changes hearts.

Just as the widow and her family were strangers in a land that was not their own, so we who are believers in Christ live in a place which is not our

157

final home. As God provided for their needs, so he has provided for ours through Jesus Christ. We who were once following the idols of our hearts have now been changed through the gospel of God: Jesus Christ crucified and resurrected for sinners. At the cross, the glory of God was displayed in life-changing grace and mercy towards sinners like us such that the Lord now causes the hearts of his people to be fully satisfied in his provision of Christ for our physical, emotional, and spiritual needs, to the praise of his supreme glory.

Josh Crawford

Connection with Newer Testament
Luke 4:24-29; Colossians 2:15

For the Kids
When countries want to display their strength, they show their armies off to the world. Ask your kids what makes armies strong. In these chapters, God displays his strength, but not by marching an army. God displays his strength by mighty demonstrations of grace. He feeds, heals, and puts to shame false worship. He displays his grace for the people's good. The greatest display of God's power for his people's good was seen in Jesus death and resurrection. God's grace was fully on display in power.

Prayer Prompts
1. We are often prone to trust in our possessions or our own abilities for provision rather than the Giver of all. Repent of the idolatry of your heart, and trust anew in your sovereign God.
2. Praise God that, in Christ, the rulers and powers and principalities have been defeated and that you are no longer enslaved to them.

◆

WEEK 20: DAY 1
2 Kings 2

Key Text

"When they had crossed over, Elijah said to Elisha, 'What can I do for you, before I am taken away from you?' Elisha answered, 'May I receive a double portion of the prophetic spirit that energizes you.'" 2 Kings 2:9

Elisha: A Double Portion of the Spirit

In 2 Kings 2, the ministry of Elijah the prophet is coming to a close. His whole purpose as a prophet was to point the sinful nation of Israel back to the one true God, their covenant God, and to remind them of the hope that was to come, even in the midst of impending judgement.

In 2 Kings 2, Elijah is passing the prophetic baton to Elisha, and throughout this passage, Elijah revisits several key places associated with the goodness of God toward Israel in passing through the Promised Land, to Jericho, and across the Jordan River. This trek serves as a reminder of the authority and power of God throughout Israel's deliverance from Egypt as it also casts hope for future deliverance from the coming judgement of exile. God does not leave his people alone at the departure of Elijah; rather, the Lord entrusts Elisha with a "double portion" of the spirit of Elijah. God does not forsake his people, for even after exile and judgment, one will come in the spirit of Elijah declaring the coming of an ultimate deliverer who is Jesus the Christ (Matt. 14:1-12). In Christ, the fulfillment of all prophetic hope is found. Christ performed great and mighty miracles just as Elijah and Elisha did, but Christ is the object of the hope to which Elijah and Elisha pointed.

Now that Jesus has, like Elijah, departed into heaven, God has not forsaken us. The Lord has sent his Holy Spirit to take up residence in his people to help us daily live for his glory. The Lord is our ultimate hope, a hope which can be found nowhere else but in him alone. We must trust the Lord for our provision through pain and suffering, in loss and sorrow, even in blessing and abundance, for he is our ultimate and final hope which will never leave us or let us down.

Josh Crawford

Connection with Newer Testament
Matthew 14:1-12

For the Kids
Elijah and Elisha were two amazing prophets in the Bible. When they were alive, all sorts of miracles happened. Imagine fire coming from heaven, waters being parted, a boy who had died being healed, oil and flour miraculously multiplied, a horrible skin disease healed, and more. They didn't have magic powers, though. It was the Spirit of God. What were some of the things Jesus did in the power of the Spirit? How do those things relate to us?

Prayer Prompts
1. In the last days, Jesus came as the final Prophet in the fullness of the Holy Spirit in order to free sinners from idolatry and sin. Praise the Lord for graciously speaking the word of life to us through his sinless, Spirit-filled Son.
2. The anointing of the Spirit in the Bible always results in proclamation of the word of God. As one in whom the Spirit dwells, pray for opportunities to share the gospel—the word of God filled with power to save both Jews and Gentiles.

◆

WEEK 20: DAY 2
2 Kings 4-5:15

Key Text
"She said to her husband, 'Look, I'm sure that the man who regularly passes through here is a very special prophet.'" 2 Kings 4:9

Elisha: Overcoming the Curse in Israel and the Nations
We rightly consider Jesus as our king. He is the perfect king from the line of David, promised from of old. However, the Bible shows us that the title of "king" does not capture the fullness of what Jesus came to do: Jesus is also our prophet and our priest.

We see the prophetic ministry of Jesus foreshadowed in the ministry of prophets like Moses, Elijah, and Elisha, Elisha being the one who we read

160

about in our passage today. We see Elisha's ministry to a widow, a barren woman, a famished land, and a Syrian commander with leprosy. Elisha models compassion in each instance, miraculously calling upon the power of God to minister to suffering people.

When Jesus comes many years later, he prophetically declared, "The time is fulfilled and the kingdom of God is near. Repent and believe the gospel" (Mark 1:15). To accompany this good news, he demonstrated the kingdom's presence by compassionately caring for widows, miraculously feeding the hungry, and lovingly healing lepers. The kingdom of God casts out all semblances of sin, suffering, disease, and death for all who bow their knee to King Jesus, Jew and Gentile alike. Jesus—our prophet, priest, and king—is making all things new. Do you look forward to that day when the new creation is complete?

Casey McCall

Connection with Newer Testament
Matthew 14:13-15:39

For the Kids
In the miracles of Elisha's day, we find that God provides what people need, gives hope, gives future, gives life, and judges sin. How did and God miraculously provide for our needs in Jesus? How did and does he give us a future? Hope? Life? How did he take care of our sin so we will not be punished for it?

Prayer Prompts
1. Praise the Lord that, in Christ, a day is coming in which Christ will do away with all sin and every effect of the curse in a new creation. The fact that you were dead in your sin but now alive is but a part of the renewing, life-giving, sin-overcoming grace of God.
2. What's striking about Elisha's miracles is that the grace of God extends beyond Israel to the nations. God's redeeming work is cosmic in its extent. Will

you pray for God to extend his new creation to the hearts of people living in places where the gospel has never been? Will you pray for missionaries to go?

◆

WEEK 20: DAY 3
Jonah 3-4

Key Text
"When God saw their actions—they turned from their evil way of living!—God relented concerning the judgment he had threatened them with and he did not destroy them." Jonah 3:10

The Mercy of God: Forgiveness of Israel's Enemies Through Repentance

The story of Jonah and the great fish is all too familiar. We recognize much of the narrative, but rarely do we recognize ourselves in foolish Jonah. In chapter 1, the word of the Lord came directly to Jonah commanding him to proclaim judgment upon Nineveh. Jonah fled because he feared the evil people of Nineveh. Fast-forward a few verses and we find Jonah being heaved overboard a ship! Jonah's plight only worsens as God himself appoints a great fish to swallow Jonah alive. Three days later, God, in his grace, delivers Jonah to Nineveh to preach the coming judgment where Jonah spoke faithfully. But something unexpected happens. The people of Nineveh repent and God spares Nineveh! Jonah is scandalized by God's forgiveness. He thinks, "This isn't fair! I had to suffer to receive grace; they should too!" While God's plan doesn't ring of fairness here, neither does the innocent Lamb of God hanging on a cross bearing the sin of his enemies. You see, the gospel reorients our understanding of the world and causes us to love our enemies rather than desire their judgment. Instead of prizing fairness, we are to treasure the scandalous grace of God in Christ.

David Prince, "When God Repents," Preached 9/30/2012, Prince on Preaching Website, Accessed 4 December 2015, Available from http://www.davidprince.com/2012/09/30/when-god-repents-jonah-33b-41/.

Connection with Newer Testament

Matthew 12:38-41; Romans 5:10

For the Kids

Were the people of Nineveh bad? Yes. Bad enough that they deserved punishment? Yes. Did God destroy them? No. Is this because sin's not a big deal to God? No! Where in the Bible do we best see the problem of sin? (The cross because that's why Jesus had to die). Where in the Bible do we best see God's mercy? (The cross because Jesus died for sinners who didn't deserve it).

Prayer Prompts

1. Praise God that he brought you, an enemy, into his family by grace!
2. Repent of harboring hatred and anger towards others, and pray for grace to love them instead.

◆

WEEK 20: DAY 4

Hosea 1-2

Key Text

"Then I will plant her as my own in the land. I will have pity on 'No Pity' (Lo-Ruhamah). I will say to 'Not My People' (Lo-Ammi), 'You are my people!' And he will say, 'You are my God!'" Hosea 2:23

Israel's Sin and God's Grace: Covenantal Adultery Meets Covenantal Faithfulness

The opening of the book of Hosea could not be more scandalous. God commands the prophet Hosea to do the unthinkable: "Go marry a prostitute" (1:2). Why? Because this is precisely what God did when he betrothed himself to Israel. God's bride, the people of Israel, have broken their marriage vows and committed adultery. So, God commands Hosea to name his children "No Mercy" and "Not My People" because God is ready to judge the adultery of Israel. God's bride has forsaken the covenant they made with him in order to prostitute themselves with idols made of wood and stone.

Despite Israel's covenantal adultery, God remains faithful. Israel will still be punished for their sin, but God will not make a complete end of them. Hosea 2 ends with God's promise to be merciful to Israel and to betroth them to him forever. This promise was fulfilled in Jesus Christ who died for his bride, the church, and was raised on the third day in victory. He has ascended into heaven until the day when he returns to consummate his kingdom and to bring his bride to the marriage supper of the Lamb. Peter reflects on God's faithfulness to his promise in Hosea and the fulfillment found by faith in Jesus Christ, saying to the church, "You once were not a people, but now you are God's people. You were shown no mercy, but now you have received mercy," (1 Pet. 2:10).

Eric Turner

Connection with Newer Testament
Romans 9:23-26; 1 Peter 2:10

For the Kids
Ask your children if they can remember a time when Mom and Dad told them to do something and they said they would do it but ultimately failed to complete the task. Remind the children that they were unfaithful to their words and that they were disobedient to their parents. This is exactly what Hosea is about. Israel told God they would love him and obey only him; yet, they did not keep their word. They disobeyed God, and they deserved his judgment. Praise God that he always loves his people, even when they disobey. Praise God that he sent Jesus to die for our disobedience so that we could be his people who love and obey him.

Prayer Prompts
1. Praise the Lord for the gift of faith he has bestowed on you—a faith that has made you, once an alienated and illegitimate child, a child of God.
2. Praise God for Jesus, our divine Reconciler.

WEEK 20: DAY 5

Isaiah 1

Key Text

"'Come now, and let us reason together,' says the LORD. 'Though your sins are like scarlet, they will be white as snow; though they are red like crimson, they will be like wool.'" Isaiah 1:18*

Message of the Prophets: Rebellion, Repentance, & Restoration

Isaiah begins with a call for hardened hearts to hear a hard word. The children of Israel have rebelled against their Father. The people of Israel have detested God's authority over them, and they scorned his Law for them. Their rebellious disease has infected them from head to toe and has caused them to suffer in agony. The misery of their sin plague has spread even to the land beneath their feet. Isaiah declares that God's judgment is coming upon them and that if they hope to survive they must repent.

God speaks through Isaiah and tells Israel how they may be healed by washing themselves in God's grace through repentance. If they will humble themselves, confess their wrongdoing, and submit to God, God will cleanse their scarlet sins until they are brilliantly bleached white. The result of their repentance will be restoration when God takes their ruined lives and their ruined land and returns them to glory.

The prophets will continue to preach this same message for the next several hundred years. They proclaim a message of our rebellion, need for repentance, and hope for restoration. Only through Jesus Christ's shed blood for us can our scarlet sins be washed clean, as John prophesies hundreds of years later: "They have washed their robes and made them white in the blood of the Lamb" (Rev. 7:14). Rebellious, sin-stained sinners may be cleansed and restored only by repentance and faith in Jesus Christ.

Eric Turner

Connection with Newer Testament

Acts 2:38-39; Revelation 7:9-17

For the Kids

Using kid-friendly finger paint, have your children put one or two drops of red paint into some white paint and mix it up. The paint should turn a shade of pink. Ask your children how they can get the red out of the paint. Ultimately, there is nothing they can do. The only way for them to have pure white paint again is for you to give them untainted white paint. Just like the paint, there is nothing we can do to remove our stain of sin. Yet, God promises to make us new and free from sin in Jesus Christ. Jesus' shed blood makes us white as snow without stain of sin.

Prayer Prompts

1. Thank God that we live in light of the cross. Unlike Israel, we have experienced the fulfillment of the promise-filled word of the prophets in the person of Jesus. Praise Christ today for his atoning work on your behalf!
2. In what areas in your life are you living like Israel, mired in rebellion while God is calling you to repentance and restoration? Pray for the Spirit to search your heart and reveal hidden strongholds of sin.

◆

WEEK 21: DAY 1

Isaiah 3-4

Key Text

"In that day the branch of the LORD will be beautiful and glorious, and the fruit of the earth will be the pride and honor of the survivors of Israel." Isaiah 4:2*

Full Vineyard to a Small Branch: A Holy Remnant Remains

A well-tended vineyard is a beautiful sight to behold. The neatly ordered trellises separate the green vines and allow them to be easily pruned in order to grow and produce delicious fruit. God often compared his chosen people, Israel, to a vine within a vineyard. They were to put roots deep down in the soil of God's grace and grow within the structure of God's law so that they would produce fruit that would bring glory to God and bless the nations. Instead, because of their sin, the trellises are full of brown dead vines and rotten fruit. The vine has withered down to one small branch, a holy remnant, which has survived. Despite the widespread decay of sin in the vineyard of Israel, God has a chosen people that have remained faithful to him. The vineyard is not completely ruined, and God has sustained a people who abide in him.

From this holy remnant, a beautiful and glorious branch will soon emerge: Jesus Christ the Messiah. Jesus is the true vine from the seed of David (John 15:1). God will prune and remove any branches that do not abide in him and bear fruit. The Vinedresser is at work to create a worldwide vineyard made up of grafted branches joined by faith and abiding to the Branch, Jesus Christ.

Eric Turner

Connection with Newer Testament
John 15:1-17

For the Kids
Find an old tree branch that you can use to demonstrate pruning. Drawing a picture if there are no trees in your yard. Show your children that pruning is an act of removing dead, unhealthy branches from a tree. Remind them that God prunes his people by removing sinful, dead people-branches from his good presence. Teach your children that, in our sin, we are cut off from God. Remind them that Jesus is the only faithful branch. Instruct them that only by trusting in Jesus will we live with God. In Jesus, we are grafted in (Rom. 11:17-24).

Prayer Prompts
1. Praise God for the Branch, the only obedient Son of God, who came to spare us from the judgment of God. Thank him that, knowing our inability to serve him faithfully, God provided a way for us to be reconciled to him.

2. Pray for those whom you know that do not profess faith in Jesus Christ. Pray that, through faith in him, they will be grafted into the Branch—eternally adopted into the family of God.

◆

WEEK 21: DAY 2
Isaiah 6

Key Text
"They called out to one another, 'Holy, holy, holy is the Lord who commands armies! His majestic splendor fills the entire earth!'" Isaiah 6:3

A Righteous Response to Seeing the Lord
There are two ways most people conceptualize God's relation to man. God is cast as either the harmless buddy or the cruel tyrant. However, the Bible paints a radically different picture of our God and us. God is more holy than you've ever allowed yourself to imagine, and you are worse than you've ever dared to believe. This is the truth that Isaiah encounters.

Isaiah was brought to the point of deepest despair upon seeing the Lord's glory compared with his own iniquity. Isaiah is experiencing repentance. It was at this moment that the seraphim touched the burning coal to Isaiah's lips, announcing his forgiveness and that his debt has been paid. The Lord then asks who will be his faithful messenger, and Isaiah exclaims, 'Here am I, send me!'

The grace of God transformed Isaiah into one who would proclaim the glory of the Lord and devote his life to preaching to people who would only hate him for his efforts. Isaiah spent his life in service to Christ because of the forgiveness he received. You see, the tongs and coal Isaiah saw point to a cross and an empty tomb. It is the gospel that drives us to preach for a lifetime with boldness.

David Prince, "Holy God and Holy Stump," Preached 3/30/2008, Prince on Preaching Website, Accessed 4 December 2015, Available from http://www.davidprince.com/2008/03/30/holy-god-and-holy-stump-isaiah-6/.

Connection with Newer Testament

Hebrews 12:14

For the Kids

Most people think that God is good. But, we sin. [Hold out your hands to demonstrate, one higher for God's goodness and one lower to represent us.] The problem is, God isn't just this good and holy; he's more holy than we can imagine. [Lift the upper hand as high as you can.] The other part of it is that when we become more aware of who he is, we realize we have a lot bigger sin problem than we realized. [Lower the other hand as low as you can.] That's why Isaiah fell down on the ground when he got a vision of God's throne. Praise God that, even though he is holy, he is full of mercy toward sinners like us through Jesus.

Prayer Prompts

1. Repent of any fear of man that would keep you from being a bold proclaimer of the gospel of King Jesus.
2. Ask earnestly for the Lord to help you devote your time and energy to him today.

◆

WEEK 21: DAY 3

Isaiah 7-8:10

Key Text

"'Therefore the Lord himself will give you a sign. Behold, the virgin shall conceive and bear a son, and she shall call his name Immanuel.'" Isaiah 7:14*

Curses and Conquering: Immanuel Will Come

King Ahaz is desperate. His rule over the southern kingdom of Judah appears to be over. The northern kingdom of Israel has allied itself with Syria in order to conquer Judah. In the midst of his plight, God sends Isaiah the prophet directly to King Ahaz with a message and a command: The Syrian/Israeli alliance will not destroy Judah; however, King Ahaz is to ask for a sign to strengthen his weak faith. King Ahaz's response is foolish. He tries to give the appearance of having great faith by not asking for a sign, but the Lord sees straight through him and his disobedient unbelief.

How often are we like Ahaz: worried about our circumstances yet unwilling to turn to God? How often do we fail to come to God under the guise that we might be putting him to the test when God calls us to pray to him continually (1 Thess. 5:17)? It's very easy to cover pride with a false humility that's actually rebellion.

God gives Ahaz a sign anyway. God's sign is unusual to say the least. The sign that God will defeat the mighty armies who oppose God's people is a warrior baby, a baby born of a virgin who will be called Immanuel, meaning "God is with us." The sign that God is with King Ahaz and his people is God himself. One day Jesus would come as the warrior-baby born of the virgin named Mary, and he would be called Immanuel. He comes in fulfillment of God's word as a sign that God has always been and always will be with us.

Eric Turner and Jon Canler

Connection with Newer Testament
Matthew 1:18-25

For the Kids
Tell your kids about the running joke that men won't ask for directions when lost. People say that men will just get more lost rather than stop and ask someone the way. The joke implies that men are too prideful to ask for help, just like Ahaz was to prideful to seek God. Sometimes we just want to appear strong, but the Bible tells us that we are strong when we are weak. We are strong when we realize that we can do nothing apart from God. At that point, God's offers us his strength. This offer is most evident in the gospel of Jesus Christ. If we try to deal with sin our own way, we become only more lost. Jesus is the way that frees us from sin.

Prayer Prompts
1. Praise the Lord that he is Immanuel, God with us. Our deliverance from sin

depended upon his willingness to take on flesh and dwell among sinners.

2. Do you trust God in the midst of your circumstances? Perhaps you are being assaulted by the enemy and your head is barely above water. Remember that God is with you. Repent of believing he isn't.

◆

WEEK 21: DAY 4
Isaiah 9

Key Text
"The people walking in darkness see a bright light; light shines on those who live in a land of deep darkness." Isaiah 9:2

For to Us a Davidic Child Is Born: Immanuel's Victory Rooted in Galilee of the Nations

Galilee of the nations refers to a region of upper Galilee that was a borderland that had many Gentiles living there. Gentiles were any nations other than Israel. Since the region was a northern borderland, it would be the first area to face the pending Assyrian army in their conquest over Israel. With this Assyrian siege on the horizon, Galilee—and all of Israel—was in the midst of great turmoil. In the previous chapter, Isaiah describes the Israelites as having no dawn, being in distress and darkness, and being thrust into thick darkness (Is. 8:20-22). The people were living in a dark time; yet, a dawn was breaking. Into the darkness, a great light shines. Isaiah describes this great light:

> "For a child is born to us, a son is given to us. Dominion shall be on his shoulder, and his name shall be called Wonderful Counselor, Mighty God, Everlasting Father, Prince of Peace. Of the increase of his dominion and of peace there will be no end, on the throne of David and over his kingdom, to establish it and to support it with justice and with righteousness, from now until forevermore. The zeal of the LORD of hosts will accomplish this." (vv. 6-7*)

171

This light will establish justice and righteousness forevermore, a promise not limited to this region of Galilee. It is a promise for the Galilee of the nations, but it is also a promise for all people. A light will shine into the darkness for the nations.

The New Testament makes it clear that Jesus is the light that will shine in the darkness for all people. He is the fulfillment of Isaiah's prophecy (Matt. 4:12-16). Centuries after Isaiah's prophesy, the apostle John describes Jesus as the true light that shines into darkness. Jesus, Immanuel, Prince of Peace, Almighty God came as a light bringing victory over darkness for us all.

Adam York

Connection with Newer Testament
Matthew 4:12-16

For the Kids
Show the kids the biggest flashlight you have. Turn off the lights and show them how bright it is, explaining that, in darkness, it can shine a long way. In the Bible, long ago, long before Jesus was born to Mary, God promised that the land of Galilee would see a great light in the midst of their darkness. That's Jesus! Galilee was where Jesus began his ministry, performing miracles and teaching to shine the light of God's good news of forgiveness of sin. Just as a bright light is for shining a long distance in darkness, the light of Jesus should be shared with people all over the world living in the darkness of sin.

Prayer Prompts
1. Praise the Lord that he is at work revealing the light of his gospel to all peoples dwelling in sinful darkness, from Galilee to us.
2. Praise the Lord that he is faithful to his word. What he promises, he will accomplish.

◆

WEEK 21: DAY 5
Isaiah 11

Key Text

"A shoot will grow out of Jesse's root stock, a bud will sprout from his roots."
Isaiah 11:1

The Spirit-Filled Branch of David: Immanuel's Victory and Reign

The woodland of wickedness is about to be clear-cut by God's judgment. What was once a mighty forest will be sawn down to stumps. God will punish his people for their disobedience and will reduce them to almost nothing. They will be conquered, destroyed, and taken into captivity. Yet, from the roots and stump of Jesse, the father of David, a Spirit-filled branch will grow. Unlike the wicked forest of God's faithless people, this branch will be righteous. God's will won't be his burden but his delight. He will not oppress the poor but will bring them justice. He will not be defeated. He will not be conquered. He will rule. He will reign. He will bring peace.

Jesus is the Spirit-filled Branch of David who springs up out of a sinful, dead world. He comes and brings life to all who trust in him. He stands tall among the forest as a signal for all to see and know the glory of God. His victory will not be a temporary one. His reign will not come to an end. Nations will come and go, empires will rise and fall, but the Spirit-filled Branch will never be cut down. He shall reign forever and ever. He shall have the eternal victory.

Eric Turner

Connection with Newer Testament

Romans 15:1-13

For the Kids

Find a picture from the internet that shows deforestation. Draw a picture of a bunch of tree stumps if you do not have internet access. Explain to your children that this process of removing trees is a picture of what God was going to do to Israel and to all who rebel against him. He will cut them down. Find another picture of a shoot from a stump. Tell your children that, even though

173

God is coming in destruction, there is still the hope of life coming from a shoot of the stump of Jesse. Jesus is the shoot. In him, there is eternal life.

Prayer Prompts

1. Ask the Lord to cause you to delight in the glory and beauty of King Jesus.
2. Praise the Lord that he has given you a living hope in Christ and that one day all who oppose him and his people will be destroyed.

◆

WEEK 22: DAY 1

Isaiah 12

Key Text

"At that time you will say: 'Praise the LORD! Ask him for help! Publicize his mighty acts among the nations! Make it known that he is unique!" Isaiah 12:4

The Song of Moses: Preaching to the Nations That the Lord Saves

It's in your home, in your car, there when you turn on the television, there when you go to church, there when you go out to eat, and even there when you go to the grocery! Music is everywhere. Music is about as pervasive as air in our world, and that should be very telling for us. Music is not just entertainment—it is spiritual warfare.

Isaiah 12 is a two-part hymn extolling the faithfulness and redeeming love of God toward his people, despite their affliction. The songs of Israel are not stand-alone pieces but tell a story throughout the Scriptures. This hymn hearkens back to the Song of Moses in Exodus 15. As Moses and the Hebrews were marching through the Red Sea, they sang a song that glorified God's faithfulness and redeeming love! Do you see the pattern? It's almost as if the song in Isaiah 12 is saying, 'Nothing has changed! We are still trusting the same God that delivered our people from the bondage of the Egyptians all those years ago!'

The same should be true of us today! Our battle cry is God's timeless faithfulness and redeeming love. But for us, one thing has changed. What the people of Israel saw in shadows and symbols, we see in pristine clarity. We have seen God's faithfulness and redeeming love in its ultimate expression—in the life, death, and resurrection of Christ. It is because of Christ we sing! But the song hasn't ended yet. Scripture tells us of a day when our song will be a 'new song,' bearing witness to the glory of Christ in his gathering of the saints from every tribe, tongue, and nation. From deliverance to persecution to consummation, God's people are proclaiming the glory of God in song and clinging to his grace.

David Prince, "Joy to the World and Other War Songs," Preached 12/13/2009, Prince on Preaching Website, Accessed 4 December 2015, Available from http://www.davidprince.com/2009/12/13/joy-to-the-world-and-other-war-songs-isaiah-12/.

Connection with Newer Testament
Revelation 5:9-10

For the Kids
Sing "God is so good," "Amazing Grace," or another selection. Tell your children that God's people have always sung of his victory and goodness—and we always will.

Prayer Prompts
1. Pray for your heart to overflow in praise to Christ today.
2. Pray for God to work mightily in a specific unreached people group so that more may be added to his singing bride.

◆

WEEK 22: DAY 2
Isaiah 19

Key Text
"The LORD will strike Egypt, striking and then healing them. They will turn to the LORD and he will listen to their prayers and heal them." Isaiah 19:22

Salvation to the Ends of the Earth: Judgment and Grace

Consider the reality that, in countries like Iran, Iraq, and Syria, there are devout Muslims, even members of terrorist organizations, who could hear the gospel today, believe, and be saved. Are you willing to pray for them? Are you willing to give your money for missionaries who would risk their lives to tell terrorists the gospel? Would you be willing to build a relationship with a Muslim family in your neighborhood or community?

Isaiah 19 teaches us that God is willing to save them. We see in this chapter God's plan for people who we might even consider our worst of enemies. The first part of Isaiah 19 describes the coming judgment God will bring upon Egypt. During this time, nothing will be able to save the Egyptians: not their idols, not their most trusted counselors, not even the Nile River. However, as outstanding as the devastation of such judgment, Isaiah then predicts an amazing display of repentance that God will grant to Egyptians.

The second part of Isaiah 19 describes a time when God's rule over Egypt will include pillars of worship to the Lord. Pagan cities like Heliopolis, the home of Egypt's sun god, will swear allegiance to the Lord. The idols of pagan gods will be toppled and replaced with altars of worship to Yahweh. These images would have been impossible for anyone in Israel to believe; yet, God uses them to show how extensive his grace among the nations will be.

Does this thought of God's grace among pagan enemy nations bring you joy? Should we repent of longing only for the judgment of our enemies instead of their salvation in Jesus?

Jeremy Haskins

Connection with Newer Testament
Ephesians 2

For the Kids
Ask your children if they have "enemies," perhaps people who aren't friendly toward them or who make fun of them at school or on an extra-curricular team. Ask your children if they would be happier if those people were punished or if those people were given grace. Teach your children that God is a God of grace,

even toward his enemies. Remind your children that, as sinners, they are God's enemies and that grace is offered to them through the cross of Jesus Christ. We should be a people of grace.

Prayer Prompts

1. Ask God to overthrow the evil prevalent within our nation and world (i.e. terrorism, abortion, racism, sexual immorality).

2. Thank God for his patience towards those who practice evil (including us!), and ask that many evildoers would find the same forgiveness and grace that you have found through the blood of the cross.

◆

WEEK 22: DAY 3

Isaiah 24

Key Text

"Look, the LORD is ready to devastate the earth and leave it in ruins; he will mar its surface and scatter its inhabitants." Isaiah 24:1

Judgment on the Whole Earth: Future Destruction of the Nations

In apocalyptic fashion, Isaiah 24 displays for us the utter devastation that will come upon the earth and upon all people before the glory of the Lord's kingdom is fully consummated. In this prophecy, Isaiah describes the earth as being desolate, scorched, barren, and even staggering around as a drunkard.

These images remind us of the connection between man's sin and the curse of death on the earth. As a consequence for sin, the earth, the place once created for communion with God, now experiences death. Such judgment will eventually reach a cataclysmic conclusion in natural devastations before the Lord's return.

Amidst such despair, Isaiah doesn't leave us hanging. God's judgment ultimately leads to hope. All sin will be punished, and the earth will be purged of unrighteousness at the coming of God's King. As those who continue to live in their rebellion are wiped out, those who trust the Lord from all over the earth will gather to worship God's King. It is his King who will ultimately make all things new. Our ultimate hope for the world is that as pervasive as the curse of death is in the world, so will be the effects of redemption at the coming of Christ.

Jeremy Haskins

Connection with Newer Testament
Revelation 18, 22:12-13

For the Kids
Ask your children to build a tower with some of their toys. Then have them knock down the tower. Teach your children that God will one day bring judgment on this world because of sin. He's going to destroy it before making it new again. Salvation from God's judgment is found only in Jesus.

Prayer Prompts
1. Praise God for his impartiality. God's judgment is just. It turns no blind eye.
2. Praise God that judgment isn't the final word for those who trust in the Lord Jesus Christ. In the midst of judgment—as in the middle of this chapter—the Lord preserves a remnant who sings for joy over God's justice.
3. Because God is both just and merciful, pray for those who do not know the Lord. Pray that they might repent of their sins and believe in Jesus so that judgment may not be their final destiny.

◆

WEEK 22: DAY 4
Isaiah 25

Key Text
"he will swallow up death permanently. The sovereign LORD will wipe away the tears from every face, and remove his people's disgrace from all the earth. Indeed, the LORD has announced it!" Isaiah 25:8

Salvation for God's People: He Will Swallow Up Death Forever

In Isaiah 25, we find ourselves in the midst of a great pronouncement feast. This would've been a fabulous social event where only the finest foods and delicacies would be served. However, at this particular feast, they did not serve porterhouses and pot roasts, but death itself was on the menu.

This meal is in honor of the gospel—that God himself will cast out the fear of death by defeating death (v. 8). To the Israelites, this pronouncement may have sounded like a promise of military action and conquest. The last thing they would have guessed is that the defeat of death would come from a slaughtered Messiah.

What the gospel promises us is not political or material conquest, but that we would be invited to God's own table in fellowship with him through Christ. Christ has swallowed up death forever in his resurrection from the grave! Now we have *access* to God through Christ. This means that we have grace for the journey until the final wedding supper of the Lamb (Rev. 19), where there will be no more death or mourning or crying or pain (Rev. 21:4). The beauty of this final feast not only lies in its benefits but also in its *membership*. The invitation to the feast is open not just to Israel, but to all the nations! Praise God that he is at work in all the world bringing sinners to his table.

David Prince, "Feasting in the Face of Death: The Victory Meal," Preached 5/31/2009, Prince on Preaching Website, Accessed 4 December 2015, Available from http://www.davidprince.com/2009/05/31/feasting-in-the-face-of-death-the-victory-mea-isaiah-25-2/.

Connection with Newer Testament
1 Corinthians 15:51-58

For the Kids
Ask your children to tell you what their ideal birthday party would be like. Who would they invite, what would they do, what food would they eat? Tell your children that, when Jesus returns, there will be an even greater party to celebrate his victory over Satan, sin, death, and the curse! Jesus himself will be there, and

the only people invited to this party will be those who know Jesus Christ as their Lord and Savior.

Prayer Prompts

1. Pray that you might have a tangible sense of God's acceptance of you through his Son.

2. Pray for a specific unreached people group, that God would bring its people into fellowship with him!

◆

WEEK 22: DAY 5
Isaiah 27

Key Text

"At that time the LORD will punish with his destructive, great, and powerful sword Leviathan the fast-moving serpent, Leviathan the squirming serpent; he will kill the sea monster." Isaiah 27:1

Return to Eden: The Crushed Serpent and the Fruitful Vine

To defeat a dragon, you need a hero. In this chapter, the prophet Isaiah speaks of a hero that is promised to Israel, a hero that will bring salvation from the dragon. The salvation described in this passage mirrors the language used in both Genesis and Revelation. The language is that of "serpent" and "sword." Isaiah's prophecy speaks of the Lord with a "hard and great and strong sword." The Lord will use that sword to punish Leviathan, which is described as a twisting serpent. With the sword, God Almighty will slay the dragon.

The promise of punishment for the serpent first appears in Genesis 3, just after Adam and Eve's fall into sin. God tells the serpent that the seed of woman "shall attack your head, and you shall attack her offspring's heel" (Gen. 3:15). This seed is Jesus the Christ, who overcame the serpent's authority during his earthly ministry as he saw Satan "fall like lightning from heaven" (Luke 10:17-20). It is this Jesus who also appears in Revelation with a sword in his mouth to judge the nations (Rev. 19). Part of the judgment is the punishment of the "dragon—the ancient serpent, who is the devil and Satan" (Rev. 20:2).

180

Here in Isaiah's promise to Israel, during the earthly ministry of Jesus, and at the consummation of the age, the Lord brings a sword of judgment down on the serpent.

A time of great fruitfulness will follow this execution of judgment. The harvest will be so great that the entire world will taste the sweetness of the fruit from the vine of Jacob (v. 6). Also, the fruit will be the sweetest kind. The produce will be the fruit of atoned guilt and forgiven sin (v. 9). The seed that will produce this harvest is Jesus Christ, the true vine (John 15:1). Jesus is the Hero who will save his people.

Adam York

Connection with Newer Testament
Romans 16:20; Revelation 20:1-10

For the Kids
In fairy tales, a brave, sword-wielding hero is often the one who defeats an evil dragon. Ask your children why they think these stories are so popular and exciting. Then talk about how they are simply a reflection of Jesus the Hero, who rescues the cosmos from the evil of the dragon, Satan.

Prayer Prompts
1. Praise the Lord that, through the cross of Christ, he has defeated the serpent who torments his people.
2. Sing out in thanksgiving today, knowing that your rescue and redemption is secure in Christ. Look with joyful anticipation to the future when all of God's people, his fruitful and beloved vine, will join together and sing to the Lord his glorious praises.

◆

WEEK 23: DAY 1
Isaiah 28

Key Text

"Therefore, this is what the sovereign master, the LORD, says: 'Look, I am laying a stone in Zion, an approved stone, set in place as a precious cornerstone for the foundation. The one who maintains his faith will not panic.'" Isaiah 28:16

Belief in Zion's Cornerstone: Israel's Only Hope from Destruction

Israel's rebellion led them into a difficult situation. The might of the Assyrian army was bearing down on them just as Isaiah predicted it would. Yet, Israel ignored Isaiah's call to repent, rest, and seek refuge in God. Since they ignored Isaiah's warning, God promised to speak to them with the foreign lips of Assyria (v. 11).

Rather than returning to and resting in God, Israel chose to make an unholy alliance with death (v. 15). Israel was taking comfort and boasting in the fact that they had aligned themselves with Egypt for protection. Isaiah makes clear this allegiance is based on lies and false assurance. The refuge the Egyptian alliance offered was constructed of wet paper. It would protect the Israelites from nothing (v. 18).

Even in Israel's rebellion, God placed a rock upon which they could stand. He laid a foundation in Zion. He promised a cornerstone that is tested, true, and plumb. This coming cornerstone was not for a weak, false sense of hope. It was a precious cornerstone full of lasting hope for all who would cling to it. But anyone who would reject the cornerstone would be caught up in the judgment.

This cornerstone is evidence that God alone saves, and no one else. The cornerstone that Isaiah speaks of is embodied in Jesus Christ, who is the only solid rock of salvation. There is no other escape from God's judgment for sinners. Rebellion against God demands judgment from God; yet, God sent his son, Jesus Christ, into the world to be our cornerstone. Whoever believes in God's cornerstone will not be put to shame.

Adam York

Connection with Newer Testament
1 Peter 2:1-10

For the Kids
Use two glass jars or glasses. Put a little sand or dirt in one, and put the biggest rock that will fit in the other. Have your children put water in both jars and observe what happens. The dirt/sand is easily moved or washed away. The rock stands firm. Share that this is true of Jesus Christ, who is the cornerstone of our salvation that our lives are to be built upon by faith in the gospel.

Prayer Prompts
1. Understand that the Lord is storing up righteous wrath against all who have sinned. These floodwaters of wrath will be poured out upon the Lord's judgment. Only those who take shelter in the Rock, Christ the Cornerstone, will be saved. Repent and believe in Christ.
2. Praise the Lord that he is gracious. All of us deserve to be eternally damned under the wrath of God; yet, he provides Jesus Christ, who endured the waters of wrath for us so that all who believe in him might be saved.
3. Pray for daily grace to build your life upon the Lord's cornerstone, Jesus Christ.

◆

WEEK 23: DAY 2
Isaiah 30

Key Text
"For this reason the LORD is ready to show you mercy; he sits on his throne, ready to have compassion on you. Indeed, the LORD is a just God; all who wait for him in faith will be blessed." Isaiah 30:18

Judah's Misplaced Trust and God's Surprisingly Gracious Patience
As the Assyrians invaded, Hezekiah has been counseled to turn to Egypt for help instead of the Lord. This should be utterly shocking for the

reader. The thought of God's people turning to Egypt for help would be a slap in the face of the Lord who once rescued them from the evils of Egypt! Here we have a picture of a disobedient son leaving the care of his father to seek the refuge of a slave master.

Isaiah declares that, for a time, God will allow his people to face judgment for being unrepentant and for seeking the protection of a pagan nation. However, once again, God promises a day when Zion will weep no more and Jerusalem will be fully restored. He will ultimately rescue his people and destroy the Assyrians. In doing so, he will prove that salvation is only found in himself.

Isaiah reminds us that salvation is ultimately only found in Jesus. We must keep from putting too much confidence in leaders and governments of this present world. Even more, we must remember salvation from our greatest enemies, the enemies of sin and death, are only found in one person. Like Israel, we only cause ourselves misery when we seek salvation, comfort, and happiness anywhere else other than God's appointed deliverer, Jesus.

Jeremy Haskins

Connection with Newer Testament
Galatians 3:1-7

For the Kids
Ask your children what makes them feel safe. Maybe it's their stuffed animal or night light. Maybe it's you as their parent. Then ask them why those things make them feel safe. Ultimately, the one who guarantees our safety is God. That is good news. He is a good Father who loves his children. He loves them so much that he sent Jesus to free his children from the bondage of sin. God wants us safe in his arms, even when we look to other people and other things first, and Jesus died to make sure that is possible.

Prayer Prompts
1. In what ways are you, like Judah, failing to remain wholeheartedly faithful to God? What works or conditions are you adding to the gospel? What are you

trusting in to save you besides Christ? Repent of anything leading you to be a "stubborn child."

2. Rejoice in the mercy of God. In Christ, we who were rebelliously stubborn have been shown grace upon grace. We see the Teacher. We know his ways. We have been and continue to be cleansed from idolatry. We are eternally blessed in Christ.

◆

WEEK 23: DAY 3
Isaiah 32

Key Text
"until the Spirit is poured out upon us from on high, and the wilderness becomes a fruitful field and the fruitful field is considered a forest. Then justice will dwell in the wilderness, and righteousness will dwell in the fruitful field." Isaiah 32:15-16*

Pouring Out of the Spirit: A Sign of the Coming Kingdom of God
Corrupt governments and deceitful politicians are nothing new. Isaiah has continually rebuked God's people for their misplaced hope in earthly rulers. Hezekiah, specifically, has sought to make alliances with foreign kings that have only proven painful for God's people.

It's reality that, until Jesus returns to fully and finally establish his rule on the earth, we will have to endure the flaws of leaders. This is why our hope cannot ultimately be in any earthly king, political party, or government structure. As good as they may be, even the best rulers are still tainted with sin.

For the believer in Christ, we live in light of this reality daily. God has graciously poured out the Spirit of our King Jesus to all who, by faith, surrender to his rule in their lives. In doing so, we 'already' taste the power of his 'not yet' consummated government as we wait for our sinless Messiah to return.

Jeremy Haskins

Connection with Newer Testament
Acts 2:16-18; Revelation 11:15-17

For the Kids
Teach your children that not everyone working in our government loves God but that we should pray for them whether they do or do not. We can pray for our current leaders and pray that God will place righteous people in positions of leadership. But, no matter what happens in these earthly matters, God will reign supreme in the end with peace, justice, and righteousness. Through Jesus, his Spirit is the down payment of our salvation in his righteous kingdom. God and his kingdom is where our hope remains.

Prayer Prompts
1. Because Jesus Christ is the King of Righteousness, pray that government officials would lead and govern under his lordship for the good of their citizens. Pray that many political and cultural leaders would come to faith in Christ.
2. Praise God that, no matter what injustices we see and experience now, we serve a righteous King who is ushering us into an eternal kingdom where all evil will be righted under the lordship of King Jesus. Sin and its effects are being crushed. Peace, justice, and righteousness will reign.

◆

WEEK 23: DAY 4
Isaiah 33, 35

Key Text
"Your will behold the king in his beauty; they will see a land of distance." Isaiah 33:17*

The Great Salvation of God: Beholding the King in His Beauty
Sometimes the very same event can produce completely different reactions from different people. A trip to the mall has that effect on my family. For my wife, a trip to the mall is a fun experience. She gets excited about the

possibility of finding sales and seeing what's new. For me, such a trip is torture, and I anticipate it with dread and trepidation.

Not everyone will respond the same way to the future return of the LORD. While many take comfort in the presence of the LORD, for many, the presence of the LORD is not good news; it is terrible news. As Christ's people eagerly anticipate their eyes beholding the king in his beauty (33:17), those who have rebelled against Christ look upon the very same event with fear and trembling and see nothing but a consuming fire (33:14).

Whether you should be excited or fearful depends entirely on the question of righteousness (33:15). The righteous see Christ's return as good news; the unrighteous have no choice but to see it as the worst possible news. We must remember that what separates the righteous from the unrighteous is not outward behavior, but a heart that has been transformed by grace through faith in Jesus Christ. Do you anticipate that day or fear it?

Casey McCall

Connection with Newer Testament
Revelation 22:3-5

For the Kids
Ask your children, "What's the most beautiful thing you've ever seen?" Have them draw a picture of what they think the "King in his beauty" will look like. Explain that while many wonderful things on this earth are a reflection of his beauty, this will be a beauty like none other we've ever experienced.

Prayer Prompts
1. Praise God that, in Christ, a day is coming where all of God's people will dwell in the full, unmediated presence of God. Faith will become sight, and we will behold our great King in the splendor of his glory, in perfect and complete joy.
2. Remember that, apart from the blood of Christ, you are a sinner who cannot dwell favorably in the presence of God. Praise him for the Savior who "walks righteously" and "speaks uprightly" on our behalf.

WEEK 23: DAY 5

Isaiah 40

Key Text

"'Comfort, comfort my people,' says your God." Isaiah 40:1

Gospel Hope for an Afflicted People: Comfort Is Coming

You are God's prize. This truth is hard to believe given our sinfulness, but it is also hard to believe because the grace of God goes beyond our understanding. We often think of our salvation as merely freedom from punishment—that God saves us and then merely tolerates us without embracing us as his own children.

Reflect on this truth: The Living Word has come, and there is real comfort for you today. When God looks at you, he sees his perfect Son and delights in you through Christ. God's love for you is not one of ignorance but of mercy and grace. God knows the depths of your darkened heart, and yet he prizes you anyway. This will liberate you from pessimism and self-centeredness today. Satan will most surely attack you today and tempt you to despise your circumstances, but Isaiah 40 shows us that the only circumstance that should shape our lives is that we are accepted and forgiven by our Warrior-King, Jesus of Nazareth.

David Prince, "You Cannot Have a Christmas Without a Highway, Voices, and Celebration," Preached 12/20/2009, Prince on Preaching Website, Accessed 4 December 2015, Available from http://www.davidprince.com/2009/12/20/you-cannot-have-a-christmas-without-a-highway-voices-and-celebration-isaiah-401-11/.

Connection with Newer Testament

Matthew 3:1-13

For the Kids

Talk to your kids about what makes a good disguise and why people wear them. Ultimately, they want to hide their identity by looking like someone else. Then, explain that, in Christ, we don't have to hide our identity because we have a total new identity. We don't have to hide our sinful selves from God because, when we believe in Jesus, we have his righteousness. Our new identity is in Christ. When God looks at followers of Jesus, he sees Jesus' righteousness instead of their sin. This is true comfort.

Prayer Prompts

1. Pray that you might have a tangible sense of God's acceptance of you through his Son.

2. Pray for a specific unreached people group, that God would bring gospel comfort to them.

◆

WEEK 24: DAY 1
Isaiah 42

Key Text

"'Behold my servant, whom I uphold, my chosen one in whom my soul delights; I have set my Spirit on him; he will bring forth justice to the nations.'" Isaiah 42:1*

The Gospel Servant: Bringing Justice and Overcoming Sin

The corruption of all God's servants is clear throughout the book of Isaiah. Israel is a rebellious servant. Israel's kings who serve on behalf of the people continually prove to be wicked and corrupt. In Isaiah 6, this prophetic servant, Isaiah, declared that he, himself, was unclean. And yet, there is hope in a servant with whom God's Spirit will fully rest. There is to be a meek, anointed one who will establish true justice and accomplish his redemptive purposes in the world.

This Spirit-filled servant is Jesus, the Christ, who, in this chapter, pronounces, "I am the Lord!" The Father confirms this kingly pronouncement at the baptism of Jesus. As the Spirit descends upon the Son, the Father declares, "Behold this is my Son in whom I am well pleased." The Father is not only claiming that Jesus is his Son. He pronounces, with the very words of Isaiah, this is his anointed King.

Despite the fact that we must endure the sin of temporary servants, despite the fact that we, in and of ourselves, are flawed servants, Jesus, the anointed servant of Isaiah 42, has established an eternal covenant with God on our behalf. As a seal of this covenant, the Spirit that rests upon God's coming King, even now, indwells all who believe in Jesus.

Jeremy Haskins

Connection with Newer Testament
Matthew 12:15-21

For the Kids
In what ways did Jesus serve others while on this earth? Summarize for your children in language they can understand the ideal servant: one who neither falters nor is discouraged (42:4), delights in God (42:1), is gentle, persevering, and brings forth justice in faithfulness (42:3). Then think about how we can be gospel servants of the Lord in our everyday lives?

Prayer Prompts
1. Praise God for sending the Servant, the one who will "establish justice on the earth" (v. 4). Unlike Israel who failed to walk in faithful covenant love before God, the Servant stands in the place of fallen mankind as both the perfect Servant and Son that Israel (and we) could never be.
2. Through the indwelling of the Holy Spirit and the spiritual inheritance we have as believers, we are able to take steps of faithful obedience to God. Pray that God would continue to make you more like his Servant.

◆

WEEK 24: DAY 2
Isaiah 44

Key Text

"'For I will pour water on the parched ground and cause streams to flow on the dry land. I will pour my spirit on your offering and my blessing on your children.'" Isaiah 44:3

Gospel Recipients: The Spirit Poured Out on Us

Isaiah 44 gives gloriously good insight into what will happen to the LORD's people, to those chosen to receive the blessings coming through the LORD's gospel servant. Isaiah declares that a day of future hope is coming in which the dry, thirsty, lifeless, and dead ground of Israel will be infused with life. A day is coming when the life-giving water of God's Holy Spirit will be poured out on God's people such that God's people will "sprout up like a tree in the grass, like poplars beside channels of water" (v. 4). A day is coming when the spiritually dead and idolatrous hearts of God's people will be made new, when God's people will be devoted to the LORD (v. 5).

The LORD is faithful to his word. After Jesus ascended to heaven after his crucifixion and resurrection, the Holy Spirit was poured out at Pentecost, giving spiritual life in Jesus to over three thousand men (Acts 2). At Pentecost, the LORD began fulfilling his promise made in Isaiah 44:1-5, and he is fulfilling his promise today to the ends of the earth by pouring out his Spirit on every tribe, tongue, and nation through the preaching of his gospel. This new life truly is the gift of God. It cannot be earned. People cannot be physically born into it. Let us be people who pray for God to give this new life to sinners, and let us be faithful to preach the gospel, through which the Spirit works to make sinners alive to God in Jesus Christ.

Jon Canler

Connection with Newer Testament

Acts 2

For the Kids

Have your children draw a picture of a desert. Is it dry, sandy, dusty, hot? Now ask them to draw what might happen if rainstorms started creating rivers in the desert. Would grass, flowers and trees grow? This is how God describes the work of his Spirit—like a desert, we were dead, and empty, but he makes us alive and fruitful!

Prayer Prompts

1. Revel in the fact that, in Christ, we have been given the Spirit of God who gives life where there is death. Instead of facing eternal destruction due to our sin, we are indwelt by the very life-giving Spirit of God. Thank God for the supremely good gift of his presence.

2. Thank the Lord for the surety and seal of your salvation. If you say, "I am the LORD's," it is because he has poured out his Spirit on you, giving you eternal life and an immeasurable spiritual inheritance.

◆

WEEK 24: DAY 3
Isaiah 46

Key Text

"'To whom can you compare and liken me? Tell me whom you think I resemble, so we can be compared!'" Isaiah 46:5

God of the Gospel: The Sovereign Lord of the Cosmos

John Calvin was right when he observed that the human heart is an idol factory. In Isaiah 46, God is speaking through Isaiah and repudiating the worship of the false gods of the day, in this case, Bel and Nebo.

We often see the practice of idol worship as a bygone historical phenomenon, but we could not be more mistaken. There are countless idols that demand our attention and worship every day. Money, power, pleasure, security, and vanity are just a few of the idols that vie for our affections.

By following after these idols, we are walking away from the righteousness that God has provided for our salvation! It is the opposite of faith! When we cling to Christ and his righteousness, we are proclaiming that Christ alone is able to deliver humanity from sin.

The good news of the gospel is that the sovereign Lord of the cosmos loves us and accepts us unconditionally. With him, nothing is meaningless. Your sufferings, your circumstances, and your burdens are given purpose. Cast your cares on the Lord, and trust him!

David Prince, "Burdens & Bowing," Preached 10/9/2011, Prince on Preaching Website, Accessed 4 December 2015, Available from http://www.davidprince.com/2011/10/09/burdens-bowing-isaiah-46/.

Connection with Newer Testament
1 Corinthians 10:1-14; 1 John 5:21

For the Kids
Ask your children what sorts of things they might treasure instead of God. Toys? Friends? Food? TV? Explain how these things are idols, and explain that our sinful hearts are constantly looking for new ones. Pray that God would help us recognize and reject idols in our lives.

Prayer Prompts
1. Pray that, as you go about your day, you would do all to the glory of God.
2. Pray for a nation that is consumed with idol worship, like the United States or Peru, that God would bring its people to repentance and belief in Christ. Pray for repentance from your own idolatries.

◆

WEEK 24: DAY 4
Isaiah 49

Key Text
"'I will make you a light to the nations, so you can bring my deliverance to the remote regions of the earth.'" Isaiah 49:6b

The Gospel Servant: A Light for the Nations
In today's text, we read of a great servant of the LORD. We read of

one who will raise up the tribes of Jacob and who will bring back the preserved of Israel. We read of a servant of God who will bring the LORD's long-awaited salvation upon the earth. But we also read of a servant who will extend the offer of salvation to the nations, to the end of the earth (v. 6).

Who is this servant? Who is this servant to Israel and this light to the nations who helps people see the LORD's salvation? It is the true Israel. It is the true people of God, as many Jewish scholars argue. Yet, the only true and faithful Israelite is Jesus Christ for he is the only one who perfectly obeyed the LORD (Matt. 4:1-11, Heb. 4:15). Jesus is this servant, this faithful Israelite, who restores Israel and who brings salvation to the nations by preaching his gospel of repentance from sin and faith in himself.

This servant, Jesus, is still at work today calling sinners from every tribe, tongue, and nation to repent of sin and to believe his gospel for the forgiveness of their sins. And he's working today through his people, his Church. The servant and his light extend to the nations as the church gives and goes to the ends of the earth preaching the gospel. So, let us be generous givers and goers who faithfully serve our Servant-King so that his gospel light shines brightly upon all nations for his glory and for their good.

Jon Canler

Connection with Newer Testament
John 8:12; Matthew 5:14

For the Kids
Go into a dark room with all the lights turned off, and ask your children to describe details about the room that they can't see. Now turn on a flashlight or light a candle and ask the same question. Describe how God has designed us to be a "light" in the world so that others can know and trust him.

Prayer Prompts
1. Praise God that salvation through his servant, Jesus Christ, extends to the nations. Otherwise we would remain dead in our trespasses and sins.

2. The Servant, Christ Jesus, is still calling the nations to repentance through the church. Ask the Lord to give you boldness to preach the gospel so that people may see their only hope of salvation—Jesus.

◆

WEEK 24: DAY 5
Isaiah 53

Key Text
"Surely he has born our griefs and carried our sorrows; yet we ourselves esteemed him stricken, smitten by God, and afflicted. But he was pierced for our transgressions; he was crushed for our iniquities; the chastisement that brought us peace was upon him, and with his scourging we are healed. All we like sheep have gone astray; we have turned—each man—to his own way." Isaiah 53:4-6*

The Gospel Servant: Atonement for Sin Through Suffering
We are not good people. God is a holy and righteous judge, and there has to be a payment for sin. This is the fundamental conflict of history, and every person must face it. The solution that God provides is that God himself would come down and be humiliated for sinners. Christ says, "I will be repulsive for you. I will be rejected by men for you. I will be punished for you." This is the truth that not only saves but also transforms. This truth redefines every category we have in our lives, whether it be success, marriage, possessions, time, and the list goes on and on and on. For you to walk faithfully with Christ today, all that is required is that you behold his glory and grace and act in light of it.

David Prince, "Why the Gospel is So Hard for Us to Believe," Preached 1/3/2010, Prince on Preaching Website, Accessed 4 December 2015, Available from http://www.davidprince.com/2010/01/03/why-the-gospel-is-so-hard-for-us-to-believe-isaiah-5213-5312/.

Connection with Newer Testament

Acts 8:26-39

For the Kids

Ask your children if they would ever consider taking the punishment on behalf of a sibling, friend, or classmate who has done something wrong. Explain how this is what Jesus does for us, for our sin. We deserved to die and be separated from God, but Jesus took our punishment instead of us!

Prayer Prompts

1. Pray that, as you go about your day, you would treasure Christ.
2. Pray that the Holy Spirit would show you new ways that you can be conformed into the image of Christ.

◆

WEEK 25: DAY 1

Isaiah 55

Key Text

"'Hey, all who are thirsty, come to the water! You who have no money, come! Buy and eat! Come! Buy wine and milk without money and without cost!'"
Isaiah 55:1

The Gospel Price: Free Grace

In spite of Israel's rebellion, God is constantly pleading with them to turn from their sins and enjoy his goodness. What's so scandalous is that they are to do nothing but repent to enjoy it. In Isaiah 55, Isaiah is clear they cannot in anyway make up for their sin and rebellion.

Here we see the logic of the gospel. Jesus has provided the life you need. He perfectly obeyed every jot and tittle of God's law for you. Jesus has provided the death you need. On the cross, Jesus was eternally punished for your sins as if he was you. This is why Jesus can personally issue the invitation to come to him and drink and never thirst again. Even though we have nothing to bring, he calls us to come and feast upon him and his provision since he is God's very bread from heaven. He is God's invitation to eternal life!

If you are too good to consider yourself a 'mooch,' the gospel isn't for you. The call of the gospel is to come and enjoy something that you could never provide for yourself. God unashamedly pleads with you to simply come. Come and enjoy his salvation. All you bring is the desperate need. Everything you get is God's infinite goodness in Christ.

Jeremy Haskins

Connection with Newer Testament
John 6:35-40, 7:37-38

For the Kids
Explain how grace is free through Jesus. We cannot be nice enough, do enough good things, or try hard enough. We cannot make it for ourselves, fake having it, or even buy it. Jesus bought grace for us through his life, death, and resurrection. Pray and thank God for this provision we cannot earn and do not deserve.

Prayer Prompts
1. Praise the Lord for free grace. There is nothing we can do to save our dead selves, but the Lord has provided the means of eternal life through Jesus Christ.
2. Repent of trying to "buy" your way into the kingdom through your works. The price is perfection, which Christ has paid for us, even in the midst of our moral imperfections. Come to him and live by grace. Buy food and drink without money.

◆

WEEK 25: DAY 2
Isaiah 57

Key Text
"For this is what the high and exalted one says, the one who rules forever,

whose name is holy: 'I dwell in an exalted and holy place, but also with the discouraged and humiliated, in order to cheer up the humiliated and to encourage the discouraged.'" Isaiah 57:15

The Gospel Condition: A Contrite Heart

In this chapter, Isaiah is describing an Israel where the number of righteous people is dwindling, and no one cares (v. 1). What is not dwindling is Israel's unrighteousness and idolatry. The Israelite people are unfaithful to the God of Abraham, Isaac, and Jacob. They covenanted with false gods and forgot the one true and living God (v. 11).

God challenges Israel's allegiance to their idols. He dares them to depend on these eyeless, earless, lifeless deities when trouble arises. God knows that help does not come from carved wood or hewn stone. Help only comes from the living God (vv. 13-14). God makes sure there is no obstacle on the path to finding refuge in him.

God's refuge is a holy place, for it is where the Holy One dwells. Therefore, the condition of those that dwell with God is the spirit of lowly contrition. In order to dwell with God, we must recognize that we, like the Israelites, have sought the support of false gods. Whether our false gods are money, comfort, family, or even our own abilities, we have worshiped at their altar. We have sinned against the living God. Yet, God removes any obstacle in the path of those who come to him.

The obstacle in our path to God is our sin; yet, God sent his Son—Jesus—to remove that obstacle. Jesus is "the Lamb of God who takes away the sin of the world" (John 1:29)! The path to God is Jesus Christ. The path to God is through confession of sin and through accepting Jesus' work on the cross, where our sin is exchanged for his righteousness. The path to God is the gospel, good news that is embraced with a contrite heart.

Adam York

Connection with Newer Testament
1 John 1:8-10

For the Kids

Ask your kids to share about a time when they felt really bad about something they did that they knew was wrong. Ask them how it felt knowing they disobeyed a rule. Then describe to them that each day we are disobedient to God and break his laws. We deserve to be punished for breaking God's good commandments. Then share that God sent his Son, Jesus, to take our punishment. So, we can come to God humbly: knowing we have sinned and broken God's law while knowing that we are forgiven for our sins in Jesus.

Prayer Prompts

1. Praise God for the fact that he revives the hearts of the lowly who feel the weight of sin rather than crushing bruised reeds. Praise him for life-giving grace through the gospel.

2. Perhaps you feel the weight of sin and your moral failures before the Lord. He is full of mercy and grace toward those who own their sin and repent of it before him. Perhaps you need to cry out for forgiveness to God.

◆

WEEK 25: DAY 3

Isaiah 58

Key Text

"'No, this is the kind of fast I want. I want you to remove the sinful chains, to tear away the ropes of the burdensome yoke, to set free the oppressed, and to break every burdensome yoke. I want you to share your food with the hungry and to provide shelter for homeless, oppressed people. When you see someone naked, clothe him! Don't turn your back on your own flesh and blood!'" Isaiah 58:6-7

Gospel Practice: A Life of Righteousness and Repentance

In Isaiah 58, Israel is rebuked for fasting in order to externally appease others. However, behind the scenes they continued to quarrel and exploit others. Fasting for God's people became a superstitious tool to manipulate God in their favor. This act of worship wasn't done from repentance of sin and a hunger for God's presence. It was done merely to look spiritual while getting God to do whatever they wanted. This is the same thing of which Jesus warned his disciples in light of the Pharisees' self-righteousness. He warned them not to simply practice their righteousness before men as a means of using God for their benefit.

How dangerous it can be with all of our spiritual resources to begin to trust in the spiritual activity itself in order to please God. With all the gifts technology has given us, how difficult is it not to think we are producing a spiritual experience by our own power? How dangerous is it with all our social media outlets to begin to self-righteously boast in our outward deeds before men through posts and pictures of all we do and feel for God?

God calls us not to examine our list of deeds before men but our hearts. He then promises, amidst all the hypocrisy of which we are prone to be guilty, if we to turn to Christ with a genuinely repentant heart, he will forgive us of such wickedness.

Jeremy Haskins

Connection with Newer Testament
Matthew 6:1-18

For the Kids
Ask your kids if they can explain the mythical genie in a bottle. Genies grant three wishes to anyone who releases them from their bottle. Let them tell you what their three wishes might be. Then make clear that God is not our "genie in a bottle." God does not give us things for doing him favors. In fact, he doesn't need anything from us. While praying, reading the Bible, and serving in a church are all good things given to us by God, they don't earn us good things from God. Similarly, we cannot earn God's salvation and acceptance. That only comes by his grace through Jesus Christ. Ask the Lord to give your children hearts of faith that hope in Jesus for salvation and that lead to obedience and repentance as a result of such gospel hope.

Prayer Prompts

1. Pray for a heart marked by genuine repentance in your next time of fasting, not a mentality of performance.

2. Ask God to forgive you for your previous acts of legalism in the spiritual disciplines. Pray that he would give you a godly mindset in your future efforts in pursing holiness.

◆

WEEK 25: DAY 4

Isaiah 60

Key Text

"The sun will no longer supply light for you by day, nor will the moon's brightness shine on you; the LORD will be your permanent source of light—the splendor of your God will shine upon you. Your sun will no longer set; your moon will not disappear; the LORD will be your permanent source of light; your time of sorrow will be over." Isaiah 60:19-20

Gospel Glory: Eternal Righteousness in God's Land

Sometimes glorious promises are given in the context of bleak circumstances. Perhaps there is no better example of this than Isaiah 60. The context? The northern part of the kingdom (Israel) was falling to the Assyrians. Judah, in the south, was full of idolatry and wickedness, and its downfall was pending. "For this reason deliverance is far from us and salvation does not reach us. We wait for light, but see only darkness; we wait for a bright light, but live in deep darkness." (Is. 59:9). All of the progress toward the promises of God—such as the conquest of the land, the establishment of peace, and the promises to David concerning his dynasty—seemed to be falling apart.

And in the midst of such circumstances, "'Arise! Shine! For your light arrives! The splendor of the LORD shines on you'" (v. 1). The promises are not forsaken! God is not shaken! He chooses this dark day to send prophecies of the most glorious time.

Listen to the hope. The people of Israel will be gathered in one place, a mighty nation. The nations will come, too. The people's hearts will be full of joy. They will not lack anything and, instead, will have an abundance. The city will be one of perfect peace, whose citizens are all righteous. And the best part, the glory of the Lord will be upon them, and he will be their everlasting light. These are the promises of the day of the new heavens and the new earth, and the promises are as true now as they ever were for all of God's people in Christ, no matter what circumstances you see around you.

Todd Martin

Connection with Newer Testament
Revelation 21:22-27

For the Kids
Give your children a flashlight, and let them turn it on to make light. Then, ask them to make darkness. Explain that darkness is not something we make; rather, it is the absence of light. We may use electricity or fire to make light and remove darkness, but the Bible says that Jesus is the true light that takes away darkness. In fact, in the new heaven and new earth, Jesus will be our light; there we will have no need of flashlights, or electricity, or even the sun or the moon. Pray with your children that, by faith, one day they too will walk by the light of the Lamb in his kingdom.

Prayer Prompts
1. Praise the Lord for the gift of faith he has bestowed on you, a faith that has ushered you into the kingdom of God.
2. Pray that God would grant saving faith to the unbelievers that you know, so that they too may experience the glory of the kingdom and the person of God.

◆

WEEK 25: DAY 5
Isaiah 61

Key Text
"'The Spirit of the Lord God is upon me, because the LORD has anointed me

to bring good news to the poor; he has sent me to bind up the brokenhearted, to proclaim liberty to captives, and release to those taken prisoner'" Isaiah 61:1*

Gospel Proclamation: Filled with the Spirit to Preach Good News

"The Spirit of the Lord God is upon me." In this text, we hear from the Spirit-filled, anointed one. Any time in the Scripture you see that the Spirit is upon someone, it is always for a purpose, for a special work or a special message. Jesus, the one speaking, is continually described throughout the gospels as working in the power of the Spirit.

What is the Spirit of the Lord God upon him for? For a good news message (and the accompanying work that makes the message a reality). It is a message of hope, healing, liberty, rescue, the favor of the Lord, justice, and comfort.

Who are the recipients of the message? The poor, the broken-hearted, the captives, the ones who are bound, those who mourn. This is a good news message for desperate people needing a Messiah. This is a description of our state in need of salvation. But, it is not the final state of those for whom the Messiah has come. The Messiah finds us as poor mourning captives, but when he is done we have "a turban, instead of ashes, oil symbolizing joy, instead of mourning, a garment symbolizing praise, instead of a discouragement" (v. 3). He clothes us with the "garments of deliverance" and covers us with "a robe of righteousness" (v. 10*).

This is not just beautiful poetic language. This is the testimony of every believer. We once were poor captives, but now we are part of the bride, children of God, citizens of the kingdom. May we continue to spread the good news message till the last day.

Todd Martin

Connection with Newer Testament
Luke 4:16-21

For the Kids

Explain the Old Testament idea of the jubilee year, that once every fifty years the Israelites were to have a year of celebration of the LORD's favor. It was to be celebrated with debts forgiven, slaves freed, and land and property returned. This is what Isaiah was to proclaim. Ask your kids if that sounds like a great year. Ultimately, Isaiah points to Jesus, the jubilee personified. He is the one who sets us free from sin and death and who forgives our debts. Jesus is our Jubilee.

Prayer Prompts

1. Pray for opportunities to be where your feet are and join the Servant-Messiah in ministering the gospel to brokenhearted prisoners of sin.
2. Praise God for his sovereign plan to send his Son to be the Spirit-anointed Servant-Messiah.

◆

WEEK 26: DAY 1

Isaiah 65

Key Text

"'For look, I am ready to create new heavens and a new earth! The former ones will not be remembered; no one will think about them anymore.'" Isaiah 65:17

Gospel Newness: A New Heavens and a New Earth

Today's key text from Isaiah 65:17 has two sides to it. 1) The Lord is creating new heavens and a new earth. 2) The former things shall not be remembered or come into mind. Both of these truths are eternal, wonderful, and beautiful. Both truths need to be remembered in our daily lives.

The first sixteen verses of Isaiah 65 are filled with condemnation toward the ungodly ones mixed with promises that God will preserve his servants. As a result, the promise that the former things will be of the past is both a serious warning to those who forsake him and, at the same time, a joyful promise to the servants of the Lord. Look around. All of the evil in the world—the murder, the abuse, the dishonorable, the wars, etc.—they are all temporary.

There is coming a day when the Lord will put an end to it all. Even better, they won't even be thought of anymore. What joy to the saved!

More so, even the rocks, the trees, the oceans, and the stars of the sky are temporary inasmuch as they will be made new. Look around! *Everything* you see is temporary. He is making new heavens and a new earth, and this new creation he makes will be perfect and permanent. But his kingdom has no end.

Let this encourage you as you strive to live for his eternal kingdom and flee from the love of the world.

Todd Martin

Connection with Newer Testament
Revelation 21

For the Kids
Ask your children to show you one of their newest toys that they frequently play with. Then you (parent) go find an older toy that your child never plays with. Teach your children how easily we forget about old, used, perhaps dirty things—clothes, toys, etc. Teach your children that a day is coming in which this old, sinful world will be forgotten because God is making all things new in Jesus, including this world. Teach them that they are sinful and can be made new in Jesus.

Prayer Prompts
1. Praise God that, through faith in Jesus, judgment is not the final word for you. Eternal life in a new cosmos is the final word.
2. The difference between judgment and blessing is faith. Who in your life doesn't live by faith in Jesus Christ? Pray for their salvation, that they may find abundant life in Christ rather than judgment leading to death.

◆

WEEK 26: DAY 2
Micah 4

Key Text

"In the future the LORD's Temple Mount will be the most important mountain of all; it will be more prominent than other hills. People will stream to it." Micah 4:1

The Coming Mountain of the Lord: The Lord Will Reign

In Micah, as in Isaiah, there are occasions where a prophecy of imminent judgment and despair is followed by a promise that looks past the near future to the 'latter days' of glory. The effect is that the zoom frame of the prophecy is expanded to remind the people of the bigger picture of hope for all who are wrapped up in the future of the kingdom. That is why, immediately after saying in Micah 3:12 that "Jerusalem will become a heap of ruins, and the Temple Mount will become a hill overgrown with brush!" (imminent judgment), Micah continues with, "In the future the LORD's Temple Mount will be the most important mountain of all; it will be more prominent than other hills." And what a glorious bigger picture is revealed! The mountain referred to is Zion, the ultimate Zion, a phrase that represents the center of the eternal kingdom of God. Notice that it has multi-national glory. "Peoples will stream to it. Many nations will come" (vv. 1-2). They are coming because they want to learn from the Lord his ways so that they can live by his laws. Do you see the parallels to the Great Commission? "[M]ake disciples of all nations…teaching them to obey everything I have commanded" (Mt. 28:19-20). Notice also the glorious picture of the law of the Lord going forth from Zion (v. 2). The contrast between the actions of people and the commandments of God has been erased by the victory of the Savior. This is the day when there is no more sin and every ounce of evil is defeated and put in the past. The result is a kingdom of perfect peace. Swords? Who needs them! Spears? Recycle them. In this kingdom, there is only peace and righteousness, forever!

Todd Martin

Connection with Newer Testament

Revelation 21:1-3, 23-26

For the Kids

Show your children a picture of Mount Everest and the surrounding mountains. Tell your children that Mount Everest is the tallest mountain in the world, which is why it is so well known compared to the rest of the mountains around it. Then tell them that days are coming and are now here when the LORD will be viewed like Mount Everest, as so supreme that his glory in Jesus will stand above all things, drawing people to come worship him.

Prayer Prompts

1. Pray for the fulfillment of Micah's vision—for the day when the nations completely submit to the righteous reign of King Jesus.

2. Pray for the many people who are not Christians to be freed from the tyranny of sin so that they too may see the Lord and his mountain exalted above other gods and their dwelling places. Pray that, in seeing the Lord, they would repent of sin, trusting Christ for life and righteousness forever.

◆

WEEK 26: DAY 3

Micah 5

Key Text

"As for you, Bethlehem Ephrathah, seemingly insignificant among the clans of Judah—from you a king will emerge who will rule over Israel on my behalf, one whose origins are in the distant past." Micah 5:2

The Redeeming Ruler of Israel: Brought Forth from Bethlehem

Here is one of the most famous Old Testament prophecies of Christ, written over seven hundred years before his birth. Most of the time this prophecy is quoted, however, only Micah 5:2 is given. After all, Micah 5:2 is packed with truth. It gives the precise town of Jesus' birth: Bethlehem. It identifies Jesus as a ruler, and he is exactly that as the King of kings. The prophecy also says his "origins are in the distant past." And indeed, the prophecies stretch back into Genesis. More so, Jesus is the Alpha, the beginning, the ageless one.

Yet notice also what the seldom-quoted verses 3-5a reveal. They make it clear that history is waiting for a childbirth, and, after that Bethlehem birth, there will be a return of "the rest of the king's countrymen" (from the nations) to the people of Israel. Together, they become one flock, and this Bethlehem baby becomes the great shepherd of strength and majesty. With Jesus as the shepherd, the flock is secure. Notice all the parallels from John 10: "I am the good shepherd … I have other sheep that do not come from this sheepfold. I must bring them too … there will be one flock and one shepherd … I give them eternal life, and they will never perish" (John 10:14, 16, 28). Micah emphasizes that the flock is secure, but the prophecy says more than that; it speaks of peace. It doesn't just say that he gives them peace; it says he is their peace. Indeed, it's in the person of Christ that we have peace. He lays his life down to give life to us. He is our Ruler, the Reconciler of nations, the Good Shepherd, our great Protector, and our Peace.

Todd Martin

Connection with Newer Testament
Matthew 2:1-12; John 10

For the Kids
Show your children their baby pictures. Talk about how they were not in control of where they were born and who their parents were. Only God controls this. Consequently, God was faithfully fulfilling his promises by having King Jesus born in Bethlehem. We can trust God with every aspect of our lives; he is in control, and he is good.

Prayer Prompts
1. Praise the Lord for his sovereignty over all things.
2. Praise God for sending the Ruler to shepherd his flock and to be our peace.

◆

WEEK 26: DAY 4
2 Kings 17

Key Text

"The Israelites followed in the sinful ways of Jeroboam son of Nebat and did not repudiate them. Finally the LORD rejected Israel just as he had warned he would do through all his servants the prophets. Israel was deported from its land to Assyria and remains there to this very day." 2 Kings 17:22-23

Exile: The 10 Northern Tribes of Israel Taken Captive to Assyria

Moses' words were actually coming to pass. In Deuteronomy 4:25-31, Moses declared that days were coming when Israel, after being in the promised land for a long time, would provoke the LORD to anger. The people would commit idolatry, and they would do what was evil in the sight of the LORD such that the LORD would send his people away from the land into exile.

In our text, Moses' prophetic words were coming to pass. After being in the land for hundreds of years, the northern kingdom of Israel began to live in unrepentant sin. They walked in all the sins of Jeroboam, in all of his sins of idolatry. Consequently, the LORD drove the northern ten tribes of Israel into Assyrian exile, just as he promised.

For the faithful, repentant Church, we can safely say that we will never face exile from God and his promises like Israel faced because we are covered by the spotless righteousness of Jesus Christ. Though we cannot be cut off, we must remember that the LORD will discipline his erring children whom he loves (Heb. 12:6). We certainly must also be reminded of the seriousness of unrepentant sin. The LORD was willing to forgive Israel had they repented seeing that he sent prophets to them time and time again calling Israel to turn from their wicked ways. But, unrepentant sin will not be overlooked. Who do you know that is unrepentant for their sins? The wrath of God remains on them. Will you call them to repent? God will grant forgiveness to all who turn from their sin, but an eternal exile in a place called hell awaits all who refuse to repent.

Jon Canler

Connection with Newer Testament

John 3:36; Revelation 20:11-15

For the Kids

Ask your children if they remember having a favorite toy taken away by their parents. Ask them why the toy was taken away. Was it because of some sin? For Israel, one of their favorite things in the world was the place where they lived. Yet, God took them away from their land because of their sin. God must punish sin. Now ask your kids if they got their favorite toy back when they confessed and turned from their sinful behavior? In the same way, God would return Israel to their land when they repented, nearly 70 years later. Drive this story home by reminding your children that they are sinners who will experience God's eternal judgment unless they repent of sin and turn to Jesus.

Prayer Prompts

1. Praise the Lord that, in Christ, we will never be exiled from the presence of God.
2. Praise the Lord that he disciplines us for our sin as he prepares us to dwell in his holy presence in the new heavens and new earth.
3. Ask the Lord to reveal places in your heart where you do not trust him, and where you rebel against him and his word. Repent of such sin.

◆

WEEK 26: DAY 5
2 Kings 22-23

Key Text

"No king before or after repented before the LORD as he did, with his whole heart, soul, and being in accordance with the whole law of Moses." 2 Kings 23:25-26

Josiah: A Righteous King Unable to Save Unrighteous Judah

After the short reign of Manasseh's son, Amon, Josiah is made king at the age of eight. The previous kings, with the exception of Hezekiah, had all done evil in the sight of the Lord, provoking him to anger against Judah. Chief among these evil kings was Manasseh (2 Kings 23:26-27; 24:4). These evil kings led the people of Israel to become like Canaanites—idolatrous people worthy of the Lord's destruction. God's own people—whom he has delivered from bondage, given his word, and called to be a distinct nation for his glory—have disobeyed and forgotten him such that they no longer read or acknowledge his word. Can you imagine?

Well, King Josiah recovers the written word of God that had been abandoned for so long by so many wicked kings, and in response, he repents and institutes great reforms in Judah by turning to the Lord. He tears down the places of false worship, purges the land of idols, outlaws child sacrifice, and restores the feast of the Passover—which was to remind the people of how God provided for them by delivering them from slavery in Egypt.

Although Josiah was a great and righteous king, he was unable to save Judah from the coming wrath of God. Israel's sin-debt had to be paid no matter the amount of future deeds of righteousness. And the same is true of us. We all sin against God, and we so easily think that we can create a few good works to outweigh our bad works in order to get out of the consequences our sin deserves. Josiah proves that theory wrong.

Israel's only hope and our only hope for salvation rests in Jesus. He would come as the sinless King who would save his people from the wrath of God by taking it upon himself. As we repent of sin and trust in him as Lord, he is there to forgive us and to give us hearts that will obey and love him. Jesus' righteousness is sufficient to save, and we are to respond by surrendering our lives to him in obedience to his word.

Josh Crawford

Connection with Newer Testament
Matthew 1:1-17

For the Kids
Ask your kids how they know when something is missing. Usually, we only miss something when we are looking for it and cannot find it. It is hard to miss something that we don't know is gone. King Josiah had no idea that the word of God was missing. He did not know it was gone. In fact, he didn't even know about it. Once he read the word of God, Josiah discovered God's grand

promises for his people and the instruction for their holiness. Sometimes we forget the glorious truth of the Bible. We don't recognize they are missing from our lives because we fail to look for them. Tell your children that you lead them in these devotions to keep the truth as it is in Jesus always before them so that they don't forget it.

Prayer Prompts

1. Praise the Lord that, in Christ, we have a King even greater than the godly Josiah who is able to deliver us from the wrath we deserve for our sins. Our King took all of our wrath, fully and finally.

2. Josiah was a man convicted of the goodness of the word of God, and it led to a purification of the land from unholy things. Ask the Lord to reveal evils in your life that need to be crucified. Repent of those sins and strive to love the Lord with all of your heart, soul, mind, and strength by the grace of God.

◆

WEEK 27: DAY 1
Habakkuk 2

Key Text
"For still the vision is for the appointed time; it hastens to the end, and it will not lie. If it tarries, wait for it, for it will surely come; it will not delay." Habakkuk 2:3*

Faith: Awaiting Salvation in the Midst of God's Mysterious Ways

"It's much better to wait." This statement ranks near the top of my list of least favorite things to hear. In our microwave meal culture, waiting is no virtue, and too often I buy into the lie. We often convince ourselves that we know what is best for us. It is a battle to see the wisdom of God in our day-to-day lives. We are often blinded by our own plans, our own priorities, and our own ambitions—so blinded that we miss seeing God's sovereign hand working in our lives for our good and his glory. The good news is that God does not make us wait simply to watch us squirm. God makes us wait in order to drive us to trust in him as a son trusts in a father. The truth is that there are no shortcuts to holiness and no expressways to maturity. Today, as you go out into the world and your head spins with possibilities, dreams, ambitions, and ideas, remember to write them down with a pencil, not a pen, and trust God along the way.

David Prince, "The Worthless," Preached 8/21/2012, Prince on Preaching Website, Accessed 4 December 2015, Available from http://www.davidprince.com/2012/08/21/the-worthless-habakkuk-25-20/.

Connection with Newer Testament
Romans 1:17, 8:22-25

For the Kids
Have you ever waited for cookies to bake? Imagine the crunchy, warm cookie fresh from the oven. Makes it hard to wait, right? What if we decided that it was too long to wait and we pulled them out? We would be so disappointed because they would be gooey and uncooked. Sometimes you will have to wait for things in life, including the fullness of our salvation. But we can trust God along the way. He has the best ending for those in Christ.

Prayer Prompts
1. Pray that you would trust God daily with your expectations and plans.
2. Reflect on and thank God for how he has brought you thus far in your Christian walk.

◆

WEEK 27: DAY 2
Zephaniah 3

Key Text
"'Shout for joy, Daughter Zion! Shout out, Israel! Be happy and boast with all your heart, Daughter Jerusalem!'" Zephaniah 3:14

From Jerusalem to the Nations: Future Judgment and Conversion

As I write this I'm listening to music in my office. Listening to music is not uncommon for me. In fact, just like many millions of people throughout the history of the world, I love music. It enables me to feel realities like few other things. Singing embeds true realities deep within the soul and provides an appropriate way for us to declare what we are feeling deep inside.

C.S. Lewis once wrote, "I think we delight to praise what we enjoy because the praise not merely expresses but completes the enjoyment; it is its appointed consummation."[5] In other words, we praise people and things because in praising our souls are brought to greater degrees of enjoyment of the object of our praise. When I sing praise to God, I am not merely expressing the delight I currently feel; my praise is bringing my soul to even greater degrees of delight than before.

Zephaniah 3:14-20 paints a glorious picture of the celebration that will be had in heaven upon God's restoration of his people in his holy city Zion. Christ, our king, will be in our midst, and we shall never again "fear disaster" (v. 15). Not surprisingly, there will be a lot of singing and praise happening on that day. However, perhaps surprisingly, God himself will be leading the choir: he will shout "for joy over you" with loud singing" (v. 17). Our God will be bringing his joy to its appointed consummation in response to his salvation of his people!

Casey McCall

Connection with Newer Testament
Matthew 28:18-20; Revelation 7:9-12

For the Kids
Ask your children why we should tell people about Jesus and why missionaries go all over the world to share the good news of the gospel. Yes, we want people

---

[5] C.S. Lewis, *Reflections on the Psalms*, (New York: Harcourt, Brace & Co., 1958), 93-97.

to be rescued from their sin and be freed from eternal punishment in hell. Yet, the main motivation for sharing Jesus is praise. God is the greatest thing in the universe and, hence, he deserves the praise of every creature. Sadly, many don't praise him. Missionaries go so that God may be glorified through praise. The first step in praising God is coming to him through Jesus. Jesus is God's Son. God is well pleased with Jesus. Therefore, if we want to praise God, we should trust in and praise his Son.

Prayer Prompts

1. Praise God that you, if you are in Christ, are part of a fulfillment of the prophecy. Praise God that his saving grace extends beyond a strip of land in the Middle East and reaches out to the ends of the earth.

2. Pray for our missionaries. Pray that God would bring many nations to faith in Christ through our efforts across the globe.

◆

WEEK 27: DAY 3
Jeremiah 2

Key Text

"'Be amazed at this, O heavens! Be shocked and utterly dumbfounded,' says the LORD. 'Do so because my people have committed a double wrong: they have rejected me, the fountain of life-giving water, and they have dug cisterns for themselves, cracked cisterns which cannot even hold water.'" Jeremiah 2:12-13

Forsaking the Lord: Israel's Transgression of the Mosaic Covenant

The state in which Israel finds itself is shocking. The kingdom was long since divided into two between Israel in the north and Judah in the south. The Assyrians had taken Israel captive, and now Judah was on the verge of a similar fate at the hands of Babylon. Yet even in this dire state, the people don't even bother themselves with calling out to God. Worse, they don't even bother to ask where he is (vv. 6-8).

They had forgotten the God that led their ancestors out of Egypt and into the promise land, the good land in which they presently dwelt. They had crafted other gods for satisfaction, protection, and pleasure (v. 28). This idolatry, rather than bringing satisfaction, only brought brokenness and spiritual poverty.

Jeremiah uses the image of sustaining water to illustrate Israel's rejection of God. Through Jeremiah, God reveals that the people have committed two evils. First, they forsook God. This forsaking was foolish since he is the only true living water. In other words, they rejected the source of satisfaction. Second, rather than returning to God, they attempted to manufacture new sources of satisfaction—idols. So, rather than experience the refreshment of living water, they foolishly attempted to quench their spiritual thirst with containers that did not hold water. Picture in your mind a dehydrated man with a spring before him yet who is sitting on the bank attempting to gather water from a pot with holes and cracks throughout it. He is rejecting the very thing that could save his life.

Sadly, many of us do the same thing. We often seek satisfaction in the broken pots, containers, and cisterns of the modern world. All the while God, through Jesus, is the fountain of living water. Will you drink deeply of the living water today?

Adam York

Connection with Newer Testament
John 4:7-15

For the Kids
Take a sizable pot and place it beside the kitchen sink. Fill the sink with some water. Give your kids paper or plastic cups in which you have poked numerous holes (or perhaps a pasta strainer). Tell them to fill the pot with the water from the sink with the cups. It should not take long for them to realize the frustration and lack of satisfaction arising from using a broken cup. Tell them this frustration and lack of satisfaction is what happens to us when we try to fill our souls with anything but God. Then, take the pot and place it under the faucet

and fill it with water. Tell them God is waiting to fill us with his Spirit if we would just stop trying with other things that will never work.

Prayer Prompts

1. Ask God to forgive you when you attempt to turn to other things for satisfaction.

2. Ask God to help you build the spiritual disciplines in your life that will guard against the temptation of forsaking him for lesser things.

◆

WEEK 27: DAY 4
Jeremiah 3-4:4

Key Text

"'Circumcise yourselves to the LORD; remove the foreskins of your hearts, O men of Judah and those who dwell in Jerusalem; lest my wrath go out like fire, and burn with none to quench it, because of the evil of your deeds.'" Jeremiah 4:4*

Restoration and Mercy: The Lord's Offer for Those Who Repent

Have you ever been wronged again and again by someone? Most of us probably haven't because we don't allow it go that far. Once someone has done the same hurtful thing a couple of times, we usually call it quits. We tend to think that people like that are unworthy of the privilege of having a relationship with us. We should rejoice that God is not like us.

In Jeremiah 3:1-5, the wicked wrongs of God's people are recorded. Again and again, Israel committed adultery against the LORD. Again and again, false gods were worshipped in place of the one true God who had saved them. Just like us today, Israel of old repeatedly followed their rebellious hearts into blatant rebellion of God. No one could blame the LORD if his anger went as far as their rebellion. No one could call him unjust for wanting to judge his people's rebellion.

And yet, God does not judge. He does not cast Israel to the side. Shockingly and amazingly, he returns their rebellion with unfathomable mercy.

If they will return, he assures them, he will still bless them with all of his promised covenant privileges. But he doesn't even stop there. Once they return, he will ensure that this type of rebellion never happens again. He will make it so that they "no longer follow the stubborn inclinations of their own evil hearts" (3:17). Jeremiah, of course, is looking ahead to the day when Christ would change the hearts of God's covenant people through his atoning sacrifice. We don't have to look to the future to experience what God has promised here. If we repent and return to him, our hearts will be changed now.

Casey McCall

Connection with Newer Testament
Luke 15

For the Kids
If a seed is planted in a field of weeds, it cannot grow to be a fruitful tree. The seed needs to be planted in broken up soil where it is given all it needs to survive without weeds that will choke it to death. We need our hearts to be like good, broken soil to receive God's truth. Pray for your children by name, that God would circumcise their hearts so that they would be able to grow strong in God's word through faith and repentance.

Prayer Prompts
1. Pray that God would soften your heart to all aspects of his word and his character. Ask him to reveal where in your life that you are still hardened to the gospel.
2. Repent of your hardness of heart and praise God for his forgiveness and mercy.

◆

WEEK 27: DAY 5
Jeremiah 5

Key Text

"'Yet even then I will not completely destroy you,' say the LORD." Jeremiah 5:18

Coming Judgment: Judah's Unrepentance Punished & a Remnant Saved

In this chapter, it is clear that God has given Judah every opportunity to repent and turn back to him. Unfortunately, the problem wasn't that Judah needed an opportunity. The problem was that the people of Judah desired their rebellion and idolatry more than God (v. 3). Though God had met the needs of the people time and again, the people chose to lust after idols (v. 7)

Their lust meant they refused to repent even after they were warned of a coming judgment (v. 6). The judgment God promises is not minor. God promises that the people will be consumed like wood by fire (v. 14). The consuming fire that will engulf the rebellious nation is the might of another nation (vv. 15-18). The Babylonians will be the instrument of God's justice. The rebellious Judah will pay mightily for their disobedience. Amazingly, even in the midst of their total rebellion and the resulting judgment, God demonstrates that he is a God of mercy. He states, "Yet even then I will not completely destroy you" (v. 18).

This one episode, with accompanying promises, reveals the depth of God's character. On the one hand, he cannot let sin go unpunished (v. 29), demonstrating his justice. Yet, he shows mercy to a nation that does not deserve it. This character of God is on display even more clearly at Calvary. God could not let sin go unpunished, and we, as sinners, deserve the punishment. Yet, God shows his mercy to us in that he took the punishment we earned and placed it on Christ through the curse of the cross. As a result, for anyone in Christ, the debt of sin has been paid and the curse of punishment removed.

Adam York

Connection with Newer Testament

Romans 5:8-11

219

For the Kids

This week, your family will see how God is working even in the darkest times of Israel's history. Help your children plant seeds in your garden or in a small cup or pot. Talk about how these buried seeds, dead-looking, don't look like anything of worth and, once planted, all we can see is the plain wet soil. However, just as something beautiful will come from these seeds, God is working a time of sadness and destruction for his people's good and his own glory. Help your children to water and monitor your seeds throughout the week.

Prayer Prompts

1. Thank God that he is a God of justice and will not let sin go unpunished. If God were not just there could be no expectation that all the bad things in the world will be made right.

2. Thank God that he is merciful. Thank him that, even though we deserve his punishment, we are forgiven through Jesus.

◆

WEEK 28: DAY 1

Jeremiah 16

Key Text

"'But for now I, the LORD, say: "I will send many enemies who will catch these people like fishermen. After that I will send others who will hunt them out like hunters from all the mountains, all the hills, and the crevices in the rocks."'" Jeremiah 16:16

As The Lord Lives: A New Exodus with Fishers of Men

The exodus from Egypt was seminal in the history of the Israelite people. It was part of their identity as God's chosen nation. Anytime the people began to doubt God or stray from his loving care, God would call his people to remember the power and goodness he displayed for them in the exodus. Sadly, by the time Jeremiah is prophesying, the Israelites have so forsaken God that remembering just won't do. Judgment is the means that God will use to remind the people that he is God and there is none like him.

The coming judgment will be one of famine, sword, and death (v. 4). It will be so destructive that people should not even bother with marriages and childbearing. Society will be so rocked by this judgment that God says to forget two institutions that are the bedrock of society. The people will be led into captivity by another nation: Babylon (v. 13). Yet, God will not leave them in Babylon. He will keep his promise to his people that they will have a promise land. God will lead his people away from Babylon with a new exodus. This new exodus will be so great that it will overshadow the one from Egypt (vv. 14-15). The new exodus, like the exile to Babylon, will be accomplished because God will send many "fishermen" to "bring them back to the land" given to their ancestors. (vv. 15-16). God is willing to show this mercy so that his name may by glorified and known (v. 21).

There is another exodus, one that far surpasses what happened in Egypt, in which God sends fishers of men out with the purpose of setting men free from bondage. Jesus tells his disciples that they will be fishers of men as they share the eternally freeing message of the gospel with men and women in bondage to sin (Matt. 4:16-22). The gospel of Jesus Christ is an exodus from the slavery of sin, and, if you are in Christ, you carry that freeing message with you. Will you be a fisher of men?

Adam York

Connection with Newer Testament
Matthew 4:16-22

For the Kids
Let each family member share what good things they think about when they think about one another. Explain that the Israelites thought about the Exodus when thinking about God. It was the greatest thing that they celebrated most often about him. But God says that he is doing something even greater now! When we think of God today, we should think first of Jesus and how he saves us from sin, which is greater than God's deliverance from Egypt.

Prayer Prompts

1. As the Lord's fishers and hunters, ask the Lord to give you boldness to share the gospel with at least one non-Christian person this week.

2. Perhaps you aren't consistently sharing the gospel. Perhaps you need to repent of things, like fear, that are keeping you from professing Christ.

◆

WEEK 28: DAY 2

Jeremiah 18

Key Text

"'There are times, Jeremiah, when I threaten to uproot, tear down, and destroy a nation or kingdom. But if that nation I threatened stops doing wrong, I will cancel the destruction I intended to do to it.'" Jeremiah 18:7-8

The Lord Promises to Relent from Wrath if Judah Will Repent

The craftsman has total control over the crafts he produces. A potter has the power to rework the clay of any of his pots. In that way, the craftsman is sovereign over his crafts. In like manner, God is completely sovereign over his creation. So, like the potter who can rework any vessel that fails to meet his expectation, God can rework any nation or people that falls short of the purpose for which they were crafted.

The purpose for which nations are crafted is to bring God glory. This is true particularly of Israel, God's chosen people (Ex. 19:6-6). Yet, God's people had rebelled. Rather that walking in God's way and worshiping him alone, they committed acts of idolatry with false gods and performed immoral acts in the name of that false worship. They turned their back on God. Therefore, God promises to remake them with the coming judgment of exile. Though there was a coming judgment, God was still willing to show mercy and to stop the judgment if the people would just repent (v. 8).

The people are not moved by his mercy. In fact, their hearts only grew harder, their necks stiffer (v. 12). They reject the blessings of God (vv. 14-16) for the judgment of God (v. 17). They chose the lies of their rebellious leaders over the truth of the obedient prophet. For this reason, the people called down their own judgment. They chose destruction over mercy.

Like the Israelite people, we too stand condemned. The Bible tells us we have all rejected God and that his judgment is upon us. Yet, he offers us mercy through repentance and belief in Jesus Christ, who takes away our sin. What is your choice?

Adam York

Connection with Newer Testament
Acts 3:19

For the Kids
Ask your kids how they would feel it they built a sandcastle then you came along and destroyed it. Ask, "Why would you feel that way?" Now ask if they would feel the same if they destroyed their own castle. Why is it different? Then, walk them through the ideas that God created all of us, that we have rejected him, that he has every right to destroy us, and that he offers grace through Jesus Christ.

Prayer Prompts
1. Ask God to forgive you when you are stubborn and reject his ways for your own.
2. Thank God that he offers grace to people that reject him.
3. Ask God for courage to share the message of his grace in Jesus with others.

◆

WEEK 28: DAY 3
Jeremiah 22-23:8

Key Text
"'Behold, the days are coming,' declares the LORD, 'when I will raise up for David a righteous Branch, and he shall reign as king and act wisely, and shall execute justice and righteousness in the land. In his days Judah will be saved,

and Israel will dwell in security. And this is his name by which he will be called: "The LORD is our righteousness."' Jeremiah 23:5-6*

Messiah is Coming: A Davidic Branch Will Save Israel

The condition of someone's heart can be measured by how that person treats poor and vulnerable people. Over and over, the Bible describes authentic faith in God as faith that cares for the orphan, the widow, and the refugee. James 1:27 says, "Pure and undefiled religion before God the Father is this: to care for orphans and widows in their misfortune." The prophet Micah reminds God's people that doing justice is one of the things that God requires from his people (Mic. 6:8).

It should not surprise us, therefore, to discover God's anger over the failure of Judah's kings to act justly. Not only were King Josiah's sons not caring for the weak and vulnerable, they were profiting off of them. The LORD condemns these wicked kings for not paying the workers who built their great houses (22:13-14). God does not grant leaders power so that they may selfishly profit. God grants leaders power so that they will use their authority to serve the people they rule. However, power is a dangerous weapon in the hands of sinful people.

Today's government systems have not improved much since those days of old. Governments and kings are still corrupt. People in power continue to get rich at the expense of the weak and vulnerable. Thankfully, our hope is not in human governments. Our hope is King Jesus, "the righteous Branch" who "shall reign as king and act wisely, and shall execute justice and righteousness in the land" (23:5). As we look out at corruption and injustice, may we look to the King who did not come "to be served but to serve, and to give his life as a ransom for many" (Mark 10:45).

Casey McCall

Connection with Newer Testament
Romans 3:20-26

For the Kids

Jesus comes from the family tree of David as our perfect King to save us and to rule forever. Check on the seeds you planted three days ago. Maybe you see sprouts. Discuss with your children how Christ is like that promised Branch growing up. Maybe you see nothing yet. Discuss with your children how Israel at this time didn't see the fulfillment of God's promises yet. Life was difficult and God was judging them, but life would still grow out of this bad time.

Prayer Prompts

1. Praise God that he has acted decisively in Jesus Christ to display his righteousness as King of kings. He has not forgotten sin. He dealt with it on the cross for all who believe and will deal with it in hell for all those who don't believe.

2. Praise God for Christ, our righteous Branch. His sinless life is counted to sinners like us so that we who deserve judgment might be saved.

3. Ask the Lord to help you walk blamelessly before him in this world knowing that the Lord is both righteous and our righteousness.

◆

WEEK 28: DAY 4

2 Kings 24

Key Text

"Just as the LORD had announced, he rejected Judah because of all the sins which Manasseh had committed." 2 Kings 24:3

Exiled to Babylon: Judah's Unfaithfulness Punished

"Don't make me count to three!" "If you do that one more time, you're going to get it!" Perhaps you heard phrases like these from your parents growing up. Perhaps you've uttered phrases like these to your own children. We say things like this when we get desperate. We want our children to obey but we really don't want to enact discipline, so we give them warnings and second chances. As parents, we must be careful with such repeated warnings accompanied by delayed or no action. Our goal should be to train our children to respond quickly and obediently to the Lord. The worst thing we could do is to give empty warnings that never come to fruition, thus training their hearts to discount warnings as meaningless.

Leading up to 2 Kings 24, God's repeated warnings through the prophets had fallen on deaf ears. Judah continued in blatant idolatry and injustice, not believing that God would act to discipline his people. God was patient, but Judah mistook his patience for leniency. 2 Kings 24 describes God's decision to make good on his warnings. He would no longer warn; he was ready to act. Babylon would be his chosen rod of discipline. His people would go into captivity under a foreign nation.

Repentance is not for tomorrow; it is always for today. God never reveals to us the date upon which his patience will end. He graciously and patiently warns us, but we must never assume that his patience is unending. He will, sooner or later, make good on his warnings. He will not tolerate our rebellion forever. "Look, now is the acceptable time; look, now is the day of salvation" (2 Cor. 6:2)!

Casey McCall

Connection with Newer Testament
Romans 1:18

For the Kids
In this chapter, as throughout Scripture, we see king after king disobey God. The Bible relates each king's disobedience to his father's disobedience. In contrast, other followers of God trusted him because of their father's legacy of faith. Tell your children about godly fathers in your life—whether it be your earthly father or another family member or a spiritual mentor—and thank the Lord for how he provides us with older generations to teach us and encourage us to obey him.

Prayer Prompts
1. Praise God for his long-suffering nature and jealousy for our hearts.
2. Meditate on the wickedness of sin and the goodness of God.

WEEK 28: DAY 5
Ezekiel 10

Key Text

"Then the glory of the LORD moved away from the threshold of the temple and stopped above the cherubim." Ezekiel 10:18

Idolatry Among the Remnant in Jerusalem: The Glory of the Lord Leaves the Temple

God has had enough. He has watched his people turn their backs on him too many times. The peoples' sin ushered bloodshed and injustice into the city (Ezek. 9:9). Finally, God gave them precisely what they wanted: a city without his presence. For centuries, the people knew God's presence was among them in the temple. They had access to God continually, but this wicked people chose to disregard and ignore this blessing. They worshiped false gods and committed all manner of immorality. Therefore, God simply honors their desire and removes his presence from them. In so doing, God is keeping the promise he made generations earlier to hide his face from his people if they sought other gods (Deut. 31:17-18).

Ezekiel explains that God's glory exits the temple, accompanied by the angelic beings that are always serving him. The cherubim escort God up from the ark of the covenant to the temple threshold (Ezek. 9:3) and then out to the east gate (Ezek. 10:19). Eventually, God's presence exited the city toward the mountains to the east of the city (Ezek. 11:22-23).

The direction of God's departure may seem insignificant, but in the next chapter, God promises to return to Jerusalem and the temple. This promise he fulfills in Jesus Christ. The New Testament recounts Jesus' triumphal entry into Jerusalem. Jesus enters the city from Bethpahage, a city on the east of Jerusalem in the Kidron Valley (Matt. 21:1-11). This valley is in the shadow of the very mountains where God's presence departed centuries earlier. Additionally, Matthew records that Jesus' first act is to enter the temple and cleanse it of wickedness (Matt. 21:12-17). God fulfills his promise to restore his glory. Jesus Christ is now the display of God's glory on earth (John 2:13-22).

Connection with Newer Testament

Matthew 21:1-17; John 2:13-22

For the Kids

Ask your kids if a friend has ever ignored them or if they have ever ignored a someone. Explain that when you ignore someone you are treating him or her like he or she is not there. When the Israelites ignored God, they treated him like he was not there. We can ignore God as well and often treat him like he is not there. What is amazing that God promises to never leave us or forsake us in Jesus Christ if we repent of ignoring him.

Prayer Prompts

1. God promised that he would return to Jerusalem and the temple. He promised his presence would again be among the people. Thank God that he keeps his promises in Jesus Christ.

2. Ask God to convict you of any sin or idolatry that is keeping you from fully acknowledging God's presence in your life through Jesus.

◆

WEEK 29: DAY 1

Jeremiah 24-25

Key Text

"'I, the LORD, the God of Israel, say: "The exiles whom I sent away from here to the land of Babylon are like those good figs. I consider them to be good."'"
Jeremiah 24:5

Good Figs and Captivity: A Seventy Year Exile Will End with the Release of God's Remnant

If you planted a tree or a garden and put a great amount of work into preparing the ground and cultivating the crop, you would expect it to yield ripe fruits or vegetables. What if it yielded a wild and useless crop? You would, of course, take the good and use it for many different things, but the bad you would most assuredly discard. That is the picture of Jeremiah 24-25. Israel is like a vine or tree that the Lord has planted in the land that produces fruit that the Lord cannot use. The people of Israel are represented by two different types of figs.

The bad figs are those people who stayed behind in the land during the exile, along with the puppet king, Zedekiah. The Lord declares that he will curse those left behind such that famine, pestilence, and violence will come upon them. Those left in the promised land will be completely destroyed from the land given to them because they obeyed Egypt and the nations around them rather than God.

The good figs are the Israelites that were exiled to Babylon. Although they are under judgement, the Lord promises a remnant will come from them, which he will restore to the promised land. The Lord will give this remnant a heart to know that he is the Lord, that they are his people, that he will be their God, and that he will do all that he has promised them.

The Lord's favor is not a matter of flesh and blood, nor is it tied to a physical location. The Israelites who stayed in the land believed that the only way they could prosper was by staying in Canaan; yet, they failed to learn the lesson the Lord taught Israel in Numbers 13-14: The Lord requires obedience on his terms, to go where he says to go when he says to go. It is better to go in faithful obedience to Babylon than to stay disobediently in the promised land, even when your history often ties God's blessing to the promised land.

God is saving a remnant for himself, and that remnant is those who put their faith in Jesus, the only good fig and the one who fulfills the Old Testament promises. This salvation does not come through our terms. It did not come through Israel's determination to stay in the land when God told Israel to go. Likewise, salvation will not come by our good works, as we tend to think, when God declares it to be by grace through faith in Jesus. May we respond to God's word on his terms, by faith, even when difficult, finding ourselves as good figs in Jesus.

Josh Crawford and Jon Canler

Connection with Newer Testament

1 Peter 1:1-10

For the Kids

What should we do with a bag of oranges with one or two rotten ones in it or a bunch of bananas with one that is too ripe? Ask your kids if they think you should throw out the whole bunch or bag. Of course, not. We discard the bad ones and keep the good ones. God does the same thing. He removes bad spiritual fruit and keeps good spiritual fruit. In other words, he keeps and protects people who are obedient, as we see in Jeremiah 24. Sadly, unlike the bag of oranges, the truth is that there is none who are perfectly good and obedient, no, not even one when it comes to spiritual fruit. The only way people can be perfectly good is if God makes them good. He has done just that by sending Jesus to remove our rot of sin and to give us life afresh. The only way we are kept by God is through Jesus.

Prayer Prompts

1. Praise God that he is merciful to his people. Exile and judgment for sin are not the end for those who trust in the Lord. Christ was exiled as a sinner and forsaken by the Father on the cross so that all who cling to him will find salvation.

2. Consider God's patience and his justice. He gave Judah ample opportunity to repent of their sins and to return to him before exercising judgment. He does the same for you. But know that God will punish your sin. Repent now and let Christ bear your sin, or refuse and bear it yourself—like Judah.

◆

WEEK 29: DAY 2

Jeremiah 29

Key Text

"'Work to see that the city where I sent you as exiles enjoys peace and prosperity. Pray to the LORD for it. For as it prospers you will prosper.'"
Jeremiah 29:7

Living as Exiles: Seek the Welfare of the City

Jeremiah 29 is a chapter of promise, bright promise for the exiled people of God. Even as they are in the heartbreak of exile, God speaks words of commitment to them: "I will fulfill my gracious promise to you and restore you," "I will hear your prayers," "I will make myself available to you," "I will bring you back" (vs. 10-14). Because of God's promises, God's people can be assured that the big picture of their future is full of good and full of hope (v. 11).

In the meantime, however, God has instruction for them. God tells his people that deliverance will come after a seventy-year exile, and he gives them a plan for how they should conduct themselves in the midst of exile: "build houses," "plant gardens," "grow in number," and "work to see the city where I sent you as exiles enjoys peace and prosperity." How strange it must have been for the exiles to hear God telling them to invest in and to seek the welfare of Babylon! As they obeyed, imagine the conversations between parents and kids: "Son, we're planting this vineyard, and we'll eat from it for a season, but it's not ours forever. This is how we follow God while we wait."

In like manner, as followers of Christ, we know we have a heavenly future that is full of hope and good because of the promises of blessing given to us in Christ. We, too, are exiles awaiting our day of final rescue in which we will be brought by Jesus to be with Jesus where Jesus is. As such, this world is not our home. Our citizenship is in heaven. Our cities and our nations are not our permanent residence. Yet as we wait, we wait actively. We build and we plant and we seek the welfare of our city. We work for the good of our temporary home as witnesses demonstrating the ways of the eternal kingdom. We improve our cities even as we speak to them of a better eternal home. This is how we actively obey while we patiently wait.

Todd Martin

Connection with Newer Testament

1 Peter 2:13-17

For the Kids

God says to pray for the good of the city. Talk to your children about where you live. Tell them what you know of the town's history or what it's known for. Talk about the groups of people: ones who don't know Jesus, the ones from other countries, the older ones, the other small kids, the poor, etc. Then pray for your city with your children as we long for the eternal city to come (Heb. 13:14).

Prayer Prompts

1. As elect exiles awaiting our eternal home, ask the Lord to help you seek the good of the place God has placed you—a good which is maximized only through Christians living and speaking as citizens of the kingdom of Christ.
2. Ask the Lord to help you love your neighbors as yourself because doing so seeks the good of your city.

◆

WEEK 29: DAY 3

Lamentations 3

Key Text

"The LORD's loyal kindness never ceases; his compassions never end. They are fresh every morning; your faithfulness is abundant!" Lamentations 3:22-23

God's Faithfulness: Hope for an Exiled People

"Jesus wept." Those two words in John 11:35 comprise the shortest verse in the Bible. And with those two words, our Lord and Savior frees us by demonstrating that sometimes the most appropriate response to tragedy is simply to grieve. Lamentations is a book of poetic grief. Jeremiah the prophet responds to the horror of the Babylonian exile of God's people with an extended lament. This lament provides us with an inspired vocabulary for our own seasons of tragedy.

Notice that Jeremiah does not try to lessen the degree of his pain and torment. He uses extreme language to describe his experience. His flesh and skin "waste away" and his bones are "broken" (v. 4). He feels surrounded as if

232

there is no escape, as if he is in chains (v. 7). He doubts that God is even hearing his prayers (v. 8). In fact, it feels like God has turned against him and is no longer on his side (vv. 10-12). It is dangerous for us to go through life pretending like everything is alright. Jeremiah teaches us to be honest. Even when our thoughts and feelings do not seem in line with truth, honesty must prevail.

The beauty of Jeremiah's lament lies in his example of preaching to himself. As he opens up about his pain to the LORD, he reminds himself of the truth of God's love and faithfulness. He will not allow his suffering to have the final word. He fights to remember the promises of God. Even in his honest doubting, he directs his gaze to the only hope he has. He refuses to let hopelessness prevail.

Casey McCall

Connection with Newer Testament
2 Thessalonians 3:3

For the Kids
Explain to your children that sleep is a good thing. Sure, it is necessary for us to be healthy and strong, but it also reminds us of our need. We cannot constantly go without sleep. We are not inexhaustible. It reminds us that we are dependent. It also reminds us that the universe doesn't depend on us. While we sleep, the world keeps going without us. Sleep is a reminder that God is in control. Therefore, mornings should be a time of praise. Each morning is a chance for a fresh recognition that God is merciful and powerful. Through his mercy and power and steadfast love, the Lord cares for his people, even in times of difficulty (like the exile was for Israel). Praise God for his faithful mercies in Christ that give hope to his people, people who are elect exiles in this world awaiting glory in the new heavens and the new earth.

Prayer Prompts
1. Praise the Lord for his faithfulness.

2. Pray that God would grant you unwavering faith in him, regardless of circumstances.

◆

Key Text

"'Say to them, "As surely as I live, declares the sovereign LORD, I take no pleasure in the death of the wicked, but prefer that the wicked change his behavior and live. Turn back, turn back from your evil deeds! Why should you die, O house of Israel?"'" Ezekiel 33:11

The Lord's Pleasure: That the Wicked Would Repent and Live

Ezekiel 33 is a revelation of God's mind and heart. In the same chapter, in close proximity, stand paradoxical yet unified teachings of human responsibility, the desires of God, and prophesied unbelief. Given alongside each other, they are a glimpse into God's love and sovereignty.

First, God tells Ezekiel that he is a watchman entrusted with warnings to give to the people. Ezekiel *must* warn the wicked people of Israel about coming judgment! Their lives are in his hands. Then, at the end of the chapter, God tells Ezekiel ahead of time that the people he is commanded to warn won't listen to him.

Yet in-between, even as God is about to tell Ezekiel that the people won't listen, God calls out to the people through Ezekiel, saying, "turn back, turn back" and "I take no pleasure in the death of the wicked" (v. 11). God's heart is revealed—a heart that loves people, a heart that takes pleasure in repentance and life.

Too often, people respond to such a combination of truths by wrestling with them solely to harmonize them theologically in their mind. Today, respond in total ways! Follow the sovereign God of love by being transformed. Ask him to stir within you his love. Follow him with a heart that loves people and yearns to see them enjoy repentance and eternal life. If we love people like the LORD loves people, we will speak to them the life-saving

234

gospel of Jesus Christ. Evangelism comes from the love of Christ for humanity. And unlike the promised rejection Ezekiel was expecting, we have been promised a response of faith. Even as some won't listen, as some will pursue other things, and as some won't be willing to pay the cost, there will be an abundant harvest from every tribe, tongue, and nation filled with those who will believe (Mark 4:14-20, Rev. 7:9-12)! Jesus will build his church (Matt. 16:18)!

Follow Jesus: love people as he does by speaking the gospel to them.

Todd Martin

Connection with Newer Testament
Matthew 4:17; John 3:16; Acts 2:38, 3:19

For the Kids
Have you ever wanted something bad to happen to someone? Maybe you told an adult what a classmate did wrong and watched with happiness as you saw him or her get in trouble. God is not like that. He will punish sinners, and he is right to do so. But, he doesn't get happy in their punishment. Instead of wanting bad things to happen to people, we should pray that they repent of sin, trust in Jesus, and find forgiving mercy. Ask God to give you a heart that loves people with the same mercy with which he loves people.

Prayer Prompts
1. Who do you know that isn't a Christian? Ask the Lord to impress upon their hearts their utter hopelessness apart from Christ. Ask the Lord to bring them to repentance so that they may not perish.
2. If you are a Christian, praise that Lord that God brought you to a place of repentance, and praise the Lord that he gave you eternal life through Jesus.

◆

WEEK 29: DAY 5
Jeremiah 31:31-40, 32:36-44

Key Text

"'But I will make a new covenant with the whole nation of Israel after I plant them back in the land,' says the LORD. 'I will put my law within them and write it on their hearts and minds. I will be their God and they will be my people.'" Jeremiah 31:33

New Covenant after Exile: The Law Written on Human Hearts

God has graciously made covenants with his people throughout history. In a covenant, God makes a solemn commitment to his chosen people, and he provides his people with a way to have a relationship with him, guaranteeing divine promises and laying out human obligations. God made covenants with Adam, Noah, Abraham, Moses, and David. Jeremiah, however, is talking about a brand-new covenant, one that is not like the covenant made with Moses on Mount Sinai (31:32). This new covenant is better than that old covenant. How is it better? Here are three ways:

The Law Will Be Written on Hearts (31:33)

When the law was given to Moses, it was written on tablets of stone, but the hearts of God's people remained unchanged with respect to their sinfulness. In the new covenant, Jeremiah prophesizes that the law will be written on the hearts of God's people. Because of what Christ has done, those under the new covenant will receive new hearts that are inclined toward obedience to the LORD.

God Will Be Known Personally and Sins Will Be Forgiven (31:34)

Because the old covenant was powerless to change hearts, those under the old covenant had no final solution to their sins and separation from God. That covenant was never intended to be the final covenant. It always pointed ahead to a better covenant. That better covenant is the new covenant about which Jeremiah prophecies. Sins are forgiven and hearts are changed because the new covenant is instituted by the sacrificial death of Jesus (Luke 22:20).

The New Covenant Lasts Forever (33:40)

The old covenant had an ending point, but the new covenant is eternal.

236

All who are covered by the blood of Jesus by faith under the new covenant are completely forgiven and made full citizens in God's kingdom forever.

Casey McCall

Connection with Newer Testament
2 Corinthians 3:4-11; Hebrews 8:6-13

For the Kids
Tie a string around your children's finger. Explain that tying a string around a finger is a practice some people use to remember things. Early in the Bible, we see that Israel had lost the word of God and forgotten it because of evil kings. It was discovered again under the good King Josiah. When the Scriptures were read, people learned of the forgotten promises of God and his requirements for his people. Here in this passage, Jeremiah is telling of a promise that can never be forgotten because it will be written on the hearts of God's people. It won't just be a string on their finger; it will be part of who they are. Praise God for this new promise that is fulfilled in all who trust in Jesus.

Prayer Prompts
1. Praise the Lord for his faithfulness. He has established this eternal, redemptive, glorious new covenant for us through the blood of Jesus.
2. Having called you his own through this covenant, ask the Lord to grant you obedience to him. If you are a Christian, remember that the law is written on your heart so that you are able and empowered by the Spirit to obey Christ.

◆

WEEK 30: DAY 1
Ezekiel 36

Key Text
"'I will put my Spirit within you; I will take the initiative and you will obey my statutes and carefully observe my regulations.'" Ezekiel 36:27

Return from Exile: New Hearts and the Moral Ability to Obey

Here in Ezekiel 36 we read about the action plan of God himself—in all his beautiful, righteous jealousy—for the glorification of his great name. The passage is full of promises of blessing and prosperity. It explains the end of exile, which is to be accomplished by the active, powerful working of God for his people and for the promised land and against their enemies. Lest we think his jealous defense is because of the people's inherent beauty or goodness, God clarifies, "It is not for your sake that I am about to act, O house of Israel, but for the sake of my holy reputation" (v. 22). Indeed, the actions of the guilty surrounding nations against the people are just the consequence of the core, larger, main problem. The main problem is with the people, their atrocious ways for which they should be "ashamed and embarrassed" (v. 32). And those ways flow from within, from within their hard, sinful hearts. God vows to fix the reproach by fixing the very root of the matter. "I will give you a new heart, and I will put a new spirit within you" (v. 26).

We often think about Jesus' work on the cross to save us in terms of his forgiveness for our sinful actions, and that is indeed a blessed reality. On top of forgiving us for what has flowed from our sinful hearts, Jesus is accomplishing a heart change in us through establishing a new covenant for us. He gives us a relationship in which we can have Holy Spirit-changed hearts. He puts his Spirit in us for a life change! He shows himself to be the one who is jealous for his people. As we live for him each day in the power of the Holy Spirit, it is a cosmic display of his lordship for the world to see! (v. 38)

Todd Martin

Connection with Newer Testament
John 14:15-31; Romans 8:11

For the Kids
Could you make the kitchen clean with a dirty, nasty sponge? Could you fix a car with broken tools? Of course not! To clean the best, you need a clean new sponge. To fix things, you need good tools. What do you need to live for God? God promised his people that he would give them a new heart and a new spirit

that is willing and able to worship him! Talk to your children about the difference God has made in your life and about how he gets the glory in the process.

Prayer Prompts

1. Praise the Lord that he has poured out his life-giving Spirit on you and has raised you from the dead through the blood of Jesus.

2. Name a few unbelievers that you know. Pray to the God of life that he would send his Spirit on those unbelievers so that they may be born again through the power of the Holy Spirit.

◆

WEEK 30: DAY 2
Ezekiel 37

Key Text
"'This is what the sovereign LORD says to these bones: Look, I am about to infuse breath into you and you will live.'" Ezekiel 37:5

Return from Exile: Resurrection of the Dead

All who are united to Christ by faith are swept into the promises of God. In Ezekiel 37, we are shown a foreshadowing of the resurrection. Ezekiel 37 is the story of Jesus Christ and those who are in him.

This life is often painful and gut-wrenching. There are many reasons to shed tears, but our tears should be full of hope. Do you realize that we have the word and the Spirit? The gospel message has the power to resurrect a valley of dry bones!

Being faithful as a Christian is marching boldly into the world with gospel hope, resurrection power, and confidence in the faithfulness of God. The joy we have in Christ is not silly. It stares in the face of death and asks, "Where is your sting?"

David Prince, "The Theology of a Graveyard," Preached 3/28/2010, Prince on Preaching Website, Accessed 4 December 2015, Available from http://www.davidprince.com/2010/03/28/the-theology-of-a-graveyard-ezekiel-371-14/.

Connection with Newer Testament
1 Corinthians 15

For the Kids
Have your children lie down and pretend to be dry bones. Tell them that you want them to get up and start moving around as you retell the story of what Ezekiel saw. Then, have your children sit back down, and talk about what this story means. God has the power to give eternal life, and he does so in Jesus!

Prayer Prompts
1. Pray that you will proclaim the gospel confidently as you go today.
2. Pray for a specific people group, that God would work among them and bring new life to them in Christ.

◆

WEEK 30: DAY 3
Ezekiel 39

Key Text
"'I will knock your bow out of your left hand and make your arrows fall from your right hand. You will fall dead on the mountains of Israel, you and all your troops and the people who are with you. I give you as food to every kind of bird and every will beast.'" Ezekiel 39:3-4

Return from Exile: Wrath on the Nations
The good news of Jesus is about grace and love and forgiveness. It's also about power! Faced with enemies, we need a savior who is a strong and skilled warrior. And that is who Jesus is!

There's a power dynamic to the gospel that is proclaimed in Ezekiel 39. What good is it to be given grace and blessing by God if a murderous enemy is able to come and take it away? And here we see a murderous enemy, a prince

240

named Gog, who is coming with hordes of people against the restored ones of Yahweh. But Gog is met with the mighty hand of God himself working for his beloved people and against her enemies. God says to Gog, "You will fall dead in the open field; for I have spoken" (v. 5). We are reminded of the words of David against Goliath: "I will strike you down and cut off your head" (1 Sam. 17:46). The parallel is continued throughout the Bible as we read of the defeated enemy armies becoming a feast for carnivorous birds.

For Christians, these are not just remote, old stories from the past. We were trapped in chains of sin and death. Jesus, with great power, conquered Satan and sin for us. We were helpless, but he came with power. Today, we have a very real, murderous enemy, a wicked prince with demonic hordes, who seeks our destruction. But Jesus is our protector and defender! We read of Gog and Magog again in Revelation 20. A day is coming in which Satan and his God-opposing minions will be finally defeated, and, on that day, the saints of God will enjoy the victorious Christ forever in the new heavens and the new earth with full security.

Todd Martin

Connection with Newer Testament
Revelation 19:11-21, 20:7-10

For the Kids
Sometimes in fairytales, things look the worst just before they get better. Often, things get better because of a courageous act by a hero. The hero puts a stop to the bad person or character. Good wins in the end. In the same way, sometimes, in the real world, it feels like badness or bad people are winning. Yet, God tells us not to worry. He sent his Hero to conquer the enemy. Jesus came to slay sin and evil. Jesus' heroic actions on the cross ensure that good wins in the end. We can be sure that only God and his people will be the forever winners in the very end. God always wins!

Prayer Prompts
1. Praise God that though you were an enemy, deserving wrath like Gog, you

have been given grace and life in order to glorify God's judging and saving character.

2. Ask the Lord for grace to trust him in the midst of persecution and trial. He will save his people!

◆

WEEK 30: DAY 4
Ezekiel 40-42

Key Text
"Then he measured its length as 35 feet, and its width as 35 feet, before the outer sanctuary. He said to me, 'This is the most holy place.'" Ezekiel 41:4

Return from Exile: A New Temple
Throughout the Bible, the idea of a temple is extremely important because the temple is the place where the LORD dwells among his people. The first temple-like place in the Bible is the Garden of Eden, for in the Garden, the LORD walked with Adam and Eve (Gen. 3:8). After choosing Israel to be his covenant, albeit sinful, people, the LORD dwelled among his people in the tabernacle (Ex. 40:34-38). Furthermore, in the days of King Solomon, a permanent temple was built unto the LORD (1 Kings 6), which was a copy of the earthly temple of the Garden of Eden (1 Kings 6:18, 29, 32, 35). The strength, success, and glory of Israel rested on the fact that the LORD chose to covenant with and dwell among them.

As we turn to Ezekiel 40-42, Israel is in exile and the temple is destroyed. The glory of the LORD had departed from the temple (Ezek. 10). Has the LORD permanently left his sinful, faithless people? In Ezekiel 36-48, Ezekiel gives the people of Israel hope by telling them that a future day is coming in which the exile will be over. There is coming a day when the LORD will pour out his life-giving Spirit on spiritually dead Israel, thus causing them to be a perpetually obedient people (Ezek. 36-37). This return from exile will ultimately lead to one final battle between good and evil (Ezek. 38-39) before culminating in a new temple (Ezek. 40-42). A day is coming, says Ezekiel, in which the temple will be reconstructed. Take hope, Israel.

Well, God was and is faithful to build a temple in which he might dwell among his people. However, God's new temple isn't made of bricks. It's made of flesh and blood. When Jesus Christ came to earth in the form of a man, he was the temple of God for he was flesh in which God was pleased to dwell (John 2). Furthermore, Jesus gives his life-giving Spirit to all who put their faith in him such that the place of God's temple is now the people of his redemption (John 14:17, 1 Cor. 3:16). And one day, when Jesus comes back, his people will be a temple-bride dwelling in the presence of God for all eternity (Rev. 21). As you share the gospel and as people come to faith in Christ, the temple of God is being built. As you disciple fellow believers and as you are discipled, the temple of God is being sanctified for the glory of God. Are you being discipled? Who are you discipling? With whom are you sharing the gospel?

Jon Canler

Connection with Newer Testament
1 Corinthians 3:16; Revelation 21:9-27

For the Kids
Ask your children where God lives. It is likely they will say, "Heaven." Then, ask them if they think God can live in their heart. The Bible teaches that, before Jesus, people could only experience God's presence through his temple. However, after Jesus and his work on the cross, the Bible tells us that the true temple of God on earth is believers who are a temple of the Holy Spirit (1 Cor. 3:16). Explain to your children that, in Jesus, they have the blessing of God's constant and consistent presence in their lives.

Prayer Prompts
1. Praise God that he is ushering in a kingdom through Christ in which his relationship with his people is so close that they become the very temple where he dwells.
2. Praise God that his temple-people, built on the foundation of Jesus as the true Temple (John 2), extends to the ends of the earth and will one day reach to every tribe, tongue, and language.

WEEK 30: DAY 5

Ezekiel 43

Key Text

"The glory of the LORD came into the temple by the way of the gate that faces east. Then a wind lifted me up and brought me to the inner court; I watched the glory of the LORD filling the temple." Ezekiel 43:4-5

Return from Exile: The Presence of the Lord in the Temple

Ezekiel opens with a description of the glory of the LORD—a glory stretching and surpassing the limits of human comprehension (Ezek. 1). His is a glory that caused the prophet Ezekiel to respond with his face in the dirt. In Ezekiel 1, Ezekiel witnessed this glory and lived to tell about it, but in Ezekiel 10-11, he witnessed the horrific vision of the glory of the LORD departing the temple. God left, but not for good. In Ezekiel 43, Ezekiel's hope and joy is restored as he sees the LORD returning from the same direction he left some twenty years prior.

The vision of the LORD's return demanded a response. The vision of the LORD's presence in the temple called a rebellious people, a people who had left God, to return to God just as God would return to them. So, the LORD called them to put away the sin in their midst (v. 9), to be ashamed of their iniquities (vv. 10-11a), and to turn to him in obedience (v. 43:11b). The chapter closes by prescribing precisely how they are to draw near to God through regular sacrificial offerings—shedding the blood of bulls and goats which serve to make atonement for the sins of the people.

The LORD would return to the temple and would require sacrifice for acceptance (v. 27). And yet, some six hundred years later, the LORD would do more than fill the Holy of Holies. He would come and walk among us such that John declared, "We saw his glory—the glory of the one and only, full of grace and truth, who came from the Father" (John 1:14). Years later, the Glory of the LORD would become our spotless Lamb of sacrifice who would shed his blood to pay the price for our sins so that we might be accepted by God.

Nate BeVier.

Connection with Newer Testament
Revelation 21:3

For the Kids
What's the most difficult thing about visiting grandparents and friends? Having to say goodbye! Nobody likes to have to say goodbye to people they love. This was particularly with Israel and their relationship with God. God's presence in their midst was their hope; yet, Ezekiel 43 shows that God's presence left the Jerusalem temple as a result of Israel's sin. Israel had rejected God for so long that he took his presence from them for a season. The good news is that God would return to dwell among his people in Jesus and in his people in the Holy Spirit. Reconciliation and presence get the last word between God and his people.

Prayer Prompts
1. Praise the Lord for the gospel! Through Christ's work on the cross, we have been reconciled to him, the holy God.
2. Pray that God would shape our church to be wholly centered upon the gospel.

◆

WEEK 31: DAY 1
Ezekiel 47

Key Text
"Every living creature which swarms where the river flows will live; there will be many fish, for these waters flow there. It will become fresh and everything will live where the river flows." Ezekiel 47:9

Return from Exile: The River of Life
We come with needs. We need healing; we need life. God shows himself over and over again to be the great provider. In the wilderness, God

caused water to flow from a rock to provide life to his people (Ex. 17). In the days of Elisha, God healed an unfruitful land by healing its water (2 Kgs. 2). Here in Ezekiel 47, we see a glorious vision of a river coming from the temple of God. It is miraculous in its source and its size. Everywhere it goes there is life and healing and blessing. Fish abound in its waters. Lush, fruitful trees drink from it on its banks. It is not diluted when it reaches the sea; instead, it transforms the sea. In this mysterious, marvelous tide there is a power of life flowing outward in blessing from the Creator of life himself.

Later in the Bible, a carpenter's son from Nazareth will call out, "If anyone is thirsty, let him come to me" (John 7:37)! Jesus speaks of living water he gives that will spring up within us to eternal life (John 4:14, 7:38).

We come with needs. Jesus comes with provision. From him, we find a marvelous power of life that transforms, a power that provides for us blessing and healing and abundant life. The picture of a river is fitting because this experience of gracious blessing from God is not a momentary act in history, but an ongoing, life-giving reality which we will enjoy from him eternally, on and on, forever in Jesus the Christ! (Rev. 22:1-5)

Todd Martin

Connection with Newer Testament
John 7:37-39; Revelation 22:1-5

For the Kids
What normally happens when something clean (like a clean shirt) touches something dirty (like a baby's hand covered with spaghetti sauce)? What happens when someone healthy spends time with someone who is sneezing and coughing? Usually, dirtiness spreads, and the sickness spreads. Not so with God! God makes the dirty one clean, the sick one healthy, and the dead one alive for all eternity through faith in Jesus Christ.

Prayer Prompts
1. Praise God that he has overcome the curse in our lives by filling our dead hearts of sin with the living waters of the Spirit.

2. Praise the Lord that he is a merciful God, the God of the living, who loves to give life to his people. Praise him as you anticipate the day when we stand in the new earth with the river of life flowing from the throne of God and of the Lamb.

3. Repent of trying to find eternal life through any means but through God and his Christ. Life comes from the Lord alone as we humbly call out to him for mercy. Pride seeks to attain to eternal life apart from the Lord.

◆

WEEK 31: DAY 2
Jeremiah 33

Key Text
"'I, the LORD, affirm: "the time will certainly come when I will fulfill my gracious promise concerning the nations of Israel and Judah. In those days and at that time I will raise up for them a righteous descendant of David. He will do what is just and right in the land."' Jeremiah 33:14-15

Fulfilling the Davidic Covenant: The Lord Is Faithful in Exile
The scene in Jeremiah 33 is a war zone. Not one house stands untouched by the result of war. The source of this hopeless scene was sin—the wasteland, a reminder of sin's destruction. Yet in the midst of the rubble, the LORD thunders forth his promise through the prophet Jeremiah that he will be faithful to undo all the destruction sin has brought forth. He promises to "restore" the war-torn city, to rebuild it to its full glory (vv. 7-11). That place of destruction would become a place where "joy and gladness" would once again be heard (v. 11).

Not only does the LORD provide a picture of restored glory, he also promises to be the very one who brings that picture to fruition. He reveals that his promise to restore and rebuild would begin with a King, a King who would fulfill the promise he made to David that one of David's own descendants would sit enthroned forever (1 Chr. 17:11-14). This King would answer the volley of sin's most destructive weapons by becoming sin for us so that we might become the righteousness of God. Some six hundred years later, in

David's city, the King was born, and they called his name Jesus. By grace and through faith in King Jesus, God restores and rebuilds what sin has destroyed.

Nate BeVier

Connection with Newer Testament
1 Peter 2:5

For the Kids
Using blocks or other household objects, build a tower with your children. Then tear the tower down. Tell your children that this fallen tower pictures Israel during Jeremiah 33: a place destructed and laid waste because of sin. Then promise your children that you will rebuild their tower better than before and actually build a better tower. Tell your children that God also promised Israel that a day was coming when he would rebuild them and restore them and prosper them and cleanse them from their sin. Teach your children that God restores and rebuilds in Jesus what sin has destroyed.

Prayer Prompts
1. Praise the Lord for his sovereignty in causing "a righteous descendant/branch" to spring up for David who will execute justice and righteousness in the land.
2. Pray that God would strengthen your trust in his faithfulness as you patiently anticipate the fulfillment of all his promises.

◆

WEEK 31: DAY 3
2 Kings 25

Key Text
"In the thirty-seventh year of the exile of King Jehoiachin of Judah, on the twenty-seventh day of the twelfth month, King Evil-Merodach of Babylon, in the first year of his reign, pardoned King Jehoiachin of Judah and released him

from prison. He spoke kindly to him and gave him a more prestigious position than the other kings who were with him in Babylon." 2 Kings 25:27-28

Jehoiachin: The Seed of David Remains in the Midst of Babylonian Captivity

When we arrive at the end of 2 Kings, things could not look more hopeless. The prophecies of Jeremiah and Ezekiel are coming to fruition as a foreign army serves as a tool of God's judgment on the people of Judah. The wicked king of Judah, King Jehoiachin, descendent of David, was taken away and imprisoned in Babylon. His uncle, the evil Mattaniah (renamed Zedekiah), took Jehoiachin's throne in Jerusalem only to see the city fall at the hands of the Chaldeans. The last thing his eyes saw before being gouged out was the death of his two sons. The Davidic line was diminishing rapidly as, one by one, the heirs to the throne were either imprisoned or killed. To make matters worse, Nebuchadnezzar had the temple burned to the ground and the entire city of Jerusalem destroyed. Along with the strongest and most skilled in Judah, everything of value was taken to Babylon.

Judah was in exile, and it appeared as if the promises of the LORD were in jeopardy. Appearances are deceiving, however, and in God's providence, a new king in Babylon, Evil-Merodach, released King Jehoiachin after thirty-seven years of being imprisoned. The Davidic line lived on even through Babylonian captivity because God was faithful to keep his promises. Matthew 1 tells of the final King born in David's line. As this King hung on a cross and died, once again it appeared as if the promises of God were defeated. But on the third day, the King rose from the dead and now sits enthroned forever.

Nate BeVier

Connection with Newer Testament
Matthew 1

For the Kids
Turn out all the lights in your house, and ask your children what they can see.

Then light a candle or turn on a small lamp. Again, ask your children what they can see. Tell your children that the situation looked very dark for Israel at the end of 2 Kings due to Babylonian captivity. Then tell them about King Jehoiachin. When all hope looked lost for Israel, this one royal descendent of David stood like the lamp you turned on. He represented hope for exiled Israel to see, and he led to the birth of King Jesus. Yes, things were dark, but the seed of David that Israel longed for was not extinguished. God is a god of hope for his people.

Prayer Prompts

1. Praise the Lord for your redemption through faith in Christ alone.

2. Pray that God would cause your hope to remain in him throughout all the tumultuous seasons of your life. Even when all seems bleak, the gospel gives a bright hope!

◆

WEEK 31: DAY 4
Daniel 2

Key Text
"Daniel replied to the king, 'The mystery that the king is asking about is such that no wise men, astrologers, magicians, or diviners can possibly disclose it to the king. However, there is a God in heaven who reveals mysteries, and he has made known to King Nebuchadnezzar what will happen in the times to come.'"
Daniel 2:27-28a

From Small Stone to Mighty Mountain: A Prophecy Regarding the Davidic Kingdom

King Nebuchadnezzar has been set up in a position of authority by the Lord and has been given a vast empire. Yet, he does not give the glory to God, but instead he sees himself as god. However, when he has dreams that he doesn't understand, he realizes that he is not in control of everything in his life. The Lord gives the king a confusing dream to point out the sin in his life.

Because of his newfound loss of control, Daniel is able to come and interpret the dream, returning all glory and honor to the Lord.

We do not rule vast empires, but we have set up our own kingdoms. Control is an alluring mistress, and we love to dance with her. But the Lord is faithful to show us that we are not in control. When we realize that we are not in control, we find that God is sovereign and worthy of all our trust.

David Prince, "Who Has the Power?," Preached 5/5/2013, Prince on Preaching Website, Accessed 4 December 2015, Available from http://www.davidprince.com/2013/05/05/who-has-the-power-daniel-2/.

Connection with Newer Testament
Mark 4:30-34

For the Kids
Ask your children who is in charge of your house? Help them realize that you control when they eat, what they eat, when you go out of town, etc. Ask them who's in charge of Mom and Dad? Help them understand that you are not ultimately in charge, God is. It's the same with kings. Through Nebuchadnezzar's dream, God was showing that he (and no one else) is really in charge forever!

Prayer Prompts
1. Consider which areas in your life you are most reluctant to relinquish control, and ask God to take control of them from you.
2. Praise God that he is sovereign and cares enough about his created order to adopt us and allow us to call him father in his vast kingdom.

◆

WEEK 31: DAY 5
Daniel 5

Key Text
"Therefore the palm of a hand was sent from him, and this writing was

inscribed. This is the writing that was inscribed: MENE, MENE, TEQEL, and PHARSIN." Daniel 5:24-25

Writing on the Wall: The Fall of Babylon to the Medo-Persians

Daniel is once again brought before a king to interpret what no other man is able to understand. King Belshazzar holds a great party to celebrate himself. However, during the party, a hand begins to write on the wall. Daniel is brought in to interpret the writing. Instead of taking the gifts the king offered, he witnessed of what the Lord had done for his father. Daniel did not fear the king or give weight to the idols that all his wealth could buy. Instead, Daniel feared the Lord, the God who had brought up and humbled kings. So, when Daniel interprets the writing on the wall, all that he said came true.

We have so many idols in our lives that demand our attention. But God has always proven that he is the only satisfaction this world holds. When we continue to build up our own kingdoms, God will humble us. But because he humbles us out of love, he is there to offer new life through repentance.

Jeremy Haskins, "Who Should I Fear," Preached 6/9/2013, Ashland Avenue Baptist Church Website, Accessed 3 December 2015, Available from http://www.ashlandlex.org/podcast/who-should-i-fear/.

Connection with Newer Testament
Revelation 18

For the Kids
Ask your children if they know what an idiom is. An idiom is a saying whose meaning is not determined by the usual meanings of the individual words. Tell you children that "kick the bucket" is an idiom, and explain why. See if your children can think of another idiom. Tell your children that the saying "writing on the wall" is another idiom. This idiom comes from Daniel 5. Explain the expression to your children using Daniel 5. Tell your children that this idiom exists because of God's control over the world. God gave the writing, and God made it happened because he is lord over all. God rules over all today in Jesus. Worship him.

Prayer Prompts

1. Pray that God reveals to you where you have built up strongholds against trusting him.

2. Praise God that Christ was sent to supply us with a new life so that we don't have to fear, but can trust the Lord instead.

◆

WEEK 32: DAY 1

Daniel 7

Key Text

"Then the kingdom, authority, and greatness of the kingdoms under all of heaven will be delivered to the people of the holy ones of the Most High. His kingdom is an eternal kingdom; all authorities will serve him and obey him." Daniel 7:27

Kingdom through Suffering: The Coming Son of Man

Daniel has a horrific vision of four beasts, each representing a rebellion that comes against the Lord. However, after he sees how great and powerful the beasts are, the text says in verse 11, "And as I looked, the beast was killed, and its body destroyed and given over to be burned with fire."* After all the hype about the beasts, their inevitable end was and will be very anti-climactic. We see the greater story, the story of God's absolute control and power, even over the evils of the world. And as proof of this, Daniel's vision continues, and the Lord shows him his plan for the salvation of the world.

As the chapter closes, the Son of Man is shown ruling over the earth for eternity. Yet, that is not all. The saints of the Most High are so intertwined with the Son of Man that the same promise that he has is relayed to the saints. Regardless of the evil that is thrown against the world, the Son of Man responds in victory.

David Prince, "Can I Ever Go Home?," Preached 6/23/2013, Prince on Preaching Website, Accessed 4 December 2015, Available from http://www.davidprince.com/2013/06/23/can-i-ever-go-home-daniel-7/.

Connection with Newer Testament

Revelation 1:9-20

For the Kids

Remind your children that Jesus is coming back soon to finally defeat his enemies, to end the suffering of his people, and to bring his kingdom to completion! Say together this poem to help your children remember what they can do to be faithful to Jesus until they pass away or Jesus returns: "Know him, trust him, stay on track, follow him, and watch for him. He's coming back!"

Prayer Prompts

1. Pray that the Lord returns soon. In the meantime, pray that we are faithful saints who witness of the Son of Man.

2. Praise God that he is victorious. Praise God that he will always fight for us and that victory is guaranteed.

◆

WEEK 32: DAY 2

Daniel 9

Key Text

"'Seventy weeks have been determined concerning your people and your holy city to put an end to rebellion, to bring sin to completion, to atone for iniquity, to bring in perpetual righteousness, to seal up the prophetic vision, and to anoint a most holy place.'" Daniel 9:24

Return from Exile: The End of Sin, Atonement for Iniquity, Everlasting Righteousness, the End of Prophecy, and A Most Holy Place

Daniel was a man of the Scriptures. He read the Scriptures. He knew the Scriptures. He believed the Scriptures. Consequently, when Daniel realized that the end of Jeremiah's prophecy of seventy years of exile was nearing its completion (vv. 1-2), Daniel prayed to the LORD to inquire about the restoration of Jerusalem and the end of exile (vv. 3-19).

In response to his prayer, the LORD told Daniel that seventy weeks or seventy sevens were decreed for Israel. After approximately 490 years (70 x 7), sin would be ended, atonement would be made for iniquity, everlasting righteousness would be ushered in, prophecy would end, and a most holy place would be anointed. Why 490 years? Because 490 years is the time needed to usher in a 10-fold, perfectly complete jubilee.

Leviticus 25 reminds us that every fiftieth year was to be a year of jubilee, a year of release from debts, a year of freedom and of restoration. For forty-nine years debts could mount, but the fiftieth year was to be a year of release. The perfect, most complete jubilee would be a ten-fold jubilee since ten is a number of completion. A ten-fold mounting of debts would take place in 490 years (49 x 10). Consequently, a most complete, perfect, ten-fold jubilee would take place after the 490 years. And what possibly could be a greater cause for jubilee and rejoicing than being released from sin into everlasting righteousness? The perfect, sin-crushing, messiah-enthroning jubilee was coming to the people of God!

After sixty-nine of Daniel's weeks came to pass, Jesus Christ, the anointed one of God, was cut off for the sins of his people on the cross to atone for iniquity. We are now living in the seventieth week awaiting the return of Jesus to usher in the celebratory jubilee in which everlasting righteousness reigns in the new heavens and a new earth with Satan and sin destroyed in a lake of fire. Until Jesus returns, persevere in the faith. In this seventieth week, war and desolations are decreed (v. 26). The people of Christ will be persecuted. Lost people will act like lost people. Stand firm. Preach the word. Eagerly await the joyous jubilee that will soon be upon us at the appearing of our Lord Jesus.

Jon Canler

Connection with Newer Testament
Luke 24:46-47

For the Kids
Ask your children if they remember the last long trip that your family took. Did they ever ask, "How much longer until we get there?" Tell your children that,

in Daniel 9, the people of Israel are in exile, and they're waiting on the messiah to come who was promised way back in Genesis 3. They're asking, "How much longer?" In Daniel 9, God gives his people a timeline for the coming messiah who would set Israel free from sin in a day of great celebration. How long, you ask? It would take 70 x 7 years. See if your children can do the math. 490 years. Using today's devotion, help your children understand the significance of 490 years as a ten-fold, ultimate celebration. Praise God that he controls the future such that he's making this promised celebration come true in Jesus.

Prayer Prompts

1. Praise God that the promises of Daniel 9 are coming to pass in Christ. Jesus, the Prince, was cut off in order to establish the new covenant through his blood, redeeming sinners like us from the great captor of sin.

2. Christ has put an end to sacrifices through his own life. Repent of trying to offer God anything in order to gain his favor.

3. Praise the Lord that a day is coming when eternal righteousness will reign and we will be unable to sin. Rejoice in imagining the glories of a world with no death, no sickness, and no pain, all because of Jesus.

◆

WEEK 32: DAY 3
Daniel 12

Key Text

"Then I heard the man clothed in linen who was over the waters of the river as he raised both his right and left hands to the sky and made an oath by the one who lives forever: 'It is for a time, times, and half a time. Then, when the power of the one who shatters the holy people has been exhausted, all these things will be finished.'" Daniel 12:7

The Last Days: Tribulation, Deliverance, Bodily Resurrection, Eternal Judgment

Daniel, now at the end of his account, gives a prediction of the end of days as delivered from the Lord. His prediction is not a maybe, but a certainty.

God reveals to Daniel a glimpse of hope. He has shown Daniel many of the horrors that will come in this world, but in Daniel 12, he speaks of the Savior to come—Jesus Christ. God is in complete control, and even though so much seems as though it is spinning out of control, he reminds Daniel that all is within his sovereign hand.

We are not very good at predicting the future, yet we are prone to attempting just that. We look at our world and make assertions of how things will be even though we are fully aware of the complete mess of a track record we have. However, God can predict the future because he controls it. And in his just love, he has revealed to us many things that do affect our lives. He has also kept from us many things that would only serve to distract and confuse us. So much of the world seems as though it is spinning out of control, yet the Lord is on his throne, and Jesus Christ, the man who stands above the churning waters in white linen, is at his right hand. There is no suffering without purpose for his people. We can trust that all things that happen end up for his glory and the protection of his people.

David Prince, "Where Is My Life Headed?," Preached 8/4/2013, Prince on Preaching Website, Accessed 4 December 2015, Available from http://www.davidprince.com/2013/08/04/where-is-my-life-headed-daniel-125-13/.

Connection with Newer Testament
Matthew 24:3-31, 25:31-46

For the Kids
Ask your children if they know what they will be doing tomorrow, or a year from now, or five years from now. We don't know the future, but Daniel reminds us that God knows the future because he controls it. We can trust God, even when bad things happen, because we know God is in control. In his control, he works all things together for good to those who love him and are called according to his purposes in Jesus.

Prayer Prompts
1. Pray that the Lord comes back soon. Pray for the ending of so many social

perversions and the systematic murder of babies. Even so, trust that he is in control.

2. Praise the Lord for his earnest protection of us. Praise him for keeping from us what could have destroyed us and for allowing us to suffer in such a way that expands his kingdom.

◆

WEEK 32: DAY 4
Joel 2

Key Text
"'Yet even now,' the LORD says, 'return to me with all your heart—with fasting, weeping, and mourning. Tear your hearts, not just your garments!' Return to the LORD your God, for he is merciful and compassionate, slow to anger and boundless in loyal love—often relenting from calamitous punishment." Joel 2:12-13

The Pouring Out of the Spirit and the Day of the Lord
Joel 2 describes the horrific scene of an army of locusts scouring the land and destroying everything in its path. The dreadful locust attack foreshadows the dreadful day of the LORD, a day on which he will advance his armies over the land in judgment for sin. Just as the locusts leave nothing untouched in their wake, all will be held accountable for their actions on the day of the LORD.

Joel 2 serves as a warning. An unavoidable calamity awaits all who do not heed the call. The only salvation from the dreadful day that approaches is a salvation from the Lord himself. Thus, Joel offers the gracious provision of the Lord saying, "'Yet even now,' the LORD says, 'return to me with all your heart—with fasting, weeping, and mourning. Tear your hearts, not just your garments!' Return to the LORD your God, for he is merciful and compassionate, slow to anger and boundless in loyal love—often relenting from calamitous punishment" (vv. 12-13).

Our only hope in light of the coming destruction is from the Commander of the armies. When we return to him with repentance, through

258

faith in his provision of Christ, we have the glorious position of witnessing the Lord of hosts relent from judgment. This relenting is made possible because Jesus bore the judgment of God in our place. And for all who are found in Christ, the day of the Lord is a day of victory, not of defeat. On that day, those who, by faith in Christ, have returned to God will have indwelling them the promised seal of the Spirit (Eph. 1:13-14)—the same Spirit who was poured out on the believers at Pentecost in Acts 2 when Peter preached the fulfillment of Joel 2.

Nate BeVier

Connection with Newer Testament
Acts 2:17-21

For the Kids
Have your children walk around the room in a circle. Then tell them to change direction and walk the other way. Do this several times. Explain that when we sin, the Bible says we are to "repent," which means to change course or to go a different way. For example, if you repent of disobeying Mom or Dad, then the next time they ask you to do something, you will obey right away. Teach your children about repentance and its role in the salvation that Christ offers.

Prayer Prompts
1. Praise the Lord for his unwavering character. Without his active goodness, he would have no reason to spare us from an eternal separation from him.
2. Pray that God would enable you to always be a person of heartfelt repentance instead of a person who merely shows an external display of repentance.

◆

WEEK 32: DAY 5
Joel 3

Key Text
"'But Judah will reside securely forever, and Jerusalem will be secure from one

259

generation to the next.'" Joel 3:20

The Glorious Future of the People of God: Holiness, Abundance, and Life

The people of God will forever dwell in peace, but that peace is gained through the victorious warfare of the Lord. In Joel 3, we hear a call for battle: "Prepare for a holy war! Call out the warriors! ... Beat your plowshares into swords ... Lend your aid and come" (vv. 9-11). The scene is of a gathering of the enemies of God's people versus the Lord and his warriors. It is the day of the Lord, and there are multitudes in the battle valley. It is the darkest of days for the enemies of the Lord, the day they meet their doom. But for the people of God, it is the day when their enemies are once and for all defeated, the day in which the peace of the kingdom is fully established. The mix of terror for some and joy for others is clearly seen in verse sixteen: "The Lord roars from Zion ... The heavens and the earth shake. But the Lord is a refuge to his people..."

Joel's prophecy ultimately points ahead to the role of Christ that we read about in Revelation 19, when the great battle takes place. It is a reminder for us that, for some, Jesus is most terrifying and dangerous. He himself will be the faithful one who—in righteousness—will make war against his enemies and the enemies of his people. But for his people, there will be terror-less joy. He makes war for—not against—his own! For them, he is the eternally victorious hero that accomplishes peace and makes all things new.

Todd Martin

Connection with Newer Testament
John 2:1-12; Revelation 19:11-21, 22:1-5

For the Kids
Put a coin in your fist, and then have your children try to pry the coin from your fingers. When your children attempt and fail, tell them that this is a picture of what security is. The coin is secure in your hand from your children because they can't take it from you. Tell your children that God promises future security

to his people. The people of Israel would live with abundance and life, in holiness, free from destructive enemies. God would rule over them for their good. Instruct your children that the promises of Joel 3 come to final fulfillment when Jesus returns (Rev. 19). Thank the Lord for the glorious future he gives to his people in Christ.

Prayer Prompts

1. Praise God that your future is filled with eternal, holy life rather than the death you rightfully deserve.

2. Pray that many from the nations would repent of sin and find life in Jesus.

◆

WEEK 33: DAY 1
Psalm 89

Key Text

"I will sing continually about the LORD's faithful deeds; to future generations I will proclaim your faithfulness. For I say, 'Loyal love is permanently established; in the skies you set up your faithfulness.' The LORD said, 'I have made a covenant with my chosen one; I have made a promise on oath to David, my servant: "I will give you an eternal dynasty and establish your throne throughout future generations."' Selah." Psalm 89:1-4

In the Midst of Exile, Hope in the Blessed Davidic King

Have you ever heard that hindsight is 20/20? When we are in the midst of a trial or difficult circumstance, we struggle for perspective. We often have a hard time seeing what God is doing in the moment. Sometimes, when our circumstances are particularly challenging, we may even wonder if God is still there. But as time goes on, the picture becomes clearer. We begin to see how that particular puzzle piece fits in the big picture. We gain perspective, and we see that God was working the whole time.

Psalm 89 is the cry of God's people looking for perspective. The psalmist knows of God's power (v. 8), and he knows of God's everlasting love toward his people (v. 1). What he's having trouble with is the question of God's promise to David to establish his offspring forever on the throne of Israel (vv. 4, 29, 36). It doesn't appear that God's promise is coming to fruition (vv. 38-51). In fact, it seems like God's steadfast love has ended as his people live under a foreign ruler with no king occupying David's throne. The psalmist is searching for answers.

You've likely been there. The question "why?" is not one that God usually answers in the moment. God has a way of using time to make things clear for his people who are seeking him. He did that in this case, too: "But when the fullness of time came, God sent forth his Son…" (Gal. 4:4*). The psalmist had no idea what God was doing. The promise to David would be upheld. David's offspring is reigning now. The covenant made with David is fulfilled in Christ. "Blessed be the LORD forever! Amen and Amen." (v. 52*).

Casey McCall

Connection with Newer Testament
Luke 1:30-34

For the Kids
Have your children cover one eye and look around the room without moving their head. Ask them what they can see. Then have them look around the room with both eyes without moving their head. Ask them again what they can see. Tell your children that, in Psalm 89, Israel was in exile, and they were struggling to view the world with two eyes through the lens of the gospel. Their difficult circumstances were certainly tempting them to focus on the present difficulties to the exclusion of all of God's great promises to them. They had to fight to see with two eyes of faith, seeing both their present circumstances and the future hope they had in a Davidic king. Help your

Prayer Prompts
1. The context of Psalm 89 is exile. There is no Davidic king. What has happened to the promises made to David? The psalmist remembers God's past faithfulness and greatness in the midst of exile, causing him to hope in God even when the present seems bleak. Remember God's faithfulness to you. Ask

God to help you trust him and remember his past faithfulness, even when the future appears uncertain.

2. Praise the Lord that he is faithful to his covenant with David. He did provide the Messiah who is seated on the throne. Exile has ended; hope has come through the deliverance of God's people.

◆

WEEK 33: DAY 2
Psalm 102

Key Text
"Nations will fear the name of the LORD and all the kings of the earth your glory." Psalm 102:15*

Psalms of Exile: Future Salvation Among the Nations

The other morning, I woke up cranky. I really cannot explain it. I was fine the day before. I was fine shortly thereafter. However, for a few hours on a Saturday morning, I had to fight negative emotions, and I had to harness frustrated tones with my wife and children. You see, I am a sinful person, and my sin does not always make rational sense. My sin does not usually ask for my permission before rearing its ugly head.

When I have days like that, psalms like this one help me see clearly. The psalmist is in trouble. His situation is emotional (v. 4), physical (v. 5), social (v. 8), and spiritual (v. 10). His pain seems to cover all the major categories. But he's fighting to keep his eyes focused on truth. He's fighting to see that God still rules "forever" (v. 12) and that God still regards "the prayer of the destitute" (v. 17). Ultimately, the psalmist lands on a truth about God that reminds me of how much God is not like us: "But you remain; your years do not come to an end" (v. 27). God doesn't wake up cranky. He's steady, and he never changes. He's the one true constant that you can always depend upon.

I can imagine Jesus praying this psalm from the cross. Abandoned by all of his friends and suffering intense agony, he fought to remember his Father's presence. He fought to remind himself of God's steadfast love. He bled and died, comforted by the full assurance that God would never jeopardize his own character. The children of God's servants would dwell secure; their offspring would be established (v. 28).

Casey McCall

Connection with Newer Testament
Matthew 28:18-20; Revelation 5

For the Kids
Have your children think about things that are constant, things that never change. One plus one always equals two. The sun is yellow. The sky is blue. The list could go on. Teach your children about how God is consistent. Teach them about how God's consistency works with his faithfulness to bring salvation to the nations in Jesus.

Prayer Prompts
1. Praise God that his salvation from exile extends to the ends of the earth.
2. Pray for people in unreached places, like Peru and North Africa and East Asia, to hear the gospel and praise the Lord.

◆

WEEK 33: DAY 3
Psalm 103

Key Text
"Bless the LORD, O my soul; and all that is within me, bless his holy name!" Psalm 103:1*

Talking to Yourself: Remembering the Lord's Grace to the Praise of His Name
David writes a psalm of command and praise here in Psalm 103. He begins by giving the command to bless the Lord. This is more than a song of praise; it is an urging from the soul to compel the reader toward giving the Lord all that he is due. Perhaps the strongest portion of this Psalm is the command

to bless the Lord, not forgetting all his benefits and his sufficiency. David sees all characteristics of God as demanding of his full affections. Psalm 103:1 says, "Bless the Lord, O my Soul." And in Psalm 103:22, David writes, "Bless the Lord, O my soul!" This repeating of the same phrase is called an inclusio, meaning everything that comes between the two phrases is of one thought. And that thought is that David is talking to himself.

The words in our minds and the words off our lips are perfect pictures of what lies in our hearts. We listen to ourselves more often and more completely than we listen to anyone else. So, when David talks to himself with the praising of the Lord, he hears himself praise the Lord. In much the same way, we must talk to ourselves about the gospel and praise the Lord with our lips, even to ourselves. This is not something for certain times and occasions. Instead, we follow what Paul tells us by taking every thought captive. All occasions completely warrant the praise of God.

David Prince, "Why You Should Talk to Yourself," Preached 3/5/2012, Prince on Preaching Website, Accessed 4 December 2015, Available from http://www.davidprince.com/2012/03/05/why-you-should-talk-to-yourself-psalm-103/.

Connection with Newer Testament
Ephesians 1; Hebrews 13:15; Revelation 19:5

For the Kids
Why is it important that we memorize Scripture? Once God's word is in our hearts, the Holy Spirit will call it to mind, and we can remind ourselves of God's truths over and over again. It will encourage us and will help us glorify God as we intentionally remember his grace. As a family, memorize Psalm 103:1.

Prayer Prompts
1. Pray that we speak the gospel to ourselves constantly.
2. Praise God that he is good, the gospel is true, and Jesus is at work in us and around us.

WEEK 33: DAY 4
Ezra 1

Key Text

"In the first year of King Cyrus of Persia, in order to fulfill the LORD's message spoken through Jeremiah, the LORD stirred the mind of King Cyrus of Persia. He disseminated a proclamation throughout his entire kingdom, announcing in a written edict the following" Ezra 1:1

A Return to the Land: Rebuilding the Temple

Imagine the astonishment! The people of Israel had been living in exile under foreign rulers for decades. They had no reason to assume that they would be permitted to return to the land that God had given them. After all, they had earned their removal from the land by being unfaithful to the covenant God made with them at Sinai. They deserved to be in exile.

But God had made promises. Particularly, God had made a promise through the prophet Jeremiah that his judgment would come upon the Babylonians (Jer. 51:11) and that the exiles would return to the land (Jer. 29:10). God had not given up on his people. So, always true to his word, God "stirred the mind of King Cyrus of Persia" (v. 1) to send Israel back to the land to rebuild the temple of the LORD.

One of the biggest enemies to faith today is the prevalence of cynicism. We train our hearts to expect the worst possible outcome and to never give people the benefit of the doubt. However, where cynicism prevails, faith is lacking. Who would have predicted that Cyrus would make such a decree? As Christians who believe in the resurrection, we should live with hopeful anticipation that God is at work all around us and that anything is possible. When times look bleak and cynicism seems to coexist with the air we breathe, we must be the ones reminding the world that our God moves the hearts of kings.

Casey McCall

Connection with Newer Testament
Matthew 19:23-30; John 2:12-24

For the Kids
Have your children imagine how they would feel if your house caught on fire and burned down. (This might be a good time to practice your family fire drill!) Now ask them how the Israelites must have felt when their temple and homes were destroyed and they were taken as prisoners. Imagine their thrill when God kept his promises to bring them back and rebuild! Thank the LORD for his grace to bring them back. Praise the LORD that, in Christ, he is preparing an eternal home for us where sin and destruction never exists, where all things are made new.

Prayer Prompts
1. Praise the Lord that he keeps his word. We can hope in his promises of future salvation because he is faithful.
2. Repent of any cynical attitudes that question God's sovereignty and God's faithfulness to his world, attitudes of unbelief.

◆

WEEK 33: DAY 5
Haggai 1-2

Key Text
"'On that day,' says the LORD who rules over all, 'I will take you, Zerubbabel son of Shealtiel, my servant,' says the LORD, 'and I will make you like a signet ring, for I have chosen you,' says the LORD who rules over all." Haggai 2:23

Exile Continues: In the Land Under a Descendant of David
Fallen human beings are extremely self-centered. We all struggle with inner battles to protect ourselves and to preserve what we self-identify as our best interests. Whether it be lying to one's parents in an attempt to protect one's innocence when accused of wrongdoing or throwing a coworker under the bus to make yourself look better before the boss, we all have an inward

bent to protect and to preserve ourselves, often to the neglect and harm of others.

In Haggai 1-2, some of the Israelite exiles have returned to Jerusalem from Babylon for the purpose of rebuilding the temple; however, these Israelites soon gave up on their temple construction task. Rather than finish the house of the LORD in order to show their utter dependence upon God, the Israelites became self-focused and spent their time building their own houses. Rather than show a repentance from the sinful selfishness that resulted in idolatry and exile, these Israelites proved that, though they were physically back in the land, their hearts were still in exile to sin. Their hearts were not permanently turned back toward God just yet.

But God was gracious to his people. The LORD spoke to his sinful people through the prophet Haggai and raised up a faithful servant in the line of David named Zerubbabel who would lead the people into obedience. Ultimately, Zerubbabel and the promises made to him would find their fulfillment in another descendant of David named Jesus who would rule over God's people, causing them to live selflessly in obedience to the LORD. In Christ, our self-seeking, inward-focused souls are freed to live in perpetual obedience to God as Christ constructs us to be his glorious temple (1 Cor. 3:16).

Jon Canler

Connection with Newer Testament
Matthew 1:1-17; Titus 3:3-8

For the Kids
Ask your children to define selfishness. It's the idea that one is devoted to caring only for one's self, even at the expense of others. Ask your children to think of a time they've been selfish, or (parent) share with them a time you've been selfish. Then explain to your children that Israel's selfishness is on full display in the book of Haggai. God had graciously allowed some of the Israelites to return to the promised land to rebuild the temple, but instead of focusing on God and his glory, the people focused on themselves by building

their own homes. The same selfishness that sent them into exile in the first place was still present in their hearts. Praise God for Jesus, the one who gives his people new hearts and who crucifies selfish tendencies.

Prayer Prompts

1. Praise God for his commitment to his word. He kept his covenant promise to David through exile, fulfilling it in Jesus. His faithfulness in the past gives us confidence to trust in his promises for the future.

2. The promise of God's deliverance never justifies unholy living. Sin should not increase so that grace may abound. Repent of any disobedience present in your life and ask God for grace to live faithfully to King Jesus.

◆

WEEK 34: DAY 1

Esther 3-8

Key Text

"'Don't imagine that because you are part of the king's household you will be the one Jew who will escape. If you keep quiet at this time, liberation and protection for the Jews will appear from another source, while you and your father's household perish. It may very well be that you have achieved royal status for such a time as this!'" Esther 4:14

Esther: An Unexpected Deliverer in the Midst of Exile

Figures like Moses, Joseph, and Esther gloriously display God's providential control over all circumstances. Even when it seems like all hope is lost, God is still working. In fact, the absence of the mention of God in the book of Esther powerfully communicates this very truth. God does not have to be acknowledged to be in control. In each case God places an unlikely hero behind enemy lines only to later provide salvation for God's people.

The story of Jesus Christ is the story of an unlikely hero who was born into this world in order to cross enemy lines and save his people from their enemy. No one would have looked at Esther as the obvious choice, and no one saw Jesus as the Messianic King. In his hometown of Nazareth, the people asked, "Is not this the carpenter's son? Is not his mother Mary? Are not his brothers James and Joseph and Simon and Judas?" (Matt. 13:55, ESV).

Esther's willingness to be used by God "for such a time as this" (4:14) to save the Jewish people from annihilation points to *the Hero* who was sent forth by God to rescue sinners "when the fullness of time had come (Gal. 4:4, ESV). It is also clear that Esther needs the grace, forgiveness, and saving mercy of God in Christ.

When times look hopeless, I must remember that God is still in control. The fate of the Jewish people in the book of Esther looked doomed, but God was at work the whole time. The crucifixion of Christ certainly looked like the defeat of his claims of being the promised King, but it was really the victory. Likewise, there will be times in my life when I am tempted toward hopeless despair. I must remember the victory that Christ has won. I must remember the promises he has made. I must look to him with hope that he will do all that he has said he will do and bring me safely into his eternal kingdom.

As I think about my own circumstances, I must remember that no circumstance is to be thought of without reference to God. Even in times when his name is not mentioned, he is providentially working all things for my good in Christ (Rom. 8:28-29). The cross and resurrection of Christ guarantees my ultimate victory. To hopelessly despair is to pretend as if Christ has not acted on my behalf. The story has been written and *the hero* has won the day. I now get to live my life—come what may—with full confidence that nothing "will separate us from the love of Christ" (Rom. 8:35).

Casey McCall, "Reading and Applying the Bible with Jesus as the Hero—Queen Esther (Esther 2:1-18)," in *Church with Jesus as the Hero*, ed. David. E. Prince (n.p.: Ashland Publishing, 2015), 44-47.

Connection with Newer Testament
Matthew 13:53-58

For the Kids
Have your children think about their car breaking down in the middle of nowhere. Imagine it's cold and snowy. Imagine you are so far away from

civilization that your cell phone doesn't work. Then imagine that, of all people, one of the children in the car was miraculously able to fix the problem. It sounds crazy. A kid would be the last person expected to save the family from disaster. Yet, Esther reminds us that God often uses unexpected people to accomplish his purposes. He uses his wisdom to shame the wise. His saving wisdom, foolish as it appears to the world, is seen mostly clearly in a bloody cross with Jesus crucified for our sins.

Prayer Prompts

1. Ask the Lord to seal Romans 8:28-29 on your heart and mind so that during difficult times, times when it looks like God isn't present, you have hope grounded in the reality that God is on his throne working all things for your good in Christ.

2. We all have the tendency to fight God for control when we are convinced in our minds that God either doesn't appear to be in control or doesn't appear to be using his control in ways that are pleasing to us. Esther reminds us that God is sovereign. Always! Repent of failing to trust him. Repent of fighting him. Repent of trying to be lord of your life.

◆

WEEK 34: DAY 2
Zechariah 3

Key Text

"'Hear now, O Joshua the high priest, you and your friends who are sitting before you, for they are men who are a sign: for behold, I will bring my servant the Branch.'" Zechariah 3:8*

The Coming Branch of the Lord: The One Who Removes Iniquity

The scene in Zechariah 3 takes place in a celestial courtroom. On one side stood the angel of the LORD, on the other stood Satan—the accuser of the brethren, and in the center stood Joshua the high priest. Joshua represents God's chosen people, and he was to be a mediator and a picture of holiness and righteousness among them. The problem, which Satan was quick to point out, was that Joshua stood before a holy God in filthy, sin-stained garments. The very one who was to be the mediator between God and the people could not do so because he himself was tainted with sin.

It seemed like a closed case. The verdict in all likelihood should have been pronounced in favor of the prosecution. But the angel of the Lord, the defender of the brethren, does something remarkable. With all the authority of heaven, he orders Joshua to be clothed in pure vestments. In light of the new evidence, the prosecution was left defenseless, and Satan stood silent for the remainder of the scene.

The angel of the LORD was not finished, however. He proceeded to make a promise that changes everything for all who "live and work according to my requirements" (v. 7). From the greatest high priest to the lowliest slave, he promises to send a Branch. And this Branch would "remove the iniquity of this land in a single day" (v. 9). The Branch has a name. His name is Jesus. And on a single day, he bore the wrath for sins by dying on the cross, thus removing the iniquity of all who would believe in him.

Nate BeVier

Connection with Newer Testament
Revelation 12:7-11

For the Kids
Tell your children how bad sin is. The Bible even says that our very best actions are like dirty clothes (Is. 64:6). Like Joshua, there is nothing we can do to make our clothes clean—it is as if we have muddy hands and we just make our clothes even dirtier! But what Jesus does for us is like trading his perfectly white, clean clothes to us in exchange for our dirty, soiled clothes to remove our sin before God. Praise the LORD.

Prayer Prompts
1. Praise the Lord for the removal of your guilt and iniquity by his grace.

2. Pray that the Holy Spirit would empower you to walk in the righteous ways of the Lord.

◆

WEEK 34: DAY 3

Zechariah 6

Key Text

"'Then say to him, "The LORD who rules over all says, 'Look—here is the man whose name is Branch, who will sprout up from his place and build the temple of the LORD.""'" Zechariah 6:12

The Coming Branch of the Lord: A Priest-King

In Zechariah 6, the Lord unfolds more information about the "Branch" who would "remove the iniquity of this land in a single day" promised in Zechariah 3:8-9. The one whose name is the Branch would be at once both king and priest. Zechariah instructs those from the house of Josiah to fashion a royal crown of gold and silver, which would serve as a reminder of the coming Branch who would be seated as king while also serving as priest to mediate peace between God and man. This Priest-King would build the temple of the LORD, and "those who are far away will come and build the temple of the LORD" (v. 15).

Jesus Christ is the Branch and the Cornerstone of the temple which is still today being built up by those who at one time were far off but who are now by the mercies of God being brought near. The words of Zechariah 6 foreshadow the fulfillment of Christ in Matthew 16:18 when Jesus states, "And I tell you that you are Peter, and on this rock I will build my church, and the gates of Hades shall not overpower it."

The Branch is at work still today branching out, using his people to build his "spiritual house" (1 Pet. 2:5). "But you are a chosen race, a royal priesthood, a holy nation, a people of his own, so that you may proclaim the virtues of the one who called you out of darkness into his marvelous light. You once were not a people, but now you are God's people. You were shown no mercy, but now you have received mercy" (1 Pet. 2:9-10).

Connection with Newer Testament

1 Peter 2:4-10

For the Kids

Have your children draw four people, cut them out, and label them: a king, a priest, a prophet, and a servant. Explain that a king is someone who is in charge of a group of people, a priest is someone who offers sacrifices to pay for the sins of the people, a prophet is someone who relays God's words to the people, and a servant is someone who serves (works for) someone else. Now, layer the four drawings and tape them together, explaining that King Jesus combines all of these roles!

Prayer Prompts

1. Pray for the Lord to reveal areas of your life that need to be brought fully into submission to the Priest-King—Jesus Christ—and for faith to obey his voice.

2. Pray for the continuing advance of God's worldwide work as he calls the nations to bow their knee in faith to the Priest-King.

◆

WEEK 34: DAY 4

Zechariah 9

Key Text

"Rejoice greatly, O daughter of Zion! Shout, O daughter of Jerusalem! Behold, your king is coming to you; righteous and having salvation is he, humble and riding on a donkey, even on a colt, the foal of a donkey." Zechariah 9:9*

The Anticipated King: Humble and Mounted on a Donkey

Zechariah 9 describes the conquest of the Messianic King. In verses 1-8, with an oracle, Zechariah charts the war path of the coming Priest-King who will sweep down from the north (from whence many of Israel's enemies came) to render the enemies of his people powerless and afraid. This King will "remove the chariot from Ephraim and the warhorse from Jerusalem, and the battle bow will be removed" (v. 10). His rule will be world-wide, and no enemy will be able to withstand his power.

The text paints a most-impressive picture of the coming Messiah. The reader is left wondering, "If this King can cut off chariots and war horses, on what mighty steed must he ride?" Verse 9 gives a most surprising answer: he comes "humble and riding on a donkey, even on a colt, the foal of a donkey." Matthew 21:1-11 tells of Jesus' fulfillment of this peculiar prophecy. While a donkey is an unlikely form of transportation for the King, the salvation and peace he promises will not be negated.

The remainder of Zechariah 9 (vv. 14-17) demonstrates the humble King displaying his true glory when he comes with vengeance and judgment. "On that day the LORD their God will deliver them" (v. 16). Revelation 19:11 tells us that, on that day, the one who is called Faithful and True will be atop a white horse treading the winepress of the fury of the wrath of God the Almighty while wielding a sword from his lips with which he will judge the nations to reign forever and ever. Until that day, the people of God will, with renewed wonder, still cry, "Hosanna in the highest! Blessed is he who comes in the name of the Lord!"

Nate BeVier

Connection with Newer Testament
Matthew 21:1-11

For the Kids
Have your children think about the donkeys and horses. Have them list the strengths and weaknesses of each. Ask them which animal would be bigger and better for a king who leads an army into war. A horse. Then ask your children how the long-awaited Messianic King should come to Israel. Once they respond, then tell them this Messianic King was coming on a donkey. Talk about the significance of coming on a donkey. Talk about how Jesus first came riding on a donkey in humility to save his people from their sins. He came to

bring peace with God to men rather than to slaughter his enemies. He came to serve, not to be served. Then tell your children about the future. Tell them that Jesus is coming back one day on a war horse to slaughter his enemies. The humble King will return as the King of kings for the world to see.

Prayer Prompts

1. Rejoice because God has come through our victorious King Jesus—the one who has saved us from our sins and who has freed us from sin's waterless pit.

2. Pray for the Lord's return, that the fullness of our salvation might be revealed for all eternity as sinners glorified in the presence of our God.

◆

WEEK 34: DAY 5
Zechariah 12-13

Key Text

"'I will pour out on the kingship of David and the population of Jerusalem a spirit of grace and supplication so that they will look to me, the one they have pierced. They will lament for him as one laments for an only son, and there will be a bitter cry for him like the bitter cry for a firstborn.'" Zechariah 12:10

Salvation from Sin Through the Pierced Shepherd

Zechariah 12-13 begins the gradual crescendo to the climatic conclusion of Zechariah 14 when the Priest-King reigns fully and finally for all time. Zechariah 12-13 reads much like an intensifying storm which begins with a soft sprinkle of rain drops and ends in Zechariah 14 with a deluge. The strength of the storm increases with the repeated phrase "on that day," and, with each repetition, the reader gains greater and greater anticipation for the culmination of the kingdom.

In the center or eye of the storm, we find our only hope "on that day." Our only hope is Jesus Christ, the one on whom they gaze, the one whom they have pierced (12:10). He is the struck shepherd (13:7) and the one from whom "a fountain opened up for the dynasty of David and the people of Jerusalem to cleanse them from sin and impurity" (13:1). He was smitten by God, wounded for our transgressions, crushed for our iniquities (Is. 53:4-5). On the cross, a Roman soldier took a spear and pierced his side, and, at once, there flowed forth blood and water (John 19:34; 37). He bled so that "on that day" we will stand alive and forgiven. Yes, we grow in anticipation for the coming King, but only in view of his mercies on the cross.

Nate BeVier

Connection with Newer Testament
John 19

For the Kids
Ask your children if they have seen God with their eyes? Ask them if they've touched God? Remind them that neither had the people of Israel up to this point in their history. Then tell your children that Zechariah 12:10 declares that God himself will be pierced. God will be struck, and a fountain shall be opened to cleanse his people from their sins. Talk to your children about how this seeming contradiction is possible and true in Jesus. Praise the LORD that Jesus was pierced to save his people from their sins. Pray for your children to trust Jesus.

Prayer Prompts
1. Praise the Lord Jesus Christ for being pierced on your behalf in order to cleanse you from your sin.
2. Pray to live, by God's grace, a holy and pure life as a cleansed Christ-follower, today and every day.

◆

WEEK 35: DAY 1
Zechariah 14

Key Text
"And the LORD will be king over all the earth. In that day the LORD will be one and his name one." Zechariah 14:9*

The Coming Day of the Lord: Judgment on the Nations and Lasting Security for God's People

What if you knew the future? What if you knew exactly what was going to happen at any given moment in your day and you also knew that the ending would turn out favorable? Would that not give you confidence? If you were able to plan and to anticipate your circumstances knowing that the outcome was secure, it would change everything. You would live boldly and confidently.

God never spells out the exact details for us like that. He wants his people to live by faith. He wants us to trust him. However, there are times in his holy word when he gives us glimpses into the future. Here's the good news: the future always turns out favorably for God's people.

Zechariah concludes his prophecy with this vision of God's blessings upon his people, curses upon his people's enemies, and a multi-national worship gathering. We may not know everything, but we at least know how it's going to end. The cross and resurrection of Jesus guarantee the trustworthiness of these wonderful promises.

How will you live in light of God's promised future? That's the question, isn't it? May the church arise and live boldly and confidently in the face of whatever may come our way!

Casey McCall

Connection with Newer Testament
Revelation 19:11-22:5

For the Kids
Ask your child to think of his or her favorite story. Is there good and evil in the story? A happy or sad ending? Explain that the Bible is telling us the story of all stories about the realities of this world. We may not know every detail about the way the story plays out in the future, but we know that God crowns his Son, Jesus, as King over all. And we know that Jesus rescues his people from their sin and defeats his enemies. Pray together that, by God's grace, your children will repent of their sin and worship Jesus as rightful King over all the earth.

Prayer Prompts

1. Biblical hope always rests in God fighting for his people because their enemies are too great. Praise God that Christ has come and has begun defeating our enemies. Look to the future with anticipation, knowing that Christ will one day destroy Satan and end sin forever.

2. Perhaps you fear what the future holds. Ask the Lord to cause the certainty of his glorious return and the glorious salvation you have received to give you confidence in his goodness for you, both in the future and today.

◆

WEEK 35: DAY 2

Ezra 7

Key Text

"For Ezra had set his heart to study the Law of the LORD, and to do it, and to teach the statutes and judgments in Israel." Ezra 7:10*

Ezra the Priest: More Exiles Released to Serve in the Temple

God's grace was upon Ezra's life and ministry (vv. 6, 9). Ezra was in the priestly line (vv. 1-5), he had exceptional knowledge of the law of God (vv. 6-9), and he was a teacher who "had set his heart to study the Law of the Lord, and to do it and to teach his statutes and rules in Israel" (v. 10). His mission among the post-exilic community was to lead a second major return to Jerusalem and implement the law of God among the believing remnant.

King Artaxerxes recognized Ezra's qualifications (v. 11) and issued a decree supporting him. Those who believed in many gods or regional gods often wanted people to appease their god[s] so that the god[s] would not become angry: "Whatever is commanded by the God of heaven, let it be done in full for the house of the God of heaven, lest there be wrath against the kingdom of the king and his sons" (v. 23*). Of course, in the believing covenant community, the king's actions were evidence of the providence of God pouring out his blessings. Ezra was honored by the Persian leader for the good of Judea and said, "Blessed be the Lord, the God of our fathers, who put such a thing as this into the heart of the king, to beautify the house of the Lord that is in Jerusalem" (v. 27*).

Ezra 7:10 provides an excellent pattern for all believers to embrace as their life mission no matter their particular role or circumstance.

"For Ezra had set his heart to study the Law of the Lord"

> The "heart" refers to a person's controlling center, the core of their being, and their driving passion. Ezra desired to be controlled by the word of God, and the same should be true for us. If it is, the law of the Lord drives us to the Bible's center—Jesus Christ. Paul explains, "Wherefore the law was our schoolmaster *to bring us* unto Christ, that we might be justified by faith" (KJV Gal. 3:24).

"to do it"

> Ezra's goal was not to win games of Torah trivia but to live out the truth of God. We must not be abstract Bible theologians. James exhorts, "Be doers of the word, and not hearers only, deceiving yourselves" (Jas. 1:22).

"to teach the statutes and rules in Israel"

> Finally, we must not come to the Scripture simply focused on ourselves, but rather we must first be focused on Christ, next focused on the believing community, and then focused on how we can apply ourselves to the biblical testimony for the glory of Christ and the good of his church. Paul said, "Be imitators of me, as I am of Christ" (1 Cor. 11:1). We must do the same, not simply seeking our own good but seeking the good of our neighbor (1 Cor. 10:24).

David Prince

Connection with Newer Testament

James 1:19-27

For the Kids

Have your child go to the mirror and examine themselves, walk away, and then draw a picture of what they saw. Explain how silly it would be for them to forget what they saw in the mirror about themselves (thinking they had three eyes or three ears, for example). The Bible too says if we hear God's word but do not act out what we've heard, it's as silly as not remembering what we have seen in our reflection. Pray for grace to be like Ezra, doers of the Bible, not just hearers.

Prayer Prompts

1. Ask the Lord to make your Bible study fruitful so that your head knowledge of the Bible might grip your heart and move you to obedience.
2. Pray that both our pastors and our church would be devoted to studying, doing, and preaching the word to one another, the community, and the world.

◆

WEEK 35: DAY 3
Ezra 9

Key Text
"Now when these things had been completed, the leaders approached me and said, 'The people of Israel, the priests, and the Levites have not separated themselves from the local resides who practice detestable things'" Ezra 9:1a

Intermarriage and Failure to Keep the Mosaic Covenant

"The human mind is more deceitful than anything else. It is incurably bad. Who can understand it?" asks Jeremiah the prophet (Jer. 17:9). The depth of the wickedness of the human heart and mind has ever confounded even the wisest of our human race. Why do we do the things that we do? That's the question Ezra is pondering in our passage today.

The people of Israel had gotten themselves into exile by their unfaithfulness to God. Yet, God continued to bless them, moving in the heart of the king of Persia to send the exiles back into the land to begin rebuilding the temple. "Everything that has happened to us has come about because of our wicked actions and our great guilt," and Ezra asks, "Shall we once again break your commandments?" (v. 13). The answer is yes. Human beings are that bad. Even in the face of immeasurable mercies, we commit cosmic treason against the Creator of the universe again and again.

Jeremiah lamented this human tendency, just as Ezra does here. However, Jeremiah also saw that God would not allow us stay in this woeful condition forever: "'Indeed, a time is coming,' says the LORD, 'when I will make a new covenant with the people of Israel and Judah…I will put my law within them and write it on their hearts and minds. I will be their God and they will be my people" (Jer. 31:31-33). The only solution to hearts as wicked as ours is the new covenant in Jesus' blood (Luke 22:20). Ezra was longing for what we get to enjoy in Christ. He was longing for new hearts for God's people.

Casey McCall

Connection with Newer Testament
2 Corinthians 6:14; 1 Corinthians 7

For the Kids
Have your children think about some of the rules that govern your house. Ask them if they've ever broken a rule, been disciplined for breaking the rule, and, yet, break the rule after being disciplined. Tell your children that this is exactly like the Israelites in Ezra 9. Remind your children that the people of Israel had committed all kinds of sin that led them into exile, but, once back in the land after the punishment of exile, they committed the same sins that led to exile in the first place (like marrying people they weren't supposed to marry). Instruct your children that no amount of physical discipline ever changes a sinful heart. New hearts must be given for people to obey God. Teach them about the new hearts available in the new covenant in Jesus blood.

Prayer Prompts
1. Ask the Lord to open your eyes to the horror of Israel's sin. Then ask the Lord to cause you to feel the same horror when you are tempted by things that would draw you away from the Lord.
2. The Israelites came back to the land and started sinning because they didn't have new hearts. In Christ, we have been given new hearts. The new exodus

that began in Ezra's day is finding fulfillment in Jesus such that now we are able to obey the Lord through the power of the Spirit. Praise God!

◆

WEEK 35: DAY 4
Nehemiah 9-10

Key Text
"'You are righteous with regard to all that has happened to us, for you have acted faithfully. It is we who have been in the wrong!'" Nehemiah 9:33

Confession & Covenant: Returned Exiles Renew their Promise
Following the public reading of the Scripture (Neh. 8), the exiles fasted while dressed in the clothing of contrition (Neh. 9). They read the book of the law (9:1-3), then the Levites led a prayer of confession (9:4-5). The psalm of confession describes the faithful works of God as he protected and guided the nation's forefathers. The purpose was to instruct and remind the people of the Lord's providence. Israel's story is a story of the Lord's relentless covenantal faithfulness.

The Lord is Creator (9:6)

The Lord chose Abraham (9:7-8).

The Lord delivered his people in the Exodus (9:9-14).

The Lord cared for and provided for his people in the wilderness wandering (9:15-21).

The Lord dealt with his people's continuing rebellion but showed mercy (9:22-32).

The Lord remained faithful in Israel's unfaithfulness (9:33-37).

The confession also emphasizes the faithlessness of the nation. Though the Israelites regularly rebelled against the Lord, God showed gracious compassion for his chosen people. Despite the Lord's patience (9:30), the time came for him to discipline his people by taking away their land and sending them into foreign bondage. All of this took place because of Israel's rebellion

283

and unfaithfulness. They admit that God had justly disciplined them by sending them into exile. Then, they pray for deliverance and enter into a covenant—"our leaders, our Levites, and our priests have affixed their names on the sealed document" (9:38)—pledging their faithful obedience to the law of God. The governor, priests, Levites, and rulers sign the document, which spells out in detail what faithfulness will mean (Neh. 10).

Notice that the repentance here is not individual but corporate. This kind of communal action seems strange in our hyper-individualistic cultural context, but it is clearly the norm in the Scripture for us to think about our lives in the plural and not merely the singular. As new covenant believers, we have a responsibility to become accountable members of a local church of Jesus Christ and to corporately obey the communal practices of baptism and the Lord's Supper, which are meant to root our lives in covenant community. Nehemiah 9 and 10 present us a vision of what covenant renewal should look like among the people of God.

1. The primacy of the word of God and our responsibility to respond to it.
2. Recognition of God's grace, blessings, and faithfulness.
3. Agreeing with God by confessing that we have sinfully fallen short of obedience and that we continue to fall short of faithfulness.
4. Declaring that our only hope is found in Jesus Christ, the only Israelite faithful to the covenant who died to pay the penalty for sinners who trust in his atoning sacrifice: "And if you belong to Christ, then you are Abraham's descendants, heirs according to promise" (Gal. 3:29).
5. Pledge our lives to Christ by faith and to love him by loving and serving his church.

David Prince

Connection with Newer Testament
Matthew 3:8; Hebrews 6:1

For the Kids

Reread the key text from today and discuss with your children what a covenant is: an agreement with promises. Explain that God has always been a covenant-keeping God. From the Old Testament to the New Testament and today, our hearts are sick with sin and only Jesus provides a way to be made well and washed of our sin. Pray with your children they would see their need to be washed of their sin, that they would confess their sin, and that they would turn (repent) from their sin to trust Jesus.

Prayer Prompts

1. Confess your sins to the Lord and ask forgiveness for the ways you have been faithless to the new covenant.
2. Praise God for Jesus Christ, the one who purchased the new covenant through his blood poured out on the cross.

◆

WEEK 35: DAY 5

Malachi 3-4

Key Text

"'I am about to send my messenger, who will clear the way before me. Indeed, the Lord you are seeking will suddenly come to his temple, and the messenger of the covenant, whom you long for, is certainly coming,' says the LORD who rules over all." Malachi 3:1

Back in Land, Still in Exile: Elijah Prepares the Way of the Lord

Malachi provides the last prophetic message from God before the close of the Old Testament period. God is the speaker in about forty-seven of the fifty-five verses in Malachi. The prophet's name, Malachi, means "God's messenger." He wrote during a time when the temple had been rebuilt (Mal. 1:13; 3:1, 10), which indicates it was composed after the Jews had returned from their captivity to Babylon. Malachi asserts that the God of justice will himself come to his temple. Malachi fulfills a priestly function as the Lord's messenger (Mal. 2:7). Malachi 3:1 is a messianic prophecy that points to the coming of

Messiah who is the "messenger of the covenant" and that promises an Elijah who will come before Christ as "the messenger" of the Messenger (3:1, 4:5). Four hundred years later, Jesus identified John the Baptist as the Elijah who fulfilled the prophecy (Matt. 3:1-12, 11:13-14). Jesus the Messiah would be deity and not a mere man, just as Isaiah had explained that the messiah would be called "Mighty God" and "Everlasting Father."

The Lord provides the Israelites a message of hope and also provides a sober warning. The Lord does not change (3:6). That fact means there is always hope, but it also means that judgment is assured for those who will not place their faith in the Lord and his gospel promise (3:2-5). The Lord is faithful even when his people are unfaithful. The final address begins and ends with commands. Malachi 3:7–10a contains two commands: first to "return" to the Lord then to evidence their turning by bringing him the tithes and offerings they had been withholding. Then in Malachi 3:10b–12, the Lord promises blessings if Judah would be faithful to him. As in all the Old Testament promises of material blessings, these applied to the nation rather than the individual. Jesus speaks directly against that kind of self-referential materialistic interpretation (Matt. 19:23-25, John 9:3). Judah had begun to call good evil and evil good (3:13-15). Whenever our minds are not guided by God's truth, all of our thoughts are distorted and we are capable of justifying all kinds of evil.

In the end, the Lord will separate the righteous and the wicked and will gather together his treasured possession (3:16–4:3). The Lord knows those who fear him (4:2-3). The book of remembrance (3:16) most likely refers to the heavenly "book of life" (Rev. 20:12). The "Messenger of the covenant" is an appropriate description of the one who is the "Word" that "became flesh" (John 1:14), the ultimate communication from God (Heb. 1:1-2), and "the mediator of a new covenant" (Heb. 9:15, 12:24). Malachi closes with a forward look to the coming Messiah. No one knew when the Messiah would come, so they simply had to expectantly wait in faith. The Church of the Lord Jesus Christ looks forward to the second coming of the Messiah. Like those in Malachi's time, we do not know the time of his return, so we eagerly wait in faith "for the happy fulfillment of our hope in the glorious appearing of our great God and Savior, Jesus Christ" (Titus 2:13). Jesus is the Hero of the Old

Testament and the New Testament, and he alone is the Hero who provides eternal hope.

David Prince

Connection with Newer Testament
Matthew 3:1-12, 11:13-14

For the Kids
Talk to your children about the work done by government officials before the President of the United States ventures into a city. There are Secret Service agents scouting the city. The president's schedule is determined. The route the president will travel is mapped out. Then, once in the city, all kinds of police cars surround the president's vehicle for protection. Not just that, the police cars in front of the president's vehicle prepare the way for the president to get to the destination as quickly as possible by getting other vehicles out of the president's way. In the same way, God promised an Elijah-like figure would come on the scene to prepare the way for the messiah and for his gospel mission. God fulfilled his promise by sending John the Baptist to prepare the way for Jesus. Praise God that his word never fails!

Prayer Prompts
1. The Lord Jesus will return soon to bring judgment on the world. Only by faith in Christ will you be able to endure the day of his coming. Repent of your sins and trust in Jesus.
2. Repentance is the lifestyle of the Christian. What sins have you committed and in what ways do you need to "return to the Lord"? Repent of your sins, and ask the Lord for grace to submit yourself to his gospel.
3. Praise the LORD that he doesn't change. He is a faithful God who forgives all who repent of sin and trust in him; this changeless reality, as demonstrated in Jesus, is the basis of our salvation and hope.

WEEK 36: DAY 1
Psalm 107

Key Text
"Give thanks to the LORD, for he is good, and his loyal love endures! Let those delivered by the LORD speak out, those whom he delivered from the power of the enemy" Psalm 107:1-2

Redemption from Exile: Give Thanks to the Lord
This Psalm serves as the introduction to the fifth and final book of the Psalms. It describes a series of adversities suffered by God's servants during the return from the Babylonian exile and God's continued intervention to deliver them in their troubles. Psalm 107 is a weapon to be wielded in the fight for God-centered wisdom. The final line declares: "Whoever is wise, let him take note of these things! Let them consider the LORD's acts of loyal love!" (v. 43). The psalm is a call to worship for every believer. In the psalm, we find not only a wonderful expression of worship, but we also find a pattern of worship, which ought to become the rhythm of every believer's walk with God.

The troubles mentioned by the psalmist involve desert wandering, being lost and needy (vv. 4-5), darkness and bondage (vv. 10-12), idolatry, conquest, and guilt (vv. 17-18), and troubles at sea (vv. 23-27). We face similar troubles today. What binds each section of the Psalm together is two refrains:

Crying Out to the Lord by Faith in Their Trouble
"Then they cried to the LORD in their distress; he delivered them from their troubles." (vv. 6, 13, 19, 28).

The Lord's Gracious Deliverance in Their Trouble
"He led them on a level road, that they might find a city in which to live." (v. 7).

"He brought them out of the utter darkness, and tore off their shackles." (v. 14).

"He sent them an assuring word and healed them; he rescued them

288

from the pits where they were trapped." (v. 20).

"He calmed the storm, and the waves grew silent. The sailors rejoiced because the waves grew quiet, and he led them to the harbor they desired." (vv. 29-30).

The Lord's grace to them in the midst of their troubles leads them to offer repeated thanksgiving: "Let them gives thanks to the LORD for his loyal love, and for the amazing things he has done for people!" (vv. 8, 15, 21, 31). They also name the new reasons to offer praise by specifically declaring what the Lord had done for them: "For he has satisfied those who thirst, and those who hunger he has filled with food" (v. 9). "For he shattered the bronze gates, and hacked through the iron bars" (v. 16). "Let them present thank offerings, and loudly proclaim what he has done!" (v. 22). "Let them exalt him in the assembly of the people! Let them praise him in the place where the leaders preside!" (v. 32).

The point of the Psalm is abundantly clear: The Lord delivers his people from everywhere and in the midst of everything because of his sovereign covenant love. Thus, all of life should be a response to his grace and a trust in his promises. If we follow him by faith, all of our problems can be turned to new reasons for praise. Augustine (354-430), an early Christian theologian, wrote that Psalm 107 teaches us "what should give us joy" and "about what we are of ourselves, what we are through the mercy of God, and about how our pride is to be shattered and his grace glorified."[6] The gracious deliverance in this Psalm leads our minds to the ultimate expression of gracious deliverance in Christ. Jesus the Hero once-and-for-all answers the problem of sin and the cry of the needy for all who trust him as Lord and Savior.

David Prince

Connection with Newer Testament
1 Thessalonians 5:18

---

[6]Augustine, *Expositions of the Psalms*, in vol. 5 of *Works of Saint Augustine: A Translation for the 21ˢᵗ Century*, trans. Maria Boulding, (Hyde Park, NY: New City Press, 2002), 223.

For the Kids

Tie your children's hands behind their backs using a rope, string, or pair of toy handcuffs. Don't hurt them, but make sure they can't get out. Knowing they can't get out, have them try to escape anyway. When they give up, untie them. Ask your children if they are thankful that you untied them. Surely they will be glad you didn't leave them bound up. Then tell your children that this is what Psalm 107 is about. God was delivering his people from their bondage and their exile, and the psalm is a call to give thanks to the Lord. Tell your children about how much more Christians should thank God. Jesus has set his people free forever from bondage to sin and death. Give thanks to the Lord.

Prayer Prompts

1. Praise God that, when you were under the wrath of God and in sin, God redeemed you from your condemnation under the Law through Jesus Christ. God redeems his people from exile; he alone is worthy of praise.

2. Ask the Lord to reveal his saving mercy to people you know who are dead in their trespasses and sins. Pray for revival among non-Christians to the praise of his glorious grace.

◆

WEEK 36: DAY 2
Psalm 110

Key Text

"'Here is the LORD's proclamation to my lord: "Sit down at my right hand until I make your enemies your footstool!"'" Psalm 110:1

The Lord of David: Eternal, Ruling, Victorious

Psalm 110 is a Psalm of David according to the title and the argument of Jesus (Matt. 22:41-46). The Psalm combines the offices of messianic king and messianic priest. In the New Testament (Matt. 22:42-45), Jesus asks the question of how this can be, how can the Lord be the son of David and yet David call him Lord? They could not answer that riddle (Matt. 22:46), but we can. Jesus, the God-man, is both David's son and David's Lord: a man like ourselves and yet "very God of very God." The resurrected and ascended Christ rules as Davidic King. He is also the eternal Messianic Priest who constantly prays on behalf of his people. When God's power controls the life of his servant, their life is refreshed, set apart to him, and he lifts their head in eternal hope.

Consider the great English Baptist preacher, Charles Haddon Spurgeon's thoughts on this magisterial psalm:

Here we see the Christ,—whom we just now saw as risen from the dead, and acknowledged as the Son of God,—seated upon the throne: "The LORD said unto my Lord, Sit thou at my right hand, until I make thine enemies thy footstool" (110:1). No sooner was Christ ascended into heaven than, out of the midst of his Church,—the earthly Zion,—the scepter of his power was stretched forth, and its might was displayed amongst the sons of men. Witness what happened on the day of Pentecost, which was but the beginning of Christ's ruling in the very midst of his enemies, who then became his friends, and yielded their hearts and lives to him; so that Jerusalem, where he had been crucified, became the very center of his kingdom on earth, from which his servants went forth to evangelize the world (110:2).

As soon as the ascended Christ began his reign in heaven, and the power of his Church began to be felt on earth, there was a willing people coming forward, in the beauty of holiness, like priests clad in their sacred robes. Such the early Christians truly were; and they were as numerous, and as refreshing, and as bright to the world as the sparkling dew of the morning. Then, indeed, had Christ the dew of his youth most clearly manifested. Multitudes of young hearts yielded to him, and his Church on earth seemed to have had a new birthday when he ascended up on high, and led captivity captive (110:3).

[The LORD] is, a priest without predecessor or successor,—a priest who was at the same time a king,—a priest of the Most High God, who was greater even than Abraham, the friend of God. Jesus our Lord is not a priest after the order of Aaron, for he came not of that line, but he was "a priest for ever after the order of Melchizedek" (110:4). When that last great day [of God's wrath] shall come, Christ shall no longer patiently wait for the overthrow of his enemies; but he shall win the complete victory over them (110:5). Thus wilt thou, O Lord, cut down all evil principles, and everything that is opposed to thee (110:6)! He shall not be wearied with thirst, as Samson was, but he shall hasten on in his mighty achievements, without pausing to rest, until he has fully accomplished the whole of his great task (110:7-8).[7]

American theologian Jonathan Edwards asserted about Psalm 110, "That Christ will rule is irrefutable, but how one will experience his rule depends on the disposition of the individual, either a joyful acceptance or a vexed resistance. For those who willingly submit to God, Christ's kingdom rule would bring 'a spiritual happiness,' in righteousness and holiness, and the favor and worship and enjoyment of God."[8]

David Prince

Connection with Newer Testament
Matthew 22:41-46; Hebrews 7

For the Kids
Talk with your children about what priests and kings in the Bible do (intercede and sacrifice, and rule and defend). Explain that Jesus is the Royal Priest who offered up his own sinless body for the sins of his people. He also rose from the dead and is with God, where he intercedes for his Church. Having conquered death, he rules over all creation as the King of kings and Lord of lords. He also protects his people from physical and spiritual enemies. Jesus is both the Messianic King and Messianic Priest of Psalm 110. Praise him!

Prayer Prompts
1. Praise the Lord that one greater than Melchizedek and greater than David has come to serve faithfully and flawlessly as our eternally victorious King. Ask the Lord for grace to trust our sovereign King, Jesus Christ.

---

[7]Charles Haddon Spurgeon, *The Metropolitan Tabernacle Pulpit Sermons*, vol. 48, (London: Passmore & Alabaster, 1902), 562-563.

[8]David P. Barshinger, *Jonathan Edwards and the Psalms: A Redemptive-Historical Vision of Scripture* (New York: Oxford, 2014), 214.

2. Pray for the continued defeat of Satan and his demonic realm.

◆

WEEK 36: DAY 3
Psalm 132

Key Text
"The LORD made a reliable promise to David; he will not go back on his word. He said, 'I will place one of your descendants on your throne.'" Psalm 132:11

The Lord Has Chosen Zion: Hope Comes in a Davidic King
What is exile? Exile is the experience of pain and suffering that results from the knowledge that there is a home where you belong, yet for the present, you are unable to return there. Psalm 132 is written out of the pain of exile. Israel has the promises of God, but for this time, that's all they have. They are estranged from their homeland and wondering how they will make it. When we read the texts that arise from Israel's exile, we should pay close attention. The New Testament says that we are "sojourners and exiles" (1 Pet. 1:1*), living in this present evil age and awaiting the consummation of the kingdom of God in Christ.

How will we survive? How will we make it through? Psalm 132 provides help. We remember God's past acts of faithfulness and his promises. And we plead with him to remember his promises to us (v. 1). What exactly has he promised? He said that a son of David would sit on the throne and rule his people forever (vv. 11-12). Israel had no idea how God would fulfill that promise, but we do. We see Jesus—crucified, resurrected, and reigning—sitting on the throne of God, and we await his return to bring us home from our exile.

Casey McCall

Connection with Newer Testament
Revelation 22:16

For the Kids

Discuss what faithfulness is with your children, and describe how God is always faithful to his promises. Tell them that we should always keep our promises as we reflect God to the world. Tell them to remember, when we and others are unfaithful, that our joy is in the unchanging, faithful God who keeps his promises toward us, promises of eternal life and hope for all who are in Christ.

Prayer Prompts

1. Ask God to seal upon your mind all the times he has been faithful to you in Christ so that, when trials come, you will persevere in faith.

2. Pray for Jesus' second coming as we long to reign with Jesus in his eternal kingdom in glorified bodies where there are no enemies and where sin is no more.

◆

WEEK 36: DAY 4

Psalm 149

Key Text

"Let them praise his name with dancing! Let them sing praises to him to the accompaniment of the tambourine and harp! For the LORD takes delight in his people; he exalts the oppressed by delivering them." Psalm 149:3-4

Salvation's New Song

This psalm opens with a jubilant command to sing to the LORD a "new song." While God's character is unchanging, the psalmist reminds us that each day provides a new expression of God's love for his people. Furthermore, God's sheer greatness means that human language would be exhausted long before his praiseworthiness could be fully described. Thus, for believers, our lives should constantly reflect "new songs" of praise to Yahweh.

Not only does the psalmist command for the singing of new songs, he also justifies the command and reveals the way in which these new songs should be sung. The psalmist is overwhelmed with God's loving kingship over his people and the ultimate victory he has promised them. Faced with the twin realities of God's powerful reign and his deep love for an imperfect people, the psalmist erupts in praise and instructs his reader to do the same. While we may be tempted to place the psalmist's commands into a box that fits with our personality traits or cultural norms, this psalm undeniably exhorts the audience to worship God in a way that is completely unrestrained: believers should dance, play instruments, and even sing joyfully from their own beds! How much more cause for rejoicing than the psalmist do we have, who live with the full knowledge of the coming of God's only Son in Jesus of Nazareth?

The command to reflect on God's holy reign and his love for his chosen people seamlessly transitions into the second half of the Psalm. In one breath, the psalmist exclaims, "May they praise God while they hold a two-edged sword in their hand." To be used as God's judges upon his enemies is in many ways a culmination of God's love and forgiveness for his own people; they are transformed from enemies into soldiers in God's own army. And just as the psalmist and other Israelites executed literal judgement upon the enemies of God, so shall the saints, through Christ, be made judges of even angels (1 Cor. 6:3).

Joe Martin

Connection with Newer Testament
Revelation 5:9-14

For the Kids
Remind your children that they should always find new ways to praise God, then model this behavior for them in your own conversations and prayers. Our children ought to be learning new things about God on a regular basis, and this psalm exhorts us to help them turn that knowledge into praise. Make your home one where every blessing and every promise of God is a reason for unrestrained praise!

Prayer Prompts
1. Consider your sin then your salvation. You have been delivered from slavery to sin and from eternal death. The Lord takes pleasure in you. Praise him for

his radical generosity.

2. Think on your daily speech and your attitude. Does your speech and attitude reflect the reality of your salvation in Christ? Repent of any grumbling and complaining in light of the reality that your greatest need has been met in Christ.

◆

WEEK 36: DAY 5
1 Chronicles 17

Key Text
"When the time comes for you to die, I will raise up your descendant, one of your own sons, to succeed you, and I will establish his kingdom." 1 Chronicles 17:11

Living in the Land After Exile: Awaiting the Davidic King

Interestingly, the books of 1 and 2 Chronicles come at the very end of the Hebrew Bible. In these books, the Chronicler recounts Israel's history, in part, to help the Israelites who have returned from exile live faithfully in the promised land.

In 1 Chronicles 17, the historian is tracing the history of the tribe of Judah from which the Messiah will rise (Gen. 49:10). In particular, the Chronicler retells the story found in 2 Samuel 7 in which David is promised a descendant who will reign over an eternal kingdom. So, why retell this particular story from Israel's past at this time?

The chronicler is reminding the returned exiles that God has made a promise to David that has yet to be fulfilled. The Messiah from the line of David and the line of Abraham first promised in Genesis 3 is still yet to come. If Israel is to be faithful to the Lord now that they have returned to the land, they must be a people who cling to the promises of God. They must live by faith in God's word, and they must diligently await the Davidic king who will rule forever over the earth.

The Davidic king, anticipated for more than one thousand years, would eventually come in the person of Jesus Christ (Matt. 1:1-16). Having defeated sin on behalf of his people, Jesus now reigns over the cosmos at the right hand of the Father as the King of kings and Lord of lords. And today, God still calls his people to exercise faith in the promises of Jesus Christ. For all who repent of sin and cling to the Davidic king by faith, the Lord promises forgiveness and life in the eternal kingdom. For all who reject this king, an eternal exile under God's wrath awaits. Are you living each moment by faith in the final king in the line of David?

Jon Canler

Connection with Newer Testament
Matthew 1:1-17; Revelation 22:16

For the Kids
Think of two small gifts you can give to your children, perhaps a couple piece of candy or a couple of coins. Tell your children that you have a couple of gifts to give them a little while later. In about ten minutes, give them one of the gifts. As you give the gift, tell your children that, when God brought Israel out of exile and back into the promised land, he fulfilled his promise to bring them out of physical bondage. Remind your children, though, that there were other promises not yet fulfilled, like the promise of the messiah through the line of David. Tell your children that 1 Chronicles 17 was written after Israel was brought back into the promised land, and it was calling Israel to wait a little longer for God to fulfill his messianic promise to David. Tell you children that the messiah from David eventually came in Jesus, who set his people free from sin. Tell your children that God is faithful to his word as you give them the second gift you promised them.

Prayer Prompts
1. Praise God that the long-awaited Messiah—the hope of Israel upon their return from Babylonian captivity—has been revealed in Jesus Christ. God's great salvation has come for the world!
2. The exiles had returned to the promised land, but the fullness of God's salvation had not yet been revealed. Much like them, we've experienced

salvation, but not in full. Ask the Lord to grant you hope in his future promises on the basis of his past grace.

◆

WEEK 37: DAY 1
2 Chronicles 15-16

Key Text
"God's Spirit came upon Azariah son of Oded. He met Asa and told him, 'Listen to me, Asa and all Judah and Benjamin! The LORD is with you when you are loyal to him. If you seek him, he will respond to you, but if you reject him, he will reject you.'" 2 Chronicles 15:1-2

Living in the Land After Exile: Faith-Based Obedience to the Lord

Remember from yesterday's devotional that the books of 1 and 2 Chronicles come at the very end of the Hebrew Bible. In these books the Chronicler recounts Israel's history, in part, to help the Israelites who have returned from exile live faithfully in the promised land. So, what might 2 Chronicles 15-16 instruct the Israelites?

In 2 Chronicles 15-16 we are reminded of the reign of King Asa. In 2 Chronicles 15, we find that Asa begins his reign over Judah well. Asa put away the idols, he repaired the altar to the LORD, and he sought the LORD (15:8, 12). Consequently, the LORD gave his people peace and rest from their enemies, very Eden-like language (15:15). However, though he began well, Asa's reign ended on a sour note. 2 Chronicles 16 informs us that Asa began to rely on the King of Syria, rather than the Lord, to fight his battles (16:2-4). Consequently, the LORD removed peace from Asa and Judah (16:9). Moreover, Asa slipped further into sin by inflicting cruelties upon the people and, it seems, altogether forsook the LORD (16:10, 12).

The Chronicler reminds Israel that faith-based obedience to the LORD should characterize their life in the promised land. Blessing will be upon the people when they trust in the LORD, when they fear him and keep his commandments. However, if the people return to the faithless ways in which they lived prior to the exile, war and unrest and cursing would come upon them. If the people are to thrive in the promised land, they must obey the Lord.

Though a remnant of Israelites returned to the land after exile, they still didn't have regenerate hearts that were needed to please the Lord always. Only after Jesus Christ came, lived a sinless life, died for sin, and was raised again was a new covenant effected that would bring new hearts and an obedient spirit (Jer. 31:31-33). For those who've placed their faith in Jesus, God grants peace with himself and the ability to obey him for eternity. The call to obey the Lord unto blessing or rebel unto judgment still exists. Submit to Jesus to find peace, or refuse him and find war with God.

Jon Canler

Connection with Newer Testament
2 Corinthians 5:7; Ephesians 5

For the Kids
Have your children do as many pushups as they can in two minutes. Once they're exhausted, discuss your children's performances. Did they start fast, doing a lot of pushups quickly, only to slow down or stop altogether by the time two minutes was up? Teach your children that King Asa's rule was similar: he started well by obeying the LORD only to stop obeying the LORD altogether by the time he was done being king. Tell your children that, even after a return to the promised land after exile, God's people still needed new hearts that were able to obey God's commands. Praise the Lord that the new covenant in Jesus blood gives new hearts to his people so that Christians can live out an obedience of faith that is pleasing to God.

Prayer Prompts
1. Ask the Lord to cause you to walk by faith and in newness of life as we await his second coming.
2. Pray for the perseverance of fellow believers. Pray especially for those who are battling doubt, sin, and persecution—that they will continue in faith with the full confidence that God will uphold all who belong to him.

WEEK 37: DAY 2
Luke 1

Key Text

"So the angel said to her, 'Do not be afraid, Mary, for you have found favor with God! Listen: You will become pregnant and give birth to a son, and you will name him Jesus. He will be great, and will be called the Son of the Most High, and the Lord God will give him the throne of his father David. He will reign over the house of Jacob forever, and his kingdom will never end.'" Luke 1:30-33

Fulfillment: The Kingdom is at Hand

Building upon the prophecies given throughout the Old Testament, the message Gabriel shares with Mary, though brief, is overflowing with the good news of who Jesus is. The time has come! "You will become pregnant and give birth to a son..." The virgin bearing a son means that this boy is Immanuel, God living among us, a flesh and blood son given to us who is also the Almighty God who will rule forever (Is. 7:14, 9:6-7). "...and you will name him Jesus". The meaning of Jesus is 'God saves.' The one who will save in ways greater than Moses, greater than all the judges, and greater than David—the ultimate Savior—is here! (Is. 25:9) "He will be great, and will be called the Son of the Most High." This is the begotten Son of God, the King of Zion who will judge all nations and put an end to the wicked. (Ps. 1-2) "[A]nd the Lord God will give him the throne of his father David." In this boy, the promises to David that seemed to have been forgotten will be completely fulfilled—the people will dwell peacefully in their own place under the permanently established throne of this eternally loved son of David. (1 Chr. 17) "He will reign over the house of Jacob forever, and his kingdom will never end." This baby will be the forever king of the kingdom of God, the only eternal kingdom, the kingdom that puts an end to all other kingdoms. (Dan. 2:44)

In short, the message is this: Mary, through your womb, a king is coming through whom all the promises of God will be fulfilled and through whom God will ultimately and eternally save his people!

Connection with Older Testament

Genesis 12:1-3; 1 Samuel 2:1-10; 2 Samuel 7:12-17

For the Kids

Have you ever had a promise broken? Have you ever broken a promise? Well, God has never broken a promise. God fulfills all of his promises just like what we read. God is saving his people in Jesus, and he will receive the glory. Remember, we can trust God because God always keeps his promises.

Prayer Prompts

1. Praise the Lord, like Mary and Zechariah, for the fact that God has finally fulfilled all of his promises of salvation in Jesus Christ. Praise God for redemption—for Christmas.

2. Ask the Lord to help you understand the Bible like Mary and Zechariah, with eyes that see the Bible as God's story of redemption as fulfilled in Jesus.

◆

WEEK 37: DAY 3

Luke 2

Key Text

"Simeon took him in his arms and blessed God, saying, 'Now, according to your word, Sovereign Lord, permit your servant to depart in peace. For my eyes have seen your salvation that you have prepared in the presence of all peoples: a light for revelation to the Gentiles, and for glory to your people Israel.'" Luke 2:28-32

The Birth of Jesus: Fulfilling Both the Law and the Prophets

Simeon was promised that he would see the consolation of Israel before he died. He was a righteous man and loved the Lord. He lived in expectation for the birth of the Messiah to come, and when Jesus was presented at the temple as a child, Simeon received him. Jesus was the consolation of

Israel. The Messiah had come. The people before Jesus waited for the coming of the Messiah as we wait for the return of Christ. They looked at the world hoping that, though so much was wrong, soon the Messiah would come and correct all things that are wrong with the world. And when Jesus came for the first time, he brought the fullness of the glory of heaven with him. And now we live in the end of days at a time where the fullness of heaven has come, and he sits on the throne at the right hand of the Father.

The birth of Jesus signals that all of the promises of God are yes and amen in Christ. Everything truly will turn out for good because the man born of woman crushed the head of the serpent. The beginning represents the entirety of what will come. We do not need to fear the future because the Messiah has come, and he will return. Yet, in the interim we wait under the sovereign authority of Jesus Christ.

David Prince, "The First Noel and Other Thoughts About End Times," Preached 12/7/2008, Ashland Avenue Baptist Church Website, Accessed 4 December 2015, Available from http://www.ashlandlex.org/podcast/the-first-noel-and-other-thoughts-about-end-times/.

Connection with Older Testament
Isaiah 52

For the Kids
Ask your kids to remember what they put on their Christmas list last year. Have them think about their excitement as they saw presents with their names on them under the tree in the days prior to Christmas. I'm sure they asked whether or not the presents contained what they asked for. Then have them recall their excitement on Christmas when one of the presents contained what was on their list. Teach your kids that the joy they experienced when they opened that present was like the joy Simeon and Anna had when they saw Jesus, born as a baby that first Christmas. Their Savior, promised of old in the Old Testament, had come!

Prayer Prompts

1. Pray that we dwell on the birth of Christ in such a way that directs us to worship the promise-fulfilling Messiah-King.

2. Pray that we are a faithful church, a church that loves in response to the way that Christ first loved us.

◆

WEEK 37: DAY 4

Matthew 1

Key Text

"'Look, the virgin will conceive and bear a son, and they will call him Emmanuel,' which means 'God with us.'" Matthew 1:23

The Last Genealogy: Old Testament Covenants and Jesus Christ

It is no accident that Jesus was born to an adoptive father. Joseph, being an honorable man, took on the dishonor of taking Mary as his wife. Joseph listened to the Holy Spirit and applied his life to the greater narrative that God was delivering in the world. The book of Matthew begins with the genealogy of Jesus, showing his lineage in a way that shadows the first book of our Bibles. This is the genesis of Jesus. And as an adopted son, Jesus would go on to set up a kingdom in which every tribe, tongue, and nation could be adopted as sons and daughters of the Lord.

The Lord says, "I will not leave you as orphans, but I will come for you." Christ has called us to adoption and to the care of orphans. This is a miraculous thing. Adoption only makes since because Jesus cares about orphans. One of Satan's greatest lies is that the only people who should be concerned with adoption are parents that are going to adopt, but the Bible tells us the opposite. In James 1:27, Jesus' brother says, "Religion that is pure and undefiled before God, the Father, is this: to visit orphans and widows in the affliction, and to keep oneself unstained from the world."* The church must care for the things God cares for, and God cares for orphans.

David Prince, "Fathers & Adoption Culture," Preached 6/15/2014, Prince on Preaching Website, Accessed 4 December 2015, Available from http://www.davidprince.com/2014/06/15/fathers-adoption-culture-matthew-118-25/.

Connection with Older Testament

Isaiah 7

For the Kids

Explain what orphans and adoption are to your children. Show them how adoption is present in the birth of Jesus. Discuss how children can care for orphans if "the church must care for the things God cares for." Ask your children what they can do. After discussing, take a moment to pray for the orphans of the world.

Prayer Prompts

1. Pray that the Lord sends out his Church to rescue the orphans of the world through adoption
2. Pray that God shows you how you need to respond to the need of those that are helpless in the world.

◆

WEEK 37: DAY 5

John 1

Key Text

"Now the Word became flesh and took up residence among us. We saw his glory—the glory of the one and only, full of grace and truth, who came from the Father." John 1:14

A New Beginning: God Becomes Flesh to Give New Life

One of man's greatest fears is this: if people really knew me, then they couldn't love me. We are desperately afraid of being found out for who we really are. So much of our lives is set up in such a way that people only see what we would have them see. However, grace takes that idea and destroys it.

Jesus, God incarnate, came to our destructive world in the humblest of all forms. As a baby, Jesus came, grew, preformed miracles, and died for those who despised him. Yet, death could not hold him, and, in his resurrection, grace was given to the world by the Savior of the same world that killed him.

The way that we know steadfast love and faithfulness is by looking at Jesus' work on the cross. In Christ, we can be both fully known and fully loved. Our deepest sins have been forgiven. We are no longer bound as slaves to sin, but we have new life in Jesus Christ. Those that have surrendered to the lordship of Jesus Christ have been set free in the world to live for a new Master. Jesus is a Master that trades our shackles for purpose.

David Prince, "The Word (Jesus)," Preached 12/23/2012, Prince on Preaching Website, Accessed 4 December 2015, Available from http://www.davidprince.com/2012/12/23/the-word-jesus-john-114-18/.

Connection with Older Testament
Genesis 1

For the Kids
Show your family pictures of animals and ask them how their human body differs from each animal body. A cat walks on all four legs, but we walk on two. A fish has scales, fins, and gills as opposed to our skin, arms, legs, and lungs. A bear has sharp claws, but we have dull fingernails. Discuss the uniqueness of the human body and, therefore, the significance that Christ came in human form. As much as he came to redeem the world, he specifically came in the form of man in order to save man!

Prayer Prompts
1. Pray that we see other believers in light of what Christ has done on the cross.
2. Pray that we do not hold others to the sins they have repented of but, instead, rejoice with others in their freedom found in Christ.

WEEK 38: DAY 1

Matthew 3

Key Text

"In those days John the Baptist came into the wilderness of Judea proclaiming, 'Repent, for the kingdom of heaven is near.'" Matthew 3:1-2

Preparing the Way of the Lord: The Ministry of John the Baptist

Preaching a powerful message of repentance accompanied by the dramatic sign of baptism, John was truly a remarkable figure in redemptive history. This passage features the ministry of John as a prelude to Jesus' own ministry, and it clearly demonstrates the weight of sin and the necessity of repentance. With a manner and ministry reminiscent of the prophet Elijah, John's appearance fulfills the prophecy of Yahweh's messenger preparing his way (Mal. 3:1).

Matthew contrasts here two distinct people(s) coming to John. First to arrive are the Pharisees, who receive a less than warm welcome from John. It is unclear whether or not any Pharisees were baptized that day; however, it is clear that John warned them that a sign such as baptism should be followed with "fruit." Just as the Pharisees should not hope for salvation in either their pedigree (as Abraham's children) or in some outward public sign like baptism, neither should we. It can be temping for Christians who show little evidence of faith in Christ to harken back to "walking the isle" as proof of their salvation. Instead of looking to the past, John urged his listeners to look to their present and abiding fruit. While believers do not "lose" their salvation, our faith is evidenced by continual fruit-bearing (Jas. 2:14-17).

In contrast to the arrival of the Pharisees was the coming of Jesus to John. Whereas John was reluctant to baptize the Pharisees due to their sin, he was reluctant to baptize Jesus due to his lack of sin. Baptism was (and is) and act that symbolizes the cleansing of sins and is accompanied by confession (v. 6). Jesus had no sins from which to be cleansed and no confession to make; yet, he sought baptism in order to fulfill all righteousness. Reflecting upon this image, Paul writes in Romans 6:4, "Therefore we have been buried with him through baptism into death, in order that just as Christ was raised from the dead through the glory of the Father, so we too may live a new life." Believers, let us follow the example of Christ in baptism and "produce fruit that proves your repentance."

Joe Martin

Connection with Older Testament
Isaiah 40:1-5

For the Kids
Speak honestly with your children about the meaning of baptism. It can be tempting for kids to seek baptism in order to please their parents or to fit in with the rest of the church, but baptism must be preceded by faith in Jesus as Lord and followed by fruits of righteousness. If your child is a believer that is yet to be baptized, encourage them to boldly follow the example of Jesus and share with him in baptism.

Prayer Prompts
1. John's message of repentance still stands today. If you haven't repented of your sins and turned to Jesus for salvation, confess your sins to the Lord and be saved by faith in Jesus.
2. Praise God that being children of Abraham is not tied to genealogy. We who are of faith, who believe in Christ, and who hope in God's promises are those children. Praise God that salvation through faith extends beyond Israel!

◆

WEEK 38: DAY 2
Matthew 4

Key Text
"Then Jesus said to him, 'Go away, Satan! For it is written, "You are to worship the Lord your God and serve only him.""" Matthew 4:10

The Temptation of Jesus: A New Adam Without Sin

Jesus boldly continues his quest to "fulfill all righteousness" (Matt. 3:15), but the mission in Matthew 4 is very dark. Chapter three concludes with Jesus rising from the baptismal waters as the Father's loving voice echoes from the heavens while the Spirit rests on him like a dove. This glorious reprieve immediately gives way to an arduous trial for the "man of sorrows" (Is. 53:3). Verses like these remind us viscerally that Jesus "did not come to be served but to serve, and to give his life as a ransom for many" (Matt. 20:28). Here, for our sake, Jesus once again gives up comfort and peace for pain and difficulty.

As he prepares for temptation at the hands of Satan himself, Jesus engages in a fast of incredible length: forty days and forty nights (calling to mind images of Moses' fasts, Israel's years in the wilderness, and the length of rain during the Noahic flood). Such a fast would have brought Jesus very near the point of physical death, but it apparently brought him even nearer to the Father. It is no surprise that the devil's first temptation not only questions Jesus' identity and power ("If you are the son of God..."), but also seeks to exploit his desire for food. The second temptation of Satan calls into question Jesus' relationship with his Father while employing Scripture, reminding us that God's word can be "twisted" by those with impure motives (2 Pet. 3:16). Finally, the "ruler of the kingdom of the air" (Eph. 2:2) promises Jesus a shortcut to glory and authority, surely the strongest temptation of three. Satan's empty and deceitful offer only required Jesus to bow in worship to him; however, Jesus knew that God's path to a crown of glory would come through a cross of shame. Praise God that we have a new Adam whose body was broken but whose knee was unbent!

Joe Martin

Connection with Older Testament

Genesis 3; Numbers 11-25 (skim to see the pattern of Israel's rebellion when tempted in contrast to Jesus' obedience as the faithful Israelite)

For the Kids

Show your children a beautifully-wrapped present (make sure nothing is in it), and offer them a trade for something valuable they have. See who is willing to give up dessert or do an extra chore or trade a prized possession. However, when they open the present, they'll see there's nothing inside! Discuss how Satan tempts us with sin by making it look good to us when it's actually worthless. Teach them that Jesus never chose the emptiness of sin so that he could provide forgiveness to us for our sin.

Prayer Prompts

1. Praise the Lord that Jesus, fully dependent upon the Spirit, withstood the temptations of Satan. He lived as the perfect Adam so that his righteousness might be applied to all who place their faith in him for salvation.

2. When you struggle with sin, look to Christ. He has defeated sin, Satan, and death. Cry out to him for grace to withstand temptation and for help in times of need.

◆

WEEK 38: DAY 3

John 2

Key Text

"Jesus replied, 'Destroy this temple and in three days I will raise it up again.'" John 2:19

In Three Days I Will Raise It Up: Jesus as the True Temple

We love the convenience of our culture today: business transactions at the push of a button, ordering our groceries from the couch, visiting our friends and family via Facetime instead of in-person, and working in our virtual offices in our homes several states away from our colleagues. The convenience of our culture spans into our Christianity as well as we listen to sermons on our phones or participate in worship services from the comforts of our own recliners or give our weekly tithes from the patio as we work on our tans.

In John 2, we see that the Jewish people had made their worship of God more convenient for themselves. Instead of sacrificing their own livestock and livelihood, they were sacrificing animals that were available for purchase right there in the temple. The Jewish people, much like us Christians today, went through cycles where they forgot who God is and what his desires are for worship. In an effort to serve themselves and their own desires for convenience, the people had distorted their worship of God into a simple business transaction.

Jesus comes in and flips their dead, convenient religion on its head. He sends away the moneychangers with the oxen, sheep, pigeons, and the like with zeal and passion that the Jews had not encountered since the time of King David. The people ask him upon what authority he cleanses the temple in this manner. He responds very simply by saying that he can run all these animals and moneychangers out of this building because this temple (building) means little in light of *this* temple, his body. With these actions and a simple statement Jesus shows that worship is not a simple, convenient business transaction. Business transactions and personal conveniences change nothing. Coming face to face with the presence of God in the person of Christ Jesus according to the word of God...*this* changes everything.

Jeremy Haskins, "Expect the Unexpected in Suffering," Preached 4/6/2014, Ashland in MC Website, Accessed 3 December 2015, Available from http://www.ashlandmc.org/podcast/expect-unexpected-suffering-john-2-13-22/.

Connection with Older Testament
Psalm 69

For the Kids
What household chores does each member of your family do? When we keep our house clean, it shows respect and thankfulness for our home and our family with whom we share it. Jesus cleans out the temple because people were sinning in it instead of respecting God. Not only does Jesus clean the temple, he reminds us that the temple is where God dwells. Because Jesus is God, he is

the temple. To rightly respect God and to thank him today requires worshipping Jesus in faith.

Prayer Prompts

1. Where are you currently treating your worship of God as a simple business transaction? Ask God to rid your life of this tendency and thank him for going to the cross to atone for our sinful worship priorities.

2. Are you actively seeking to come face to face with the presence of God? Ask God for a heart of worship that seeks to be in his presence at all times.

◆

WEEK 38: DAY 4
John 3

Key Text

"For this is the way God loved the world: He gave his one and only Son, so that everyone who believes in him will not perish but have eternal life." John 3:16

For God So Loved the World: Born Again into Eternal Life

Do you ever sit around in awe of the fact that other people love you? Other people love you in spite of your sins, faults, and failures. Let's take it one step further. Do you ever sit in absolute wonder that the Creator of the universe loves you? Not only does he love you, but he loves you so much that he is willing to sacrifice his favorite possession, the One who is most like him, for *you*, a person who naturally despises and rejects him. John 3 unpacks this truth for us.

God's love shows a conscious commitment and a willingness to give everything he has without expectation of receiving anything in return. This fact is such a foreign concept to us in our culture as we consistently move from one relationship to another once we've gotten everything we can from the previous relationship. We tend to use others for our own personal gain. Our behavior is the very opposite of God's. Thankfully, through faith and trusting in the perfect life of Christ, we can be in right relationship with that one perfectly righteous being and see what real love looks like. Then, when we get a taste of this love, we begin to be transformed. We will be able to give everything away for the sake of others expecting nothing in return because we know we have everything we could ever imagine: eternal life and the love of our heavenly Father through faith in Christ alone.

Jeremy Haskins, "The Solution—He Gave," Preached 12/21/2014, Ashland in MC Website, Accessed 3 December 2015, Available from http://www.ashlandmc.org/podcast/solution-gave-john-3-16-18/.

Connection with Older Testament
Exodus 34:6-7

For the Kids
John 3:16 is an excellent verse for your family to memorize in order to succinctly treasure and share the gospel. If your children can read, write the verse on index cards (one word per card) for them to arrange in order and read. Then flip over one card at a time, reading the entire verse each time until they can say it entirely with no words showing. If your children are younger, repeat the verse with motions so they can memorize it. Discuss how big and strong the love of God is—big and strong enough to cause him to send his own Son to die in order to save us!

Prayer Prompts
1. Are you willing to give the way that God gives? Pray that God would make you give and love expecting nothing in return.
2. Does the truth that you were perishing and God saved you in Christ affect the way you see the world? Pray for a deeper understanding of your need for Christ and what he has done for you.

◆

WEEK 38: DAY 5
Luke 4

Key Text

"'The Spirit of the Lord is upon me, because he has anointed me to proclaim good news to the poor. He has sent me to proclaim release to the captives and the regaining of sight to the blind, to set free those who are oppressed.'" Luke 4:18

Jesus in Nazareth: Proclaiming Liberty and Fulfilling Scripture

"Then Jesus, in the power of the Spirit, returned to Galilee, and news about him spread throughout the surrounding countryside" (vv. 14-15). Jesus' name was spreading; he was becoming famous in the region. As he was teaching in the synagogues around Galilee, he was "praised by all."

Typically, a famous person is celebrated in their hometown. Not so with prophets! When Jesus reaches his hometown of Nazareth, an initial positive response quickly turns dangerous as people attempt to throw him down the cliff.

And what was the message that got them so angry so quickly? Jesus compared them to the other widows in the time of Elijah who weren't miraculously fed, to the other lepers in the time of Elisha who weren't healed. Instead of learning from Jesus' words and submitting to the words of the prophet in front of them (as the widow of Zarephath did and as Naaman the Syrian did), these Galileans confirmed what Jesus was saying by turning against the Son and attempting to kill him. They completely missed the glory of the message from Isaiah that Jesus had read a few moments before in their midst. Here was the One who, in the power of the Spirit, was proclaiming *good* news, liberty, and recovery of sight. But, they were not willing to see that they were the poor, the captives, and the blind.

Jesus' message angers some and blesses others. When we see ourselves for who we are, understand who Jesus is, and call upon him, we experience liberation, healing, and the Lord's favor.

Todd Martin

Connection with Older Testament

Isaiah 61

313

For the Kids

Imagine if Jesus had been your brother and he said he was the Messiah sent to rescue you. Do you think you would have been confused and angry like the people of Nazareth? Show you children that Jesus really is who he says—he really is our good news Savior.

Prayer Prompts

1. Pray for someone you know who needs to be set free from sin by the gospel of Christ. Pray that you would be the one to proclaim liberty to the captives.
2. Praise God that Jesus has power over sin and the curse. We can look forward to the new heavens and the new earth where sin will be no more because we see that Jesus has power over the curse and over the effects of sin.

◆

WEEK 39: DAY 1

Matthew 5-7

Key Text

"'But above all pursue his kingdom and righteousness, and all these things will be given to you as well.'" Matthew 6:33

The Sermon on the Mount: Faith-Based Ethics in the Kingdom of God

"'Indeed, my plans are not like your plans, and my deeds are not like your deeds'" (Is. 55:8). The way of the kingdom, the eternal way, does not come naturally to us, nor does it make natural sense to us. That is what makes the Sermon on the Mount so challenging to us. As Pastor David Prince once wrote on Matthew 5-7, Jesus here "turns the wisdom of the world upside down."[9]

---

[9]David Prince, "Christians and Culture: Truth, Beauty, Goodness and the Great Commission," Published 3/19/2015, Prince on Preaching Website, Accessed 28 December 2015, Available from http://www.davidprince.com/2015/03/19/christians-and-culture-truth-beauty-goodness-and-the-great-commission/.

Jesus describes those who are walking in the eternal way—the poor in spirit, those who mourn, the meek, those who hunger and thirst for righteousness, the merciful, the pure in heart, the peacemakers, those who are persecuted for righteousness' sake. This is a list of characteristics none of us would have selected! But look at the promises of the kingdom—theirs is the kingdom of heaven, they shall be comforted, they shall inherit the earth, they shall be satisfied, they shall receive mercy, they shall see God, they shall be called sons of God. How glorious are the rewards of the way of the kingdom!

Jesus gives great warnings. Watch out! These are common pitfalls that keep people from life and lead to eternal destruction. 1) Do not minimize the law of God or the seriousness of your sin. 2) Do not live for other people's opinions. 3) Do not focus on possessions, either by laying up treasures or by being consumed with worry. 4) Do not focus on other's faults, neglecting yours. 5) Beware of false prophets.

Instead, what should we do? Ask, knock, seek, enter by the narrow gate, build our lives upon his words. "Pursue his kingdom and righteousness" (Matt 6:33)

Todd Martin

Connection with Older Testament
Exodus 20

For the Kids
Many children really want a lot of things. They want this new toy or that new game. They think a lot about what they want to have or do. But Jesus told the people the way of wisdom. What did he say they should be wanting? His kingdom and his righteousness. Help your children understand how to seek first the kingdom of God and his righteousness and why this kingdom and righteousness are worth seeking above all else.

Prayer Prompts
1. Ask the Lord to reveal the motives behind your actions. Is it merely to have a good reputation or is your primary motivation the glory of God?

2. Perhaps you need to repent of "appearing to please God."

3. Ask the Lord to increase your faith. He is good. He is sovereign. He can be trusted in a fallen world more than material things that so easily ensnare us. Repent of trusting in yourself. Find provision and comfort in the God who rules the universe for your good if you are in Christ.

◆

WEEK 39: DAY 2
Matthew 8

Key Text

"When Jesus heard this he was amazed and said to those who followed him, 'I tell you the truth, I have not found such faith in anyone in Israel!'" Matthew 8:10

The Priority of Faith: Entering into the Kingdom of Heaven

"I tell you, many will come from the east and west to share the banquet with Abraham, Isaac, and Jacob in the kingdom of heaven, but the sons of the kingdom will be thrown out into the outer darkness" (vv. 11-12). This prophecy points ahead to the multi-national, multi-ethnic, global expansion of the Church. It points to the crowd spoken of in Revelation, when there will be an "enormous crowd that no one could count, made up of persons from every nation, tribe, people, and language, standing before the throne and before the Lamb" (Rev. 7:9). It points to the great marriage supper of the Lamb, when the crowd will cry out, "Hallelujah! For the Lord our God, the All-Powerful, reigns! Let us rejoice and exult and give him glory because the wedding celebration of the Lamb has come" (Rev. 19:6-7). On that day, Abraham will be there, as will Isaac, Jacob, the centurion, and all others who have trusted Christ. What a glorious day! But not everyone will be there. Some of the 'sons of the kingdom' (ethnically Jewish) will be cast out. What's the difference between those who are included in the great crowd and those who are in the outer darkness? Faith.

The faith of the centurion is a foreshadow of the faith of all those from the nations who trust in Christ. He is one who 1) knows he is not worthy, 2) comes to Jesus for help, 3) believes in Christ's power, and 4) trusts his word.

316

That is the testimony of every believer, and there is a seat at the table for all who do likewise.

Todd Martin

Connection with Older Testament
Genesis 15:6

For the Kids
Take your children outside, lock the door to your house, and make sure to take a key with you. With the door locked, have your children try to get inside your house. When they realize they can't, that they need a key, use your key to open the door. Explain to your children that, in our sin, we are locked out of the kingdom of heaven. Jesus is the door to the kingdom, and the door is opened by the key of faith in Christ. Using the centurion as an example and using the last paragraph of today's devotion, show your children what faith pleasing to God looks like.

Prayer Prompts
1. Praise the Lord for the gift of faith he has bestowed on you: a faith that has ushered you into the kingdom of God.
2. Pray that God would grant saving faith to non-Christian people you know, such as your children, extended family, friends, neighbors, and coworkers.

◆

WEEK 39: DAY 3
Matthew 9

Key Text
"'But so that you may know that the Son of Man has authority on earth to forgive sins'—then he said to the paralytic—'Stand up, take your stretcher, and go home.'" Matthew 9:6

The Miracles of Jesus: The Son of Man's Power over the Curse

There are so many different ways that one can assert power and great authority. Some people believe they need to be the craziest or the loudest to show they have power and authority, while others act as dictators where they slander their opponents and gossip about their competition. In Matthew 9, we see Jesus declare that he has all authority and is all-powerful. He does not shout it from the rooftops or go to the most powerful and famous people in Jerusalem. He goes to the outskirts of town, or as we may call it today, the down and out, redneck parts of town. Here it is that he asserts his power and authority through radical and outrageous compassion. He is unbelievably kind and merciful to all through proclaiming the gospel and healing every disease and every affliction. Most assuredly people were shocked and amazed at his service and mercy towards these people. What if we, the people of God, chose to show this same compassion and mercy to our culture and neighbors? What would happen? What kind of reaction would we get? Let us assert the preeminence of Christ by being radically and outrageously compassionate.

Jeremy Haskins, "Conquering with Compassion," Preached 10/14/2012, Ashland in MC Website, Accessed 3 December 2015, Available from http://www.ashlandmc.org/podcast/conquering-with-compassion-1/.

Connection with Older Testament
Micah 6:8

For the Kids
Have your kids sit in a chair, and then tie their hands behind their back so that they cannot untie the knot. Let your kids try for a minute to undo the knot. Once they cannot, go undo it for them. Let them know that God placed a curse on the world in Genesis 3 that no one could undo, like their knot. But then Jesus came to save them to undo the knot as the Great Rescuer. He has the power of God.

Prayer Prompts
1. When was the last time that you shocked someone with your unbelievable

compassion and mercy? Ask the Holy Spirit to give you shockingly outrageous compassion for your neighbors this week.

2. How do you respond to the compassion and grace of others? Pray that you would become humbler and receive outrageous compassion and grace humbly.

◆

WEEK 39: DAY 4

Matthew 12

Key Text

"'For the Son of Man is lord of the Sabbath.'" Matthew 12:8

Lord of the Sabbath: Interpreting the Law in Light of Christ

The Sabbath was meant for freedom. After the Israelites had been under Pharaoh's oppression for 400 years, laboring for him day in and day out, God sets them free. Then he gives them the Law at Sinai. Included in the Law is Sabbath. One day in seven was to be dedicated especially for rest and worship. Unlike under Pharaoh, the peoples' worth in the eyes of the true God was not in their production but in their person. God valued the people not for what they could do but, rather, for who they were as his people. Sabbath was a weekly reminder to the people of their identity before God.

Sadly, by the time Jesus was alive, Sabbath had been turned into a burden. The religious leaders had applied countless laws to its observance. Once again, people were being measured on what they could do over who they were. The laws were so detailed that the Pharisees accused Jesus of breaking the Sabbath because he rubbed his hands together with grain between them (Luke 16:1). Jesus took this accusation as a moment to clarify his purpose and the intent of the Law in light of it.

He reminded the Pharisees that the Sabbath was about mercy and freedom (v. 7). It was never meant to be a burden. How does he know? Jesus is "Lord of the Sabbath." His yoke is easy, his burden light (Matt. 11:30). He offers freedom and mercy. He came to fulfill the Law (Matt. 5:17). Jesus reminds the people that the Law was never meant to earn favor with God; rather, it was to be a blessing because God has already favored his people.

Connection with Older Testament

Exodus 20:8-11; 1 Samuel 21:1-6

For the Kids

Have your kids do a physical activity until they cannot continue, pushups for example. Then when then want to rest, make up rules that dictate how they can rest. For example, do not let them sit down. Tell them they are not allowed to breath heavily. Anything they attempt to do, don't allow it. Then explain that is what the religious leaders had done to the Sabbath during Jesus' time. Yet, Jesus came to remove the burdens the religious leaders had placed on the people. He did so by fulfilling the Law and dying to take away our sins.

Prayer Prompts

1. Praise God that Jesus is greater than both the Law and David. Praise the Lord that he fulfills the Law so that we might be freed from its bondage.

2. Ask God to forgive you when you attempt to influence him with your effort to win his approval.

3. Ask God to help you learn what it means to rest in Jesus, the Lord of the Sabbath.

◆

WEEK 39: DAY 5

Matthew 13

Key Text

"Then the disciples came to him and said, 'Why do you speak to them in parables?' He replied, 'You have been given the opportunity to know the secrets of the kingdom of heaven, but they have not.'" Matthew 13:10-11

Kingly Wisdom: Parables of the Mysterious Kingdom of God

Jesus' parables have a double effect. To some—such as the Pharisees—the parables keep the message of God's kingdom hidden, and to others—such as the disciples—they reveal powerful truths. Getting a clear explanation of the parables is an exclusive blessing, a gift. The disciples are privileged in that way, and so are we, through what is recorded for us in Scripture. Consider the following truths that are revealed:

1) Kingdom work begins with the word of the kingdom, which must be understood.

2) The reality of the kingdom divides people into two groups. There are the sons of the kingdom, and there are those outside the kingdom. The sons are the ones who understand, the fruitful. The other group, those outside, are represented in the various parables as the unfruitful, the weeds, and the bad fish. Their destination is to be burned in the place where there is "weeping and gnashing of teeth." (vv. 30, 40-42, 50)

3) The sons of the kingdom gain the kingdom through great cost (giving of all they have) but the kingdom they gain is of immeasurably greater value.

4) The kingdom, though it starts small, will grow astonishingly, as seen in the fruitful crop of a hundredfold, in the leaven throughout the flour, and the growth of the tiny mustard seed into a great tree.

5) History is marching toward a day of 'harvest,' which will be a joyful day for the sons of the kingdom and a day of destruction for those outside the kingdom.

How shall we respond to Jesus's teaching about God's kingdom that is already here in Jesus but not yet established in full? Seek to understand him. In wisdom, count all else loss and embrace his kingdom. In the process, you'll become a fruit-bearing part of the story of the growth of the kingdom as we await the day of harvest.

Todd Martin

Connection with Older Testament
Isaiah 6; 1 Kings 4:29-34

For the Kids
Ask your children how they feel when you share a secret with them (such as

what's inside someone's birthday package). Why do they feel special? They feel special because not everyone knows the secret, and they wouldn't know if you didn't tell them. When God helps us understand something about the ways of his kingdom, it's a special gift! How do we honor the gift? By listening in faith!

Prayer Prompts

1. Ask the Lord for his wisdom to help you better understand the mysteries of the kingdom so that you might better understand the Bible and live as more faithful citizens of the kingdom.

2. Praise the Lord that he has revealed the secrets of the kingdom of heaven to us—that he has given us eyes to see and ears to hear of the glorious reality of the eternal kingdom of God.

◆

WEEK 40: DAY 1
Matthew 14

Key Text

"Then those who were in the boat worshipped him, saying, 'Truly you are the Son of God.'" Matthew 14:33

A New Exodus in Christ: Wilderness Manna and Sea Crossing

Upon hearing of John the Baptist's heinous murder at the hands of Herod the tetrarch, Jesus went to a desolate place to grieve. Yet, the ministry pressed in on him. Followers soon surrounded him. Rather than push them away, he taught them. These events led to a display of Jesus' divine power.

At first glance, this series of events is amazing. Jesus feeds more than 5,000 people with a few loaves of bread and a couple of fish! He walked on water! It becomes even more amazing when you move beyond a first glance. The New Testament is replete with examples of how Jesus Christ is a second, better Moses. The book of Hebrews moves this idea from illusion to statement (Heb. 3:1-6).

Moses led his people out of the bondage in Egypt by crossing the Red Sea. Once in the wilderness, Moses appealed to God for food. God gave the people manna from heaven. Here in this chapter, we see Jesus crossing a sea and providing food, but, unlike Moses who must appeal to God, Jesus preforms these works in his own power. Jesus created the sea (Col. 1:16). He is the bread of life (John 6:35). In this one chapter, we see Jesus taking up and surpassing Moses' ministry.

Jesus is better than Moses because he is God. He is not just a prophet. He is God's Son who came to free his people from their bondage to sin. The freedom that Jesus provides is greater than being freed from Pharaoh's physical oppression. Jesus frees us from eternal damnation. He is greater than Moses.

Adam York

Connection with Older Testament
Exodus 14-16; 1 Kings 17:9-16; 2 Kings 4:42-44

For the Kids
Ask your kids what makes something better. Why do people stand in line for things like new phones? Why do new computers work better than old ones? The reason people are willing to stand in line is because they believe a new phone can do more and is better than what they have currently. New computers work better because they are superior. Similarly, Jesus is superior to Moses. He did something Moses could not. He removed our sin through his death on the cross.

Prayer Prompts
1. Praise the Lord that he has provided for us an exodus from sin and death through faith in Christ. Jesus is the long-awaited Messiah.
2. Ask God to remind your family daily that all we need is in Christ.

◆

WEEK 40: DAY 2
John 6

Key Text

"Jesus said to them, 'I am the bread of life. The one who comes to me will never go hungry, and the one who believes in me will never be thirsty.'" John 6:35

The Bread of Life: Jesus is the True Manna

We all are very aware of our needs, and a sense of scarcity or fear of poverty can motivate us to work or even cause some to be anxious. Jesus' message of fulfilling our deepest needs was so often misunderstood because our perceived needs are so temporal. Many of Jesus' followers could not see past their immediate desires, and this new prophet seemed a promising source of continual provision. He reminded them of Moses and of God's provision of manna for the Israelites in the wilderness. The promise of food and healing seemed to them the ultimate prize.

But Jesus had much bigger things in mind. He saw them desperately grasping for the things that don't last, and he offered something that would last forever. He used the known to teach them the unknown, taking physical realities to communicate spiritual truths. Their hunger and thirst were just glimpses of their real helplessness. God's feeding of their forefathers was a picture of his ultimate provision that would later come.

And now, Jesus is offering the final solution to their hopeless situation, the *food* and *drink* that would not just keep them alive but would give them real life. Jesus held up their daily physical provision as a symbol pointing to their need to trust and believe in the sacrifice of his body and the spilling of his own blood for their salvation. Even having enough bread could not save them from death, but he was offering "living bread."

John Martin

Connection with Older Testament
Exodus 16

For the Kids
As you sit down today to eat a meal, talk to your children about why we eat.

324

We eat to get energy. We eat to remove hunger pains. We eat to keep our bodies alive. These are all good reasons to eat. Then ask your children to think about why it is people still die even though we eat food that our bodies need to stay alive. Use this as an opportunity to talk about sin. Then teach your children that Jesus is the bread of life who came down from heaven. His body is the bread that gives eternal life over sin to all who surrender their lives to him.

Prayer Prompts

1. Praise God that he provided his only Son as the bread of life, broken for your soul's satisfaction and salvation.

2. Pray for the spiritual and physical needs in your life and the lives of others to be satisfied by and through Jesus Christ.

◆

WEEK 40: DAY 3

John 8

Key Text

"Jesus said to them, 'I tell you the solemn truth, before Abraham came into existence, I am!'" John 8:58

Before Abraham Was, I AM: The Divinity of Jesus

In John 8, the Lord Jesus provides for us one of the most shocking statements pertaining to who he is as a person. Reminiscent of the LORD revealing himself to Moses as I AM (Ex. 3:14), Jesus declares himself to be of the same essence as the LORD by stating that he existed as the eternal I AM before Abraham and before Moses. And with this declaration of his divinity, his Jewish audience immediately sought to stone him to death.

Lest we think too critically about the Jews, we must remember that it is an act of God's revealing grace that any of us see and believe in Jesus as God. The Old Testament was very foggy about the coming messiah with respect to his divinity. In fact, most faithful Jews would likely have not expected the messiah to be divine. Only by God's grace do any of us understand and accept that Jesus the Christ is both God and man. Let us be thankful for God's grace to us that causes us to understand the truth about Christ. Let us be merciful to those such as Muslims, Jehovah's Witnesses, and others who are blinded to the truth that Jesus is God. Let us take the gospel to them boldly, pleading with the Father to reveal truth so that the blind may see and live by faith in the person and work of Jesus, the great I AM.

Jon Canler

Connection with Older Testament
Exodus 3:1-14

For the Kids
Ask your children, "How old is Jesus?" Was he alive before Mom and Dad were? Before Grandma? Before Grandma's grandma? Yes! Jesus was alive before everyone. When we celebrate the birth of Jesus at Christmas, we celebrate a special time because he was born a baby. But, it wasn't his beginning! He was there before the world was made. He always was, he is, and he always will be. He is God, the ageless one. There was never a time in which he began. How does it make you feel to know that Jesus always was?

Prayer Prompts
1. Rejoice in the fact that Jesus is so much more than a wise teacher. He is God. He has freed us from God's curse on sin because he is able as God to do so. We can endure life in a fallen world because our King is sovereign over the world and works all things for our good.
2. Pray for those you know who don't see Jesus as I AM. Pray that they would rightly come to understand who Jesus is and turn to him by faith to be saved.

◆

WEEK 40: DAY 4
John 10

Key Text

"'I am the good shepherd. The good shepherd lays down his life for the sheep.'" John 10:11

The Good Shepherd: Loving His Sheep to Death

In John 10, we see one of the most beautiful descriptions of our need for and dependence on Christ: the shepherd and his sheep. Sheep are unintelligent, totally dependent, helpless, and slow creatures. They even eat things that may harm them. However, the sheep are the most prized possession of the shepherd. If the sheep are harmed, the shepherd is harmed as well. The shepherd has wholly committed himself to the sheep for he has chosen them out of the world and will care and fight for them. The shepherd is the protector, provider, and keeper of the sheep. The sheep know this as well for they are always prepared to change their direction based solely on the voice of their shepherd. His voice directs their every movement. Sheep are not self-sufficient or capable of making their own decisions. They do not pick and choose which directions they follow. If the sheep go their own way, they will inevitably lead themselves down a path of destruction.

The same is true for us. We are the sheep in need of Christ, the great Shepherd. The best thoughts and ideas we have ever had apart from Jesus would lead us to destruction as well. The battle that we fight every day of our lives is the same as the sheep: do I desire and am I prepared to change every decision of my life based on the word of the Shepherd? Or do I pick and choose which commands I follow?

David Prince, "Knowing God as Shepherd," Preached 9/13/2015, Prince on Preaching Website, Accessed 4 December 2015, Available from http://www.davidprince.com/2015/09/13/knowing-god-as-shepherd-john-101-15/.

Connection with Older Testament

Ezekiel 34; Psalm 23

For the Kids

Think of the jobs of a shepherd and sheep in a field. What should the shepherd do? (feed the sheep, protect the sheep, lead the sheep, etc.) What should the sheep do? (follow) Who has the hardest job? The shepherd! Good news! Jesus says he is committed to us to be the Good Shepherd. Our only task is to follow him in his goodness toward us!

Prayer Prompts

1. Thank God that he has committed to be your Shepherd.
2. Ask God to enable you to respond to everything he says today.

◆

WEEK 40: DAY 5

John 11

Key Text

"Jesus said to her, 'I am the resurrection and the life. The one who believes in me will live even if he dies'" John 11:25

I Am the Resurrection and the Life: Jesus' Power over Death

In John 11, we see Jesus coming to the funeral home to see his friend Lazarus. We have all been to a funeral home and know what to expect there. We will see mourners who have an "others-centered" focus on the people who are still living instead of the dead. All will encourage the living to delight in the memories that God has given them and tell them to focus on the community of people who are here to support and love them. All of us do this because, in the face of death, we look for some source of comfort and a sense of peace.

This is also what Martha expected of Jesus as he approached her. He, however, gave her the ultimate source of comfort and sense of peace. He states that he *is* the life and the resurrection. In this very short and simple statement, Christ turns the idea of mourning and hope on its head. He states that the goal is not to think about provisions for the here and now, but instead the goal is always to worship, magnify, glory, and exalt in the person of Christ. He *is* comfort. He *is* peace. Without him, these things do not exist. He reminds us that the focus must always be on him. Without him, we have nothing. However, with him, we have everything.

David Prince, "When Jesus Shows Up at the Funeral Home," Preached 4/18/2010, Prince on Preaching Website, Accessed 4 December 2015, Available from http://www.davidprince.com/2010/04/18/when-jesus-shows-up-at-the-funeral-home-john-1117-27/.

Connection with Older Testament

Psalm 16

For the Kids

Talk to your children about baptism. Ask if they know why we put people under water and bring them back up? [Lower your hands and bring them up with each of the following three sentences, to help them imagine the motion.] First, it shows us that two thousand years ago, Jesus died and rose again!. Second, it shows us that the person who has trusted in Jesus has changed; the way they used to be is gone, and their life is new because of Jesus. But third, it also shows the future. Jesus said that, even if someone dies (and we all do eventually), if they believe in Jesus, they will live! There's eternal life in Jesus, the resurrection and the life!

Prayer Prompts

1. Where do you look for comfort in your times of unbelievable grief and pain? Pray that God will remind you to look to him for ultimate comfort and peace in all of your pain.

2. Do you find yourself struggling to worship Christ in all things? Pray that the Spirit would give you a God-centered heart that seeks Christ's magnification in all things.

◆

WEEK 41: DAY 1

Matthew 16

Key Text

"But he turned and said to Peter, 'Get behind me, Satan! You are a stumbling

329

block to me, because you are not setting your mind on God's interests, but on man's.'" Matthew 16:23

Peter's Confession: A Disciple Called Satan

A disciple called Satan?! What are we to make of this? In Matthew 16, we see Jesus ask the disciples the question that all of us have to answer: Who do you say that Jesus is? Is he a prophet? Is he a forerunner of the Messiah? Or is he the Messiah himself? In order to answer this question, however, we must understand what Jesus must do to truly understand who he is. That is the challenge that we all face when answering this ultimate question.

All of us are in danger of separating who Christ is from what he must do. Christ knew that we needed our sins forgiven. And he knew that there was only one way, one plan to complete that. That plan always was, from the beginning of time, for the Son of Man to go to the cross. However, Satan tempted Christ repeatedly to embrace the kingdom without the cross, thereby nullifying the plan. Satan always desired for Christ to bypass the cross because that means that he would win.

Do you see why Peter was called Satan? Peter desired to bypass the cross in order to receive the kingdom. In this statement, he was in league with Satan, as are we when we believe that, as sons of God, no suffering should come to us. The kingdom that we sometimes desire does not include the call for us to carry our cross. This desire comes when we set our minds on the things of man and not the things of God. So how do you answer this question? Who do you say that Jesus is?

David Prince, "A Disciple Called Satan: When Knowing Jesus is not Enough," Preached 2/22/2009, Prince on Preaching Website, Accessed 4 December 2015, Available from http://www.davidprince.com/2009/02/22/a-disciple-called-satan-when-knowing-jesus-is-not-enough-matthew-1613-23/.

Connection with Older Testament

Isaiah 53

For the Kids

Talk to your children about something really painful that you've experienced. Ask them if they too can give an example. Then ask them if they thought the pain and suffering had any good with it. Remind your children that suffering, as painful as it is, is part of God's plan for us. Our greatest good, our salvation, is dependent on a crucified Christ who died for our sins. And our being made like him for all eternity is dependent on suffering that leads us to die to ourselves daily. Pray for wisdom to see God's good purposes for us in our suffering. Pray for grace to reject the satanic logic that says we can have a crown of glory without a cross of shame.

Prayer Prompts

1. Pray that God would allow you to always set your mind on the things of God instead of the things of man.

2. Praise God for the suffering in your life that points your heart and mind to him.

◆

WEEK 41: DAY 2

Matthew 17

Key Text

"While he was still speaking, a bright cloud overshadowed them, and a voice from the cloud said, 'This is my one dear Son, in whom I take great delight. Listen to him!'" Matthew 17:5

The Transfiguration of Jesus: The Prophet Greater than Moses

In Matthew 17, we encounter the transfiguration of Christ. Can you imagine the scene? Peter, James, and John are standing at the foot of a mountain seeing manifestations of glory. Glory is emanating from Christ making him bright and shining. Then Moses and Elijah appear, and Peter volunteers to build three tabernacles to mark this point in history. There is only one problem with his desire: there are not three equal players in redemptive history. There is only one. Moses appeared to show that Christ fulfilled the Law of Moses, and Elijah appeared to show that Christ fulfilled the message of the prophets. Jesus is fulfilling all of redemptive history with his life. At this moment, we see that the issue is no longer what the Law and the prophets say. The issue is what the Law and the prophets point to—Christ. Christ is everything we need. He is our hope. He is the answer to all of our longings. We need to abandon trust in ourselves and follow him. There are no other gods because there is no other name other than Christ.

David Prince, "Making God in Our Image: Our Idols and The Voice from the Mountains," Preached 7/10/2011, Prince on Preaching Website, Accessed 4 December 2015, Available from http://www.davidprince.com/2011/07/10/making-god-in-our-image-our-idols-and-the-voice-from-the-mountains-exodus-203-matthew-171-8/.

Connection with Older Testament
Deuteronomy 18:15-22

For the Kids
Imagine that three people showed up at your house from the office of the President of the United States to give you good news. Imagine two of them coming with official badges such that you knew these people were sent by the president. Then imagine the third person, who you knew was important, surprisingly showed a shiny badge that said he was the president himself! How would you respond? Would you not respect the two people who were part of the president's staff but honor the president because the president is superior to the staff? That's the point of today's reading. Moses and Elijah were great prophets, men sent by God to point to Jesus. But Jesus is God, which means he alone is to be worshipped being superior to Moses and Elijah.

Prayer Prompts
1. In what parts of your life do you trust in self instead of Christ? Ask the Spirit to enable you to abandon self and trust Christ.
2. Ask God to help you listen and obey the word of Christ today.

WEEK 41: DAY 3

Matthew 18

Key Text

"Then Peter came to him and said, 'Lord, how many times must I forgive my brother who sins against me? As many as seven times?' Jesus said to him, 'Not seven times, I tell you, but seventy-seven times.'" Matthew 18:21-22

Kingdom Citizenship: Pursuing Repentance and Forgiveness

When you compare the world in which we live with the kingdom of heaven that Jesus describes, it seems like the kingdom of heaven is completely upside down from this world. Jesus says that the greatest in his kingdom are children, that the kingdom is so worth your while that you should maim yourself, if necessary, to enter it. According to the kingdom economy, you should leave ninety-nine sheep to find one that is lost. The kingdom ethic requires wild and lavish forgiveness. All of this seems backwards. In truth, the fallen, sinful world in which we live is what is upside down and backward.

Therefore, we who live in this upside down and backwards world are those who need to be righted. It is not the kingdom of heaven that needs to conform to us. We must conform to the kingdom of heaven. We must repent of the backward way in which we have lived. We must turn to live like citizens of the kingdom of heaven. Living thusly is impossible apart from Jesus, the King of the kingdom.

Because we have rejected the kingdom way of life, we have incurred a massive debt we cannot repay. Only the King can forgive it. Like the servant in the parable who owed 10,000 talents (equivalent to $6 billion in today's money), there is nothing we could ever do to pay off our debt. The King must forgive us. Amazingly, he does, and he invites us into his kingdom through repentance from sin and faith in the King. Since we have been so lavishly forgiven, we should be a people who lavishly forgive. In other words, we should be people who live as citizens of the kingdom of heaven.

Adam York

333

Connection with Older Testament
2 Chronicles 7

For the Kids
Share with your children about some appropriate-to-share sin that God has forgiven you. Share with them how thankful you are that God has forgiven you. Now share with them some appropriate-to-share sin that someone committed against you. Help them to see how being forgiven by God in Christ (immense debt paid for you) frees you to forgive others (lesser debt paid by you).

Prayer Prompts
1. Thank God that he lavishly forgives us in Christ.
2. Ask God to help you live as a citizen of the kingdom of heaven who practices repentance and forgiveness daily.

◆

WEEK 41: DAY 4
Matthew 19

Key Text
"Jesus said to him, 'If you wish to be perfect, go, sell your possessions and give the money to the poor, and you will have treasure in heaven. Then come, follow me.'" Matthew 19:21

Clinging to Jesus: The Only Way for Sinners to Enter the Kingdom
In Matthew 19, we see the story of the rich young ruler. This young man approaches Christ and asks what he must do to inherit eternal life. Jesus says it very simply: you must obey the commandments and love your neighbor as yourself. Boldly, the ruler replies that he has kept all of the commandments from an early age.

In this statement, he shows that he has a very superficial and surface understanding of the commandments. He wasn't thinking anything of his desires, thoughts, and longings, but instead was focusing only on his specific acts as though a desire is not an act and as though a thought is irrelevant to God. He could not have been further away from a true understanding of the commandments. He was saying these things to the God who created the commandments, to the One who is the ultimate fulfillment of the commandments!

In truth, if he is not bowing before Christ in faith, he does not love God as the commandments demand. If he does not love his neighbor in the same fashion that Christ loves his neighbor, then he is not meeting the demands of the commandments either. Truthfully, there is not one moment apart from Jesus that anyone has ever kept and obeyed any of the commandments. Do you hear that? No one…ever!

Ultimately, Jesus tells the young ruler that he must repudiate his idol (his possessions) and, in turn, follow him. Sadly, the ruler is unable to fulfill that command. But he now knows the truth, the truth that there is only one way for a sinner to inherit eternal life. That one way is to cling to the only one who has ever fully met the demands of every commandment—Christ himself. Trust him with your life and follow him, for there is no other way to meet the demands of the commandments.

David Prince, "Jesus & the 10 Commandments: God, Men, & Things," Preached 7/3/2011, Prince on Preaching Website, Accessed 4 December 2015, Available from http://www.davidprince.com/2011/07/03/jesus-the-10-commandments-god-men-things-exodus-201-2-matthew-1916-22/.

Connection with Older Testament
Exodus 20:1-3

For the Kids
Have your children imagine walking into a bank with a lot of money to deposit. Have them imagine asking the teller if they could go into the bank's safe by themselves to drop off the money. Ask them if they think the bank would let them in the safe by themselves. Tell them that the answer is no. It doesn't matter how much money you have, there's only one way to get in the safe: going with a bank worker who has authority to bring them in. Tell your children

that the kingdom of God works the same way. No amount of money or good works gets you in. Only Jesus can give access. We must cling to Jesus alone or remain outside of the kingdom.

Prayer Prompts

1. What idols are you still clinging to in your life? Ask God to cause you to repudiate and avoid them.

2. What is your understanding of the commandments? Are you more aligned with the rich young ruler or Christ? Pray for a deeper understanding of the Law and your lack of ability to meet its requirements.

◆

WEEK 41: DAY 5

Luke 19

Key Text

"So he ran on ahead and climbed up into a sycamore tree to see him, because Jesus was going to pass that way." Luke 19:4

Zacchaeus: Salvation and Self-Forgetfulness

In Luke 19, we are introduced to Zacchaeus. Zacchaeus was a very prominent man in a very notorious way. He was a chief tax collector and, accordingly, was very wealthy. Because of his wealth, he had a very high social standing with his peers in Jericho. In this section of Scripture, however, we do not see a man acting as a man with a very high social standing. We see him climb up a tree just so he could see Christ. This was a very undignified (not to mention strange) thing for a man of his wealth to do. In fact, he was acting more like a child than he was a wealthy man.

As a parent, I have seen firsthand that a child does not obsess about the viewpoints of others. They are not concerned about their social standing or the way that anyone sees them. In this way, children and Zacchaeus, in this situation, are self-forgetful. Zacchaeus was so enamored by his desire to see Christ that he ignored social norms and the thoughts of those around him. He got lost in the good news of Christ!

In the instant that he saw Christ, the way that Zacchaeus viewed the world changed. He no longer started with himself and saw the world out. All that mattered to him was Christ. His world no longer revolved around himself. Instead, his world was now centered and focused on Christ, and he did not care what he looked like to the world around him.

When we start with us and see the world out, we are always self-conscious. This is a fight that we will always battle. We cannot see the world from us out and follow Christ. We are to see the world God out, cross out, others out, and then consider the way we fit in that story. In order to win this battle, the gospel gives us the gift of becoming self-forgetful because we are humbled in the sight of God. This is what we see from Zacchaeus in Luke 19.

David Prince, "The Gospel Freedom of Being Fools for Christ's Sake," Preached 4/26/2015, Prince on Preaching Website, Accessed 4 December 2015, Available from http://www.davidprince.com/2015/04/26/the-gospel-freedom-of-being-fools-for-christs-sake-luke-191-10/.

Connection with Older Testament
Ezekiel 34:11

For the Kids
Ask your children if there is something they really want. (Wait for answers, such as a particular toy, a movie, a game, etc.). Explain that when we are so focused on the things we want, it's hard to think about anything else. This is the way we should be about Jesus because of who he is and what he has done for us! Pray with them that God will help them want Jesus more than anything else in this life.

Prayer Prompts
1. Do you have self-forgetful humility? Pray for the Spirit to transform the way you view other's opinions of you and your faith.
2. Pray for the Spirit to grant you the ability to be lost in the good news of Christ.

WEEK 42: DAY 1
Matthew 21

Key Text
"This took place to fulfill what was spoken by the prophet" Matthew 21:4

The King Has Come: Jesus's Triumphal Entry into Jerusalem

The time had come. After a long wait, the promised one was here. Jerusalem had awaited this moment for centuries. The one to restore God's people had arrived. Celebration was the appropriate response, so crowds gathered around and followed Jesus. They laid branches on the road as a welcome mat. They chanted, "Hosanna to the Son of David! Blessed is the one who comes in the name of the Lord! Hosanna in the highest!" The whole city was in an uproar (v. 10).

In the midst of the fanfare, Jesus came striding into the city on a donkey, hardly a kingly steed. In this case, however, it was this lowly steed that carried the King of kings and the Lord of lords. The crowds that were so jovial didn't even get it. They saw Jesus as just a prophet (v. 11). Their inability to see meant that, in just a few days, the same crowds would curse Jesus rather than praise him. Rather than bless him, they will chant, "Crucify him!"

Jesus entered the city on a lowly donkey because he is a king who did not come to be served, but came to serve and to give his life a ransom for many (Mark 10:45). This King's mission was to give of himself, which he would do most supremely a week later upon the cross. Celebrating Jesus as a conquering king was a few days premature. Jesus' ultimate victory would be won through his death, burial, and resurrection as he conquered death and gave victory over sin to any who believe in him.

Adam York

Connection with Older Testament
Zechariah 9

For the Kids

Make a list of the typical characteristics of a king with your kids. Maybe the list would include things like castles, royal clothes, or a kingdom. Then compare those characteristics with the King of kings, Jesus. Then, share why Jesus is a different king, a king who came riding on a donkey. He is the king of a different kingdom. His kingdom is marked by service, mercy, grace, forgiveness, and the death of all evil.

Prayer Prompts

1. Thank God that he keeps his promises. He promised a savior, and he fulfilled his promise in his Son, Jesus.
2. Ask God for the courage to live a life of service like our King.

◆

WEEK 42: DAY 2
Matthew 22

Key Text

"He said to them, 'How then does David by the Spirit call him "Lord," saying, "The Lord said to my lord, 'Sit at my right hand, until I put your enemies under your feet'"?'" Matthew 22:43-44

Jesus: Son of David and Lord of David

The religious leaders of Jesus' day had a very specific agenda regarding what to do with Jesus. They saw Jesus as a threat to their authority and even to their assurance of their own standing with God. They knew he was challenging the self-assurance of their own goodness. If they could prove him wrong, they could keep their pride and autonomy intact.

The Sadducees and Pharisees thought they could outsmart Jesus with trick questions and false pretenses, but they were stumped by his knowledge and insight. He could not be fooled and lured into a linguistic trap or logical error, but it wasn't merely a matter of being outwitted.

The issue then, as now, is about Jesus' identity, not just his teaching. His authority did not come from his superior knowledge and debate skills. Once his opponents were silenced, he got to the source of their misunderstanding. He was not a mere man clamoring for influence or power. He was something much more. His question in Matthew 22:42 was asked in order to expose the error in their thinking. While they could readily accept that their coming Messiah would be a decedent of the revered King David, it seems never to have occurred to them that this same Messiah would be even *greater* than David.

These experts in the Scriptures had missed something, and they were still missing it even as the Messiah stood in front them. God's Messiah had an authority they had not imagined, a nobility beyond their assumptions. He was no mere "Teacher" (v. 16); he was their King.

John Martin

Connection with Older Testament
Psalm 110

For the Kids
Ask your children this riddle: What is black, white, and read/red all over. Let them think about it for a while knowing that they will think "read/red" is a color (red) before they think about "read/red" in relation to reading a book. If they don't guess it, tell them the answer is a newspaper. Then tell your children that Matthew 22 contains something like a riddle. How is it that a son of David could also be lord over David? Explain this by teaching your children how Jesus is the eternal God and how he became a son of David when he took on flesh in Mary's womb.

Prayer Prompts
1. Praise God for faithfully fulfilling his promises to send one from the line of David to rule and reign as the King of kings and Lord of lords.
2. Pray for Jesus Christ to be received as King and Lord in the lives of the unbelievers you know.

◆

WEEK 42: DAY 3
Luke 22

Key Text
"Then he took bread, and after giving thanks he broke it and gave it to them, saying, 'This is my body which is given for you. Do this in remembrance of me.'" Luke 22:19

The Lord's Supper: Jesus as the Passover Lamb and Blood of the New Covenant

Jesus' final hours before the crucifixion were filled with events and meaning. God's plan, which he had orchestrated through centuries, was coming to a crescendo. The timing was no coincidence.

Since the inception of the nation of Israel, the people of God had been celebrating the Passover meal, a recognition of God's spectacular intervention in their suffering under generations of slavery. God had worked wondrous miracles seen by millions, and his salvation culminated in the threat of death for every first born in the land. For the Jews, their protection from the angel of death came from a sacrificial lamb whose blood on the door of their homes would cause the wrath of God to *pass over* them. The result was their freedom from Egypt's bondage.

For ages, the people of God celebrated this redemption, which looked forward to another redemption. But as usual, many would miss the grand scale of God's redemptive work. Jesus' Passover meal with his disciples was not a recognition of Israel's political past; it was the institution of a new covenant sealed by his own blood (v. 20). Jesus was the Passover Lamb, but his death would not merely free God's people from an oppressive dictatorship to regain national sovereignty. It would free them from slavery to sin and bring them into the very kingdom of God.

John Martin

Connection with Older Testament

Exodus 12

For the Kids

Talk to your children about why we celebrate Memorial Day, Thanksgiving, or Christmas. It is to remember and celebrate something important that has happened. Explain that Jesus calls us to remember the most important event in history—his death on the cross. We do this during the Lord's Supper, where we remember that Jesus's body was broken and his blood was poured out on the cross for our sins.

Prayer Prompts

1. Pray for God to impress upon your heart and mind the greatness of his grace in passing over our sins and placing them on his Son, Jesus Christ.
2. Pray for opportunities to share this good news with the unbelievers in your life.

◆

WEEK 42: DAY 4

John 13

Key Text

"Because Jesus knew that the Father had handed all things over to him, and that he had come from God and was going back to God, he got up from the meal, removed his outer clothes, took a towel and tied it around himself." John 13:3-4

The Lord's Supper: Jesus as the Servant Cleansing Us from Sin

Before his death, Jesus knew that he would soon be returning to his Father and to the glory of being in God's presence. Jesus shocks his disciples with an outrageous act of humility: washing their feet. This was a job that was beneath anyone but a foreign slave, and Peter could barely stomach the idea of the Messiah humiliating himself like this.

But as often before, Jesus is using something they understood to demonstrate a deeper spiritual truth. In his divinity, Jesus had humbled himself to take on humanity so that he could wash away the sins of his people and give them what only he deserved—the inheritance of the kingdom of God. The King of creation had become a servant for their sakes, and this humble act was visually portraying what he had done and was doing.

Visualizing the image of our sovereign King stooping down to our feet with a dirty towel wrapped around him should be startling but not without purpose. It should wake us up from the stupor of self-serving agendas and of grasping for advantage at the expense of others. When we think about the lavish service and shocking humility of Christ, how can we be condescending? What justification is there for self-importance? The incomprehensible gift of salvation through Jesus' humiliation and death gives us freedom to accept any dishonor, to submit to any disgrace for the sake of serving others. There is something far greater than pride in store for those who do (v. 17).

John Martin

Connection with Older Testament
Leviticus 16

For the Kids
Ask your children why we take baths. After they respond, make sure they know that we take baths to stay clean and to take care of our bodies. Instruct your children that our sin makes us spiritually dirty before a perfectly clean God. We deserve to be wiped away in judgment, but Jesus comes to cleanse from sin all who trust in him. And once cleansed through Jesus' service to us, it frees us to serve others. Help your children think about how they can serve others in light of what Jesus has done.

Prayer Prompts
1. Praise the Lord that he has served us by sacrificing his body and blood to cleanse us from our sins before God.

2. Ask the Lord for grace to help you see your life in terms of servanthood, laying your life down for your brothers and in sisters in Christ and serving those who don't know Christ so that they might see a picture of his grace through you.

◆

WEEK 42: DAY 5
John 14-16

Key Text
"'I will not abandon you as orphans, I will come to you.'" John 14:18

The Coming Holy Spirit: The Comforter of the Church in the Last Days

Jesus is leaving. He is marching to a cross to die. He is not going to be there in his physical presence anymore. Things are changing. All of these things are happening; yet, Jesus says in John 16:7, "But I tell you the truth, it is to your advantage that I am going away. For if I do not go away, the Advocate will not come to you, but if I go, I will send him to you."

The Helper is defined for us as the Holy Spirit. He is not *a* spirit but *the* Spirit. The Spirit of Christ is not an impersonal or electrical force, but rather a person. To have the Spirit of Christ is to have Christ not just with us, but in us. To be filled with the Spirit is to have the word of God dwelling richly in you (Col. 3:16)!

Jesus tells us that we, as believers in this age, are in the most privileged moment in redemptive history. The Holy Spirit is not only our Helper, Comforter, and Advocate, but he is the Spirit of truth. He is at work helping us, aiding us, and clarifying the truth. As we call upon him, we grow in the knowledge of the truth. When the Spirit of God dwells in us, it changes what we do. The Spirit of Christ is constantly at work convincing us of the gospel truth that as believers in Christ, we are forgiven and covered in righteousness.

David Prince, "The Helper (Spirit/Church)," Preached 12/30/2012, Prince on Preaching Website, Accessed 4 December 2015, Available from http://www.davidprince.com/2012/12/30/the-helper-spiritchurch-john-1415-24/.

Connection with Older Testament

Ezekiel 11:19, 36:26-27

For the Kids

Ask your children to think of a time when they had a rough day. Maybe they didn't do so well on a test. Maybe they didn't make the team. Maybe a friend or a family member got hurt. Ask them if anyone came up to them speaking words of encouragement. Similarly, the Holy Spirit of God is a person who comforts all Christians. He brings to our minds the good news of the truth as it is in Jesus to encourage us when we are tempted to live like Jesus hasn't risen from the grave on both good days and rough days.

Prayer Prompts

1. Pray that you will be reminded of your legal Advocate with the Father through Jesus Christ and of your forgiveness and imputed righteousness when you are being accused or accusing yourself.
2. Pray that God will help you richly dwell in his word and teach you his truth so that you may develop a courageous mentality because you have the Holy Spirit of Christ dwelling in you.

◆

WEEK 43: DAY 1

John 17

Key Text

"'I am praying on behalf of them. I am not praying on behalf of the world, but on behalf of those you have given me, because they belong to you.'" John 17:9

345

The Lord's Prayer: Salvation, Sanctification, and Preservation of Christians

Have you ever had a conversation where you just ran out of things to say? Even married couples can lose interest in talking such that they silently sit in a restaurant. Many find God to be the most difficult person to talk to. But not Jesus. When he prays, there is plenty to talk about. The depth of the relationship and the weightiness of the subjects show us a pattern for our own prayer life as well as a startling glimpse into the mind of Christ. We see what he is thinking about and what he cares about most.

Much of what we see him praying for is about us! His followers are not just mentioned briefly in a long list of wants. He is deeply concerned for us and pleads with God on our behalf. Not vaguely, he specifically prays about our salvation, sanctification, and preservation.

Imagine praying about something like Jesus did. Picture yourself with the same intensity and passion in your prayer life. If the idea seems foreign, think about how to align your thoughts with Christ. Consider the urgency of the salvation of others and even the urgency of your own salvation. What could possibly be more important in your conversations with the Father?

Pray with a passion for spiritual growth. Think about the significance of growing in Christ in your life and in the lives of those around you. What if you saw fathers and mothers maturing in their faith? Can you see the difference it would make in their children's lives? And pray for the preservation of the saints. Christians have an enemy, and Jesus prayed earnestly for our protection (v. 15). When we care and pray about the things Jesus does, we can see amazing things happen.

John Martin

Connection with Older Testament
Numbers 6:22-27

For the Kids
In John 17, Jesus prayed for us! How cool is that? By looking at his prayers for those of us who are Christians, it helps us understand what he thinks is most

346

important for us. In turn, let's pray the same things for our friends and fellow believers.

Prayer Prompts

1. Praise God that Jesus' prayers are heard and affirmed by God. Take comfort, O Christian, that God will preserve you in trial and will cause you to endure to till the end.

2. The answering of Jesus' prayer is the desire and delight of our God. Pray this prayer for other Christians.

◆

WEEK 43: DAY 2
Luke 23

Key Text
"'And we rightly so, for we are getting what we deserve for what we did, but this man has done nothing wrong.'" Luke 23:41

The Crucifixion: The Suffering Servant Slain for the Sins of His People

They were known as bandits, robbers, and criminals. They were terrorists. They had the same background and the same agenda. They are in the same situation; yet, they differ in their prayer directed towards Christ on the cross. The way the first criminal viewed life was with a desire to save himself. He offers a prayer without faith and without repentance. It is a prayer that uses a logic that is not so unfamiliar to us. The logic behind his prayer is "if God really loves me, he will do this…".

While the one criminal was railing against Christ, the other was silent. Something has gone on with this man. There is a reverence and humility towards God. He does not assert his rights; rather, he is confessing his sin and guilt. The basis for the first terrorist's logic is simple: real kings save themselves. The second terrorist understands that there is a kingdom beyond the cross.

We think that what makes the most sense is a king who would save himself, but if Jesus were a king who saved himself, we would be without hope.

The gospel is God's work in the world saving sinners, and, for the one who would come to him in reverence and humility confessing sin and acknowledging the perfection of Jesus, there is salvation now and forever! There is heaven!

The good news is that there is a King who does not save himself but dies for his people. There is no kingdom without a cross.

David Prince, "A Terrorist Meets Jesus: The Good News of a King Who Does Not Save Himself," Preached 4/5/2009, Prince on Preaching Website, Accessed 4 December 2015, Available from http://www.davidprince.com/2009/04/05/a-terrorist-meets-jesus-the-good-news-of-a-king-who-does-not-save-himself-luke-2326-43/.

Connection with Older Testament
Isaiah 53

For the Kids
Why did Jesus *have* to die? Being all-powerful, wasn't there another way? Was there something else he could have done? Knowing that Jesus could have saved himself from the cross but didn't helps us understand that this was the best way—God's way. Jesus dying on the cross for our sins was always God's plan to save us sinners.

Prayer Prompts
1. Pray for a reverent and humble spirit when you are faced with trials, suffering, and hardships knowing that King Jesus took on your sin and shame and died for you. Pray that you would be given wisdom from God when remembering his sacrifice on the cross.
2. Pray for the boldness to share this gospel, which is foolishness to the world but the power of God to those who are being saved.

◆

WEEK 43: DAY 3
Luke 24

Key Text

"Then he said to them, 'These are my words that I spoke to you while I was still with you, that everything written about me in the law of Moses and the prophets and the psalms must be fulfilled.' Then he opened their minds so they could understand the scriptures" Luke 24:44-45

The Resurrection: A Crucified and Resurrected Messiah Fulfilling the Old Testament

Christ has called us to the mission that he has shown us. The teachings of the Old Testament and of Jesus have unfolded before the disciples and ourselves. Jesus is showing us that all of the Scriptures are about himself and that he has not come up with something new. Rather, he is fulfilling what has already been given. The Scriptures cannot be understood without Jesus at the center.

Jesus shows us in this passage that he has been resurrected and his redeemed people will one day be resurrected with him in the new heavens and the new earth. For now, we are in our ordinary physical bodies, and we are to surrender them for the sake of the mission! It doesn't matter who you are. If you are in Christ, you are a witness of the things to come. We are to serve God in our daily, ordinary lives, and, through this faithfulness to him, the world will be changed. The ordinariness of our lives is not a barrier to the mission, but rather a means by which we look to the nations and accomplish the mission given by Christ.

David Prince, "Expect the Unexpected in Mission," Preached 4/27/2014, Prince on Preaching Website, Accessed 4 December 2015, Available from http://www.davidprince.com/2014/04/27/expect-the-unexpected-in-mission/.

Connection with Older Testament

Genesis 3:15

For the Kids

As the *Jesus Storybook Bible* says in its title: "Every story whispers his name."[10]
Many things in the Old Testament might seem like they're not connected to
the gospel of Jesus, but in reality, Jesus is at the center of the entire story God
has written! He's the hero, and everything that happens before and after his
time on earth points toward him and God's plan for saving us. Show your
children how Jesus is the serpent-crushing, Genesis 3:15 seed of the woman.
Teach them how Jesus is a greater Joshua who gives eternal rest. Instruct them
how Jesus is a greater savior-king than David.

Prayer Prompts

1. Pray that your heart and mind will be focused on Christ's mission to every
nation and that you would be a witness wherever you are in your daily life.
2. Praise the LORD for his faithfulness. Christ is risen! Scripture is fulfilled.
Satan is cast down. Sins are forgiven through the death and resurrection of
Jesus. Praise the LORD that we can enjoy eternal life with him because Jesus
has been raised in fulfillment of the Scriptures.

◆

WEEK 43: DAY 4

Matthew 28

Key Text

"Then Jesus came up and said to them, 'All authority in heaven and on earth
has been given to me. Therefore go and make disciples of all nations, baptizing
them in the name of the Father and the Son and the Holy Spirit, teaching them
to obey everything I have commanded you. And remember, I am with you
always, to the end of the age.'" Matthew 28:18-20

The Great Commission: Making Disciples and Baptizing Them

Up until the resurrection, the disciples were leisurely following Jesus

---

[10]Sally Lloyd-Jones and Jago Silver, *The Jesus Storybook Bible: Every Story
Whispers His Name* (Grand Rapids: Zonderkids, 2007), title.

around a geographical pattern. He would stop and teach them, and they would sit and learn. They are obviously interpreting all that he teaches them in light of how it will benefit themselves and help them have a better life. They didn't quite get it. After the resurrection, we find a radical group of followers who are no longer self-focused, leisurely learners. The resurrection of Jesus Christ changed everything!

This was a transition point in redemptive history. Jesus summoned and taught his disciples by giving them a glorious commission. All authority in the entire cosmos is his. Some will go to the ends of the earth, and some will go next door. His commission is for us to go and make disciples, baptizing and teaching them as a declaration to the world that Christ has all authority and the gospel triumphs and is marching to the ends of the earth!

Far too many of us live our lives like pre-resurrection disciples. When we function passively and self-centeredly, concerned more about our comfort and safety and how our lives can be better, we are living as though the resurrection never happened. Post-resurrection disciples are always aggressively, strategically seeking to make disciples effectively from all the nations of the world. We are called to be global gospel warriors, declaring the gospel without limits.

David Prince, "From Leisurely Learners to Global Gospel Warriors," Preached 8/22/2009, Prince on Preaching Website, Accessed 4 December 2015, Available from http://www.davidprince.com/2010/08/22/from-leisurely-learners-to-global-gospel-warriors-matthew-2816-20/.

Connection with Older Testament
Daniel 7:13-14

For the Kids
Ask your children where missionaries go to tell people about Jesus. They will probably name a few different far away countries that they know. Remind them that God doesn't just call "missionaries." He calls everyone to "be where our feet are," telling our neighbors, friends, and families about the gospel of Jesus. Have your children consider what this passage calls them to do if they are

Christians (pray for non-Christians, tell others about Jesus, etc.) and what it calls them to do if they are not Christians (believe the gospel, follow Jesus, etc.).

Prayer Prompts

1. Pray for a passion to get the gospel to the nations and to see the global vision which knows no bounds.

2. Pray for God to use you as a witness for the gospel wherever he has planted you, whether it be at work, in your neighborhood, school, or family. Pray that he would use you from your own backyard to the ends of the earth.

◆

WEEK 43: DAY 5

Acts 2

Key Text

"Now when they heard this, they were acutely distressed, and said to Peter and the rest of the apostles, 'What should we do, brothers?' Peter said to them, 'Repent, and each one of you be baptized in the name of Jesus Christ for the forgiveness of your sins, and you will receive the gift of the Holy Spirit.'" Acts 2:37-38

The Holy Spirit Poured Out: The Age of Salvation Inaugurated

When the world thinks of power, they think of those with money, fame, education, and preference. When the promised Holy Spirit comes, all of this changes. A small band of poor, uneducated Galileans becomes filled with the Holy Spirit, and the world is turned upside down. God sends the gracious power of the Holy Spirit to fill his people and dwell in them. This is true for every believer!

As promised, Christ has not left us as orphans. He is always dwelling in us by his Spirit. There are things that always captivate our hearts and minds, but the Spirit of Christ disrupts our sin patterns by his Spirit, bringing us to conviction and conforming us into the image of Jesus. In Acts 2, the judgment from the Tower of Babel (Gen. 11) with the confusion of the languages and the scattering of people has been reversed! There is a reversal because when

Christ sent his Spirit, it was the creation of a new people, a new identity, and a new community. We who are filled with the Spirit speak; and our message is that "Jesus Christ is Lord."

David Prince, "Kingdom Power," Preached 5/6/2012, Prince on Preaching Website, Accessed 4 December 2015, Available from http://www.davidprince.com/2012/05/06/kingdom-power-acts-21-13/.

Connection with Older Testament
Genesis 11; Ezekiel 36-37; Joel 2:28-32

For the Kids
Hold a light bulb in your hand and ask your children what it will take to light up the bulb. Can the bulb light itself up? No, it must be connected to electricity! Just as the light bulb needs power from outside of itself, we need the Holy Spirit to empower us for God's work. We can't do it on our own! Praise God for the person and work of the Holy Spirit, the one who convicts us of sin, who gives us new life, who leads us to repentance and faith, who comforts Christians, who empowers us to reflect Jesus, who equips us for God's work, and so much more.

Prayer Prompts
1. Pray that you will live each day remembering that the Spirit of Christ is in you and that he will lead, guide, convict, and comfort you as you are being conformed into Christ's image.
2. Pray that you will be a bold witness who speaks the glorious gospel of Christ into the world with confidence knowing that the Spirit is dwelling in you.

◆

WEEK 44: DAY 1
Acts 3-4

Key Text
"'But the things God foretold long ago through all the prophets—that his

Christ would suffer—he has fulfilled in this way."' Acts 3:18

The Gospel Proclaimed in Jerusalem

This is the second major time that Peter has borne witness to Christ. Peter makes it clear that a witness always testifies of Jesus. Peter tells the people that the healing of the lame beggar (3:1-11) is not by his own personal display of power; rather, he glorifies Jesus by tying him to the God of Abraham, Isaac, and Jacob. Peter is testifying that every word in the Bible is fulfilled in Jesus and that he is the only way to salvation. Because Peter sees that all of the Bible is about Jesus, he is saying "Look! See what Jesus is doing!" Without Jesus, the law of God is not comforting; it is crushing. Without Jesus, the sacrificial system is meaningless. Jesus is a King who gives his life for his subjects and a God who dies for sinners.

Because of what God did through Jesus, our sins can be obliterated, and there is an eternal rest to come (3:19). Like Peter in his daily life as a witness, we too can say, "See! It is all about Jesus!" Jesus is the final word of God (Heb. 1:1-2), and he demands a response from us. There is no neutral response. The answer is either faith or rejection. If the answer is faith in the Son whom the whole story of the Bible is about, Jesus Christ is at work in them. We testify to him every day.

David Prince, "Kingdom Witness," Preached 5/20/2012, Prince on Preaching Website, Accessed 4 December 2015, Available from http://www.davidprince.com/2012/05/20/kingdom-witness-acts-311-26/.

Connection with Older Testament

Deuteronomy 18:15-22

For the Kids

Teach your kids that the book of Acts tells the story of the gospel of Jesus going out to the ends of the earth by the power of the Holy Spirit. Tell your children that the gospel started going out from the city of Jerusalem, as seen in Acts 3-4. Pull out a map of the world. Show them where Jerusalem is in the world. Then show them where your city is in the world. Thank God that the

Spirit has brought the gospel all the way from Jerusalem to your city over the past 2,000 years.

Prayer Prompts

1. Pray that God will give you a zeal to be a witness to him in everyday life and that you will point people always to Jesus in your work, school, conversations, and relationships.

2. Pray that you will always respond in faith to God and his final word in Christ no matter the circumstance or cost.

◆

WEEK 44: DAY 2

Acts 8

Key Text

"Philip went down to the main city of Samaria and began proclaiming the Christ to them." Acts 8:5

Philip: Israel Reunited and the Spirit Poured Out on Samaria

Just before Jesus ascended, he gave his disciples some of the greatest promises of Scripture: "But you will receive power when the Holy Spirit has come upon you, and you will be my witnesses in Jerusalem, and in all Judea and Samaria, and to the farthest parts of the earth" (Acts 1:8). These promises were not just for the eleven remaining disciples; they were for all of Jesus' followers, as is demonstrated in the fact that it is Philip whom God uses to begin a great work among the Samaritans.

God's promise of the power of the Spirit was seen in Philip's work as he preached the good news of the kingdom. The Spirit's power was not only in the activity of preaching, however. The preaching was accompanied by the same great healings and casting out of demons that God had given as signs accompanying the ministry of Jesus and his apostles.

It is what happens next that is truly amazing. When Peter and John show up and pray for them, not only are these Samaritan Christians recipients of forgiveness of sins and of a future with Jesus, they also become recipients of the Holy Spirit. In other words, they are empowered with the same Spirit to also become witnesses for Christ. As a result, no one could argue that they were second-class believers. The Samaritans were not just recipients of kingdom work; they became fellow kingdom workers!

For the first time in over 950 years, since the division of Israel after King Solomon, Samaritans in the north and Judeans in the south became united together in one kingdom. And this time, the union is much better than the union under the kingship of David or of Solomon. This time, the unity is in the eternal kingdom of the King of kings, the son of David, the true Israel, Jesus Christ himself.

Todd Martin

Connection with Older Testament
Ezekiel 37:15-22

For the Kids
Grab a stick about a foot long and a piece of string. Using the stick, tell your children about the people of Israel and how they were one united people from the time of the exodus until King Solomon. Then break the stick in half. Teach your children that Israel was divided after Solomon into two kingdoms as a result of sin: the northern kingdom of Israel/Samaria and the southern kingdom of Judea/Jerusalem. The kingdoms were divided even until Jesus arrived, but God promised that a day was coming when the two kingdoms would be one again (Ezek. 37:15-22). Now splice the two sticks back together using the rope. Once together, teach your children that the unity of the two kingdoms has come now in Christ, which we see on display in Acts 8. Praise God that the gospel brings back together people divided as a result of sin. Praise God that he's faithful to his promises.

Prayer Prompts
1. Pray, regardless of the place or circumstance where God sets you, even in the midst of persecution, that you would be a bold and joyful witness for Christ.

2. Praise God that he is faithful to his Old Testament promises of salvation to Israel and to us through Jesus Christ, the true Israel. Thank God for the new covenant fulfillment of the pouring out and indwelling of the Spirit.

◆

WEEK 44: DAY 3
Acts 9

Key Text
"'For I will show him how much he must suffer for the sake of my name.'"
Acts 9:16

Saul: Conversion and Calling to Preach the Gospel to the Gentiles

Saul was an enemy of the church and threatened them with abuse, imprisonment, and murder. He was the face of persecution to those who were called the "Way." These were those who were changed by Christ and had a new resolve, a new purpose, and a new family. Saul was sincere about his religion, but his sincerity and faith was placed in the wrong object. It was not in Christ. Jesus appeared to Saul and changed him on the Damascus road by humbling and making blind the man who was bold, confident, and zealous. He was given the same new resolve, purpose, and family of those whom he persecuted.

Paul had previously genuinely believed that he was serving God by persecuting the church until he was saved by the amazing grace of God. This goes to show that it is not your own faith that saves you but rather the object in which your faith is placed. This has eternal consequences. The object that leads to eternal life is Jesus Christ (John 14:6). As a believer in Christ, you have the same radical resolve and purpose as Paul and the believers of his day because you are indwelt by the same Spirit and covered by the same grace of God. Your purpose is to be a witness for Christ in every aspect of your life.

The man who inflicted the Christians of his day became one who suffered for the sake of Christ as a chosen instrument of God. We too are instruments of God and are called to the same mission of reaching the nations with the gospel.

357

David Prince, "Kingdom Conversion," Preached 6/17/2012, Prince on Preaching Website, Accessed 4 December 2015, Available from http://www.davidprince.com/2012/06/17/kingdom-conversion-acts-91-19/.

Connection with Older Testament
Psalm 1

For the Kids
Ask your children if they have ever been bullied or if they have ever seen anyone being bullied. Now have them imagine what it would be like if one day the bully apologized for being so mean and starting being kind to everyone all of the time. Have them imagine what it must have felt like when the apostle Paul went from being a persecutor of Christians to becoming a Christian himself. It's hard to love and pray for our enemies, but it becomes easier when we imagine what they might be like if they became fellow believers someday and when we remember God offers forgiveness to his enemies. Pray that God's amazingly powerful grace in Jesus would save our enemies.

Prayer Prompts
1. Pray to be filled with a sense of gospel purpose every single day knowing that God has strategically placed you where you are to be a witness of the gospel.
2. Pray for reconciliation with your gospel family of brothers and sisters whenever it is needed. Pray for unity in your relationships with others who are difficult to get along with and for unity specifically in your church.

◆

WEEK 44: DAY 4
Acts 10-11:18

Key Text
"But the voice replied a second time from heaven, 'What God has made clean, you must not consider ritually unclean!'" Acts 11:9

Cornelius: The Gospel Breaks Down Jewish Barriers to Go to the Gentiles

In Acts so far, there is a newness in Christ's fulfillment of the Law. Christ has been pointing believers in different directions and breaking down different barriers. Word has been getting out, starting in Jerusalem then Samaria and now throughout the world, that Gentiles are receiving the word of God.

Cornelius was a Roman Gentile who, by the grace of God, helped break down the barrier as Peter recalls his conversion to the Jews who are questioning him in chapter 11. Peter gives an account of the vision which led him to the conversion of Cornelius. It is clear by Peter's response to the vision that he initially found the idea of killing and eating animals that were given to him repulsive. What was the point of these food restrictions and laws that Peter and the Jews abided by? They were always meant to point to Jesus Christ and his fulfillment of those laws. Christ shows Peter that there is a people who are unified by faith in Christ from every tribe, tongue, and nation. These are a people who would have their sole identity not in cultural distinctions, but in Christ alone.

We are to look at every person with no distinction. God will not be stopped in his mission of spreading the gospel to every tribe, tongue, and nation, and we must not stand in his way. We cannot stop God. We must join him in his mission which is constantly shaking our expectations and putting us out of our comfort zones.

David Prince, "Kingdom Vision," Preached 6/24/2012, Prince on Preaching Website, Accessed 4 December 2015, Available from http://www.davidprince.com/2012/06/24/kingdom-vision-acts-111-18/.

Connection with Older Testament

Isaiah 66:19-21

For the Kids

Have your children think about what defines your family. Teach your children that, for faithful Jews, their identity as the people of the Lord was rooted in many external distinctions. They were to be distinct with the food they ate, so, for example, they didn't eat bacon. They were to be distinct with the way they conducted themselves, so they would not act like Gentile (non-Israelite) people. Yet, God gives a vision to Peter (an Israelite) in Acts 10 to take the gospel to those unclean, not-like-me Gentiles. Tell your children that the gospel was always intended to go to all peoples, Jews and Gentiles, from every tribe, tongue, and nation (Gen. 12:1-3). Tell them that the gospel is shocking because it tears down so many barriers of distinction that we create to look better than others, and it creates one new people called the Church, a distinctly diverse people who witness to the glory of God. If you are a Gentile, praise God that the gospel is for you too!

Prayer Prompts

1. Pray that God will break down any barriers or prejudices you may have in order to continue in his mission of the gospel.

2. Instead of criticizing the work of God in something you are not used to or comfortable with, pray that God will use you in reaching those who are not like you or in places that you have never been.

◆

WEEK 44: DAY 5

James 2

Key Text

"For just as the body without the spirit is dead, so also faith without works is dead." James 2:26

Cruciform Wisdom: A Generic Faith Doesn't Justify

Have you ever considered that your faith could be worthless? It's a strange and scandalous thought. Yet this is exactly what James warns us about in James 2:14-26.

Authentic faith always results in heartfelt works done to the glory of God, while worthless faith produces nothing. James comments that this worthless faith is akin to the faith demons have in God: They know the right theological answers but are condemned nonetheless. Even having strong doctrine doesn't necessarily mean sound (or any!) faith; a worthless faith may produce a well-organized theology that one might spout before men, but authentic faith leads to good theology *and* good works. The demons' right belief alone cannot save them, and the same is true for any one of us who does not have authentic faith.

When was the last time your faith in Christ drove you to act in a way pleasing to God? Drove you to an act of obedience? To an act of compassion or charity? Are you guilty of talking about the things of God but never acting to do them? Bonafide faith results in sincerely-done good deeds. The word of God declares to us unapologetically that anyone with real faith cannot help but be led to act in such a way that displays his faith to the world through his works.

Casey McCall, "Cruciform Works," Preached 10/14/2014, Ashland Avenue Baptist Church Website, Accessed 4 December 2015, Available from http://www.ashlandlex.org/podcast/cruciform-works-james-2/.

Connection with Older Testament
Genesis 15, 22:1-19; Joshua 2

For the Kids
Ask your children how they know you love them. Do they know it just because you tell them? Or is it because how you treat them shows them what your words say? Explain to them the Bible says our faith is similar. We cannot simply say we believe. What we do shows what we believe. Do your works reflect great faith in Jesus by displaying obedience to him?

Prayer Prompts
1. Confess and repent of hypocritical, dead faith.
2. Pray for a continual biblical faith which would result in good works done in and through yourself and your church.

◆

WEEK 45: DAY 1
Acts 13-14

Key Text

"While they were serving the Lord and fasting, the Holy Spirit said, 'Set apart for me Barnabas and Saul for the work to which I have called them.' Then, after they had fasted and prayed and placed their hands on them, they sent them off." Acts 13:2-3

To the Ends of the Earth: Paul's First Missionary Journey

Acts 13-14 tells the story of Paul's first missionary journey. As Paul travelled about preaching, he taught the Jews the story of their people and pled with them to see that the goal of that story was the person Jesus Christ himself.

Our life stories are far different from the people in this passage to whom Paul preached. We have modern day responsibilities such as paying bills, going to school, providing for our families, teaching our children well, or perhaps seeking that promotion at work. But the temptation is the same as in Paul's time: to seek these things in order to make a name for ourselves instead of for our Savior.

It's easy for us to long to rise to the top of an empire of success and be greater in our own minds than we actually are, at the expense of Christ. Are the everyday tasks just things you mark off a checklist or ways in which you seek to be an active part in the coming of the kingdom of Christ? The reality is I could have money, a house, a great reputation, and well-mannered kids—and it all be in vain. Jesus can't just be another character in the story; he is *the* character in the story.

Jeremy Haskins, "Kingdom Preaching," Preached 7/8/2012, Ashland in MC Website, Accessed 3 December 2015, Available from http://www.ashlandmc.org/podcast/kingdom-preaching/.

Connection with Older Testament

Psalm 117

For the Kids

God doesn't ask us to stop what we're doing to go and tell people about the gospel. He calls us to share his good news with those in our lives no matter where we are or what we are doing. Help your child make a list of daily or weekly things you do in which you can honor Christ intentionally where you are and in the places you go.

Prayer Prompts

1. Pray for God to give you grace to view all of life's tasks and goals through the lens of the kingdom of God and to do all things to him, through him, and for him.

2. Plead with God to help you see Christ daily as the centerpiece in the story of history and as the centerpiece in the story of your own life.

◆

WEEK 45: DAY 2
Galatians 3

Key Text

"Now it is clear no one is justified before God by the law, because the righteous one shall will live by faith." Galatians 3:11

Defending the Church from Legalism: The Righteous Shall Live by Faith

In verse 11, Paul is going to quote another verse from the Old Testament, "Now it is clear no one is justified before God by the law, because the righteous shall live by faith." (Hab. 2:4). It is impossible to be declared righteous before God by the law because you can't do the law. No, the only way you can be declared righteous is by faith. The righteous live their lives by faith. If you choose to rely on the law, you must live on the basis of the law. If you are choosing to live your life by your own achievements, by your own standard, by your own effort, then you have to deal with the consequences of that. That is the standard by which you will be judged by God, and no one will be justified on that basis.

And so, we get to verse 13 and Paul tells us the glorious good news that God has provided a way, and it's not about you. It's not about your effort. It's not about your ability, and it's not about your achievement. It is based solely on Christ—the only one who could ever be perfect. Jesus said, "I am going to take the place of those undeserving sinners. I am going to hang on the tree under the wrath of God, cursed by God, taking the punishment that people deserve, and I am going to take it upon myself so that these people can be forgiven and declared righteous by my perfection." Jesus here says, "I am going to be treated as if I committed all the sins of all my people on all the earth in all of history so that my people can be treated as if they lived my perfect life."

The sinless Son of God hung on a tree and endured the wrath of God so that, by faith, you and I could be saved, so that we might receive the promised Spirit through faith. This is how you get in: not by your own effort and not by your own performance, but by the Spirit through faith in Jesus Christ.

Casey McCall, "Set Free by the Spirit," Preached 7/19/2015, Ashland Avenue Baptist Church Website, Accessed 4 December 2015, Available from http://www.ashlandlex.org/podcast/set-free-by-the-spirit-galatians-3/.

Connection with Older Testament
Genesis 15:6; Habakkuk 2:4

For the Kids
Have your child think about rules at school or in the home. Ask them if they perfectly obey all the time. Explain that, while rules in the Bible—such as the Ten Commandments—are good, God calls us to more than rule keeping, which is impossible for sinners like us. He calls us to faith in Jesus. The gift of faith allows us to believe Jesus kept all the commandments perfectly knowing that we never can. Faith allows us to tell God the truth about how sinful we are and how desperate we are for him to save us, which pleases God and results in the forgiveness of sin through the sinless person and work of King Jesus. Pray for Christ-centered faith for your children.

Prayer Prompts
1. Repent of any personal effort, work, achievement, or ability that you are trusting in for salvation in the place of Jesus Christ.

2. Praise God for the salvation he has granted to us by faith in his Son Jesus Christ.

◆

WEEK 45: DAY 3
Acts 15

Key Text
"On the contrary, we believe that we are saved through the grace of the Lord Jesus, in the same way as they are." Acts 15:11

The Jerusalem Council and the Abolition of the Law

"What do I have to do?" From getting a degree to winning someone's heart, we so often want to boil life down to a set of tasks that we must accomplish. If we can find out the actions required to meet a goal, then it puts us in control. We have a mission and the reward that we believe will be worth the effort.

That thinking is nearly universal in humans throughout history and has led to great accomplishments. But when it comes to being restored to God, everything is different. There is nothing we can do. There are no steps, no tasks, no mountains to climb, hurdles to jump, or goals to achieve. We must simply accept a free gift or have no hope at all. But for some, that's hard to accept.

The Jews saw God welcoming outsiders into his kingdom without any prerequisites. These Gentile outsiders didn't know the Law and the prophets, they hadn't heard all the stories about Old Testament heroes, they hadn't memorized Scripture, and certainly they hadn't obeyed all the commandments since childhood. And yet, God was giving them free admission into his family. Surely these newcomers had to do something!

But Peter pointed out, "We believe that we are saved through the grace of the Lord Jesus, in the same way as they are" (v. 11). No one was better off than the outsiders. The Mosaic Law and the old covenant was recognized as firmly abolished. All are equally dependent on grace for salvation under the new covenant in Jesus' blood.

Connection with Older Testament

Jeremiah 3:16, 31:31-33

For the Kids

Help your child write out the Ten Commandments if he or she is old enough. Ask your child to think about ways they have broken the Law. Explain that the Law (the Ten Commandments) was given to show us our sin and our need for a Savior. We are guilty, but Jesus never broke the Law. His perfect life, his death, and his resurrection save us from our sins because he fulfilled the Law. Ask God to give your child a heart that trusts in Jesus and his law-keeping, a heart free from the impossible task of trying to earn favor with God through our own works.

Prayer Prompts

1. Praise God for the freedom you have from the Law. Through the blood of Christ, you are accepted before God, despite your past disobedience to the Law.

2. Praise God for the freedom you have to obey the Law as a means to reflect the character of God for his glory in the world.

◆

WEEK 45: DAY 4

Acts 16-18:23

Key Text

"The God who made the world and everything in it, who is Lord of heaven and earth, does not live in temples made by human hands" Acts 17:24

To the Ends of the Earth: Paul's Second Missionary Journey

In Acts 17, we find Paul in the thick of his second missionary journey. Along the way, he finds himself at Mars Hill, the cultural epicenter of religious thought and ideas in the city of Athens. Surrounded by many idols and belief systems, his spirit was provoked to preach.

The people in Acts 17 were building idols, trusting them, and attributing to them power to carry out their human desires. Paul's sermon centers on the fact that God does not need man to be sustained, but that man needs God for life and breath and everything.

Even in our familiarity with this truth, we all struggle with making idol replacements every day. We all try to maintain control over our own lives and circumstances in a way that only God rightfully can and should. Remember today that God is sovereign over not only your life, but the whole universe. Give up any idolatrous tendencies and efforts to be sovereign over your own life. Trust that God has wisdom to direct all things well. Choose to do everything for his glory as well as your good.

David Prince, "2009: The Year of Living Upside Down," Preached 1/4/2009, Prince on Preaching Website, Accessed 4 December 2015, Available from http://www.davidprince.com/2009/01/04/2009-the-year-of-living-upside-down-acts-171-8/.

Connection with Older Testament
Isaiah 44, 66:1

For the Kids
Ask your child to think of a time they made something: a craft, a sand castle, Legos, etc. Discuss how foolish and silly it would be if your child began to worship this object. "I am lonely, so I will love and worship my Lego rocket." Explain that we are just as foolish, and even sinful, when we worship anything other than God. He made us, so worship him in Christ!

Prayer Prompts
1. Recognize and turn away from any of the ways in which you try to take the place of God in your own life.

2. Be grateful to God that he does not need anything from us to fulfill his perfect purposes in our lives and that he is completely sovereign over all things in the world.

◆

WEEK 45: DAY 5
2 Thessalonians 1:5-2:16

Key Text
"They will undergo the penalty of eternal destruction, away from the presence of the Lord and from the glory of his strength" 2 Thessalonians 1:9

Encouragement for a Persecuted Church: Christ Will Bring Judgment

The church at Thessalonica was a persecuted church that faced many afflictions because of their faith in Christ (2 Thess. 1:4). One way that Paul encouraged these enduring believers was by reminding them that a day is coming when affliction will be over. There is coming a day when persecution will be finished for the people of God. There is coming a day when King Jesus will descend from the heavens to "repay with affliction those who afflict you, and to you who are being afflicted to give rest" (1:6-7). There is coming a day when those who don't know God will suffer the punishment of eternal destruction, away from the good and merciful presence of the LORD (1:9). But until this day, endure knowing that, through suffering, God is making his people worthy of his calling for the glory of Jesus (1:11-12).

Are you afflicted because of your faith in Jesus? Are you persecuted? Take hope. Your affliction is temporal. Be courageous. Your persecution is purposeful in preparing you for glory. Be encouraged. Jesus is coming to gather you to himself in a place where sin and suffering are no more for all eternity, in a place where all those who hate God will not exist. Don't be alarmed. You're following in the footsteps of your Savior, just as Jesus promised would happen (John 15:20).

Jon Canler

Connection with Older Testament

Exodus 23:22; Joel 3:1-8; Isaiah 63:1-6

For the Kids

Discuss with your children the importance of doing difficult things even when our stomachs tell us we don't want to. We must be courageous, and we must practice doing the uncomfortable to be ready for when we may be called to suffer for Christ's sake. Remind them that serving Christ in all circumstances can only happen through the grace of God, and we should pray for his grace. Remind them that we can endure hardship knowing that the hardship makes us look like Jesus and knowing that Jesus will bring it to an end at the right time.

Prayer Prompts

1. Ask the Lord to impress upon your heart and mind the glories that await his return so that, in dwelling upon future grace, you may have hope to live in obedience to Jesus today regardless of your circumstances.

2. Pray for those who persecute you, that they may be extended the same grace of God that you were also given when you were an enemy of God.

◆

WEEK 46: DAY 1

Acts 18:24-20:1

Key Text

"This became known to all who lived in Ephesus, both Jews and Greeks; fear came over them all, and the name of the Lord Jesus was praised." Acts 19:17

To the Ends of the Earth: Paul's Third Missionary Journey

Paul set out with a message to proclaim to the world. The message was called good news, but the response wasn't always positive. In Ephesus, it nearly caused a riot! Why was there so much chaos and upheaval when the message was so good?

Paul himself had been one of those who used violence to attack the very message he was now proclaiming. The gospel message was powerful. He knew it could undermine social structures, political powers, and the stability of his nation. But then Paul discovered it was true. When he took the message around the world, he began to see the gospel's dramatic power first hand.

As he traveled from city to city, Paul could see the fear, resentment, and anger that came from telling people that Jesus is the Son of God who died for sin and was raised from the dead. The gospel is a message almost too good to take in, yet it is threatening to so many. It threatens one's status. It makes people accountable. It forces people to make a choice. It even jeopardized the livelihood of many in Ephesus. In a world that has turned its back on its Creator, people develop entire philosophies, religions, and economies in opposition to him. It's no wonder that the gospel causes division and strife wherever it is proclaimed and understood.

While we are also called to proclaim this good news to the people in our circles, we should not expect joy and acceptance at every encounter. We can expect, however, that we will see some gospel fruit. Even in all the chaos, Paul experienced that "the word of the Lord continued to grow in power and to prevail" (19:20).

John Martin

Connection with Older Testament
1 Samuel 16:14-23

For the Kids
Ask your children what they know about magic from movies and books they have seen. Explain that men may attempt to imitate God through magic, but only God can do whatever he pleases. Through faith in Christ, we receive the Holy Spirit, who is all the power we need to serve God and share the gospel. The gospel is better than magic; it's the power of God that brings people to eternal life.

Prayer Prompts

1. Pray that the Spirit of Jesus Christ would save many souls in your city and to the ends of the earth so that the name of Jesus would be worshipped.

2. Jesus is not your magic genie. Repent of using Jesus and Christianity as a means of furthering your kingdom, much like the sons of Sceva.

◆

WEEK 46: DAY 2

1 Corinthians 8

Key Text

"yet for us there is one God, the Father, from whom are all things and for whom we live, and one Lord, Jesus Christ, through whom are all things and through whom we live." 1 Corinthians 8:6

Life Under the Gospel: Freedom in Christ to Build Up the Brothers

"I know my rights!" As a nation of freedom-loving people, we can quickly become irate when the least of our inalienable rights are infringed upon. We enjoy so many protections in the law, and yet, there are so many disputes and legal battles for the rights of individuals against each other, organizations, and corporations. One of freedom's boundaries is the point at which it infringes on the rights of others.

The believers in Corinth also had rights as followers of Christ. They were set free from being slaves to sin, to the law, and to pagan superstitions. They knew that there was nothing to the idols and that there was nothing to fear about offending them. But their freedom was to be tempered by one thing according to Paul: love.

Some will say, "It doesn't matter what people think. What matters is that my conscience is clear." But Scripture says it *does* matter. We cannot simply do anything we want without regard for the faith of others, even when their misunderstanding is caused by their own ignorance.

True followers of Christ are governed by the law of love. It sums up the Law and the prophets. We are to ask not what we are allowed to do but how we can build up others in Christ, how we can pour out on others the love and grace we've been given. In that sense, love is less of a boundary. We are free to love lavishly.

John Martin

Connection with Older Testament
Deuteronomy 10:19

For the Kids
Ask your children to get the loudest toy they have. Ask your children if it's okay for them to play with the toy. Sure they can. Then ask your children if it's okay to play with that toy after everybody has gone to sleep for the night. The answer is (hopefully) no. Teach your children why this is the case: parents limit the time the toy can be played with in order to serve everyone in the family so that the family can rest at night. This is loving. Tell your children that this principle is what 1 Corinthians 8 teaches. There are all kinds of things that Christians can do (like playing with the loud toy), but there are things Christians shouldn't do at certain times (like playing with the loud toy at night) in order to help fellow Christians continue to live by faith in Christ. Encourage your children to give up a privilege this week in order to serve the family.

Prayer Prompts
1. Pray for God to give you a greater heart of love for your brothers and sisters in Christ that results in sacrificial service for them.
2. Pray for the Lord to grant you wisdom and conviction about any rights that you need to give up for the sake of others.

◆

WEEK 46: DAY 3
1 Corinthians 10

Key Text
"So whether you eat or drink, or whatever you do, do everything for the glory

of God." 1 Corinthians 10:31

Life Under the Gospel: Do All Things for the Glory of God

In 1 Corinthians 10, we read that we should do all things for the glory of God. It is a wonderful command that pushes us to do all things for the sake of Christ. But how exactly do we go about living it out?

In our culture, we see immorality all around us, and the knee-jerk reaction is to ensure that we do all things in a good, honest, moral manner. But to think that the fulfillment of this command, the line between the glory of God and the sin of man, is found solely in living morally is to fall pitifully short of what God is commanding us to do here.

God is calling us to make a paradigm shift and bring attention to the worth, value, grace, mercy, and love of God through every thought, word, deed, and intention we have. This goes far beyond the scope of morally-driven actions. It encompasses all of our hearts and minds, causing us to act and speak as we ought in every situation not just for the sake of doing what is right, but for the sake of declaring that Christ is reigning and that he is worthy of our lives. Will we see the difference? The glory of God realized in us is at stake.

David Prince, "Eating, Drinking, Cutting Grass, Work, Class, Shopping and the Gospel: Why the Kingdom Means More than Morality," Preached 8/29/2010, Prince on Preaching Website, Accessed 4 December 2015, Available from http://www.davidprince.com/2010/08/29/eating-drinking-cutting-grass-work-class-shopping-and-the-gospel-why-the-kingdom-means-more-than-morality-1-corinthians-1031-33/.

Connection with Older Testament
Psalm 115

For the Kids
Talk about where each family member spends their days. Discuss what it may look like to glorify God in serving him where he has placed you. One way to glorify God is to speak highly of him and tell of his love for us in sending his Son to die for us. Encourage your children to share the gospel with those that

God has placed around them: a sibling, classmate, teammate, etc. Another way to glorify God is to be thankful for your current circumstances, even the ones you wouldn't have picked for yourselves. Give thanks to God for his goodness to you.

Prayer Prompts

1. Pray that the gospel would be a greater treasure to you than any earthly thing, enabling you to do all for the glory of God.

2. With thanksgiving, recognize that God has freed us in Christ to enjoy all things so long as we can do so for his name's sake.

◆

WEEK 46: DAY 4

1 Corinthians 12-13

Key Text

"And now these three remain: faith, hope, and love. But the greatest of these is love." 1 Corinthians 13:13

Life Under the Gospel: Use Spiritual Gifts for the Unity of the Body

1 Corinthians 13 is often known as the "love chapter" of the Bible. It is frequently read at wedding ceremonies or as brotherly encouragement to love and behave. Yet, the reason why it is placed where it is in the Bible is rarely understood.

The city of Corinth was a place of affluence, individualism, pride, and social success. The Corinthian church reflected all of these cultural attributes. Inside the church, the people used spiritual gifts to bolster themselves instead of to build up the body of Christ. Thus, Paul wrote the words in chapter 13 in order to rebuke the Corinthians—to teach them that amazing gifts are nothing apart from love.

When your identity is gained by what you do instead of rooted in the cross of Christ, then you will not love, and your ministry will come to nothing. Do you have a lot of spiritual gifts? That's great. Or maybe you don't have a lot of gifts. The beauty is that, in Christ, you have love, and that's better than all the gifts. Actually, without love, the gifts are nothing, and so are we. So, whom have you loved lately?

David Prince, "Church of the Less Excellent Way? What You Need More than What You Think You Need," Preached 9/12/2010, Prince on Preaching Website, Accessed 4 December 2015, Available from http://www.davidprince.com/2010/09/12/church-of-the-less-excellent-way-what-you-need-more-than-what-you-think-you-need-1-corinthians-1231b-133/.

Connection with Older Testament
Leviticus 19:9-18

For the Kids
Have your children list strengths and abilities for every member of your house. Have your children think about how those strengths are actually used. Does Dad use his physical strength to fix things that break? Does Mom use her mental ability to keep the bills paid? Do your siblings use their abilities to do chores? Then think about how awful things would be if everybody used their strengths and abilities for themselves. Teach your children that the Holy Spirit gives gifts to every Christian to use for serving the Church, not for serving themselves. Just as Jesus used his rights and gifts as God for the well-being of his Church, so Christians are to use God-given gifts and abilities to serve one another. Pray about how you can use your gifts and abilities to serve others in love today.

Prayer Prompts
1. Ask the Lord to give you a heart that desires to use your gifts for the good and advantage of others instead of for self-recognition and identity.
2. Pray for church members to use their gifts to lead and serve for the building up of the church and for the glory of Jesus, being driven by the love of Christ.

◆

WEEK 46: DAY 5
1 Corinthians 15

Key Text
"For since death came through a man, the resurrection of the dead also came through a man." 1 Corinthians 15:21

Life Under the Gospel: The Centrality of the Resurrection
In 1 Corinthians 15, Paul reminds Christians of the importance of the resurrection of Jesus. Paul declares that the resurrection of Jesus is of first importance to the Christian faith, that it is absolutely fundamental to the heart of the gospel, and that without it the gospel falls apart (v. 3). Why is the resurrection so crucial to grasp? If Christ has not been raised, our faith in Christ is useless because we would still be dead in our sins (vv. 14-17). Not only would we still be in our sins, seeing that Christ would be subject to sin and death like us rather than Lord of them, we would be sinning by declaring a resurrection from God that God did not accomplish. If Christ has not been raised, there is no hope for future life beyond the grave for any of us (vv. 18-19). Apart from the resurrection, we are of all people most to be pitied (v. 19).

But praise God for the resurrection! Praise God that Christ's death has atoned for our sins and that his resurrection over sin and death gives us hope that, one day, we will be raised to new life where sin and death are no more! Let us, therefore, contend for the faith once for all delivered to the saints, a faith deeply rooted in the resurrection. Let us hold fast to the miraculous realities of the gospel, such as the incarnation of God in human flesh and the resurrection of the dead from the grave, knowing that apart from them we lose the gospel, the benefits of salvation, and the very presence of God himself. Let us cling to what is revealed to us in the gospel even when the world calls it foolish.

Jon Canler

Connection with Older Testament
Isaiah 53:10

For the Kids
Why is it so important that Jesus has been raised from the dead? If he had not been raised from the dead, what would that mean for us? When hard times come, how does knowing that Jesus is no longer in the tomb encourage us?

Prayer Prompts
1. Praise God that Jesus Christ is risen. If he was still in the grave, death, sin, and Satan would still have power over him. Consequently, we too would still be dead and doomed in our sins.
2. Ask the Lord to help you live in light of the reality of resurrection. Pray for grace to respond to adversity in light of the resurrection when things don't go according to your plan.

◆

WEEK 47: DAY 1
2 Corinthians 3-4

Key Text
"But since we have the same spirit of faith as that shown in what has been written, 'I believed; therefore I spoke,' we also believe, therefore we also speak." 2 Corinthians 4:13

Ministry in Christ: The Superiority of the New Covenant
In 2 Corinthians 4:13, Paul says that we believe the gospel and so we go forth speaking it. The gospel was something that Paul believed in to the point that it captivated his heart and mind, and so he was compelled to speak it in all that he did. It was not an auto-repeat message or memorized gospel pamphlet. He didn't add it on to all of the "regular things" he spoke about. Every conversation was highlighted by and came back to the life-changing reality of the gospel. To Paul, it truly was good news that he could not contain within himself.

How often does your belief in the gospel drive you to speak the good news before others? Do you share how Christ has redeemed you and changed your life? Daily gospel talk should be a natural habit for every follower of Jesus. We are, Paul says, clay pots. Hardened clay pots could be used as trash cans, but instead, we are holding the glorious grace of God. This must drive us to speak and declare the light of Christ. If we truly believe the gospel, we will be compelled to share it with others. When did you last speak about the gospel?

David Prince, "Chatting the Good News Every Day," Preached 9/18/2011, Prince on Preaching Website, Accessed 4 December 2015, Available from http://www.davidprince.com/2011/09/18/chatting-the-good-news-every-day-2-corinthians-47-16/.

Connection with Older Testament
Jeremiah 20:9

For the Kids
What are some things you do every day? Do you talk with classmates? Do you choose who to sit by at lunch? Do you participate in a sport? Do you participate in a family? What are some ways you can talk about Jesus in your daily routine tomorrow?

Prayer Prompts
1. Repent of any lack of obedience to speaking the truth of the gospel to others.
2. Ask God to give you an intentional mindset that looks for and takes opportunities to speak the gospel to those within your realm of influence.

◆

WEEK 47: DAY 2
2 Corinthians 5

Key Text
"Therefore, we are ambassadors for Christ, God making his appeal through us. We implore you on behalf of Christ, be reconciled to God." 2 Corinthians 5:20*

Ministry in Christ: Ambassadors of Reconciliation

Have you ever watched the news when the United States sends an ambassador to another country? When the ambassador goes, he is fully representing the one who sent him.

How often do we think of ourselves as ambassadors on behalf of God? If you are in Christ, then God has appointed you to be just that. 2 Corinthians 5 states, "In Christ God was reconciling the world to himself, not counting their trespasses against them, and entrusting to us the message of reconciliation. Therefore, we are ambassadors for Christ, God making his appeal through us."*

The depth of what this means for us should be gripping. An ambassador is sent because the sender entrusts a message to him. In this case, the sender is God himself, and the message is the gospel. All those born of God are ambassadors, and the recipients are anyone and everyone with whom you come into contact every day of your life. How seriously do we take this commission in our daily lives? Would you take a request to be the ambassador for the United States more seriously than you do to deliver the gospel of the grace of God on his behalf?

David Prince, "INTENTIONAL: Making it Our Aim to Please Christ," Preached 1/6/2008, Prince on Preaching Website, Accessed 4 December 2015, Available from http://www.davidprince.com/2008/01/06/intentional-making-it-our-aim-to-please-christ-2-corinthians-51-10/

Connection with Older Testament
Isaiah 6

For the Kids
When you go to the playground, school, or anywhere away from Mom and Dad, you are an ambassador for your family. You represent them in the way you talk and handle yourself. Christians are ambassadors for Jesus. How do they represent Jesus to other people? Help your children who are Christians think of one way to be a more faithful ambassador of Jesus today.

Prayer Prompts

1. Think about your neighbors. Think about the nations. You are an ambassador on behalf of God to them in some way. Ask God to help you see yourself as a messenger on his behalf.

2. Thank God that, while he does not need any ambassadors, he has graciously chosen you to carry and deliver his message to everyone whom he has placed in your life.

◆

WEEK 47: DAY 3

Romans 1:1-3:20

Key Text

"What then? Are we better off? Certainly not, for we have already charged that Jews and Greeks alike are all under sin" Romans 3:9

The Gospel: All Have Sinned and Are Under the Wrath of God

Paul's letter to the Romans starts out much like his other letters: "Grace and peace to you from God our Father and the Lord Jesus Christ" (1:7). But, his letter to the Romans is not just another letter. It is a deeply theological letter that clearly sets forth the best news the world has ever heard: the good news of Jesus Christ. Before Paul gets to the good news, though, he informs us of the bad news that surrounds all of humanity apart from Christ.

Romans 1:18 declares, "For the wrath of God is revealed from heaven against all ungodliness and unrighteousness of people who suppress the truth by their unrighteousness." Paul wants us to know that, in order to understand what Jesus has accomplished on the cross, we must understand the depth of our sin. Just like Adam and Eve in the Garden of Eden, we choose to follow our own desires and our understanding of the world while we ignore the word of God. Paul puts it this way: "[F]or we have already charged that Jews and Greeks alike are all under sin, just as it is written: 'There is no one righteous, not even one, there is no one who understands, there is no one who seeks God" (3:9-11). Consequently, we are all under the judgment of God in our sin, a judgment of eternal death (Gen. 2:17, Rom. 2:2-3).

380

Now, if Paul's letter to the Romans ended with Romans 3:20, we would all be left to despair. But it doesn't! There are many more glorious chapters of redemption, grace, and application in Jesus to follow that only make sense and give hope in light of the first few chapters of Romans. Jesus came so that Paul's letter to the Romans would give us delight instead of despair once we grasp the dread under which we stand in our sin.

Chad Lindon

Connection with Older Testament
Genesis 2:15-17, 3:11-24; Psalm 14

For the Kids
Exclaim to your kids, "Don't look over there!" Ask your kids what they wanted to do (or tell them what they actually did). They wanted to look; it's only natural. Ask them if they know what else comes naturally. Sin—to think, say, or do anything in disobedience to God. It is in our nature to sin. Can you think of a time that you've sinned? Help your children understand the terrible problem with sin in our relationship to God, in our relationship with others, and in relation to the judgment we deserve.

Prayer Prompts
1. Praise God that he sent us a Liberator to free us from our sins and from the judgment we deserve.
2. Ask the LORD to reveal remaining sin in your life so that you might repent of it.
3. Perhaps you've never admitted that you're a sinner—that you're "under sin." Confess your sin to God, turn away from sin, and turn to Christ for your soul's salvation.
4. Pray for those you know who are still "under sin." Pray that God would convict them of their sin and lead them to eternal life in Jesus Christ.

WEEK 47: DAY 4
Romans 3:21-5:21

Key Text
"For all have sinned and fall short of the glory of God, being justified as a gift by his grace through the redemption that is in Christ Jesus, whom God put forward as a propitiation by his blood through faith." Romans 3:23-25a*

The Gospel: Justification Before God Is Provided Through Faith in Jesus Christ

These chapters are almost overwhelming in their gospel richness. Paul, under the inspiration of the Holy Spirit, is in the midst of a withering critique of works-based salvation and a simultaneous celebration of the glory of faith-based salvation in Christ. While volumes could be written on the beauty and depth of this passage, its essence is easily understandable and attainable. To quote a description often spoken of the gospel, "It is like a pool shallow enough so that a child can play, but deep enough for an elephant to swim." Staying in the shallow end for now, these passages teach two essential truths: man is hopelessly lost, and Christ is mighty to save.

While many in Paul's time and our own are prone to confidence in their good deeds, these passages offer a strong corrective by reminding us of our utter depravity (wickedness), regardless of whether we are a Jew or "Greek" (Rom. 3:9-18). Christ, on the other hand, is entirely righteous, and he imparts his righteousness to us exclusively through faith. We also know that in this one imparting event, Christ did not just give us his righteousness. Rather, God also "made the one who did not know sin to be sin for us" (2 Cor. 5:21). This incredible transaction is the essence of the gospel, and it is a constant reminder that there is no room for boasting among true Christians (3:27). Glory to God alone!

Joe Martin

Connection with Older Testament

Genesis 15:6; Habakkuk 2:4

For the Kids

Imagine that you stole a toy from your best friend. Now think about how you would feel if your parents found out what you had done. You would be guilty of sin against your friend, and you would feel guilty, right? Would you try to do anything to make up for it? Maybe give the toy back? If so, would giving the toy back undo the fact that you stole the toy in the first place? No, it wouldn't. You would still be guilty. On top of that, imagine that you would be chastised because of your sin. Then, just before you were going to get chastised for stealing, imagine your friend steps in and says to you, "I haven't done anything wrong here. In fact, I was wronged. But I promise to take the punishment you deserve, and I promise to let you go free like you never sinned. All you have to do is trust this promise." How would you feel? Would you trust the good news promise? This is what God promises us in Romans 3:21-5:21. We are all sinners before God, but he offers to pay the penalty of our sins and to give us his sinlessness (to justify us) if we surrender our lives to Jesus. Made right with God for all eternity, not by works but by faith. Good news to trust indeed!

Prayer Prompts

1. Thank God for the righteousness of Christ that is yours through faith in Jesus.

2. Pray for God to grant you a deeper joy and peace from knowing that your sins are forgiven and that the righteousness of Christ has been credited to your account.

◆

WEEK 47: DAY 5

Romans 6

Key Text

"We know that our old man was crucified with him in order that the body of

sin might be brought to nothing, so that we would no longer be slaves to sin"
Romans 6:6*

The Gospel: Freedom from Sin as a Result of Justification

Have you ever felt enslaved to sin? That, even as a Christian, sin seems to find you despite the fact that you are supposed to be set free from it? It can sometimes feel like you can't fight anymore, like giving up is the only option. These are times when we have to set aside our feelings in favor of the declaration of God's word about who we are in Christ.

You might have been struggling with the same sin for years and feel as though you are permanently enslaved, but the truth is that you're not. You don't have to live in sin anymore. You don't have to yell at your kids, or give your spouse the cold shoulder, or visit that website, or pick the bottle back up, or covet and struggle with the desires of this world anymore. You don't have to do these things, and you have the means not to do them. Even though sin will be present until the end of time, you have the Holy Spirit in you. You are a new creation in Christ, and sin is no longer your master. We know this because Romans 6:10 states, "For the death, he died he died to sin once for all, but the life he lives, he lives to God." So then, since you are in Christ, consider yourself dead to sin but alive to God in Christ!

Casey McCall, "Free at Last! Saying Goodbye to Snakes, Sin, and Slavery," Preached 7/28/2013, Ashland Avenue Baptist Church Website, Accessed 4 December 2015, Available from http://www.ashlandlex.org/podcast/free-at-last-saying-goodbye-to-snakes-sin-and-slavery-romans-61-14/.

Connection with Older Testament
Genesis 4:7

For the Kids
Let your children play a quick game of tug-of-war with one another. As Christians, we have two natures pulling us in different directions—our new self toward holiness and our old self toward sin. Now, play another round but with you on one team. Your team will easily win with your extra power. Discuss how

we have power in Christ to live in freedom from sin and power to obey the Lord.

Prayer Prompts

1. Repent from living in any way that would show belief or acceptance of willing enslavement to sin.
2. Ask God daily to help you walk in the power of the Spirit as you declare war against all sinful desires.

◆

WEEK 48: DAY 1

Romans 7

Key Text

"So, my brothers, you also died to the law through the body of Christ, so that you could be joined to another, to the one who was raised from the dead, to bear fruit for God." Romans 7:4

The Gospel: Freedom from the Mosaic Law as a Result of Justification

It is sometimes confusing how the Mosaic Law figures into the Christian life. Are we now free from the Law, or are we still bound by the Law? This question is part of what Paul was addressing in Romans 7. If the wife of a man were to marry another man, that act would be an act of adultery. But if her husband were to die, then she would be free to marry another man. This analogy Paul uses to explain what happens when we repent and trust in Jesus (vv. 1-3). When we surrendered our lives to Jesus as Lord, we died to the Law and now belong to another to bear fruit for God instead of bearing fruit for death (vv. 4-5). While we lived in the flesh, we were held captive by the Law, but now, in Christ, we serve in the new way of the Spirit rather in the letter of the Law (v. 6). So, what does all of this mean for us?

We all have a desire to earn favor with God. The problem is that we could never fulfill the Law in order to earn favor with God because we all fall drastically short of God's perfection (Rom. 3:23). When we work to earn God's favor, we are working for nothing! It's like digging a hole and filling it back up again. We will never satisfy God with our actions. God knows this. He knows that we fall short and deserve his wrath. But he loved us so much that he sent Jesus the Christ to fulfill the Law for us. Now, by faith in Jesus, we are declared in the right before God, and we are free to live a life that is pleasing to God because we are in Christ, not because we impress him with our good deeds. Let's honor God by trying not to earn his favor. He chose us, and we are his children by grace. Live and die there, under grace, free from the Law.

Chad Lindon

Connection with Older Testament
Isaiah 61

For the Kids
Choose an activity for your children to race to complete that uses their hands or feet, but bind those body parts (for example, tie up their feet for a short race, tie up their hands for a play-dough creation race, etc.). You can bind one child and not the other, then switch, or let everyone try the activity unbound then bound. Is it easier to do what you needed to do when you were tied up or when you were free? Tell them that, when we trust Christ, we are not tied up by trying to keep laws to earn favor with God, and we are not tied up by sin anymore. Rather, we are free and empowered to obey him because Christ makes us right with God and gives us a new heart and the Holy Spirit.

Prayer Prompts
1. Praise God that Jesus has freed your sinful heart from the futility of trying to keep the Law, and praise God that Jesus has given you a new heart that can produce good fruit in obedience to God.
2. Being freed from the Law does not mean that we are freed to live however we choose. Repent in the areas of your life where you have succumbed to unrighteous, anti-gospel thinking, and serve the Lord in the power of the Spirit.

WEEK 48: DAY 2

Romans 8

Key Text

"For the law of the life-giving Spirit in Christ Jesus has set you free from the law of sin and death." Romans 8:2

The Gospel: Freedom from Death by Life in the Spirit

I once spoke with a family who adopted a teen girl who had been terrified that she was going to age out of the system with no family. When the girl first came home with the family after the judge had declared legally that she was their child, she was still full of fear. In the morning, when the parents woke up and went to her bedroom, she would be sitting on the bed, and her room would be immaculate. And often she would say something like, "See how clean my room is. Can I stay?" This idea that she had to earn her place to stay in the family broke her adoptive parent's hearts. They told her, "We love you because you are our child no matter what you do! Nothing will change that!" The first time the parents got up in the morning and saw that she had not cleaned her room, they high-fived one another. It's not that they didn't want her to clean her room; it is just that they did not want her to do it as a servant's wages. After all, she now possessed a son's inheritance, and she did not have to earn it.

What about you? Salvation is by grace alone from beginning to end. If the almighty Judge has declared you righteous because his Son has paid your penalty in full, and if he then stepped down from the bench, not only forgiving your debt, but also declaring you now his Son with full rights to his inheritance, what is there to fear? What can you be lacking if the one who owns everything has adopted you as a son, united you to his only begotten Son, and given you the Spirit of adoption?

David Prince, "Grace Alone: John Calvin and the Good News of Adoption," Published 11/6/2017, Prince on Preaching Website, Accessed 22 November 2017, Available from http://www.davidprince.com/2017/11/06/grace-alone-john-calvin-good-news-adoption/.

Connection with Older Testament

Psalm 143:10

For the Kids

Tell your kids that adults do all kinds of things to avoid death. Ask your kids if they know why adults try to avoid death. It's because people fear the finality of death. Tell your children that God takes the fear of death away in Jesus by raising him from the dead. Tell your children that, through faith in Jesus, the Holy Spirit will work in us to free us from death and from fear of death as adopted sons of God.

Prayer Prompts

1. In thankfulness, praise God for the life-giving Spirit of adoption that dwells in us.
2. Pray for a mind wholly captive to the things of the Spirit of God.

◆

WEEK 48: DAY 3

Romans 9-11

Key Text

"It is not as though the word of God has failed. For not all those who are descended from Israel are truly Israel" Romans 9:6

The Gospel: The Faithfulness of God

The Christian's salvation depends upon Romans 9-11. These three densely-packed chapters about Israel's relation to God in light of Christ often provoke discussion about God's sovereign choice in election (9:1-29), Israel's unbelief (9:30-33), the gospel of salvation to all people (10:1-21), the remnant of ethnic Israel (11:1-10), the Gentiles' in-grafting to the people of God in Christ (11:11-24), and the mystery of Israel's salvation (11:25-36). Yet, in the midst of all the details laid out, Paul's big picture demonstrates that God is faithful to his word, to his promises, and to his covenant with Israel. If Israel's current state looks like the word of God has failed, the problem is not with the word of God; it's with the reader of the word.

Understanding the faithfulness of God to his promises in the midst of these three chapters is vital to the Christian's salvation. If God is indeed faithless, if his promises to Israel have failed, Christians have no hope. How can we trust a God who promises to save us from our sins for all eternity through faith in Jesus Christ if this same God has a track record of failing to keep his promises? We can't! We need to see that God is faithful, that he is trustworthy, and that our hope is not in vain in light of Israel's circumstances, and Romans 9-11 provides this assurance for us. Take heart, Christian. God is faithful.

Jon Canler

Connection with Older Testament
Lamentations 3:22-24

For the Kids
Have you ever had a friend make a promise to you that they did not keep? Were you hurt when they didn't keep their word? Do you think you will quickly believe them in the future if they make another promise to you, or will you not be sure whether or not you can trust them? In Paul's day, many people thought that God made promises to Israel that he did not keep, so some people questioned whether or not God could be trusted. Paul wrote Romans 9-11 to help up see that God does keep his promises, which means we can trust him when he promises to save us from our sins through faith in Jesus.

Prayer Prompts
1. Praise God that he is faithful to his promises such that we can trust him for life and salvation that he promises to us in Jesus.
2. Pray for the fullness of Gentile and Israelites to be saved through the preaching of the gospel to the ends of the earth.

WEEK 48: DAY 4
Romans 12-13

Key Text
"I urge you therefore, brothers, by the mercies of God, to present your bodies as a living sacrifice, holy and pleasing to God, which is your spiritual worship. Do not be conformed to this world, but be transformed by the renewal of your mind, that you may discern by testing what is the will of God, what is good and pleasing and perfect." Romans 12:1-2*

Gospel-Centered Minds: Living and Loving in Light of Salvation
"Brothers" is very pointed and scandalous and is meant to shock the world around us. Our standing before our holy God is not bound up in us as individuals, but in Jesus, and he has made us a community of brothers by "the mercies of God." We are the transformed y'all. The Church is a community project. We are to live as the community of the kingdom. Private Christianity is false Christianity. Family is at times exhausting, but we are still united to one another. Our service is not pleasing to God if it is only inward or only outward. We are to offer our whole selves to God as a "living sacrifice." If your service in the Church is at times not exhausting, it is because you do not see the Church as family. God has ordained it that we would be sanctified by loving people who we would not be ordinarily drawn to love.

David Prince, "Brothers - The Scandalous Community," Preached 10/16/2011, Prince on Preaching Website, Accessed 4 December 2015, Available from http://www.davidprince.com/2011/10/16/brothers-the-scandalous-community-romans-121-2/.

Connection with Older Testament
Malachi 3:1-4

For the Kids
Have your children think about why they go to school. They go to learn truth

about the world and how to think about God's created order. While school may not always teach us rightly about God's world, school is meant to transform our minds and to shape the way we think and live. Likewise, as followers of Jesus who have been saved by his grace, we have the Bible and the Holy Spirit to renew our minds in truth to live rightly in light of the truth of the gospel. This means, in part, that, rather than living for and loving ourselves, we're freed to live in love for God and others. Have your children think about how they might love others today in light of the gospel with renewed minds.

Prayer Prompts

1. Ask God to help you think of your church correctly: as real, blood-bought family.

2. Ask God to help you call the members of your church "brothers," and ask for wisdom to sacrificially serve them with renewed minds.

◆

WEEK 48: DAY 5

Colossians 1:15-23

Key Text

"For God was pleased to have all his fullness dwell in the Son and through him to reconcile all things to himself by making peace through the blood of his cross—through him, whether things on earth or things in heaven." Colossians 1:19-20

The Sufficiency and Preeminence of Jesus

We are all prone to add things to the gospel. Oh, we may say that justification is by grace alone through faith alone, but we're so prone to think that, once we are reconciled to the Lord by faith in Christ, we stay in God's good graces through works we perform.

Such was the case in the Colossian church. There was a false teaching creeping into the church that began to add Jewish practices and Gentile philosophy to the gospel (Col. 2:8-23). Consequently, Paul begins his letter to the Colossians by reminding them of the sufficiency and preeminence of Jesus

(vv. 15-23). Jesus is supreme over both the creation and the Church (vv. 15-18) on the basis of the fact that the fullness of God dwells in him and on the fact of his work of reconciliation (vv. 19-23). Paul reminds the Church that Jesus is sufficient for the fullness of our salvation. No extras are needed. Repent of trying to add things to faith in Christ for your standing before God. Remember simple gospel math: Jesus plus nothing is everything.

Jon Canler

Connection with Older Testament
Genesis 1

For the Kids
Take a few minutes to teach your children gospel math and why it is important.

Prayer Prompts
1. Ask God to give you an understanding of the supremacy of King Jesus in everything.
2. Ask God to help you find your identity in King Jesus and nothing else.

◆

WEEK 49: DAY 1
Ephesians 2:1-3:13

Key Text
"But now in Christ Jesus you who used to be far away have been brought near by the blood of Christ." Ephesians 2:13

The Mystery of the Gospel: One New Man of Jews and Gentiles
A genuinely Christian attitude toward racial and ethnic diversity is not one of toleration, but celebration. The human race was made in the image of God (Gen. 1:27, Acts 17:26). The entire human race shares a common descent as the fallen children of Adam (Gen. 3:17, 1 Cor. 15:22). The Church of the

Lord Jesus Christ is made up of redeemed image bearers described as "one new man" (Eph. 2:15), a people whose identity is found in being united by faith to Christ (Eph. 2:11-22). The glory of the triumphant kingdom of Christ is demonstrated by the multi-ethnic diversity of worshippers who exult, "Worthy are you to take the scroll and to open its seals, for you were slain, and by your blood you ransomed people for God from every tribe and language and people and nation" (Rev. 5:9*).

The inclusion of ethnically diverse peoples in the household of God is God's intention, fulfilling his gospel promise (Gen. 3:15, Gen. 12, 15, Ps. 67, Acts 2, Rom. 4, Gal. 3, 4, Eph. 2, 4, Rev. 5, 7, 14). Culturally derived worldviews which root identity in race and ethnicity are directly at odds with the gospel of Jesus Christ and must be subordinated by those who truly say, "Jesus is Lord." A vital way that local churches reflect the glory of his kingdom is through being intentionally multi-ethnic outposts of the kingdom who celebrate diversity in Christ, including diversity of skin color. Where racism is embraced, or racist hatred is tolerated, the mind of Christ on display in the incarnation and subsequent crucifixion is rejected.

The Bible says that the new heavens and new earth will be an eternal display of the multi-ethnic grace of God, and it also has a name for the place where people just want to cling to self and be with their own kind; the Bible calls that place hell.

David Prince, "Never Trump: Opposing Racial Injustice Now, Tomorrow, and Forever," Published 3/3/2016, Prince on Preaching Website, Accessed 22 November 2017, Available from http://www.davidprince.com/2016/03/03/never-trump-opposing-racial-injustice-now-tomorrow-forever/.

Connection with Older Testament
Psalm 67

For the Kids
When God created us, he gave us our own special color of eyes, hair, and skin. He put us in a land with our own language and way of life. One of the most special things about the Church is that people who are different are loving and

worshipping the same God. Jesus came to save all kinds of people and wants us not only to love him, but to love and welcome each other! Thank God for the way he brings all kinds of people from all kinds of different backgrounds into one diverse community for his glory.

Prayer Prompts

1. Ask God to help you remember who you were apart from Jesus Christ.
2. Ask God to help your church to be committed to demonstrate the peace of Christ to all ethnicities and peoples.

◆

WEEK 49: DAY 2
Philippians 4

Key Text
"I am not saying this because I am in need, for I have learned to be content in any circumstance. I have experienced times of need and times of abundance. In any and every circumstance I have learned the secret of contentment, whether I go satisfied or hungry, have plenty or nothing. I am able to do all things through the one who strengthens me." Philippians 4:11-13

The Provision of God in the Gospel: Joy and Contentment in All Circumstances

Considering the extraordinary events that unfolded in the life of the apostle Paul, it is interesting here to see him giving advice to "normal" Christians on how to carry out their everyday lives. He first pleads for fellow Christians to live in peace, both with each other (vv. 2-3) and with those who may be outside the body of Christ (v. 5). Both exhortations echo his command in Romans 12:18, "If possible, so far as it depends on you, live peaceably with all people."

The peace Paul described in Philippians 4 is attained, in part, through the orientation of our minds. Though there are innumerable selfish desires and anxieties we could dwell on, we must instead make every effort to focus on that which is just, pure, lovely, commendable, excellent, and praiseworthy (v. 8).

When our thoughts are on the things of God, our tongues and actions will follow and only then will we live in that peace "that surpasses all understanding" (v. 7).

Thus, happiness and peace for Christians comes only when we forget ourselves and, instead, give our love and priority to God and to others: "All the law and the prophets depend on these two commandments" (Matt. 22:40). This orientation away from self was clearly alive in the heart of Paul who, though he had faced numerous hardships and had already been in need, hungry, and brought low (v. 12), was writing in hope that two church members would resolve an argument (v. 2).

Joe Martin

Connection with Older Testament
2 Kings 14:10

For the Kids
Do you have days when things are going wrong? Maybe your bike has a flat tire, you can't find your favorite toy, it's rainy and cold and you wanted to play outside? It can be hard to be happy in all circumstances. But Christians can be happy in good and bad times because Christ's eternal gospel is all-satisfying. Pray for the Lord to cause you to be satisfied in Jesus no matter what.

Prayer Prompts
1. Praise God that he has provided more than we deserve in Christ. Meditate on the gospel and find joy. Are you lacking in joy? Ask God to help you to behold the glory of the gospel so that in all things you might be content.
2. Repent of grumbling. You've been given eternal life in Christ rather than the hell we all deserve. How can we complain when we've been given so much?

◆

WEEK 49: DAY 3
1 Timothy 3; Titus 1

Key Text

"The reason I left you in Crete was to set in order the remaining matters and to appoint elders in every town, as I directed you." Titus 1:5

Overseers and Deacons: Instructions for Leadership in Christ's Church

Paul dedicated his ministry to maintain the health of Christ's Church at all costs. God is not a God of chaos, but a God of order. He has appointed elders to oversee the health and order of his church, fleshed out specifically in the local church. The New Testament does not allow us to pit the Lord Jesus against the local church.

Paul did not see his mission as complete until new believers were organized into local churches under the leadership of elders (pastors). The unity and health of the local church is so important to the gospel that God has given us pastors to guard against anyone or anything that would tear the church apart. To maintain healthy doctrine and unified community, pastors must champion the truth that Jesus is enough in their teaching and also in their daily lives. As church members, we are to humbly follow our pastors, knowing they are a gift from God to his Church. We are to follow their example by matching our lives to our profession and promoting unity and not discord in the church.

Casey McCall, "Health," Preached 10/06/2013, Ashland Avenue Baptist Church Website, Accessed 4 December 2015, Available from http://www.ashlandlex.org/podcast/health/.

Connection with Older Testament

Exodus 18:21-22

For the Kids

Pastors are men who love God and who lead our church under the authority of God. When the pastors preach to us, they are teaching us what the Bible means. Let's pray for our church and for our pastors!

Prayer Prompts

1. Thank God for our pastors and their families as they are given to us by God.
2. Ask God to make you a promoter of gospel unity.

◆

WEEK 49: DAY 4

2 Timothy 3:1-4:8

Key Text

"I solemnly charge you before God and Christ Jesus, who is going to judge the living and the dead, and by his appearing and his kingdom: Preach the message, be ready whether it is convenient or not, reprove, rebuke, exhort with complete patience and instruction." 2 Timothy 4:1-2

An Approved Man of God: Preach the God-Breathed Word

In 2 Timothy 3:1-4:8, Paul describes two forces in conflict for Timothy's heart: the world and the word of God. We must be careful to accept the full-force of God's word when Paul warns Timothy of the last days when people will be "lovers of themselves" and "lovers of money" (3:2), "without self-control" (3:3), and "loving pleasure" (3:4). In an era of "selfies," social media, bottomless buffets, unprecedented wealth, and great comfort, we must honestly ask ourselves whether Paul would caution Timothy against excessive interactions with us. At the very least, along with Timothy, we must humbly consider the example of Paul, who was at the time of this writing persecuted, abandoned, imprisoned, cold, and lonely—all for the sake of Christ.

Although Timothy is advised to avoid some people and situations altogether (3:5), he is also called to influence the world for good through the preaching of the word (4:1-5). The teachings of God and the example of Paul are partially to help Timothy navigate the treacherous world in which he lives, but they are also given so that Timothy can influence others in that same world. The same is true for us. We must know the God-breathed word in Jesus Christ if we are to be "capable," "equipped for every good work" (3:16-17).

Joe Martin

Connection with Older Testament

Ezra 7:10

For the Kids

The Bible gives important instructions for our pastors. First, they are to seek God to help them as they study the Bible. Then, they are to do what the Bible says. The pastors are then ready to teach their church everything God has taught them. Say a prayer of thanks for our pastors. Pray that the pastors would faithfully preach the word of God, the truth as it is in Jesus.

Prayer Prompts

1. Pray for your pastors and teachers to faithfully submit to and preach God's word.

2. Pray for your heart and mind to be prepared to hear and obey the word taught to you this week.

◆

WEEK 49: DAY 5

Hebrews 1-2

Key Text

"but of the Son he says, 'Your throne, O God, is forever and ever, and a righteous scepter is the scepter of your kingdom.'" Hebrews 1:8

Jesus: The Preeminent and Eternal Ruler of All

Angels are second in power only to God. That is why the introduction of the letter to the Hebrews is so shocking. Angels are mighty. In 2 Kings 19:35, a single angel wiped out 185,000 Assyrian soldiers in one night! Angels are terrifying warriors of light. This explains the reaction of the shepherds in Luke 2:9 who "were absolutely terrified" when an angel appeared to them. Angels stand in the presence of God, ready to serve him and calling to one another, "Holy, holy, holy is the LORD who commands armies! His majestic splendor fills the entire earth!" (Is. 6:3). No wonder the Colossians were tempted to worship angels (Col. 2:18). Even John wanted to bow down before an angel and worship him (Rev. 19:10).

What is incredible about the beginning of Hebrews is that the Spirit-inspired author tells us that, as mighty and glorious as angels are, they are nothing when compared to Jesus Christ. The author repeatedly demonstrates how Jesus is greater than angels in every way imaginable. He is preeminent, surpassing all, distinguished above all beings, even spiritual beings. The logical conclusion is that if Jesus is greater than angels, and angels are second in power only to God, then Jesus Christ must be God!

Angels do not hold the position of Son of God, only Jesus does (1:5-6). Angels do not have authority as the eternally existing ruler of all, only Jesus does (1:8). Angels do not have the power to create and sustain the world, only Jesus does (1:10). Angels did not die for sins nor were they raised to life in victory over Satan for our salvation; only Jesus has done that (2:14). Truly, Jesus is the preeminent one, surpassing all angels and human beings. He alone deserves all of our worship and praise. Behold his glory today and give him the honor he deserves!

Eric Turner

Connection with Older Testament

2 Samuel 7:14; Psalm 2:7, 45:6-7, 102:25-27

For the Kids

Pull out old photos of you and your children, or use your phone to take a picture. Help your children understand that a photo is an image. In the photos you're looking at, you see a representation of you and your children. Likewise, Jesus is the image of the invisible God. He is the exact imprint of his nature (Heb. 1:3). When we see Jesus, we see God himself. This means, in part, that Jesus is greater than angels. This means that Jesus is to be worshipped. Pray that your children would see the supremacy of Jesus and would worship him rightly.

Prayer Prompts

1. Praise Jesus Christ because he is our Creator God.

2. Pray for grace never to neglect the great salvation given through faith in Jesus Christ.

◆

WEEK 50: DAY 1
Hebrews 3:1-4:13

Key Text
"For he has been considered worthy of more glory than Moses, as much as the builder of a house has more honor than the house itself." Hebrews 3:3*

Don't Return to Judaism: Jesus as Superior to Moses and Joshua

By the time Hebrews was written, many former Jews who became Christians were experiencing persecution for their faith, and these Christians were considering returning to Judaism to escape persecution. In the book of Hebrews, the author is trying to persuade his audience not to return to Judaism by showing the superiority of Jesus to everything associated with the old covenant in Judaism.

In Hebrews 3:1-4:13, Jesus is shown to be superior to two of the most key figures in the old covenant: Moses and Joshua. On the one hand, Jesus is greater than Moses because Jesus is the Son of God who builds the house of God (Church) under the new covenant whereas Moses was a servant of God who represented the house being built (Israel) under the old covenant. In both his person (son vs. servant) and in his work (builder vs. that which is built), Jesus is superior to Moses. On the other hand, Jesus is also greater than Joshua because Jesus offers a rest to God's people that Joshua could not offer, namely a superior Sabbath rest that allows God's people to rest from their works, like God, because of the finished work Jesus provides on their behalf.

While afflictions and other worldly circumstances often call us to abandon the gospel for the sake of temporary comfort and pleasure, hold fast to Jesus. Jesus is greater than the old covenant of Judaism. He's also greater than all of the other works-based systems of religion and their prophets the world has to offer. Mohammed, while a prophet of Islam, was a mere man while Jesus is God. Gandhi may have been a good teacher, but Jesus always

400

revealed truth. Jesus and his gospel is greater than all. Hold fast to him in all circumstances by faith and find soul-satisfying rest.

Jon Canler

Connection with Older Testament
Numbers 12:7; Psalm 95:7-11

For the Kids
Ask your children if they've ever had arguments with friends along the lines of "My dad is better than your dad." It's easy, in many cases, for us to think highly of our parents because of how good they are to us and because of how they provide and protect for the family. For the former Jews who are now Christians being written to in Hebrews, the temptation was to think of spiritual fathers, like Moses and Joshua, as most important. Hebrews 3:1-4:13 teaches us that, as important as people like Moses and Joshua are, Jesus is greatest, which means he's also greater than our parents. Because Jesus saves, let's honor our parents, but let's worship Jesus. Help your children think about how to honor and worship rightly.

Prayer Prompts
1. Thank God that, in Christ, you are part of his eternal building, never to be destroyed or torn down. Christ protects us from both the wiles of Satan and the righteous and just wrath of God.
2. Pray for the Lord to strengthen his building across the globe so that all peoples and nations may hear the gospel and come to faith in Christ.

◆

WEEK 50: DAY 2
Hebrews 4:14-5:10, 6:13-7:28

Key Text
"For here is the testimony about him: 'You are a priest forever in the order of Melchizedek.'" Hebrews 7:17

Don't Return to Judaism: Jesus as Superior to the Levitical Priesthood

The author of Hebrews continues to build his case for the superiority of Jesus Christ. He began by proving how Jesus is vastly greater than angels, Moses, and Joshua. Now, he argues for how Jesus is superior to the entire Levitical priesthood. The contrast could not be starker. The Levitical priests died and had to be replaced. Jesus is eternal. He died but was resurrected, and he will never be replaced as our Great High Priest. Levitical priests were sinners and, as such, had to make daily sacrifices not only for the people, but for themselves. Jesus was sinless and, as such, was able to offer himself as a perfect one-time sacrifice for us. Levitical priests maintained the old covenant, but Jesus has instituted a new superior covenant of grace.

The evidence is overwhelming: Jesus is clearly superior to the Levitical priesthood. Our response is to trust in him as our eternal Great High Priest who permanently secured our salvation by sacrificing himself. Unfortunately, in many ways we are still tempted to return to the old Levitical priesthood. For example, we obey God's word and then feel secure of our salvation because of our own obedience. Or we do something we know we should not do and then we promise God that we will do something good in return to make up for it. By doing so, we try to offer little sacrifices for our sins instead of trusting that all our sin debt has been finally paid through Jesus Christ's sacrifice. We don't need to return to the Levitical priesthood because our Great High Priest has come and graciously offered himself for us so that by faith in him we are saved!

Eric Turner

Connection with Older Testament
Psalm 110

For the Kids
Have your children think about sweeping the house. Does sweeping the house ever really stop? No. You'll sweep today, the dust will pile up tomorrow, and you'll sweep again and again and again. You'll never get to a point where sweeping will permanently clean your house. Likewise, the Old Testament

priests constantly offered sacrifices to God because those sacrifices never permanently made an end to sin. But Jesus did! Praise God that Jesus has offered a final sacrifice for sins as the Great High Priest.

Prayer Prompts

1. Praise God for the eternality of Jesus' priesthood. We now have access to the holy presence of God forever through our resurrected Mediator.

2. Because Christ is our Priest, we live under his new law: the freeing law of Christ that is rooted in grace. Repent of trying to live by works when the law of Christ demands that we live by faith in the promises of God.

◆

WEEK 50: DAY 3
Hebrews 8

Key Text

"For if that first covenant had been faultless, there would have been no occasion to look for a second." Hebrews 8:7*

Don't Return to Judaism: The New Covenant as Superior to the Mosaic Covenant

Before a great or beautiful building can be constructed, scaffolding must first be assembled. This external structure allows workers to more easily create the intended design. While the scaffolding typically precedes the construction of the actual building, it serves a temporary purpose and is eventually disassembled. The sacrificial system of the Old Testament is similar to scaffolding: It helped God's people to grasp the seriousness of sin and the need for atonement, but it was ultimately incomplete and, by itself, unable to truly cleanse from sin (Heb. 10:4).

The author of the letter to the Hebrews was trying to show his readers that, just because the old sacrificial system came first, it was not better. In fact, the old system was not even truly first! Before Aaron (the first high priest) ever entered the Holy of Holies, Hebrews reminds us that the ritual proceedings and architecture under the old covenant were merely copies and shadows of the heavenly things (v. 5).

The author of Hebrews concludes by citing Jeremiah 31 to demonstrate the superiority of the new covenant. This new covenant is not only a replacement for the old covenant; it is a superior replacement that renders the old covenant "obsolete" (v. 13). As the author notes, the new covenant is "enacted on better promises" (v. 6). And although Abraham and the Israelites received great promises from God, nothing can compare to the promises of the new covenant where Christians receive the righteousness of Christ, are granted eternal life, are co-heirs with God's own Son, and even judge angels because of the spotless blood of Jesus Christ.

Joe Martin

Connection with Older Testament
Jeremiah 31:31-40

For the Kids
Have your children think about the most disgusting flavor of ice cream they can imagine. Then ask them if they could ever love that flavor. Could they eat it every time it was offered to them? Could they talk about how good it is to others? Tell your children that, physically, they have the ability to put the ice cream in their mouth and the ability to use their words to talk about ice cream. The problem is that they wouldn't have a heart that would want to do such things freely and with joy. This is a lot like the old covenant. God's people had the physical ability to do all that the covenant required; they just didn't have the heart to want to do it. So, they didn't. But the new covenant in Jesus' blood is better than the old covenant. In the new covenant, the Lord gives his people the heart needed to want to do his works as he writes the laws on the hearts and minds of his people. The new covenant in Jesus is better. Praise God that he gives his people the ability to rightly serve him forever in the new covenant.

Prayer Prompts
1. Praise God for the fact that we can each know him intimately because of the

superiority of the new covenant mediated by Jesus Christ.

2. The Lord has given you, Christian, a new heart that is enabled to obey him. Ask him for grace to obey, even when sin and temptation tell you otherwise.

◆

WEEK 50: DAY 4
Hebrews 9

Key Text
"But when Christ appeared as a high priest of the good things that have come, through the greater and more perfect tent—not made by hand, that is, not of this creation—he entered once for all into the holy places, not through the blood of goats and calves but through his own blood, having obtained an eternal redemption." Hebrews 9:11-12*

Don't Return to Judaism: Jesus as Superior to the Temple
As the tabernacle was a holy place, it was also a bloody place. In order to purify, the tabernacle blood had to be sprinkled as a sin offering. Animals were slain, and their blood was poured out daily as a constant visual reminder of the need for cleansing the guilt of sin. The holiest place was only entered once a year by the high priest, only after a sufficient amount of blood had been spilt. Hebrews 9 begins by talking about this bloody tent where priests went to meet with God, and then the author shows us how Christ has surpassed it.

When Jesus Christ offered himself as the perfect, eternal sacrifice for sins, he did not enter into a bloody tent made by human hands. Rather, he entered directly into the presence of God in heaven. The blood of animals provides a momentary cleansing from sin, but Christ's blood provides an eternal cleansing from sin. The old covenant rituals were outward and visual, but only Christ's atoning work combines an outward visual sacrifice on a cross with an inward purification of the conscience.

On this side of the cross, we no longer need to load up our goats and bulls to go to the tent on Sunday mornings. No more blood needs to be shed on our behalf because Christ's death was completely sufficient for all time. Now we respond in worship and by recruiting the nations to join the choir to declare with us for eternity, "You are worthy to take the scroll and to open its seals because you were killed, and at the cost of your own blood you have purchased for God persons from every tribe, language, people, and nation" (Rev. 5:9).

Eric Turner

Connection with Older Testament
Leviticus 16

For the Kids
Use building blocks or Legos to build a miniature house that looks like your house as best as you can. Then ask your children to compare your miniature house to your real house. In what ways are they similar? In what ways are they different? Show your children how your actual house is much superior to the Lego house, which is only a copy. Teach your children that the Jewish temple is like the Lego house. It was an imperfect copy of the dwelling place of God in heaven. Instruct your children that Jesus himself has entered into heaven, the place where God dwells in full glory, and he appears in the presence of God for his people on account of his death for their sin. This means Jesus' sacrifice was a supreme sacrifice brought into the superior temple.

Prayer Prompts
1. Consider that, in Christ, you have continual access to the throne of God through the spotless blood of Christ poured out for you before the Lord.
2. Praise the Lord that, in Christ, we have a sacrifice that actually purifies our consciences. His death enables us to fully serve God instead of performing empty works. We're set free to serve.

◆

WEEK 50: DAY 5
Hebrews 10

Key Text
"And every priest stands day after day serving and offering the same sacrifices

again and again—sacrifices that can never take away sins. But when this priest had offered one sacrifice for sins for all time, he sat down at the right hand of God" Hebrews 10:11-12

Don't Return to Judaism: Jesus as the Superior Sacrifice

The author of Hebrews begins Hebrews 10 by demonstrating the insufficiencies of the old covenant sacrificial system. Specifically, the old covenant system required repeated "maintenance" without even the ability to fully realize its purpose: the forgiveness of sin. This is in stark contrast to the new covenant in Jesus Christ, who "by one offering has perfected for all time those who are made holy" (v. 14). Hebrews 10:14 is a thesis statement for much of Hebrews 10, for much of the letter to the Hebrews, and for much of the New Testament.

The perfection of Christ's sacrifice has ushered in a new era for God-fearers. We no longer watch from a distance while an earthly high-priest cautiously enters the Holy of Holies. Instead, the tears in Jesus' body have literally torn the temple curtain so that we now "have confidence to enter the sanctuary by the blood of Jesus" (v. 19). The perfect and eternal nature of Christ's sprinkled blood has transformed his people into a nation of priests who possess more purity than any ritualistic cleansing could ever provide.

In light of the eternal and perfect cleansing that Christ's blood offers Christians, the author of Hebrews, pre-empting any potential distortions of his words, offers some important commands and stern warnings: hold fast to our faith (v. 23), stir one another up through meeting together (vv. 24-25), and avoid deliberate sin (v. 26).

Though the warnings in Hebrews 10:26-31 are stern, faithful Christians should not "throw away [their] confidence" (v. 35) nor should they make the grave mistake of assuming that their continued works are the means by which they avoid the wrath of God. The author of Hebrews encourages his Christian readers to remember their past (vv. 32-34) as a source of evidence of their faith and urges them to refuse to "shrink back" (v. 39).

Joe Martin

Connection with Older Testament

Psalm 40:6-8

For the Kids

Use a flashlight to create hand shadows on the wall with your children. Teach your children about how shadows work. The shadows always reflect and point to the true form, in this case, your hand. Teach them that the Old Testament sacrifices for sin were shadows. They never took away sin. They simply pointed to the true sacrifice that would take away sin. Then tell your children that Jesus' death on the cross was the true form to which the Old Testament shadows pointed. Rejoice that God remembers the lawless deeds of his people no more because of Jesus.

Prayer Prompts

1. Pray for God to help you draw near and have communion with him based on the once-for-all-time sacrifice of his Son.

2. Pray for opportunities to encourage and meet together with other believers to celebrate and spread the gospel.

◆

WEEK 51: DAY 1

Hebrews 11

Key Text

"He considered the reproach of Christ greater wealth than the treasures of Egypt, for he was looking to the reward." Hebrews 11:26*

Don't Return to Judaism: The Saints of the Old Lived by Faith

I was recently asked an email question: *"I listened to your most recent sermon today and wanted to ask, what would you say the differences between faith and courage are?"* I thought the answer below might be helpful to others as well.

Let's start with basic and simple definitions. Courage is acting on the premise that there is something more important than fear; it is not the absence of fear. Faith is cognitive and volitional trust; a trusting in, relying on, or a clinging to.

A biblical/theological understanding of faith clarifies that the faith which glorifies God has as its object Jesus and his gospel of the kingdom. Also, the something-more-important-than-fear that provides courage is someone— the triune God. We rightly fear him in a reverential way that leads to worship knowing that his sovereign power is for us in Christ. Courage is related to faith because faith is the foundation and motivation of all courageous deeds that can be counted as acts of worship.

What Moses said to the people at Mt. Sinai provides clarity (Ex. 20:20*):

"Moses said to the people, "Do not fear, … "
Be courageous in the face of all non-ultimate, temporal fears.
"for God has come to test you, … "
This clause is a call for faith; trust in, rely on, and cling to God and his gracious promises.
"that the fear of him may be before you that you may not sin."
Fear of the ultimate–godly fear–is the rightly-directed reverential awe of worship.

Saving faith is directed at its object–God in Christ and his kingdom. True saving faith is rooted in a godly fear that the believer never overcomes because God is ultimate and we are always needy sinners who appropriately worship God through Christ as Lord of all.

The courage that honors God is not the absence of fear, but rather, it requires fear. There is no need to be courageous if you are not afraid of something. Biblical courage is directed at obeying the Lord, who is more important than fear, in our daily lives in spite of temporal things, situations, and people that bring natural fearfulness.

David Prince, "The Relationship Between Faith and Courage," Published 1/14/2016, Prince on Preaching Website, Accessed 22 November 2017, Available from http://www.davidprince.com/2016/01/14/the-relationship-btween-faith-and-courage/.

Connection with Older Testament

Exodus 2

For the Kids

Talk to your children about the times they have conquered difficulty trusting you (perhaps in things that they are afraid of such as water, heights, or bike riding). Help them see that it can be the same way in life for God. When they trust him no matter what he calls them to do or what situations they find ourselves in, despite any fears, we call that faith.

Prayer Prompts

1. Ask God to give you eyes of faith.
2. Thank God that he knows what is best for you and does everything for your good.

◆

WEEK 51: DAY 2

1 Peter 1:13-2:12

Key Text

"But you are a chosen race, a royal priesthood, a holy nation, a people of his own, so that you may proclaim the virtues of the one who called you out of darkness into his marvelous light. You once were not a people, but now you are God's people. You were shown no mercy, but now you have received mercy." 1 Peter 2:9-10

Pilgrim Life: Be Holy as God is Holy on the Basis of Jesus' Death

Most of us live life with a microscope, looking at our circumstances and problems and seeing them as ultimate. As believers, we are to live our lives with a telescope looking at the privileges that we have in Christ. When we are overwhelmed with our standing in Christ, we will look at everything with gospel hope, and we will live like a missionary right where we are. Our call is to order our lives to reach people with the gospel of Christ. Our fuel for the task is to tell ourselves every day that we are God's beloved by his grace. As God's beloved, we have been transported into a new kingdom, and we have become temporary residents on this earth. This means that our lives are not meant to just fade away into the background, but must rather be markedly different. As pilgrims, we must distant ourselves from our flesh and our sinful desires. We are to see ourselves as our greatest problem. We are to live in such a way that our lives proclaim that this life is not the end as we give up on our rights so that those around us will give glory to our God.

David Prince, "Only Foreigners Will Win the World for Jesus: A Genuine Call to Missional Living," Preached 10/25/2009, Prince on Preaching Website, Accessed 4 December 2015, Available from http://www.davidprince.com/2009/10/25/only-foreigners-will-win-the-world-for-jesus-a-genuine-call-to-missional-living-1-peter-211-12/.

Connection with Older Testament
Leviticus 20:22-27

For the Kids
Ask you kids to describe what makes your family, well, your family. Maybe you have certain traditions you keep. Maybe there are certain sports teams you follow. Maybe there are certain meals you enjoy as a family. Make a "My Family Does ____" list. Once the list is made, tell your children that God's family is to look and act in distinct ways too. Christians are called to be holy, set apart and devoted to telling others about the greatness of God in Christ. Help your children understand what people in God's family do by explaining some of the commands from 1 Peter 1:13-2:12.

Prayer Prompts
1. Thank God that he has made you his beloved.
2. Ask God to open your eyes to see everything with gospel hope.

WEEK 51: DAY 3

2 Peter 1

Key Text

"And we have the prophetic word more fully confirmed, to which you will do well to pay attention as to a lamp shining in a dark place, until the day dawns and the morning star rises in your hearts" 2 Peter 1:19*

Pilgrim Life: Guard Against False Teachers

You and I live in the most privileged time in the history of the world. For the past 2,000 years, God's people have been able to live in light of the fullness of God's revelation in Christ. Under the old covenant, God's people struggled to see how it would all come together. They heard God's promises, but they never saw them come to fruition. In fact, it often looked like it was impossible. But here we sit, right in the middle of the story, but from the vantage point of knowing that all the promises of God find their 'Yes' in Jesus (2 Cor. 1:20).

Peter writes to the Church as an "eyewitness of his grandeur" (v. 16). He's referring to his experience of Christ's transfiguration (Matt. 17), when he saw Christ's glory and heard the voice of God confirming Jesus as his Son. Peter wisely connects his experience with the Old Testament Scriptures. Certainly, his mind went to Psalm 2:7 where the LORD says to his anointed, "You are my son!" Peter understands the significance of what he saw. Men don't make up their own interpretations of prophecy. God himself fulfills his word through his Spirit (v. 21). Our job is to listen and delight in what God chooses to reveal.

Casey McCall

Connection with Older Testament

Exodus 19:5-6; Psalm 2

For the Kids

Ask your children if they've ever been taught or told something that was false. For example, maybe a friend told them a story that just wasn't true. Then ask your children how they found out the truth. Did they ask a more knowledgeable or trustworthy person? A teacher or parent perhaps? Then explain that there are people who tell stories about God and Jesus that aren't true. You might give the example of someone wanting to use religion and Jesus to become popular or rich. Then ask your children where they can go to find the truth about God and Jesus. The answer is the Bible. Read 2 Peter 1:16-21 to your children, and help them understand that even the apostles who saw Jesus face to face tell us to pay attention to the prophetic word, the Bible, in order to know what's true and what's false about Jesus.

Prayer Prompts

1. Ask God to grant you grace so that you may heed his word rather than competing false voices that vie for your attention.
2. Ask God for grace to understand his word more clearly and to apply it correctly in light of the gospel each time you read it.

◆

WEEK 51: DAY 4
1 John 2-3

Key Text

"Now by this we know that God resides in us: by the Spirit he has given us." 1 John 3:24b

Test for Assurance of Salvation

We live in a world full of uncertainty. We don't know what tomorrow is going to bring, so we often live life asking a lot of questions. "Will I get married?" "Will I get that job I applied for?" "Will my sickness be cured?" To make matters more difficult, we live in a sinful world in which promises made today are often broken tomorrow. Fortunately, for those who've repented of sin and trusted in Jesus Christ for salvation, the LORD does not want his people to be uncertain about their great salvation. In 1 John, the LORD reveals three tests through which those who "believe in the name of the Son of God…may know that you have eternal life" (1 John 5:13).

How does the Spirit assure Christians of their salvation in a world full of uncertainty? First, assurance come through obedience to Christ (2:1-6, 3:1-10). Second, assurance come through loving other Christians (2:7-17, 3:11-24). Third, assurance comes through acknowledging that Jesus is the Christ come in the flesh (2:18-26, 1 John 4:1-6). Assurance of salvation does not come from some kind of mystical experience with tingly feelings. Assurance is a gift of the Holy Spirit given to those who stake their lives on the truth of the gospel and who, consequently, seek to live out the gospel in love for God and in love for other Christians. Be encouraged, people of Christ, that the LORD desires for us to know that we have eternal life!

Jon Canler

Connection with Older Testament
Deuteronomy 30:1-10

For the Kids
Tell your kids that every family has traditions. There are certain things that your family does that identifies who you are. Discuss some of those things that you do that identify who you are as a family. Tell your children that one way they know they belong to your family, as opposed to another, is because they do activities fitting with your family. Likewise, God wants his children to know that they are part of his family by reminding them of what his family does: they love him as Father, they love each other, and they believe in Jesus. Just as we can know who our physical families are, God wants his people know who their spiritual family is.

Prayer Prompts
1. Ask God to remind you daily that, in his Son, we have everything; we are, therefore, free to love others and to obey the Lord.

2. Praise the Lord that he wants his children to know that they are his redeemed and beloved in Christ. Our assurance and confidence in God's salvation is God's desire.

3. Do you hate the church, rebel against God, and reject Jesus as the Christ? Do you think you can save yourself? John tells us that you have no grounds for assurance. Repent of your sins and trust in Jesus as your Savior. Find salvation. Find confident assurance in him.

◆

WEEK 51: DAY 5
Revelation 1

Key Text
"Then I turned to see the voice that was speaking with me, and having turned I saw seven golden lampstands, and in the midst of the lampstands one like a son of man, clothed in a long robe and girded with a golden belt around his chest." Revelation 1:12-13*

The Last Things: Jesus as Daniel's Son of Man
So many Christians live as if things in this world couldn't be worse. They look at all the evil and all the danger that our world is filled with and then grumble, complain, and act as if there's no hope for our sin-filled cosmos.

When John wrote Revelation, life was extremely difficult for Christians. Jews persecuted Christians for abandoning Judaism (Rev. 2:8-11). Gnostic false teachings were developing that would lead people astray from the pure gospel of Jesus Christ (Rev. 2:1-7). Even more, the Roman government was actively persecuting Christians by arresting them as political prisoners (v. 9). And John reveals in Revelation that things were going to get worse before they got better (Rev. 13:1-18).

Yet in the midst of it all, John was no pity-seeking, hopeless, cowardly Christian. John was fully convinced that Jesus Christ is the Lord of the Cosmos, no matter how bad things appear to be (v. 5). As Lord, Jesus reigns over sin and death (vv. 5, 18). As Lord, Jesus reigns as the Son of Man prophesied by Daniel, the Son who would be God Almighty (vv. 12-16; cf. Dan. 7:9-28).

Though evil increases and assaults the people of God, Jesus is on the throne where he is ruling and reigning (v. 5), preserving his people (Rev. 7:1-17), and working all things according to his purposes until he returns to make a complete end of all things evil (Rev. 19:11-21). This world is not out of control. Jesus is on the throne as the Ancient of Days working all things for his own glory and for the good of his people. What better time to be alive could be possible?

Jon Canler

Connection with Older Testament
Daniel 7

For the Kids
Ask your children what they worry about. Prod into why they worry. Is it because they aren't in total control? Is it because they don't trust God? Help them to see that one of the most beautiful truths, especially when times get difficult, is that God is on the throne. He has the future in his hands, and all is working exactly according to plan for the good of his people. Pray that Jesus' lordship over all creation would give you freedom from cowardly fear to firmly trust him.

Prayer Prompts
1. Behold and worship Christ in his splendor. He is to be glorified as the all-knowing and all-powerful God, the Ancient of Days.
2. Fear not in the midst of your circumstances because Jesus died and is alive forevermore. Cast your anxiety on him. Ask for grace to trust him more.

◆

WEEK 52: DAY 1
Revelation 2-3

Key Text
"He who has an ear, let him hear what the Spirit says to the churches. The one

who conquers will not be hurt by the second death." Revelation 2:11*

The Last Things: Perseverance in Persecution

One of the main themes of Revelation is that believers must boldly and courageously endure persecution in order to receive the final reward of the kingdom. This theme of perseverance is prominent throughout Revelation 2-3 as John reminds the churches that eternal blessing awaits only those who "conquer" in faith even unto death (2:7, 11, 17, 26; 3:5, 12, 21). Those who deny the gospel and submit to the beast, the false prophet, and Satan under persecution will face God's wrath for eternity (Rev. 14:9-12).

So, how exactly do Christians hold fast to the gospel under the temptations to abandon Christianity that come through persecution? We look to Christ who is the "faithful witness," the one who persevered in trusting the Father through Satan's temptations, even to death, and who was consequently raised from the dead to rule the cosmos (Rev. 1:5). As a result of his resurrection, Christ, the faithful witness, actively works to preserve his blood-bought people so that his death is not in vain (Rev. 7:1-12, 11:1-2, 13:7-8, 14:1). We fight to persevere by faith because Christ is at work displaying his sovereignty over all things in the cosmos, even over Satan and sin, by preserving the faith of those for whom he died unto their deaths. Constantly look to Christ and find that his conquering and preserving work will give you grace to persevere unto the end whereby you may conquer and inherit the kingdom.

Jon Canler

Connection with Older Testament
Psalm 145:18-21

For the Kids
Talk to your children about being persecuted for the sake of Christ. Remind them that others may tease them or make fun of them for going to church or talking about God. Encourage them to be faithful to talk about God and live a life for him even when other people do not understand. Eternal life with Jesus is the reward of enduring persecution until the end.

Prayer Prompts

1. Ask the Lord, the "faithful witness," to grant you grace to boldly endure persecution that you experience as a result of living in line with the kingdom of Christ. May his grace cause us to inherit the eternal blessings promised to the seven churches.

2. Confess any fears you may have about enduring physical suffering for the sake of Christ. Ask the Lord to seal in your heart the fact that you have died to yourself and are alive to Christ, our enduring example.

◆

WEEK 52: DAY 2

Revelation 6:1-8:5

Key Text

"Then the kings of the earth, the very important people, the generals, the rich, the powerful, and everyone, slave and free, hid themselves in the caves and among the rocks of the mountains. They said to the mountains and rocks, 'Fall on us and hide us from the face of the one who is seated on the throne and from the wrath of the Lamb, because the great day of their wrath has come, and who is able to withstand it?'" Revelation 6:15-17

The Last Things: Judgment on the World

John goes to great lengths in Revelation to communicate that the Lord and his Christ are sovereign over the cosmos, all in an attempt to encourage afflicted Christians who are prone to question the Lord's rule over a wicked world. One such way the absolute rule of God is displayed in Revelation is through a repeated demonstration of God's comprehensive judgment on evil through the seal judgments (6:1-8:5), the trumpet judgments (Rev. 8:6-11:19), and the bowl judgments (Rev. 15:1-16:21). When war, famines, and plagues come upon the earth, John makes it clear that the Lord is behind the calamity, unleashing judgment upon the world as a display of his holiness upon sinful rebels. There is coming a day when all who boldly oppose Jesus Christ will seek to hide in fear from "the face of the one who is seated on the throne, and from the wrath of the Lamb" (6:16). The Lord will pour out his righteous wrath, and he will vindicate his people and his great name! Fear not, Christian!

So, what of Christians during the days of God's final judgment? What will these days look like for God's people? Exactly like the exodus generation, God's people will be persecuted by those opposed to God (6:9-11; cf. Ex. 1:8-22); however, also like the exodus generation, God's people will be preserved from falling away from Christ while also being protected from God's wrath on the unrighteous until God's judgment is poured out in full (7:3; cf. Ex. 7:22, 9:4, 26, 11:1-8). As a result of God's judgment, God's people will be released forever from all evil into a new heavens and earth as the greater-than-Moses-exodus is fulfilled in Jesus Christ (7:15-17; cf. Ex. 15; Jer. 16:14-15).

Jon Canler

Connection with Older Testament
Exodus 8:21-24; Isaiah 24

For the Kids
Ask your children to give an example of a time when they were wronged—someone hit them, took a toy, made fun of them, etc. Have them recall the hurt and the longing for justice, for wrongs to be punished and made right, that they likely had. Remind them that one day Jesus will come and will right every wrong. Jesus will bring judgment on the earth for all who have not claimed him as Lord and Savior. Even so, pray with your children for fellow sinners who have wronged them to be given mercy in Jesus. Pray with your children for those who do not know Jesus—that they will come to know him before it is too late.

Prayer Prompts
1. Praise God that his justice and judgment are coming upon all those who persecute his people and who rebel against his lordship. Praise God that justice and righteousness will reign and that injustice and rebellion will be crushed.
2. Praise God that his people are sealed and protected from the divine wrath of God. Who can stand on the day of the wrath of the Lamb? All who are in Christ

can withstand because of his seal upon us. Our salvation from sin and from the Lord's wrath is secure!

◆

WEEK 52: DAY 3
Revelation 19

Key Text
"Then I saw heaven opened, and behold, a white horse! The one sitting on it is called Faithful and True, and in righteousness he judges and makes war." Revelation 19:11*

The Last Things: The Return of the Righteous King

Revelation 19:11-21 gives us an extended look into what King Jesus will do when he returns to the earth. The picture painted by John is quite alarming. The same Jesus who came to earth nearly two thousand years ago to seek and to save the lost as a humble, self-sacrificial servant (Luke 19:10) will return as a violent Warrior-King who will make war on his enemies (v. 19). Though the kings of the earth will come out to fight Jesus, the encounter will be so lopsided in favor of Jesus that John doesn't even record a battle scene. Jesus will simply speak a word such that everyone and everything opposed to his righteous rule will be slaughtered as his robe is stained with the blood of his enemies (vv. 13-15). The iron rod of Psalm 2 will be used to triumph over the rebellious nations such that the winepress of God's wrath will be poured out in full (v. 15). Revelation 19:11-21 clearly emphasizes that the return of Jesus will be filled with judgment on all who oppose him.

If you are a Christian, rejoice because our King is coming to rule over our enemies and over those who persecute us. The sufferings and afflictions we face will one day be overcome and vindicated (vv. 1-10). If you are not a Christian, see what kind of judgment awaits you at the return of Christ, and repent of refusing to submit to him as Lord. Turn to Jesus while salvation is near so that you may receive mercy and forgiveness while there is time.

Jon Canler

Connection with Older Testament

Ezekiel 38-39

For the Kids

Explain to your children that God is a merciful and gracious God. Yet, God is also holy, and he cannot tolerate sin. For now, God is patient, even though sin is all over the earth. He's kindly and patiently leading people to repentance. But, there will be a day when God says "no more" to the sin on the earth. On that day, Jesus will come on his war horse, and he will defeat sin, Satan, and every other enemy. Pray with your children by thanking God for his judgment on sin. Thank him for escape from judgment in Jesus.

Prayer Prompts

1. When Jesus returns, he is coming to destroy all who stand opposed to him and his kingdom. There will be no mercy. Perhaps you need to repent of your opposition to Christ and turn to him by faith before the day of his coming.

2. Christian, rejoice that a day is coming when God will act decisively for his glory to eradicate evil. Satan, his beastly minions, and all who are "of the world" will be judged. Those who persecute and hate the church will be eradicated by King Jesus under his eternal wrath.

3. Praise God that, in Christ, you will be saved from the judgment that is to come. Jesus has paid it all.

◆

WEEK 52: DAY 4

Revelation 20

Key Text

"And I saw the dead, the great and the small, standing before the throne. Then books were opened, and another book was opened—the book of life. So the dead were judged by what was written in the books, according to their deeds."
Revelation 20:12

The Last Things: The Final Judgment

As we come to the end of the Bible in Revelation 20, we see that God will deal with his enemies finally and forever (vv. 13-15). On the one hand, this pending judgment should be a sobering wake up call for evangelism knowing that people whose names are not written in the Book of Life will be damned forever and thrown into the lake of fire (v. 15). There are people that we know who are headed for this tragic outcome for eternity apart from Jesus, and this coming judgment should give us a yearning to share the gospel of Jesus Christ with those around us so that they might be saved from the wrath that is to come.

On the other hand, Revelation 20 should cause Christians to rejoice. There is coming a day when evil will be destroyed. There is coming a day when satanic temptation will be no more. A day is coming when dominions and powers that hold sway over this cosmos will be cast into eternal judgment. There is coming a day when persecution for the people of God will be put to death. Oh, take comfort, Christian, in the fact that a day is coming when we will be free from fallen, sinful things as our great God judges his cosmos in righteousness.

Chad Lindon and Jon Canler

Connection with Older Testament
Psalm 92; Isaiah 66:15-24

For the Kids
Discuss with your children the fact that God is just and that justice is good. For example, if someone breaks into your house and hurts your family, then it is good and right for that person to be punished. When we sin, we disobey God, and that sin deserves punishment. For sin against an eternally perfect God, God's punishment is eternal destruction. Explain that God is also loving and that he sent his Son to prove his love, to save sinners who will trust in Jesus (John 3:16).

Prayer Prompts

1. Praise God that, in Christ, you have security against eternal death because Christ paid for the eternal punishment that you deserve on the cross.

2. Ask the Lord to help you live in light of coming judgment, focusing on the kingdom. Ask him to help you feel the weight of judgment which would compel you share the gospel with the lost.

◆

WEEK 52: DAY 5

Revelation 21-22:5

Key Text

"And I heard a loud voice from the throne saying: 'Look! The residence of God is among human beings. He will live among them, and they will be his people, and God himself will be with them.'" Revelation 21:3

The Last Things: The New Heavens and the New Earth

The book of Revelation emphasizes over and over that it is the word of God and that everything written in the book will happen. We can be certain of all of its promises. We will dwell with God. There will be no barriers to our access to God. There will be no more sin. There will be no more death. There will be no more disease. There will be no more war. We will serve Jesus. The new heavens and the new earth will go on forever, and we will never grow tired of any of its sure realities.

Jeremy Haskins, "The End," Preached 1/6/2013, Ashland in MC Website, Accessed 3 December 2015, Available from http://www.ashlandmc.org/podcast/the-end/.

Connection with Older Testament

Isaiah 66:22-23

For the Kids

Help your children understand how glorious the new heavens and new earth will be! It will be a place greater than we can ever imagine. There will be no tears, no pain, no suffering, no sadness, and, most importantly, we will be in the presence of God our Father! Pray with your children by thanking God for saving sinners so we can spend eternity with him.

Prayer Prompts

1. Ask God to set your mind on the future kingdom and to give you a longing for its coming.

2. Be amazed that God would allow you, a sinner, to be a part of the new heavens and the new earth!

BIBLIOGRAPHY

Augustine. *Expositions of the Psalms*. In vol. 5 of *Works of Saint Augustine: A Translation for the 21st Century*. Translated by Maria Boulding. Hyde Park, NY: New City Press, 2002.

Barshinger, David P. *Jonathan Edwards and the Psalms: A Redemptive-Historical Vision of Scripture*. New York: Oxford, 2014.

Bayly, Lewis. *The Practice of Piety*. Primary Source Edition. Charleston, SC: NABU Press, 2013.

Haskins, Jeremy. "Conquering with Compassion." Preached 10/14/2012. Ashland in MC Website. Accessed 3 December 2015. Available from http://www.ashlandmc.org/podcast/conquering-with-compassion1/.

_____. "Expect the Unexpected in Suffering." Preached 4/6/2014. Ashland in MC Website. Accessed 3 December 2015. Available from http://www.ashlandmc.org/podcast/expect-unexpected-suffering-john-2-13-22/.

_____. "Kingdom Preaching." Preached 7/8/2012. Ashland in MC Website. Accessed 3 December 2015. Available from http://www.ashlandmc.org/podcast/kingdom-preaching/.

_____. "The End." Preached 1/6/2013. Ashland in MC Website. Accessed 3 December 2015. Available from http://www.ashlandmc.org/podcast/the-end/.

_____. "The Promise." Preached 11/4/2014. Ashland in MC Website. Accessed 3 December 2015. Available from http://www.ashlandmc.org/podcast/the-promise/.

_____. "The Solution—Gave." Preached 12/21/2014. Ashland in MC Website. Accessed 3 December 2015. Available from http://www.ashlandmc.org/podcast/solution-gave-john-3-16-18/.

_____. "The Spiritual Discipline of Not Forgetting." Preached 4/27/2014. Ashland in MC Website. Accessed 3 December 2015. Available from http://www.ashlandmc.org/podcast/spiritual-discipline-forgetting-deuteronomy-4-32-40/.

_____. "VBS as Warfare in a Foreign Land." Preached 7/21/2013. Ashland in MC Website. Accessed 3 December 2015. Available from http://www.ashlandmc.org/podcast/vbs-as-warfare-in-a-foreign-land/.

_____. "Who Should I Fear." Preached 6/9/2013. Ashland Avenue Baptist Church Website. Accessed 3 December 2015. Available from http://www.ashlandlex.org/podcast/who-should-i-fear/.

_____. "Worship is the Mission." Preached 6/22/2014. Ashland in MC Website. Accessed 3 December 2015. Available from http://www.ashlandmc.org/podcast/worship-mission-psalm-67/.

Lewis, C.S. *Reflections on the Psalms*. New York: Harcourt, Brace & Co., 1958.

Lloyd-Jones, Sally and Jago Silver. *The Jesus Storybook Bible: Every Story Whispers His Name*. Grand Rapids: Zonderkids, 2007.

McCall, Casey. "Cruciform Works." Preached 10/14/2014. Ashland Avenue Baptist Church Website. Accessed 4 December 2015. Available from http://www.ashlandlex.org/podcast/cruciform-works-james-2/.

_____. "Free at Last! Saying Goodbye to Snakes, Sin, and Slavery." Preached 7/28/2013. Ashland Avenue Baptist Church Website. Accessed 4 December 2015. Available from http://www.ashlandlex.org/podcast/free-at-last-saying-goodbye-to-snakes-sin-and-slavery-romans-61-14/.

_____. "Health." Preached 10/06/2013. Ashland Avenue Baptist Church Website. Accessed 4 December 2015. Available from http://www.ashlandlex.org/podcast/health/.

_____. "Reading and Applying the Bible with Jesus as the Hero—Queen Esther (Esther 2:1-18)." In *Church with Jesus as the Hero*, ed. David. E. Prince, 41-48. n.p.: Ashland Publishing, 2015.

_____. "Set Free by the Spirit." Preached 7/19/2015. Ashland Avenue Baptist Church Website. Accessed 4 December 2015. Available from http://www.ashlandlex.org/podcast/set-free-by-the-spirit-galatians-3/.

_____. "The Majesty of Mundane." Preached 8/11/2013. Ashland Avenue Baptist Church Website. Accessed 4 December 2015. Available from http://www.ashlandlex.org/podcast/the-majesty-of-mundane/.

_____. "The Seed." Preached 5/3/2015. Ashland Avenue Baptist Church Website. Accessed 4 December 2015. Available from http://www.ashlandlex.org/podcast/the-seed-genesis-3/.

Prince, David. "A Disciple Called Satan: When Knowing Jesus is not Enough." Preached 2/22/2009. Prince on Preaching Website. Accessed 4 December 2015. Available from http://www.davidprince.com/2009/02/22/a-disciple-called-satan-when-knowing-jesus-is-not-enough-matthew-1613-23/.

_____. "A Terrorist Meets Jesus: The Good News of a King Who Does Not Save Himself." Preached 4/5/2009. Prince on Preaching Website. Accessed 4 December 2015. Available from http://www.davidprince.com/2009/04/05/a-terrorist-meets-jesus-the-good-news-of-a-king-who-does-not-save-himself-luke-2326-43/.

_____. "Blessed Warriors." Preached 11/3/2013. Prince on Preaching Website. Accessed 4 December 2015. Available from http://www.davidprince.com/2013/11/03/blessed-warriors/.

_____. "Blessed! No Matter What." Preached 10/26/2014. Prince on Preaching Website. Accessed 4 December 2015. Available from http://www.davidprince.com/2014/10/26/blessed-matter-numbers-23-24/.

_____. "Brothers - The Scandalous Community." Preached 10/16/2011. Prince on Preaching Website. Accessed 4 December 2015. Available from http://www.davidprince.com/2011/10/16/brothers-the-scandalous-community-romans-121-2/.

_____. "Burdens & Bowing." Preached 10/9/2011. Prince on Preaching Website. Accessed 4 December 2015. Available from http://www.davidprince.com/2011/10/09/burdens-bowing-isaiah-46/.

_____. "Can I Ever Go Home?" Preached 6/23/2013. Prince on Preaching Website. Accessed 4 December 2015. Available from http://www.davidprince.com/2013/06/23/can-i-ever-go-home-daniel-7/.

_____. "Chatting the Good News Every Day." Preached 9/18/2011. Prince on Preaching Website. Accessed 4 December 2015. Available from http://www.davidprince.com/2011/09/18/chatting-the-good-news-every-day-2-corinthians-47-16/.

_____. "Christians and Culture: Truth, Beauty, Goodness and the Great Commission." Published 3/19/2015. Prince on Preaching Website. Accessed 28 December 2015. Available from http://www.davidprince.com/2015/03/19/christians-and-culture-truth-beauty-goodness-and-the-great-commission/.

_____. "Church of the Less Excellent Way? What You Need More than What You Think You Need." Preached 9/12/2010. Prince on Preaching Website. Accessed 4 December 2015. Available from http://www.davidprince.com/2010/09/12/church-of-the-less-excellent-way-what-you-need-more-than-what-you-think-you-need-1-corinthians-1231b-133/.

_____. "David and Goliath We Never Knew You: The Good News that the Bible is Not All About You." Preached 3/8/2009. Prince on Preaching Website. Accessed 4 December 2015. Available from http://www.davidprince.com/2009/03/08/david-goliath-never-knew-good-news-bible-1-samuel-17/.

_____. "Eating, Drinking, Cutting Grass, Work, Class, Shopping and the Gospel: Why the Kingdom Means More than Morality." Preached 8/29/2010. Prince on Preaching Website. Accessed 4 December 2015. Available from http://www.davidprince.com/2010/08/29/eating-drinking-cutting-grass-work-class-shopping-and-the-gospel-why-the-kingdom-means-more-than-morality-1-corinthians-1031-33/.

_____. "Expect the Unexpected in Mission." Preached 4/27/2014. Prince on Preaching Website. Accessed 4 December 2015. Available from http://www.davidprince.com/2014/04/27/expect-the-unexpected-in-mission/.

_____. "Family Worship." Published 3/23/2013. Prince on Preaching Website. Accessed 4 December 2015. Available from http://www.davidprince.com/2012/03/23/family-worship/.

_____. "Fathers & Adoption Culture." Preached 6/15/2014. Prince on Preaching Website. Accessed 4 December 2015. Available from http://www.davidprince.com/2014/06/15/fathers-adoption-culture-matthew-118-25/.

_____. "Feasting in the Face of Death: The Victory Meal." Preached 5/31/2009. Prince on Preaching Website. Accessed 4 December 2015. Available from http://www.davidprince.com/2009/05/31/feasting in-the-face-of-death-the-victory-mea-isaiah-25-2/.

_____. "From Leisurely Learners to Global Gospel Warriors." Preached 8/22/2009. Prince on Preaching Website. Accessed 4 December 2015. Available from http://www.davidprince.com/2010/08/22/from-leisurely-learners-to-global-gospel-warriors-matthew-2816-20/.

_____. "God-Centered Living." Preached 11/10/2013. Prince on Preaching Website. Accessed 4 December 2015. Available from http://www.davidprince.com/2013/11/10/god-centered-living-numbers-147-234/.

_____. "Grace Alone: John Calvin and the Good News of Adoption." Published 11/6/2017. Prince on Preaching Website. Accessed 22 November 2017. Available from http://www.davidprince.com/2017/11/06/grace-alone-john-calvin-good-news-adoption/.

_____. "Grumbling Against God." Preached 7/27/2014. Prince on Preaching Website. Accessed 4 December 2015. Available from http://www.davidprince.com/2014/07/27/grumbling-god-numbers-12/.

_____. "History." Preached 6/2/2013. Ashland Avenue Baptist Church Website. Accessed 4 December 2015. Available from http://www.ashlandlex.org/podcast/history/.

_____. "Holy God and Holy Stump." Preached 3/30/2008. Prince on Preaching Website. Accessed 4 December 2015. Available from http://www.davidprince.com/2008/03/30/holy-god-and-holy-stump-isaiah-6/.

_____. "I'm Snakebit." Preached 10/5/2014. Prince on Preaching Website. Accessed 10/5/2014. Available from http://www.davidprince.com/2014/10/05/im-snakebit-numbers-211-9/.

_____. "In the Wilderness with Jesus." Preached 10/27/2013. Prince on Preaching Website. Accessed 4 December 2015. Available from http://www.davidprince.com/2013/10/27/in-the-wilderness-with-jesus/.

_____. "INTENTIONAL: Making it Our Aim to Please Christ." Preached 1/6/2008. Prince on Preaching Website. Accessed 4 December 2015. Available from http://www.davidprince.com/2008/01/06/intentional-making-it-our-aim-to-please-christ-2-corinthians-51-10/

_____. "Jesus & the 10 Commandments: God, Men, & Things." Preached 7/3/2011. Prince on Preaching Website. Accessed 4 December 2015. Available from http://www.davidprince.com/2011/07/03/jesus-the-10-commandments-god-men-things-exodus-201-2-matthew-1916-22/

_____. "Joy to the World and Other War Songs." Preached 12/13/2009. Prince on Preaching Website. Accessed 4 December 2015. Available from http://www.davidprince.com/2009/12/13/joy to-the-world-and-other-war-songs-isaiah-12/.

_____. "Just Say Something." Preached 9/28/2014. Prince on Preaching Website. Accessed 4 December 2015. Available from http://www.davidprince.com/2014/09/28/just-say-something-numbers-20/.

_____. "Kingdom Conversion." Preached 6/17/2012. Prince on Preaching Website. Accessed 4 December 2015. Available from http://www.davidprince.com/2012/06/17/kingdom-conversion acts-91-19/.

_____. "Kingdom Power." Preached 5/6/2012. Prince on Preaching Website. Accessed 4 December 2015. Available from http://www.davidprince.com/2012/05/06/kingdom-power-acts-21-13/.

_____. "Kingdom Vision." Preached 6/24/2012. Prince on Preaching Website. Accessed 4 December 2015. Available from http://www.davidprince.com/2012/06/24/kingdom-vision-acts-111-18/.

_____. "Kingdom Witness." Preached 5/20/2012. Prince on Preaching Website. Accessed 4 December 2015. Available from http://www.davidprince.com/2012/05/20/kingdom-witness-acts-311-26/.

_____. "Knowing God as Shepherd." Preached 9/13/2015. Prince on Preaching Website. Accessed 4 December 2015. Available from http://www.davidprince.com/2015/09/13/knowing-god-as-shepherd-john-101-15/.

_____. "Making God in Our Image: Our Idols and The Voice from the Mountains." Preached 7/10/2011. Prince on Preaching Website. Accessed 4 December 2015. Available from http://www.davidprince.com/2011/07/10/making-god-in-our-image-our-idols-and-the-voice-from-the-mountains-exodus-203-matthew-171-8/.

_____. "Never Trump: Opposing Racial Injustice Now, Tomorrow, and Forever." Published 3/3/2016. Prince on Preaching Website. Accessed 22 November 2017. Available from http://www.davidprince.com/2016/03/03/never-trump-opposing-racial-injustice-now-tomorrow-forever/.

_____. "Only Foreigners Will Win the World for Jesus: A Genuine Call to Missional Living." Preached 10/25/2009. Prince on Preaching Website. Accessed 4 December 2015. Available from http://www.davidprince.com/2009/10/25/only-foreigners-will-win-the-world-for-jesus-a-genuine-call-to-missional-living-1-peter-211-12/.

_____. "Pilgrims March." Preached 10/12/2014. Prince on Preaching Website. Accessed 4 December 2015. Available from http://www.davidprince.com/2014/10/12/pilgrims-march-numbers-2110-35/.

_____. "Raising Cain in the Church." Preached 2/13/2013. Prince on Preaching Website. Accessed 4 December 2015. Available from http://www.davidprince.com/2013/02/13/raising-cain-in-the-church- genesis-41-10/.

_____. "Seeing God's King: Understanding Power in the Kingdom of Christ." Preached 2/22/2009. Prince on Preaching Website. Accessed 4 December 2015. Available from http://www.davidprince.com/2009/02/22/seeing-god's-king-understanding-power-in-the-kingdom-of-christ-1-samuel-161-13/.

_____. "The First Noel and Other Thoughts About End Times." Preached 12/7/2008. Ashland Avenue Baptist Church Website. Accessed 4 December 2015. Available from http://www.ashlandlex.org/podcast/the-first-noel-and-other-thoughts-about-end-times/.

_____. "The Gospel Freedom of Being Fools for Christ's Sake." Preached 4/26/2015. Prince on Preaching Website. Accessed 4 December 2015. Available from http://www.davidprince.com/2015/04/26/the-gospel-freedom-of-being-fools-for-christs-sake-luke-191-10/.

_____. "The Helper (Spirit/Church)." Preached 12/30/2012. Prince on Preaching Website. Accessed 4 December 2015. Available from http://www.davidprince.com/2012/12/30/the-helper-spiritchurch-john-1415-24/.

_____. "The King of the Cosmos." Preached 3/15/2015. Prince on Preaching Website. Accessed 4 December 2015. Available from http://www.davidprince.com/2015/03/15/the- king-of-the-cosmos-genesis-1/.

_____. "The Manliness of Adoption: Testosterone and Pure Religion." Published 9/9/2010. Prince on Preaching Website. Accessed 4 December 2015. Available from http://www.davidprince.com/2010/09/09/the-manliness-of-adoption-testosterone-and-pure-religion/.

_____. "The Problem—We Take." Preached 12/14/2014. Prince on Preaching Website. Accessed 4 December 2015. Available from http://www.davidprince.com/2014/12/14/problem-take-2-samuel-121-7a/.

_____. "The Relationship Between Faith and Courage." Published 1/14/2016. Prince on Preaching Website. Accessed 22 November 2017. Available from http://www.davidprince.com/2016/01/14/the-relationship-between-faith-and-courage/.

_____. "The Temple (David)." Preached 12/2/2012. Prince on Preaching Website. Accessed 4 December 2015. Available from http://www.davidprince.com/2012/12/06/the-temple-david-2-samuel-74-19/.

_____. "The Theology of a Graveyard." Preached 3/28/2010. Prince on Preaching Website. Accessed 4 December 2015. Available from http://www.davidprince.com/2010/03/28/the-theology-of-a-graveyard-ezekiel-371-14/.

_____. "The Word (Jesus)." Preached 12/23/2012. Prince on Preaching Website. Accessed 4 December 2015. Available from http://www.davidprince.com/2012/12/23/the-word-jesus-john-114-18/.

_____. "The Worthless." Preached 8/21/2012. Prince on Preaching Website. Accessed 4 December 2015. Available from http://www.davidprince.com/2012/08/21/the-worthless-habakkuk-25-20/

_____. "2009: The Year of Living Upside Down." Preached 1/4/2009. Prince on Preaching Website. Accessed 4 December 2015. Available from http://www.davidprince.com/2009/01/04/2009-the-year-of-living-upside-down-acts-171-8/.

_____. "Treacherous Tongues." Preached 7/13/2014. Prince on Preaching Website. Accessed 4 December 2015. Available from http://www.davidprince.com/2014/07/13/treacherous-tongues-numbers-11/.

_____. "When a Donkey Talks." Preached 10/19/2014. Prince on Preaching Website. Accessed 4 December 2015. Available from http://www.davidprince.com/2014/10/19/donkey-talks-numbers-

22/.

_____. "When God Repents." Preached 9/30/2012. Prince on Preaching Website. Accessed 4 December 2015. Available from http://www.davidprince.com/2012/09/30/when-god-repents-jonah-33b-41/.

_____. "When Jesus Shows Up at the Funeral Home." Preached 4/18/2010. Prince on Preaching Website. Accessed 4 December 2015. Available from http://www.davidprince.com/2010/04/18/when-jesus-shows-up-at-the-funeral-home-john-1117-27/.

_____. "Where Is My Life Headed?" Preached 8/4/2013. Prince on Preaching Website. Accessed 4 December 2015. Available from http://www.davidprince.com/2013/08/04/where-is-my-life-headed-daniel-125-13/.

_____. "Who Has the Power?" Preached 5/5/2013. Prince on Preaching Website. Accessed 4 December 2015. Available from http://www.davidprince.com/2013/05/05/who-has-the-power-daniel-2/.

_____. "Why Gospel Movies are Not Visual Enough." Preached 9/13/2009. Prince on Preaching Website. Accessed 4 December 2015. Available from http://www.davidprince.com/2009/09/13/why-gospel-movies-are-not-visual-enough-leviticus-161-16/.

_____. "Why the Gospel is So Hard for Us to Believe." Preached 1/3/2010. Prince on Preaching Website. Accessed 4 December 2015. Available from http://www.davidprince.com/2010/01/03/why-the-gospel-is-so-hard-for-us-to-believe-isaiah-5213-5312/.

_____. "Why You Should Talk to Yourself." Preached 3/5/2012. Prince on Preaching Website. Accessed 4 December2015. Available from http://www.davidprince.com/2012/03/05/why-you-should-talk-to-yourself-psalm-103/.

_____. "You Cannot Have a Christmas Without a Highway, Voices, and Celebration." Preached 12/20/2009. Prince on Preaching Website. Accessed 4 December 2015. Available from http://www.davidprince.com/2009/12/20/you-cannot-have-a-christmas-without-a-highway-voices-and-celebration-isaiah-401-11/.

_____. "Your Foolish Life Now! One Easy Step into a Life of Folly." Preached 1/25/2009. Prince on Preaching Website. Accessed 4 December 2015. Available from http://www.davidprince.com/2009/01/25/your-foolish-life-now-one-easy-step-into-a-life-of-folly-1-samuel-13/.

_____. "Zeal & Hope." Preached 11/2/2014. Prince on Preaching Website. Accessed 4 December 2015. Available from http://www.davidprince.com/2014/11/02/zeal-hope-numbers-25/.

_____. sermon series on Judges sent via text message link to Dropbox to editor 5/27/2015.

Roberts, Vaughan. *God's Big Picture: Tracing the Storyline of the Bible*. Downer's Grove, IL: InterVarsity Press, 2002.

Ryken, Leland. *Worldly Saints: The Puritans as They Really Were*. Grand Rapids: Zondervan, 1990.

Spurgeon, Charles H. *The Metropolitan Tabernacle Pulpit Sermons*, vol. 48. London: Passmore & Alabaster, 1902.

67116940R00260

Made in the USA
Middletown, DE
14 September 2019